THE DOMESTICATION OF DESIRE

THE DOMESTICATION
OF DESIRE

WOMEN, WEALTH,
AND MODERNITY IN JAVA

SUZANNE APRIL BRENNER

PRINCETON UNIVERSITY PRESS

PRINCETON, NEW JERSEY

Copyright © 1998 by Princeton University Press
Published by Princeton University Press, 41 William Street,
Princeton, New Jersey 08540
In the United Kingdom: Princeton University Press,
Chichester, West Sussex
All Rights Reserved

Library of Congress Cataloging-in-Publication Data

Brenner, Suzanne April, 1960–
The domestication of desire : women, wealth, and modernity
in Java / Suzanne April Brenner.
p.   cm.
Includes bibliographical references and index.
ISBN 0-691-01693-3 (cl : alk. paper) —
ISBN 0-691-01692-5 (pb : alk. paper)
1. Ethnology—Indonesia—Surakarta. 2. Social change
—Indonesia—Surakarta. 3. Women—Indonesia—Surakarta.
4. Surakarta (Indonesia)—Social conditions. I. Title.
GN635.I65B69 1998
306′.09598′2—dc21   97-46124 CIP

This book has been composed in Janson

Princeton University Press books are printed
on acid-free paper and meet the guidelines
for permanence and durability of the Committee
on Production Guidelines for Book Longevity
of the Council on Library Resources

http://pup.princeton.edu

Printed in the United States of America

10 9 8 7 6 5 4 3 2 1

10 9 8 7 6 5 4 3 2 1
(pbk.)

TO MY PARENTS

Howard Brenner and Lorraine Brenner Kulok

WITH LOVE AND GRATITUDE

CONTENTS

FIGURES

All photographs are by the author.

ACKNOWLEDGMENTS

I HAVE ACCUMULATED many intellectual and personal debts in the course of carrying out this project. And it is with a mixture of relief and regret that I let this book go, since it has become part of me in a very real sense, providing a sense of continuity through the otherwise dramatic changes in my life. To those who have helped me along the way, I offer my deepest thanks.

I owe my greatest intellectual debt to James Siegel, whose own thinking about Indonesia, Java, and anthropology inspired me to think about each of these in ways I would otherwise never have imagined. I am especially grateful for his encouragement over the years and his unwavering enthusiasm for this project. I also wish to thank Benedict Anderson for taking so much interest in my work, for the unstinting time and moral support that he has offered me, and for teaching me the importance of looking at Indonesia through a historical lens.

F. G. Bailey, Michael Meeker, and Tanya Luhrmann each read part or all of the manuscript and offered me very useful advice and gentle criticism; I have also been very lucky to have them as colleagues. Indeed, I am thankful to the entire faculty and staff of the Anthropology Department at the University of California, San Diego, for being so supportive since I came to UCSD in 1991.

When I was desperate to find time away from teaching in order to finish a draft of this book, I had the good fortune to be invited to spend a year as a member at the Institute for Advanced Study in Princeton. It was there that I first met Clifford Geertz, whose work had been (without his knowing it) a source of inspiration to me since my undergraduate days. It was a pleasure to finally get to know him after all these years and to share his considerable insights on anthropology, Indonesia, and many other subjects. I was also delighted to spend time in the company of Joan Scott, who is a model for any aspiring feminist scholar. Other colleagues at the Institute who provided me with intellectual companionship include Suzanne Kaufman, Debbie Keates, Fred Myers, Lilia Labidi, Peter van der Veer, Henry Abelove, Linda Zerilli, and the other members of the "Modernization" seminar. Also deserving of thanks is Debbie Koehler, who, along with the rest of the staff at the Institute, did everything she could to facilitate my work.

During the research and writing of this book in its various forms I have had the help and friendship of many people. In Indonesia, special thanks go to Ny. Nora Yap Goenawan, Halim H.D., Bapak and Ibu Suhardiman

Tjokrosoehardjo, Ibu Budi Maknawi, Ibu Darsono Priyosoemarto, Bapak and Ibu Abdul Somad, and Bapak Sutrasno, along with countless others. I am also indebted to Professor Umar Kayam, who sponsored my research in his capacity as director of the Center for Cultural Studies at Gadjah Mada University. Others who helped me through this project in various ways include Amrih Widodo, Coeli Barry, Carol Block, Martijna Briggs, Budi Susanto, Alex Dea, Farha Ciciek, Alan Feinstein, Nancy Florida, Jan Hostetler, Webb Keane, Kathryn March, Mary Pat Olley, Paschalis Laksono, John Pemberton, Marc Perlman, Danilyn Rutherford, P. Steven Sangren, Saya Shiraishi, Takashi Shiraishi, Thoriq Addibani, Gigi Weix, John Wolff, and Philip and Tinuk Yampolsky. With Leslie Morris and Ward Keeler I shared the joys and frustrations of fieldwork; I benefited greatly from their ideas and companionship.

Ward Keeler, Patsy Spyer, and Mary Steedly each quickly and unselfishly read the entire manuscript and offered me valuable comments. Mary Murrell of Princeton University Press has been extremely helpful in expediting the review and publication of this book; my thanks as well to Madeleine Adams and Alice Falk for their excellent editorial assistance.

Funding for the research and writing of this book came from many sources. My fieldwork in Solo, Indonesia, from March 1986 to August 1988 and subsequent write-up were sponsored by a Social Science Research Council Dissertation Research Grant, a Fulbright-Hays Dissertation Research Fellowship, a Woodrow Wilson Research Grant in Women's Studies, and a Foreign Language and Area Studies Fellowship awarded through the Southeast Asia Program at Cornell University. The University of California, San Diego Academic Senate provided me with a faculty research grant to conduct further fieldwork in Solo in 1992; I also received a Faculty Career Development Program Grant from UCSD in 1993. The Institute for Advanced Study, with partial funding from a National Endowment for the Humanities fellowship, supported my writing of a draft of the manuscript in 1995–96. I obtained permission to conduct research through the Indonesian Institute of Sciences (LIPI) and received institutional sponsorship from the Center for Cultural Studies (Pusat Penelitian Kebudayaan) at Gadjah Mada University.

Finally, my deepest debt is to the members of my family, who have been my greatest source of support, and to my husband John Opferkuch, who, although he entered this project relatively late, has helped by providing me with emotional support, humor, and welcome distractions through the trying process of getting it finished.

Parts of this book were published in earlier versions. Part of chapter 2 appears in my article "Competing Hierarchies: Javanese Merchants and the *Priyayi* Elite in Solo, Central Java," *Indonesia* 52 (October 1991): 55–83.

Part of chapter 4 was published in my article "Why Women Rule the Roost: Rethinking Javanese Ideologies of Gender and Self-Control," in *Bewitching Women, Pious Men: Gender and Body Politics in Southeast Asia*, edited by Aihwa Ong and Michael Peletz, 19–50 (Berkeley: University of California Press). Copyright © 1995 by The Regents of the University of California. Both articles are used with permission.

A NOTE ON THE USE OF FOREIGN TERMS
AND PROPER NAMES

Because fieldwork for this study was conducted in both Javanese and Indonesian, terms appear here from both languages. Unmarked foreign-language terms and quotations are Javanese, or both Javanese and Indonesian; others have been identified as Indonesian (I.) or Dutch (D.). A number of Arabic loanwords appear in the text; since these have been adopted into Javanese and Indonesian I have not considered it necessary to mark them. Neither Indonesian nor Javanese distinguishes the plural form from the singular; for the sake of smoother English sentences, however, I have taken the liberty of pluralizing some Indonesian and Javanese words by adding -s (for example, I have pluralized *bécak* as *bécaks*).

The names of people used in this study are pseudonyms except for the names of well-known figures, but all place names are real. Lest there be confusion about the names "Solo" and "Surakarta," it should be mentioned from the outset that these are interchangeable. Both designate the same city, although Surakarta tends to be used in official contexts, whereas Solo is used more commonly in daily speech.

All translations are my own unless otherwise noted. A glossary of selected terms appears after the endnotes.

THE DOMESTICATION OF DESIRE

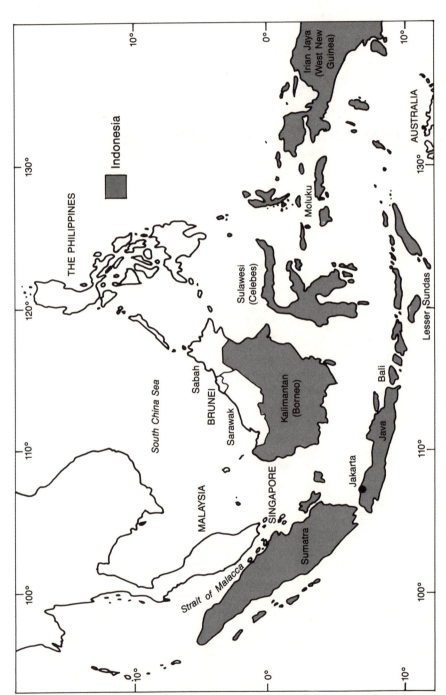

1. Map of Indonesia. From S. Errington 1989, [xv], used by permission.

INTRODUCTION

SOLO, a densely populated city of about half a million people, seems to epitomize the fitful process of "development" that is so characteristic of Indonesian cities. Located in the interior of Java, an island with roughly the area of New York State but inhabited by well over a hundred million people, Solo (also known as Surakarta) has the feeling of a once-sleepy provincial city that has been rudely awakened by the tremors of modernization emanating from Jakarta, Indonesia's political and economic hub. Bicycles, *bécaks* (bicycle-powered pedicabs), and an occasional oxcart or horse-drawn carriage crowd the roads alongside new BMWs, motorcycles, and double-decker buses. Multimillion-dollar textile factories compete for cheap labor with small batik workshops that are run much as they were in the nineteenth century. At night, hundreds of makeshift food stalls selling everything from skewers of grilled *saté* to hot milk and toast take over the sidewalks, obscuring the modern department stores, banks, and hotels that local officials proudly point to as signs of Solo's urban sophistication.

While I lived there in the latter half of the 1980s, it seemed that almost everywhere I looked, "modernization" was taking place, if somewhat haphazardly, right before my eyes. Pasar Singosaren, a large, busy bazaar housed inside a distinguished old building, was torn down and replaced by a multilevel shopping mall, its unfortunate vendors relocated to other markets or left to fend for themselves by selling their wares on the sidewalks. An elite housing complex, "New Solo" (Solo Baru), was being constructed on the former site of farmlands a few miles south of the city; billboards portrayed it as the ultimate in modern suburban living. Several upscale nightclubs and restaurants opened to cater to the middle and upper classes'

increasing penchant for Western-style entertainment and conspicuous consumption. Rumor had it that the city's quiet airport was going to be upgraded to an international airport, foreshadowing much greater change, and that the local and national governments had great plans for making Solo a major tourist destination and a showcase of development, *pembangunan* (I.), the obsessive goal of the current regime.

Even in its best efforts to imitate Jakarta's cosmopolitanism, though, Solo was not entirely successful. Less than a mile north of where I lived was a small, air-conditioned shopping mall, the first to open in Solo. Here at Purwosari Plaza, local teens had their choice of the latest cassettes of American rock music, Jamaican reggae, or Indonesian pop that blared at painful volume from stereo speakers. Well-heeled urbanites could buy toasters, jars of Nescafé, or Australian cheese at the Mickey Morse [sic] supermarket on the top floor (which had, not surprisingly, a logo bearing a striking resemblance to a Disney character). But many of the mall's stores were unoccupied or nearly deserted. On the ground floor, a restaurant called Dallas Fried Chicken stood perpetually without customers, a sad imitation of the more popular Kentucky Fried Chicken chain that had opened in some Indonesian cities. The prices at the shops and restaurants were too high, some of the would-be customers complained, and the goods no better than what they could buy elsewhere at a cheaper price. The mall was just far enough from the center of town, moreover, that even those who could afford it generally shopped in more convenient places. Solo was still a rather conservative city, and consumerism had not yet become the way of life here that it had in metropolitan Jakarta.

In the midst of all of the city's efforts at development, abortive or successful, Laweyan, the neighborhood in the southwest corner of Solo where I lived for more than two years, had the eerie feeling of a place stuck in time.[1] A short walk westward from the house in which I lived, past a few tiny shops selling cooked food and basic household provisions, was a small open-air market, always muddy during the rainy season. Customers bargained fiercely there with the vendors, surrounded by their piles of goods, for the best prices on papayas, mangos, shallots, or chilies. Across the street, two or three older women with warm smiles and deep lines etched into their faces sat on straw mats on the sidewalk, selling faded, second-hand sarongs and observing the movements of the local residents, including my own. Some days, braving the onrush of traffic (one unmistakable sign of change) to cross the congested road that bisected the neighborhood, I would walk past those women and, after we had exchanged greetings, continue southward past the small Islamic prayer hall on the corner into the kampong, a maze of narrow streets and alleys crowded with houses and workshops. Inside the kampong the quiet came as a relief after the honking horns and exhaust fumes of the main road; it was broken only by the wheels of a bicycle as it scattered the gravel in its path, or by the periodic call to prayer that issued from crackling loudspeakers at neighborhood mosques and prayer halls. Usually a *bécak* driver or two sat napping in the shade, waiting for a fare. My purpose there was to visit friends and acquaintances, or to buy some sweet rice porridge with coconut milk from a woman who set up a little stall in front of her house in the mornings—at about three cents a bowl, it was a bargain, especially because it always came with twenty minutes or so of free local gossip.

As I wandered through the dusty alleys, most of the larger homes were hidden from sight by high walls that badly needed a new coat of whitewash. An open front gate might offer a rare glimpse of an old, gracious wooden house built in Javanese style, or, more commonly, one of the hybrid dwellings mixing Javanese and European aesthetics and building materials that had been built by the neighborhood's textile merchants and entrepreneurs from the 1920s through the 1960s. Many of the houses had batik workshops attached to them—sometimes I would catch the acrid smell of hot wax in the air when I passed one that was still in use—but most of the workshops were empty, their large dye vats covered with cobwebs. A number of the homes were still inhabited by the less-prosperous descendants of the original owners, but their peeling paint and cracked stained-glass windows hinted that the current occupants could barely afford to maintain them. Some of the houses had been vacant for years. Gradually decaying in the tropical climate, they stood as dilapidated monuments to the neighborhood's more affluent days.

I was swept by a wave of nostalgia every time I set foot in that kampong. Even then I realized the inherent contradictions involved in feeling so nostalgic for a past that is not one's own, knowing that I was guilty of a misplaced romanticism. But there was a poignancy about the place that is difficult to convey in words—a poignancy that one might feel at driving through a deserted mining town, or visiting the archaeological ruins of a once-vibrant city—and that sometimes overwhelmed my efforts at academic detachment. Nostalgia seemed to permeate the air in Laweyan, as pungent as the smell of hot wax, and it was hard not to succumb to it.

People in the community, especially those who were old enough to remember better times, often reminisced about the days when the neighborhood had been a place of thriving businesses, wealthy entrepreneurs, and constantly employed workers. Those quiet alleys had teemed with life not so long ago, I was told, filled with the sounds of residents and batik workers coming and going, and of *bécaks* arriving with piles of white cambric cloth and large blocks of wax and leaving with neat stacks of finished batik sarongs, bound for the marketplace. The streams that cut through the neighborhood had run dark blue and brown back then, stained with the runoff of the dyes used in making batik. No one had really minded the pollution;

these were signs of a prosperity from which everyone in the neighborhood had benefited, from entrepreneur to worker. Now, the homes themselves radiated a silent wistfulness for those times: the decor of many of them had remained unaltered for decades, as if the current inhabitants feared that any change would permanently erase the memory of the community in its heyday.

Even as I gazed upon the specter of Laweyan's history, however, I could not possibly imagine that I was seeing a place that had been untouched by modernity, for these were the remains of a community that had been born and nourished in the distinctly modern social and economic conditions of urban Java under late colonial and early postcolonial rule. The ghosts that haunted these back alleys were those of Javanese petty capitalists and wage laborers, people whose day-to-day lives were often more directly affected by global economic recessions than by fluctuations of the rice harvests in the nearby villages. Modernity had also entered the community through commodities: automobiles, piped water, radios, and eventually telephones and televisions were standard features of many Laweyan households long before they were accessible to most other Indonesians. Some people still had old Mercedes-Benzes that had been kept in near-perfect condition for years, waxed to a brilliant shine and ready for any outing.

The neighborhood, then, felt more like a museum commemorating a once-modern past than a remnant of some premodern era. The impressive homes built by Laweyan's elite were testimony to the modern age as it had burst upon the scene in the early decades of this century. Influenced by the art deco movement, whose streamlined, curvilinear forms and bold angularity triumphantly announced the arrival of a new era, the architectural styles of the brick and cement houses that were constructed in the late 1920s and after stood in sharp contrast to the intricately carved wooden homes with steeply arched roofs that had been built earlier in a more traditional Javanese style. The later homes, although incorporating elements of Javanese architectural design, were more Western in appearance than Javanese. They made a clear statement about the orientation of their owners: these people had not been looking backward to their village roots. Instead, they were looking ahead to the future, and to the West as an exemplar of progress and modernity.

But at some point in the intervening years, Laweyan had been transformed from an icon of the modern into a site of nostalgia, a place that was distinctly out of step with the rapid cadence of urban development in Indonesia. Other residents of Solo commonly associated the neighborhood with an "old-fashioned Javanese" as opposed to a "modern Indonesian" way of life. It was not hard to see why. Most middle-aged and older Laweyan women had clung to wearing Javanese dress, consisting primarily of an ankle-length batik sarong (*jarik, tapih; kain,* I.) and a *kebaya,* a long-sleeved, tailored overblouse, even as the majority of urban middle- and upper-class women abandoned it for Western-style clothing. The dialect of Indonesian (*bahasa Indonesia*, I., the national language) spoken here was considered by other urbanites to be rather archaic and heavily influenced by Javanese, suggesting a lack of modern sophistication; on several occasions, when I unwittingly slipped into a Javanese expression in the midst of speaking Indonesian with Solonese from outside the neighborhood, they laughed and remarked that I spoke Indonesian "just like someone from Laweyan."[2] People from other quarters of the city also told me that if I wanted to find traditional foods of the kind eaten in the villages, Laweyan was the place to look for them. Despite its automobiles, television sets and VCRs, and even an occasional satellite dish, Laweyan was perceived by other Solonese as an urban neighborhood that in some ways had more in common with the hinterland—invariably identified with "Javanese tradition"—than it did with the rest of the city.

Laweyan's reputation for being old-fashioned was not undeserved. Having read a Dutch account of the neighborhood's batik firms from 1930, I was struck by how little they seemed to have changed since that time. The organization of the industry, the setup of the workshops, and the attitudes of the entrepreneurs were all startlingly similar to what the author had described more than half a century earlier.[3] Photographs of batik workers from the late 1920s and early 1930s might just as easily have been taken in the 1980s. Considering all the dramatic changes that had shaken Indonesia since the 1930s—the global depression of that decade, the Japanese occupation during World War II, the Revolution and independence in the mid- to late 1940s after more than 300 years of colonial domination, the political and economic upheavals of the 1960s, and the rapid economic development that had been taking place since the 1970s—the sense that very little had changed in more than fifty years was astonishing. The decline of the community's prosperity was obvious, but one had the feeling that if the batik industry had remained profitable, the neighborhood might have stayed more or less the same for another half century or longer.

Far from evolving into full-fledged industrial capitalists poised to take advantage of Indonesia's economic growth, most of Laweyan's entrepreneurs and their businesses had turned into quaint relics of the past. It seemed that memory had become one of the community's few remaining assets: although the neighborhood had once been famous for its abundant wealth, by the time I lived there most of the wealth had dried up—as everyone knew. While much of Solo was being swept up by the tide of development unleashed by President Suharto's New Order regime, Laweyan appeared to have done all it could to keep development at arm's length, trading its erstwhile modernity for a recalcitrant traditionalism. Why, I wondered, had Laweyan allowed itself to be recast as a signifier of tradition rather than as an active participant in modernization? I was anxious to learn the story of Laweyan's past, but it was revealed to me slowly, in bits and pieces, for the neighborhood did not give up its secrets easily. It was a narrative without a clear beginning or end, parts of which I, as an outsider to the community, would never learn. I had to be satisfied with what I could glean from people's answers to my incessant questions, as well as from their silences, which were sometimes just as informative.

This book is an exploration of modernity and its reversals—what I call the making of the "unmodern"—in an Indonesian city. It traces the social dynamics that brought Laweyan into being as a self-consciously (if somewhat unevenly) modern community in late colonial Java; it then analyzes the factors that contributed to the community's decline beginning in the 1960s. I wish to show how Javanese in this merchant enclave created their own distinctive forms of modern social life, but also how, under certain circumstances, modernness can give way to traditionalism, turning back the trajectory of progress usually associated with modernization.

Besides documenting the history and social relations of this distinctive community, my aim is also to illuminate the connections between the values and practices that we often call "domestic"—that is, those associated with family and household—and those that are linked to the extradomestic spheres of the community, the market, and the state. By concentrating on the family, its internal dynamics, and its relationships to other social domains and institutions, I examine modernity from the inside out, so to speak, showing how the most intimate sides of family life are interwoven with the most abstract forces of market exchange and state policy. I am especially concerned with exposing the limitations of models of modern life that hinge on sharp divisions between "domestic" and "public" spheres, or between "family" and "economy"—divisions that, despite many recent criticisms, are so closely wedded to the Western concept of modernity itself that they have proven very difficult to dissolve. Through an ethnographic investigation into the life of a Javanese community that for over a century has been deeply involved with modern institutions and social processes (such as global capitalism, national and international political movements, and colonial and postcolonial bureaucracies), I offer a picture of an alternative engagement with modernity that both draws on and significantly differs from its Western counterparts, one that is not based on the functional or ideological division of public and private spheres.

An equally important focus of the book, closely tied to the themes that I have just mentioned, concerns the issue of gender and how it is linked to the processes of modernization and traditionalization. My argument, simply stated, is that an understanding of gender is central to grasping the ways in which Javanese in this particular social field participated in modern urban life and social institutions—especially the market—while simultaneously turning them into recognizably "Javanese" social forms. Understanding the centrality of gender here hinges on recognizing the connections between the family and the spheres of economy and politics. Issues of gender are also key to making sense of why the members of this once-progressive merchant community found it so difficult to continue to modernize during a period when the Indonesian state had made modernization its primary agenda.

I am interested in how social constructions of gender (including ideas about personhood, male and female nature, and the proper roles of men and women in and outside the family) are related to such practices as market exchange and the conversion of wealth to status under conditions of incipient capitalism. The book will highlight women's roles in generating material wealth and symbolic capital for their families through their engagement in the marketplace; as I will argue, it is through women's actions that the forces of the market are "domesticated," or converted to the signs of value in a Javanese sense. This very process, however, has also contributed to Laweyan's profound ambivalence toward modernization, for reasons that will become clear as the book unfolds.

Thus I place women and gender at the heart of the study, a study that does not confine itself to questions of gender alone but recognizes the centrality of gender to all aspects of social life. One cannot fully comprehend the ways in which economic value, social prestige, or cultural capital are created in Javanese society without considering the gendered roles assigned to males and females. Nor can one understand how the social transformations associated with modernization are experienced and internalized by families and individuals. The approach I have chosen leads me to reevaluate some of the ethnographic commonplaces about gender and status that have dominated the literature on Java; it also exposes the weakness of Western models that presume the division between the family and the economy to lie at the heart of modern social formations. Although the book takes Java as its focus, my objective is to demonstrate the potential value of a gendered approach to analyzing social change in any location.

MODERNITY AND ITS DECLINE

How do we *know* modernity when we see it? For all the attention that the topic of modernity has attracted in recent years, the answer to this deceptively simple question remains elusive. As a periodizing concept, the term "modernity" is used somewhat loosely to refer to a distinct historical epoch ("the modern age"), to a set of sociological or technological indicators of "modernization" or social complexity, or to the existence of particular forms of subjectivity that are supposedly unique to the present (that is, the modern) era. Although the term is often applied unproblematically, as if modernity could be identified objectively, it is in the end as much a subjective as an objective condition, defined by its perceived relationship to the past in a given social and historical setting as well as by other, more tangible criteria. Furthermore, it has become increasingly clear over time that "other" modernities do not, and will not, follow the same course as Western modernity—which is itself inappropriately spoken of in the singular, given the diversity of experiences and social forms that have been lumped into the category of "the modern." How, then, might we begin to approach alternative modernities that do not mirror our own?

My usage of the term "modernity" in this book will reflect the overlap of meanings that is common in discussions of this concept. I consider this overlap essential, in fact, because I want to capture a sense of the modern as something experienced subjectively by individuals through their awareness of becoming part of a new age and a new way of life, but which also reflects the objective changes in social institutions and social relations that have everywhere been associated with modernity, such as the rise of capitalism, industrialization, and global markets; growing bureaucratization and the expansion of the state into everyday life; and increasingly complex divisions of labor and social classes. What we need to consider is how the effects of these transformations are experienced, understood, and transformed once again in accordance with local and national histories, cultures, and social relations. Some of the best anthropology in recent years has worked toward this goal, but there is still much to be done. Rather than aiming at a comprehensive analysis of modernity in its various aspects, my book offers an ethnographic treatment of how and why one Javanese community both embraced modernity and held it at bay over the course of nearly a century. I examine the external political, economic, and social conditions that affected the community as well as the internal social and cultural dynamics that shaped people's responses to these external influences. Through this dialectic, I bring into focus some of the dilemmas that have accompanied modernization in Indonesia, which surely have their parallels in other places and times.

One of these dilemmas centers on the ambiguous place of the market and those associated with it. The market is a persistent figure for the modern age, a place where the unfettered circulation of money and commodities is said to break down traditional social hierarchies and distinctions. It is sometimes thought to bypass the constraints of culture or history; governed by the logic of capital, it gradually comes to govern the logics by which society itself operates. This image of the market, while compelling, also has its limitations. In Java as elsewhere, one often finds that the market is entangled with local social and cultural forces in ways that do not fit well with classic images of capitalist development. In nineteenth- and early-twentieth-century Java, for instance, the demands of colonial capitalism simultaneously pushed Javanese toward and held them back from full engagement with the modern market. This contradiction resulted in a certain ambivalence among Javanese toward money and the market, which I treat in chapter 2 and after.

The traces of this ambivalence can still be seen today in the attitudes and practices of the old Javanese merchant class, including the merchants of Laweyan, and in the broad failure of this class to turn into a full-fledged capitalist bourgeoisie in postcolonial Indonesia. In this book I suggest that for merchants of Solo, the value of money lay less in its role as capital than in its ability to be converted to the signs of status and a historically produced value. I consider how they transformed money to locally meaningful forms of value and how this transvaluation of money sometimes worked against the modernizing movements typically associated with the market. I discuss in chapters 2 and 3 how Laweyan's internal hierarchies both reflected and transfigured the hierarchies of the wider society, creating a social system in which wealth rather than rank or aristocratic title was the primary basis for commanding deference and respect from others. The logic of the market, then, was incorporated into local social logics at the same time that it transformed them.

A further dilemma resulted from Laweyan's inability to sustain its own modernization over time, leading to a basic paradox: a community that once prided itself on its own modernness could over a few decades be transformed into a bastion of "tradition." We often take two things for granted when we talk about modernity. First, we assume that it has to be *achieved*—that the stasis of "traditional" society has to be overcome by the social, political, economic, and psychological processes that create modern social institutions and modern forms of subjectivity. Second, it is often taken as a given that the state of being modern is the end product of an evolutionary progression in which the present supersedes the past, for once and for all. When modernity has been achieved, it cannot be reversed: once modern, we *stay* modern.

Whereas the transition from tradition to modernity is usually assumed to be linear and unidirectional, this book looks at an urban community of Javanese merchants that has been gradually transformed in the "wrong" direction—from a community that represented an emergent modernity in late-nineteenth- and early-twentieth-century Java to what is often characterized as an anachronistic bastion of "tradition" in the 1990s. In the imagined transition from "tradition" to "modernity," some locales become the targets of modernization and development, while others become sites of nostalgia, remnants of a past era that are seen as marginal to the present one.[4] In a "developing" country like Indonesia, these places are typically seen as stubborn pockets of local tradition in the midst of a national and global modernization, uncomfortable reminders of a "backwardness" that has neither been overcome by the march of progress nor been deemed worthy of recuperation as a generically emblematic Tradition in the cultural projects of the nation-state.[5] But when we look closely at some of these sites, the term "traditional" (a concept that has itself been much problematized in recent anthropology) does not seem to fit them well at all.

Laweyan, a neighborhood that was known until recently as a major Indonesian center for the production of batik textiles, is one such site. Formerly one of Solo's wealthiest districts but now in decline, Laweyan exemplifies for more cosmopolitan Indonesians a passing way of life that centered around family firms—a lifestyle and mode of production that are increasingly irrelevant to the workings of modern Indonesian society and economy. Although it evokes a sense of longing for a would-be traditional past, I propose in chapter 1 that Laweyan's emergence as an entrepreneurial community in the late nineteenth century and its subsequent history can only be understood through its engagement in the social dynamics of modernity.

Thinking about Laweyan has made me think more about the problems inherent in the concept of modernity, especially in its evolutionary assumptions. Is it possible, I have wondered, to avoid the traps of evolutionary models of modernization, while still retaining a meaningful conception of modernity? It has also made me realize how fragile modernity is, at least in some of its aspects, and how easily it can be undone. While the Indonesian government is obsessed with the idea of modernizing Indonesia, the community of Laweyan has clearly been *de*modernized. What I saw there was less a nostalgia for tradition than a nostalgia for modernity, which was what I found so curious about the place. This book, then, begins with Laweyan's modern origins in the late period of Dutch colonial rule and works forward in time toward its traditionalized (but not traditional) present—a point at which, it seems, the community is once again on the verge of being absorbed into a newer modernity, one in which it can participate only peripherally.

Why would an entire community allow itself—and I do believe that there is an element of local agency involved here, if not exactly deliberate choice—to become gradually demodernized, at precisely the moment when modernization and development are the goals most ardently pursued by the Indonesian state? I attempt to answer this question as best I can, through a necessarily circuitous route. I show, for example, how the construction of an imagined "ancestral" tradition—a tradition that turns out to be tied, oddly enough, to the production of commodities for the market—deflects the modernizing agendas of the so-called New Order Indonesian regime. A space is then created in which nostalgia replaces "development" or "progress" as the dominant ethos of the community. This "backward" transformation has taken place through the interaction of factors both internal and external to the community, which illustrate the mutual entanglement of culture and politics in colonial and postcolonial Indonesia. I analyze these factors by looking at Laweyan within the larger political and cultural economies of Solo, Java, and Indonesia.

For the moment, however, I would like to consider more broadly how traditionalism, or something akin to it, might itself emerge out of modernity, confounding the master narratives of modernization theory, which hold that tradition invariably gives way to modernity in an orderly, sequential progression. I find it useful to think of modernity as Marshall Berman does (1988), less as a chronologically determinate stage of social evolution, the climax of the process of development, than as the social experience of a state of flux, a constant process of tearing down and building up that is rife with internal contradictions (see also the comments on Berman in Osborne 1995). In addition to its being a particular form of social experience, however, "modernity" also marks a unique type of temporal consciousness, a reflexive understanding of time that stresses the *newness* of the present era and its "qualitative transcendence of the past" (Osborne 1995, 11; see also Habermas 1987, esp. chap. 1; Felski 1995). Or, as Peter Osborne has written, "Modernity is a form of historical time which valorizes the new as the product of a constantly self-negating temporal dynamic" (1995, xii). "Modernity," by this definition, is not a state that is achieved once, definitively and in perpetuity. It must constantly be renewed, because yesterday's modernity is today's past, and therefore must itself be overcome if one is to retain a notion of the modern as the ever-new. Thus, modernity "is permanent transition" (14):

> "Modernity," we have seen, plays a peculiar dual role as a category of historical periodization: it designates the contemporaneity of an epoch to the time of its classification; yet it registers this contemporaneity in terms of a qualitatively new, self-transcending temporality which has the simultaneous effect of distancing the present from even that most recent past with which it is thus identified. It is this paradoxical doubling, or inherently dialectical quality, which makes modernity both so irresistible and so problematic a category. (13–14).

This dialectical aspect of modernity, while serving as a source of the constant regeneration of the modern, also creates a certain instability. Failure to fulfill the need for unceasing renewal can lead to a failure of the modern, a decline and even a retrogression as "newer" modernities surmount older ones. The once modern, then, may give way to what might best be thought of as the "unmodern," since it is certainly not the "premodern" nor, exactly, the "postmodern." The very term—like the "undead," those restless souls that exist in a world between life and death—suggests being trapped in limbo, neither "traditional" nor "modern," not progressing on a straight path from the former to the latter. As Osborne observes, "in its perpetual anxiety to transcend the present, modernity is everywhere haunted by the idea of decline" (19).

Laweyan seemed to epitomize the unmodern in the making, a place haunted by the specter of past modernities and their failure. The collective historical consciousness of the community had become oriented over time toward creating and maintaining a continuity with the past, rather than toward creating a rupture with it. The goal was not, as in modernist visions of progress, to transcend the past but rather to join it to the present. Laweyan found its legitimation in its sense of history: the past animated the present—at the same time, though, that it threatened to stifle it. Ironically, the more "unmodern" the community became, the more its members sought to validate their way of life through their connection to history. And as long as the present remained in the grip of the past, modernity would continue to elude them, receding into the past even as it stretched out, ungraspable, before them.

By situating Laweyan within the historical contexts of late colonial Java and postcolonial Indonesia, I suggest that the community's attachment to the past should be seen not as the result of a perverse archaism but as a strategy to claim cultural legitimacy and autonomy for itself, even as it became increasingly marginal to the mainstream of "modern" Indonesian society. The merchants of Laweyan resisted the state's attempts to domesticate them and their families through its development schemes; they seemed to prefer a marginal autonomy to being directly subjected to state control. This attitude appears to have evolved during the late colonial period and to have continued, though for varying reasons and under changing circumstances, down to the present day. Understanding the origins of the Javanese merchant community's relationship to the Dutch colonial state and its Javanese representatives, the class of bureaucratic and aristocratic elites known as *priyayi*, sheds light on the more recent reluctance of the *sudagar* or merchant class to participate fully in the contemporary state's modernizing moves. I examine this relationship in chapter 2 by looking at the ambiguous position of the indigenous bourgeoisie in the hierarchies of late colonial Javanese society. I also explore the position of women in defining as well as bridging the gap between the two classes, suggesting that the differences between women's roles in the two groups were often more symbolic than real.

Rethinking the Domestic Sphere

How does one trace the movements of a particular community through the broad sweeps of modernization (and, in this case, demodernization)? In this book I have chosen to focus, although not exclusively, on a domain that is sometimes paid inadequate attention in efforts to map modernity and its effects on society: the domestic sphere (a term that I prefer to others, for reasons that I discuss below). If modernity works, as has often been noted, through public spaces and institutions—factories, government offices, schools, city streets—it also works, perhaps most deeply and immediately, through the home and the family (see, e.g., Foucault 1978; Comaroff and Comaroff 1992). A basic concern of this book is to analyze how women and the domestic sphere have been involved in the complex transformations associated with modernity in Java. A key issue is not only how the family responds to external modernizing influences, but also how it fundamentally shapes the forms that modernity takes and the significance it acquires in any location.

My inspiration comes in part from the work of feminist scholars in various disciplines who have addressed related issues for periods and places far removed from twentieth-century Java, such as Linda Nicholson (1986), Nancy Armstrong (1987), Mary Poovey (1988), Joan Scott (1988), and Rita Felski (1995). Each of these authors has been concerned at some level with analytically breaking down the divisions that are often assumed to exist between the "domestic" or "private" sphere and the "public" sphere—that is, with showing how the public is always radically implicated in the private, and vice versa—and simultaneously exposing the reasons and means by which these stubborn divisions came to occupy such an important ideological place in Western society and thought. Lingering notions of the domestic sphere as a private, self-contained domain that stands at a complete remove from the public sphere have been exploded by the research of these and other scholars, who reveal in detail how domestic economies of production, reproduction, consumption, and affect are shaped through their interaction with larger political economies and ideological systems.[6]

Although the concept of the domestic sphere has to some extent fallen out of favor both in anthropology and in feminist studies, largely because of well-deserved criticisms of the resilient but problematic domestic/public dichotomy (e.g., Rosaldo 1980; Nicholson 1986), my study suggests that it is worthwhile to retain the idea. I prefer the term "domestic sphere" to "family" or "household" in some contexts because it can encompass both of these and more. The notion of an encompassing sphere rather than a social unit or collection of persons better allows for the inclusion of individuals, practices, and functions not generally associated with "the family" or "the household" in modern society, such as those associated with domestic economic production. I use the term to designate both a physical and conceptual space that centers on the home and family, but which in Java can also be expanded outside the confines of the home to include practices that may be linked conceptually to home and family even if they take place within the domain that we usually call "public." In using such a term, one must of course investigate the meanings, ideologies, and practices associated with it in its distinct historical and cultural settings, rather than take the meaning of "domestic" for granted. The "domestic sphere" is a Western construct, not a Javanese one, but for analytical purposes I find it useful in the Javanese setting.

Retaining a notion of the domestic sphere, then, does not necessarily imply accepting its absolute separation from, containment by, or subordination to the public sphere. Indeed, I argue for a reconceptualization of the domestic sphere and of the public/private opposition usually associated with it. By revealing the significance of the domestic in a Javanese community, I also aim to cast a new light on the notion of "the domestic" itself and the possibilities that might be contained within it.

What makes Laweyan so compelling a site for a study that focuses on the domestic is the extent to which local society revolved around women and a particular configuration of the domestic economy. Laweyan women, famed for their prowess as batik merchants and entrepreneurs, played defining roles in the family as well as in the community. They ran the family firms and market stalls, often with little or no help from their husbands; they also viewed themselves as the primary guardians of the household, assuming the burden of maintaining the family's material, social, and spiritual well-being. Much of the book is dedicated to exploring how women's centrality in the family and household was tied to their key roles in managing the family firms and in conducting the social life of the community, which were in turn linked to culturally specific ideas about gendered subjectivity.

I expand the concept of "domestic economy" to include not only material consumption and production but also the management and control of human passions, spiritual substance, and cultural value. In chapters 4 and 5, I show that in Javanese merchant households, these various aspects of domestic economy were so deeply intertwined as to be almost inseparable. In their positions as entrepreneurs and merchants, mothers, and wives, women were crucial in bringing together these economies; they saw themselves as the managers simultaneously of the family firm and of the material economy of the household, as well as the domesticators of the forces of desire—typically associated with men and money—which, if left uncontrolled, threatened the welfare of the family and the social order more broadly. (I am intentionally playing with the double meaning of the word "domesticate," to suggest the idea of bringing something under control as well as turning it into something of value to the family. At the same time, women were deeply involved in the harnessing of a certain kind of spiritual value and in its perpetuation from generation to generation. To be sure, women's willingness to attend to matters of money that many Javanese men would find demeaning might be seen as diminishing their broader social status. Yet women's roles in producing and conserving wealth for their families, and in converting money into an object of cultural value, were also essential to the production of the family's status and to its positioning in the hierarchies of Javanese society.

The domestic sphere in Laweyan, then, was the nexus of an economy that was simultaneously material, cultural, and social, and that extended out from the heart of the family to the marketplace, to the wider society and back again. Women stood at the center of this nexus; as the primary agents of domestication in the household, they, often to a greater extent than their husbands, took on the responsibility for generating material, cultural, and social value for their families. But the cultural logics that placed women in the role of "domesticator" were quite different from those that have linked women to the domestic sphere in the West, where, as Nancy Armstrong writes, "We are taught to divide the political world in two and to detach the practices that belong to a female domain from those that govern the marketplace" (1987, 9–10). In Solo, where the marketplace *itself* is frequently conceived of as a female domain, the logic of this division fails. Women's association with money and the market, which is informed by culturally and historically specific ideas about gender, subjectivity, and economy, destabilizes the distinctions between the market and the home that have characterized the modern West. Rethinking the significance of the domestic from this angle presents alternative ways of understanding the relationships between everyday practices, subjective experiences, and the larger cultural, political, and economic forces with which they interact.

This concentration on the domestic sphere rather than on the more public social and political domains (which has been more common in studies of Java) offers a new perspective from which to view Javanese society. The importance of women in Javanese systems of status and prestige has often been underestimated because of lack of attention to the ways in which social and cultural value are produced and reproduced through the family. Moreover, in the particular sector of Javanese society on which I focus here, the domestic sphere was not only a major site of the family's material and cultural production, but also the locus of its power in the community and wider society. In chapters 6 and 7, however, I also point to the difficulties in sustaining the power of the domestic under the more recent "modernizing" conditions of New Order Indonesia (which is no longer so new, the current regime having entered its fourth decade), where, through the impact of ideologies of national and capitalist development, the domestic sphere is rarely seen as an important site of material production or as the source of the family's power in society.

What I am suggesting, in effect, is that we move the domestic sphere and the domestic economy from their generally peripheral status in studies of modern society and economy to the very center. Yet the economy that I have in mind is an economy that is not contained by that term's conventional meanings in the modern West. As Nicholson and others have pointed out, since the nineteenth century the widespread belief that the family is a natural haven from the harsh world of the market has led to the assumption that home and family are necessarily distinct from the domain of "the economy" (Nicholson 1986, 121). It is worth remembering, though, that prior to industrialization the family/household was an economically productive unit (122; Tilly and Scott 1978), and that the very word "economy," derived from the Greek *oikonomia*, "household management," carries within it the figure of the domestic.[7]

When we think about economy in its original sense, as a managing of the household, and then think about "home" as a key site for the generation and conservation of the most elemental kinds of value, the term "domestic sphere" takes on a new significance. Instead of seeing it as a sphere that is both subsumed by and subordinate to the public sphere, we can consider it as a central sphere of production, cultural as well as material, in its own right. We should not lose sight, though, of the extent to which the domestic is molded by its involvement with that which is ordinarily defined as "public"—and that ultimately the distinction of the two domains is an artificial one, useful only for analytical purposes. In this study I will demonstrate the mutual engagement of the domestic and the public, and their final inseparability, through the details of ethnography. I know of no better way to break down such an obstinate division.

GENDER AND SUBJECTIVITY

Exploring the roles of women and men in particular forms of "the domestic" requires an understanding of the ways in which historically and culturally specific notions of gender work through the family (as well as through other social institutions and relationships) to produce subjectivities that are locally recognizable as "female," "male," or something else. In recent years a number of scholars have called insistently for studies that treat gender and subjectivity as processes generated in discrete locales and through particular histories; they assert that neither gender nor subjectivity are fixed across time or location (e.g., de Lauretis 1987; Scott 1988, 1992; Kondo 1990; Probyn 1990; Butler 1992; Flax 1993; Barlow 1996). By analyzing the linkages between constructions of gender, subjective experience, and their broader sociohistorical milieu in Java, I will apply the insights that have been offered by these scholars to a densely textured ethnographic setting.

Even though I use the term "woman" throughout this book without attempting to deconstruct it systematically, I also try to make clear that the women about whom I write do not constitute an undifferentiated category of "Javanese women."[8] They are women who are defined in very concrete ways by their class locations in Javanese/Indonesian society and by their occupations, as well as by their positions in the family. Furthermore, they are identified, and identify themselves, by their membership in particular communities in a specific historical period. I cannot justify making sweeping generalizations about *all* Javanese women based on research undertaken primarily in one urban community, nor would I want this ethnography to be read as a general statement about Javanese women. On the contrary, I insist that the specifics of time and place are critical; one of my fundamental aims is to tease out the relationship of historical and social context to certain configurations of gender and subjectivity. In doing so, I also hope to demonstrate that modern subjectivity takes a wide variety of forms—some of which might not ordinarily be judged "modern" at all by most Western standards. My point is not to argue for some timeless, quintessentially Javanese sense of self but to show how gender and subjectivity are constructed in a particular place and time. In chapter 7 I juxtapose those contextually specific patterns with the dominant gender ideologies of the current Indonesian regime and its stereotypes of modern women and men, to underscore the contrast between state-driven ideas about the correct roles of women in their relationships to husbands, children, and the nation and those ideas that I saw revealed in the daily lives of people in Solo.

While I would deny that Laweyan represented a generic, ahistorical Javanese authenticity, it would also be misleading for me to suggest that there was no "Javaneseness" at all to the ways in which people in Laweyan chose to live their lives. Such a notion would, I believe, be dismissed outright by people in Laweyan themselves, for they had strong ideas about what being "Javanese" meant and were quick to condemn others who did not act according to their standards of "proper" Javaneseness. To be sure, there is no monolithic entity out there called "Javanese culture"—their ideas about being Javanese were certainly not identical to those of people from other sectors of Solonese society, let alone from other parts of Java, nor were their ideas internally consistent within the community itself, as I discuss in some detail in chapter 4 with regard to dominant Javanese gender ideologies and their alternatives. But it would be a mistake not to acknowledge the extent to which Laweyan people's conceptions about what it means to be Javanese inform their actions and modes of thinking about the world.

So, for example, I maintain throughout the book that an overriding concern with status and hierarchy—which has often been noted as a basic feature of Javanese society, especially in the part of Central Java where I have worked (see C. Geertz 1960; Siegel 1986; Keeler 1987; J. Errington 1988)—permeated the lives of people in Laweyan, palpably shaping all social relationships. Ideas about gender, too, were played out against the backdrop of certain recognizably Javanese notions of personhood, including, among other things, a preoccupation with the ability of individuals to exercise control over their base instincts and passions. Rather than identifying these as timeless facts of Javanese culture, however, I wish to consider how fairly loose guidelines for living in Javanese society translate into concrete modes of thought and action that are very much affected by changing social and political circumstances, as well as by the subject positions of individuals—their sex, class, generation, and so on. As I will seek to make clear in the chapters that follow, it is precisely the flexibility that such vague guidelines offer which enables members of a rather marginal community such as Laweyan to assert their essential "Javaneseness" even as those outside the community question it, or which allows women and men in the same community to hold simultaneously contradictory, yet somehow compatible, conceptions of gender and human nature.

One issue that I treat in some depth concerns how subjective understandings of desire and its control—a matter that is usually thought of as intensely personal—relate to more "social" and even "economic" matters: a family's placement in the status hierarchies of the community, the ability of women or men to accumulate wealth for their families, and so on. It is here that that we see how thoroughly intertwined the domestic and the public, the personal and the social, really are. I am interested in how notions of desire and self-control become attached to certain ideas about gender—how, in short, subjectivity is gendered in a particular context. This involves understanding how desire is constituted and managed in the family, which I regard as a locus for the control of desire, as well as in the wider society. Women and men, I propose, view themselves somewhat differently in relation to the control of human desires, instincts, and emotions, and this has widespread ramifications for their actions in the family and in society (see Peletz 1996). People in Solo commonly express the idea that human passions need to be properly channeled for social and personal purposes, but the question of *who* most needs to control their passions, and *how* those passions should be controlled, generates quite a bit of controversy.

The domesticating roles that Laweyan women often play in the family are intimately tied to these ideas about gender and self-control, and these ideas also influence their actions in other realms of social life. Women's domination of the marketplace as merchants and consumers, their self-assigned roles as the conservators of spiritual and material ancestral inheritances, and their willingness to assume responsibility for perpetuating the rituals and exchanges that hold Laweyan together as a community are all related in some way to conceptions of gender and subjectivity that focus on the family. What defines males as men, fathers, or husbands, and females as women, mothers, or wives, is not only their biological sex, their style of dress, or their marital or parental status, but also their relationship to gendered notions of desire and self-discipline as they are constituted, first and foremost, in the family.

Attention to issues of discipline and desire is especially valuable for understanding gender, subjectivity, and social change in the contexts of Javanese society and New Order Indonesia. Several authors have noted that ideas about the control of desire and other strong emotion through self-discipline and reason are strongly interwoven with Javanese conceptions of self, power, and hierarchy (C. Geertz 1960; Anderson 1990c; J. Errington 1984; Keeler 1987); they also lie at the heart of Javanese gender ideologies asserting the "natural" superiority of males over females (Djajadiningrat-Nieuwenhuis 1987; Keeler 1987, 1990; Hatley 1990). The New Order regime, drawing on these themes of discipline and control but removing them from their original contexts and meanings, has heavily emphasized the need for self-discipline and the suppression of individual desire among its citizens toward the interrelated goals of creating order (ketertiban, I.) and fostering the development (pembangunan) of a modern nation. The state's messages of self-discipline and self-sacrifice are broadcast even more emphatically to women than to men, stressing the importance of motherly selflessness and the restraint of personal desire for the sake of family and nation.

I am intrigued by the interplay of these distinct but overlapping understandings of desire and discipline, and the ways that these have contributed to the creation of "modern" forms of subjectivity in Indonesia. By examining notions of discipline and desire as they are applied in certain contexts of Javanese/Indonesian life, I consider the ways in which local constructions of gender run counter to state-generated gender ideologies that are presented as alternately "traditional" (thereby representing a comforting stability and imagined continuity with the past) and "modern" (and therefore in keeping with the state's goals of development and modernization). Ideas about what form the domestic sphere should take, as well as the gendered roles that its inhabitants should occupy, are shifting as the domestic sphere is subjected, to an ever-greater extent, to the interventions of the state, the mass media, and the emerging forces of capitalist development in Indonesia.

CAPTURING THE LOCAL

Whatever theoretical contributions this book may make, it is in the end an ethnographic study of one urban community. The decision to focus my research on a particular neighborhood seemed an obvious and unproblematic one when I began this project, for this was something that had been done by many other anthropologists before me. It also seemed a useful solution to the daunting problem of how to go about establishing myself in a fairly large city where I initially had very few acquaintances. However, the debates that have emerged in anthropology since I began my research have led me to think about the possible problems inherent in such a study. To speak of "the neighborhood" suggests the intimacy of face-to-face interactions; gemeinschaft rather than gesellschaft (Tönnies 1957); a "real" community as opposed to an imagined one (Anderson 1991). It evokes the sense of a place where social relations exist in forms that are direct and open rather than indirect and mystified—potentially lulling one into the dubious notion that social life is more transparent at this level than it is at more encompassing levels of social organization.

Does concentrating on a single neighborhood or village merely foster the illusion that these are cohesive and insular communities that exist prior to, or independent of, the effects of larger social, political, and economic formations and processes—the nation-state, the global economy, transnational informational flows, and so on? Should we avoid these pitfalls by avoiding studies of local communities altogether? I would argue, on the contrary, that the value of such studies is that they offer a means of deciphering at close range the ways in which local communities and the individuals who constitute them engage in, and are affected by, the processes that in turn constitute regional, national, and global political and cultural economies. If we do not take "the neighborhood," "the village," or "the community" for granted but rather ask how they come to be created as social entities and reproduced—or how they fail to reproduce themselves, as one might say of the community in which I worked—and how the neighborhood, too, serves as a locus of ideology, of power, or of social change, then we can better understand how a given place participates in the larger social and political economies within which it is embedded.

Laweyan is a community that often positions itself at odds with the current regime and the powerful capitalist ventures that the regime supports. Many of its residents see themselves as the guardians of valuable cultural traditions that are being eroded by the relentless forces of change foisted upon them by the state or by modernization. It is hard for me at times not to romanticize Laweyan's past or to mourn its plight as a community that has been broken down by the ravages of capitalism, modernization, and the intrusions of a too-powerful regime. What must be kept in mind, however—and this is a point to which I will be returning—is that Laweyan's very existence and survival as a community depended for close to a century on forces quite similar to those that have contributed to its decline. This is not a pristine, "natural" community that has been dragged only recently into the grasp of the state or the global economy. It is a community that was spawned by the conditions of late colonialism and that was raised to maturity by the early postindependence state. Despite its own ideologies of autonomy, it has never been a truly independent, self-contained community. I want to make clear that the concept of "community" itself has its own genealogical and ideological foundations, which extend far beyond the actual spatial boundaries of the neighborhood, linking it to much larger social, political, and economic contexts.

Ultimately, the national and the global are always mediated and experienced through the local, and what anthropologists still seem to do best, after all these years, is to study the local. I see no reason to abandon this strength of the discipline, particularly at a time when scholars in many fields are arguing in favor of specificity over generalization, condemning metanarratives, and calling repeatedly for historically grounded studies of the local. This may indeed be where anthropologists can make some of their most significant contributions to social theory, including feminist theory, and to the understanding of social processes and transformations. We should also heed Elspeth Probyn's reminder, however, that "the local exists nowhere in a pure state. The local is only a fragmented set of possibilities that can be articulated into a momentary politics of time and place" (1990, 187). The goal of studying the local should not be to reify it, to glorify it, to freeze it in time, or to turn it into a representative site that stands for others "just like it." Rather, by capturing the evanescence of one place at one point in time, we should hope for no more than to begin to gain insight into the complex dynamics of society at a historical moment of contradiction and change. If this seems too modest a goal, I would suggest that it is a more difficult and significant task than it may initially appear— and that it is the best place to start if we are to understand how, ultimately, modernity enters the lives of those who do not yet take it for granted.

Chapter One

A NEIGHBORHOOD COMES OF AGE

THIS CHAPTER introduces the neighborhood of Laweyan, both as a site of ethnographic inquiry and as a community that was born out of the social and economic transformations of late colonial Java. Located on the periphery of Solo, a city long known among Javanese and Westerners alike as a preserve of "authentic" Javanese culture and courtly traditions, Laweyan emerged as an enclave of textile entrepreneurs and merchants that was famed less for its cultural purity than for its remarkable wealth. By focusing on the development of the batik industry, the source of Laweyan's wealth, the chapter demonstrates how fully Laweyan was integrated into the economics and politics of colonial society by the early decades of the twentieth century. Viewing Laweyan as a product of an emergent modernity sets the stage for the later exploration of why the processes of modernization in the community came to be reversed over the course of only a few decades.

CULTURAL AUTHENTICITY AND THE ETHNOGRAPHIC COLLAGE

When foreign visitors to Solo step off the train at Balapan Station, they are quickly approached by *bécak* drivers offering to take them to one of the two palaces located within city limits, the Kraton Surakarta (Surakarta Palace) and the Mangkunagaran.[1] It is assumed that tourists will make these their first and perhaps only stops, for Solo is best known as a center of Javanese court culture. The royal seat of Surakarta, known in everyday parlance as Solo, was established in the mid–eighteenth century by Sunan (King) Pakubuwana II (r. 1726–49), a ruler of the once-powerful Mataram dynasty of Java. Pakubuwana II (whose name translates roughly as "Axis of the Universe"; Florida 1995, 2) had initially come to the throne in Kartasura, about seven miles to the west, where the capital of Mataram had been located since 1680. After an armed rebellion against the allied forces of Pakubuwana II and the Dutch East India Company led to the sacking of the palace at Kartasura in 1742, the rebels were finally put down with the help of Pakubuwana's brother-in-law, a Madurese prince who was an ally of the Company. Forced to cede a large portion of the lands under his control to the Company in return for its support, Pakubuwana was restored to the throne by the Dutch in 1743, but with his power much diminished.

Instead of attempting to rebuild the palace at Kartasura, which appeared to be an ill-fated site from which to rule, he decided to move the entire court a short distance east to Solo, at that time a swampy village on the banks of the Solo River (Bengawan Solo). The building of the new palace at its present site was completed in 1745, and Pakubuwana and his courtiers had taken up residence there by early 1746.[2] In 1755 the old kingdom of Mataram was divided into two realms, Surakarta and Yogyakarta. In 1757 a minor royal house was founded in Solo to placate a rebellious relative of the ruling family. The new palace was called the Mangkunagaran after its chief prince, who took the name Mangkunagara I ("Holds the Kingdom on His Lap").[3]

Although the royal houses of Solo ruled at the pleasure of the Dutch, which rendered them impotent from a political and military standpoint, socially and culturally they continued to wield considerable influence in Java, and especially in Solo itself. This cultural influence continued after Indonesian independence in 1949, although to a lesser extent than under colonial rule.[4] In particular, the palaces have been viewed as sites where "authentic" Javanese culture and language have been preserved in their loftiest and least corrupted forms. The association of the palaces with high Javanese culture extends to the city more broadly: Solo prides itself on being a place that upholds time-honored Javanese linguistic and cultural traditions. The classical Javanese arts flourished here during the colonial period (and, to a somewhat lesser degree, after independence), including dance, gamelan music, lyric poetry, shadow puppetry, and batik making. Solo's residents are renowned for speaking the most elegant style of Javanese language and for following the most refined forms of social etiquette; they are alternately admired and mocked for these qualities by people in other parts of the island.

Many Westerners have been equally convinced of Solo's cultural superiority and authenticity. In 1904, for instance, the Dutchman H. H. van Kol wrote of the Residency of Surakarta, the colonial district that included the city of Solo: "Here beat the heart of Java, and nowhere else does as much of Javanese life, of Javanese customs and traditions, still exist as in these lands where the old architecture of the Hindus worked its most beautiful temples, still an object of respect and admiration for anyone who has a feeling for beauty and art. One still finds the flower of the Javanese nobility here, and language and religion are preserved in the forms truest to the original" (1904, 1149). Van Kol's statement reflected a widespread belief among Dutch colonial officials and scholars that Solo, especially the palace of the sunan, was the truest heir to the venerable cultural, linguistic, and artistic traditions of pre-Islamic Java, which they felt had existed at that time in their "purer" Indianized forms.[5] The conviction that Solo was a repository of these hallowed cultural traditions, albeit in rather degenerate forms, lent an official colonial stamp of legitimacy to Solonese culture and in particular to Solo's aristocratic elites, who were seen as the guardians of high Javanese tradition.

Today, Solo still attracts those in search of "true" Javanese culture: Solo's teachers of *kebatinan*, Javanese mysticism and meditation, draw pupils from North America, Europe, and Australia, and others come from abroad to study Javanese dance and music. What had attracted me to this city, however, was less its aristocratic ambience or its status as a preserve of "genuine" Javanese culture than the dense and irregular texture of its everyday life. To my eyes, Solo is, above all, a city of contrasts and contradictions. It is a place of aristocrats, but also of bazaar merchants and street peddlers, mystics and university students, veiled Muslim women and highheeled prostitutes, flamboyant transvestites and drably uniformed civil servants. Although the vast majority of the local population is Javanese, there are also ethnic Chinese and Arabs (most locally born), a handful of Indians, and Indonesians who have migrated to Solo from various parts of the archipelago. In addition, there is a small but constant presence of foreign tourists, students, and consultants. This vibrant and sometimes strange mixture of people and lifestyles does not, as I see it, detract from Solo's famed cultural authenticity—for this *is* the real Solo.

Trying to navigate through Solo's social intricacies was a challenge to me: I am an urban anthropologist because I am intrigued by the complexity and dynamism of cities. The anthropologist of the city knows that any effort to attain ethnographic closure is bound to fail; she must content herself with the profusion of often wildly random snapshots that her mind's eye takes and later reassembles in a sort of ethnographic collage. It was this sense of open-endedness, of unexplored and sometimes unexplorable possibilities, that I found fascinating about Solo. Doing fieldwork here—and writing about it—meant, both literally and metaphorically, wandering about half-lost through the city's labyrinthine streets and alleys, peering into windows and doors left ajar, and making new acquaintances through purely chance encounters. You do not capture the city, confining it neatly to the ethnographic page; you follow its lead, knowing that while one alley might prove to be a dead end, the next might take you in a halfdozen directions that you had never imagined pursuing. My wanderings in Solo took me to bazaars and graveyards, workshops and palaces, mosques and roadside food stalls, wedding halls and amusement parks. I found myself in the homes of local Javanese, Chinese, and Arabs; merchants, batik workers, domestic servants, aristocrats, intellectuals, bureaucrats, *bécak* drivers, and a healer (*dhukun*) of snakebites who fed me dried cobra meat and offered to put a live scorpion in his mouth in exchange for two American dollars. "Theory" seemed very remote while I was in the midst of these ethnographic peregrinations, for what sort of theory could adequately account for and integrate the tremendous richness and complexity of life in an Indonesian city?

But as enlightening as wandering can be, one also feels the need for a place, if only a narrow grid of city streets, where one comes to recognize familiar people and sights, and where one is in turn recognized by others. For this reason as well as others, I chose to live and anchor my research in one neighborhood. Calling Laweyan rather than some other place "home" had definite implications for my research. It gave Java a certain hue for me: the ways that I think about Javanese and Indonesian society have been filtered through my experiences in that one neighborhood, and those experiences have obviously colored my account of Java in this book. Since Laweyan was an unusual neighborhood in many respects, I could not take for granted that what I saw there was typical of Solo or of Java more generally. I see this as a positive thing, because it forced me to focus on the specific rather than to seek the general. To the extent that I was tempted to draw ethnographic generalizations about "Javanese culture" from my experiences in Laweyan, I had to remind myself that *these* Javanese could not necessarily be assumed to represent *other* Javanese, which then raised the question in my mind: who, if anyone, could be called "typical" or "representative"? By sustaining the tension between the specific and the general rather than assimilating the former to the latter, I was compelled to consider the effects of local histories on what one might otherwise gloss with such broad terms as "culture," "gender," or "social relations."[6]

I had initially taken up residence in Laweyan for a particular reason: to learn about the entrepreneurial community that was involved in the production and trade of batik textiles, and especially about the roles of women in that community. Solo was one of the foremost centers of batik production in Java, and Laweyan, in the southwest corner of the city, had at one time contained the largest concentration of batik workshops in Solo. There were indications in the available literature that women were very active in the batik business as entrepreneurs, traders, and workers, and I wanted to explore how their position in this industry might be tied to more general social and cultural constructions of gender in Java, especially the reputed association of women with matters of money. By 1986, the year I arrived in Laweyan, most of the businesses had folded, or "rolled up their mats" (*gulung tikar*), the local euphemism for bankruptcy. A few were still operating, though, and since I was as interested in the history and social relations of the community as I was in the actual workings of the industry, I was not discouraged from living there despite the small number of functioning firms. On the contrary, I wanted to learn why the batik business had declined and what was becoming of the community in the wake of these changes.

What was it that made Laweyan different from other neighborhoods of Solo? Unlike certain other ethnic groups in Indonesia, for whom trade is a well-accepted, even esteemed, way of life, Javanese are generally not known as merchants. As Clifford Geertz points out in his study of two Indonesian market towns, the market has tended to form its own rather separate cultural universe in Java, while "the status of the trader in the wider society has been ambiguous at best, pariah-like at worst" (1963, 44). Especially in this heavily agrarian region of Java, removed from the old ports of trade on the north coast of the island, well-established communities of Javanese entrepreneurs and merchants are fairly rare, and only a few ever rivaled the former wealth of Laweyan. Physically, the neighborhood was distinguished by its large, ornate homes, which smacked of old wealth. Located at the edge of town, in a site that had been considered "village" (*désa*) rather than "city" (*kutha; kota*, I.) in the living memory of its older inhabitants (but which was now quite urban), the properties on which the homes and workshops were built were also much more spacious in Laweyan than those usually found in the center of the city, where land was at a premium.

But it was not just the size of the properties or the opulence of the homes that made the neighborhood distinctive. The looming walls surrounding the houses and workshops in the kampongs and on the main road created an aura of secretiveness, of closure to the outside world, which set this neighborhood apart from most others in the city. That Laweyan's merchant community did indeed have a reputation for being closed and suspicious of outsiders made the walls into more than just physical barriers between the neighborhood's residents and those who lived outside: they were symbols of difference, of people who kept themselves at a remove from the rest of society. Oddly, while Laweyan was often said by outsiders to epitomize an old-fashioned Javanese way of life, its residents were also considered by some to be far outside the Javanese mainstream—not "typically" Javanese at all. Quite a few eyebrows were raised when I told other Solonese that I was living and conducting research in Laweyan; the neighborhood's inhabitants were rumored to have peculiar ways that set them apart from other Javanese, and some people from outside the community clearly wondered if I had not made a mistake in choosing to do research among people who did not fit their image of true Javanese.

Like people of Arab or Chinese descent, some of whose families had lived in Solo for generations, the merchants of Laweyan tended to be perceived as marginal to the local society. Some Solonese were convinced that Laweyan's residents were not originally from Solo or its environs, that they came from some other part of Java known more for trade, such as the north coast of the island. Others questioned whether they were really Javanese at all. A Javanese historian from a local university who was conducting research in Laweyan announced to me in all earnestness that after interviewing many people in the neighborhood and inspecting the architectural style of their homes, he had finally come to the conclusion that they really *were* ethnic Javanese, something that he had seriously doubted at the outset of his study. One woman from a nearby city even told me in a hushed voice that she had heard that people in Laweyan had tails![7]

Depending on whom one spoke to, then, and in what context, the people of Laweyan were usually depicted either as ultra-Javanese or as not-quite Javanese. In either case, they were clearly marked off as different, members of a marginal community who were always linked with another time (through their old-fashionedness) or another place (outside Solo, even outside Java). Although the residents of Laweyan themselves had a strong sense of their own Javanese identity, some of them also did not consider themselves appropriate representatives of what they thought of as "Javanese culture" (*budaya Jawa, kabudayan Jawa*), which they tended to equate with what we would call "high culture." A number advised me to go to the palaces to conduct my research, for *there* were preserved the standards of Javanese culture that had been passed down from time immemorial. (Besides, they knew that foreigners tended to gravitate to the palaces, so they were convinced that if I were a proper foreigner, I should be doing the same.) They saw their own version of culture as a pale imitation of the real thing: they were "just merchants," after all, and merchants didn't really have culture, as they understood the term.

BEHIND HIGH WALLS

My first image of Laweyan was of the fortresslike walls, huge houses, and closed atmosphere for which it was famous. A friend of a friend had escorted me there early one evening, only a day or two after I arrived in Solo, so that I could inquire about a room that he had heard might be available. We rang at the front gate of an imposing home, most of which was obscured from view by a high wall. A servant received us and led us into an open sitting area at the front of the house. I was amazed at the size and style of this house, which was unlike any that I had seen before. Like most Javanese houses it was only one story high, but it extended back so far that I could not see where it ended. Most of the rooms were built around an open courtyard, which allowed air to circulate freely and made it surprisingly cool inside. The house had a look of faded grandeur. Dating to the 1930s or so (and obviously quite modern for that time), it was built of sturdy materials and had fine decorative touches in the tilework and windows, but it was sparsely furnished and rather run-down. Considering its size—it could easily have accommodated several families—the house was inhabited by very few people.

After introducing ourselves to the owner, a widow of about seventy, we were shown room after empty room that might be let out, we were told, to a boarder. In the course of discussion, I was informed that the heavy iron gates out front were pulled shut and locked at nine o'clock every night, making it difficult for anyone to enter or leave the house. Anticipating that this might prove inconvenient for all parties involved—I experienced some claustrophobia, I admit, at the thought of being locked up every night inside that house, which I found a little spooky—we decided that it would be best for me to look elsewhere for a place to live. Another few weeks were to pass before I would actually move to the neighborhood, but that first glimpse inside the walls of Laweyan left a lasting impression on me.

The house that I finally settled in was of a very similar style, built behind a high wall in a rectangular shape around an open courtyard, but the atmosphere was less somber and more inviting. It belonged to a kind couple in their fifties, Bapak and Ibu (Mr. and Mrs.) Wiyono,[8] and had been built by Pak Wiyono's parents in the mid-1930s. At the time that I moved in, the couple lived there with two unmarried daughters in their early twenties, two teenage sons, and two young grandsons who had been entrusted to the Wiyonos' care. From time to time one of the Wiyonos' three oldest children, who lived in other cities, would come to visit for a few days, often with a spouse and a couple of children in tow. During the course of my stay there, the household would expand and contract as several of the other children married and were joined by their spouses or left to live elsewhere with them. New grandchildren also joined the household for a short time until their parents moved into their own homes. This shift in household composition was not unusual; although a single nuclear family forms the core of many Javanese households, it is common for other relatives or spouses to live with the family for short or extended periods of time.

Along with the members of the Wiyonos' immediate family, an assortment of employees also lived there or came in to work during the days. There were two ancient live-in housekeepers, frail-looking women with teeth stained red from chewing betel, who had cooked, cleaned, and looked after the children for many years (and had barely spoken to each other for almost as long, for reasons that were never clear to me). One of them appeared perpetually amused at the unpredictable behavior and gawky movements of the new American who had invaded her turf; the other seemed at a loss to know what to make of me and kept her distance. Another live-in employee was a boy in his late teens who helped mind the small shop in front of the house, ran odd errands for the family, and was occasionally aroused late at night to chase through the house after a marauding rat. During the daytime, a feisty, energetic woman from a nearby kampong came in to wash and iron all of the family's clothing by hand, usually accompanied by her small, shy daughter. Two or three older men dyed batik sarongs in the spacious workshop attached to the back of the house and did whatever maintenance work around the house the Wiyonos thought necessary. The oldest of these men, Pak Joko, patiently tolerated the constant indignity of hearing his name called shrilly by the family's pet myna bird, which was fond of imitating Bu Wiyono as she summoned Pak Joko to do some task or other.

Although the composition of the household shifted often during the time that I lived there, the Wiyonos' home was always a lively place. From the terrace in front of my upstairs room, which looked out over the small courtyard (and the tall mango tree that grew right in the middle of it), I had a perfect view of all the comings and goings of the household, which were considerable. Along with the regular daily routines of its members, which I soon came to memorize, the days were punctuated with the activities of others who came there for various reasons. Peddlers selling cooked food or other wares would come around on bicycle or on foot, sometimes with huge baskets or large pots strapped to their backs (the one I recall best was the woman on a bicycle who never failed to ask me in the politest Javanese if I would buy her banana fritters, which I often did). Every Thursday morning a steady stream of beggars in broad conical hats and torn clothes would make their rounds from house to house on the street. Coming up to the front gate in small groups, they called out loudly in stylized piteous voices to attract the attention of those inside, and one of the old servants would shuffle over to the gate to hand them small coins from a cup that had been set out for that purpose.

Other people appeared at the house intermittently. Friends and relatives of the Wiyonos frequently dropped by to chat. During months in the Javanese Islamic calendar when exchanges of food are customary, servants of the Wiyonos' neighbors, friends, and kin often came by to drop off a box of pastries or other delicacies for the family to enjoy, together with a calling card from the sender. Periodically a young village woman would arrive at the house carrying a small bundle of cloths that she had decorated with wax for the batiking process, but that had not yet been dyed; these she would sell for the cost of the materials and a minimal payment for her labor to Bu Wiyono, who scrutinized each piece carefully through her thick glasses. Later, Bu Wiyono would have them dyed in the workshop out back and sell the finished batik sarongs to traders in Pasar Klewer, Solo's immense textile bazaar.

Anthropologists are often proud of the physical hardships that they endure for the sake of scholarship. I will be the first to admit, though, that as far as field sites go, mine was no hardship post. Some of my more intrepid friends who came to visit, fellow anthropologists who had chosen to do fieldwork in more remote parts of Indonesia, would tease me about the comfort of my living situation as they regaled me with their experiences of traveling between distant islands in boats that nearly capsized, or chewing betel to stay awake for ritual ceremonies that lasted three days and nights. I bore this teasing with good humor, since I am a dyed-in-the-wool urban anthropologist with great admiration for, but little desire to emulate, those dedicated researchers who are willing to set themselves off in isolated places for months or years at a time.

Besides, for the research that I had set out to do, my living situation was, in fact, ideal. Both Bapak and Ibu Wiyono were third-generation batik entrepreneurs whose families had lived in Laweyan for decades. They were well liked and respected in the community and had extensive contacts with people both in and outside of Laweyan, which, along with their patient willingness to answer my unending questions, greatly facilitated my work. Pak Wiyono quickly understood my interest in the history of the community, and he graciously introduced me to older people in Laweyan who might otherwise have been reluctant to be interviewed by a stranger, let alone a foreigner. Bu Wiyono cheerfully let me tag along with her when she attended the weekly neighborhood *arisan* (a rotating savings club), as well as the innumerable weddings, funerals, and other ceremonies that demanded so much of her time. From Bu Wiyono and the many other *ibus* whom I met through her, I learned about the lives of the women of the community in countless ways. These were, I believe, some of the most valuable lessons of my research.

The Wiyonos made me feel welcome in their home from the start, and I remained with them for the duration of my stay in Solo. Living with the Wiyonos gave me a recognizable place in a community that was known for its wariness of outsiders—and that undoubtedly would have been suspicious of an unmarried woman in her twenties living alone. That a well-respected local family had opened its doors to me in turn opened many other doors which otherwise probably would have remained closed. Living with this family also helped me gain an understanding of how Laweyan was woven together as a community—and why the threads of this community were slowly unraveling.

ORIGIN STORIES

According to local lore, Laweyan was a center of trade long before the founding of the court at Surakarta in 1745—some sources say by the sixteenth century or earlier. Located between two waterways (now just small streams) that were used to transport agricultural produce and other goods east to the Solo River, a major river connecting the interior of Java with the north coast seaports of Surabaya and Gresik, Laweyan was apparently an entrepôt and the site of a thriving market. It is said that the market at Laweyan specialized in the trade of indigo, woven cloth, thread (one local etymology for the name "Laweyan" connects it to the Javanese word for thread, *lawé*) and, according to one source at least, opium.[9] Although the old marketplace no longer exists, some support is lent to this folk history by the fact that there are still two adjacent kampongs in Laweyan called, respectively, North-of-the-Market (Lor Pasar) and South-of-the-Market (Kidul Pasar), indicating the site where the marketplace probably stood.

Laweyan's first appearance in the written annals of Javanese history links it to the political affairs of the sixteenth century. According to several Javanese court chronicles, the parcel of land called Laweyan was originally given as a royal appanage in the late 1540s to a certain Kyai Ageng Anis (Great Lord Anis) as a reward for his loyal service to the family of the sultan of Demak, who ruled from Java's north coast.[10] What Kyai Ageng Anis is best remembered for, however, is not his role as a vassal to this particular sultan but as a revered ancestor to others. His grandson, Senapati Ingalaga, was the founder of the Sultanate of Mataram, the last powerful Javanese kingdom established prior to colonial rule, as well as the dynasty from which the present-day royal houses of Surakarta and Yogyakarta are directly descended. Kyai Ageng Anis is considered the first settler (*cikal bakal*) of Laweyan even though the area was already inhabited when he and his entourage settled there. As one Javanese author notes, little is known about Laweyan before the time of Kyai Ageng Anis because it was inhabited only by "common folk, just ordinary people" (*golongané wong cilik, wong lumrah baé*) who "left no traces" of their existence. Only after Laweyan was honored by the presence of Kyai Ageng Anis, "who subsequently gave issue to the great Kings of Mataram in the land of Java, until the era of the palaces of Surakarta and Yogyakarta," did it finally acquire a history (Samsudjin 1981, 27–28).

Kyai Ageng Anis was buried in Laweyan, behind a mosque that still exists today, Mesjid Laweyan.[11] Both the cemetery and the mosque are the property of the royal house of the sunan of Surakarta; the cemetery, which dates back four centuries, is said to be the oldest in Solo. It now contains the graves of many members of the Solonese nobility, has the official status of a royal cemetery, and is tended by a retainer of the palace.[12] The site attracts visitors from all over Java, who come to the cemetery to meditate, make offerings, and to entreat the spirits of Kyai Ageng Anis and others buried there for their help with personal matters of money, love, career, or health.

What became of Laweyan between the mid–sixteenth century and the late nineteenth century is not entirely clear. Stories told in Laweyan and in the Kraton, the sunan's palace, claim that the area was still inhabited by wealthy merchants when Sunan Pakubuwana II stopped there as he fled eastward from Kartasura after his palace was sacked in 1742; he was also buried in the royal cemetery at Laweyan when he died in 1749.[13] However, very few of the present-day merchants of the community claim to have roots that extend back more than three or four generations in Laweyan.[14] There is little doubt that the area has been continuously inhabited since before the days of Kyai Ageng Anis, but whether it has served without interruption as a center of trade since then is questionable.[15]

In the final decades of the nineteenth century and the first decades of the twentieth century, Laweyan once again becomes the focus of historical attention. Now, however, Laweyan appears not in the chronicles of the Javanese palaces but in the reports of Dutch colonial bureaucrats of the Netherlands East Indies' government, which by this time had established full control over Java and other parts of the Indonesian archipelago. By the early 1900s, Laweyan had become known as a center of batik cloth production (and, in the 1910s and 1920s, as a hub of political activity as well). From a quiet, sparsely inhabited settlement on the edge of town, still bordered by wet rice fields, Laweyan had developed around the turn of the century into one of the preeminent centers of the batik industry in Solo and, in fact, in the whole of the Netherlands East Indies.

THE DEVELOPMENT OF THE BATIK INDUSTRY IN SOLO

Batik, a wax-resist technique for dyeing cloth, had flourished in the courts of Central Java from at least the early seventeenth century.[16] Batik making was a leisurely, refined activity of noblewomen, but it was also practiced by artisans who earned their livelihood from this craft.[17] In Java the art of batik making reached its highest level of sophistication; Javanese batik became a much sought-after commodity throughout the region, where fine textiles were greatly valued as prestige goods with ritual as well as economic and political significance. Until the mid– to late nineteenth century batik cloth had been a luxury item, restricted as daily wear to men and women of the upper classes.[18] Nonelites generally wore clothing made of coarse, locally woven cloth, not batik (Wertheim 1956, 12–13; Raffles [1817] 1965, 1:87). Although batik cloth was produced as a commodity in the eighteenth and early nineteenth centuries by artisans attached to the courts and by village women during slack periods of agricultural activity, it was still too costly to be worn by most of the Javanese population, except for special ceremonial occasions.[19]

In the early nineteenth century, European manufacturers had attempted to tap the potentially lucrative market in Java by producing cheap imitation batik fabrics. According to one source, the first effort to introduce European imitation batik to the Indonesian market was made in 1812 by none other than Thomas Stamford Raffles, lieutenant-governor of the colony during the brief period of British rule (1811–16). English textile-printing firms began to produce imitation batik cloth printed with synthetic dyes for export to Java in 1814.[20] Firms in the Netherlands followed suit not long thereafter: in 1835 a batik factory was set up in Leiden with Javanese workers; others soon sprang up elsewhere in Holland. Swiss companies also manufactured imitation batik, which found an eager market in Java because of its low price relative to genuine batik (Kitley 1987; Robinson 1969).

This imitation batik might have led to the demise of the Javanese batik industry—or, more accurately, to its failure to develop from a smale-scale industry into a major, centralized industry—had it not been for the invention in the mid-1800s of the *cap* (pronounced something like "chop"), a handheld copper stamp used for applying wax designs to cloth.[21] The *cap*, simple as it was, revolutionized the batik-making process by sharply cutting the amount of labor time needed to produce a piece of batik. Batik makers had previously relied on the *canting*, a small, handheld tool with a bamboo handle and a spouted copper reservoir, which works a bit like a fountain pen, for drawing designs on cloth with molten wax.[22] *Canting* work is laborious and painstaking; it can take from a few days to as long as six months to finish waxing a single sarong (about two and a half meters in length), depending on the quality of the work and the intricacy of the design. Consequently, *batik tulis*,[23] hand-drawn batik, can be very expensive.[24] The use of the copper stamp to apply wax to cloth made it possible for an individual to wax twenty sarong-sized lengths of cloth in a single day; by the existing standards of batik making, this was nothing short of mass production (Koperberg 1922, 148).

The invention of *batik cap*, as batik made by the stamping process is known, gave new life to the batik industry, enabling it to hold its own against the competition of European imitation batik. Because *batik cap* was relatively cheap, a much larger percentage of the population could now afford to purchase batik. It was also considered aesthetically superior to the imitation batik, in part because of its use of the natural dyes that many Javanese preferred for their deep tones and relative colorfastness.[25] *Batik cap* thus eventually supplanted the market for the imported imitations. As Koperberg writes, "Instead of the imitation batik pushing aside the indigenous batik industry, the opposite happened, namely, the transformation from a craft to an industrial business, through which, at the same time, a bulwark was erected for the preservation of an important piece of national culture" (1922, 148).

The invention of the *cap* did not just change the technical aspects of batik production. It transformed the whole organization of the industry, particularly the organization of labor. *Batik tulis* had been made exclusively by women, although the dyeing and finishing were usually done by men.[26] While the actual dyeing of the cloth was generally carried out in the entrepreneur's workshop in the city, most of the waxing was done on a putting-out basis. A village woman would work on a piece of batik at home in her spare time—which is to say, when she was not working in the fields, cooking, caring for her children, or looking after her household's other needs—in order to supplement the family's income. The money earned from making batik often provided a substantial portion of her family's income, especially during slow periods of agricultural activity. There were some workshops in the city where women and girls (usually young and unmarried) were brought together from the villages to do batik work, but overall the putting-out pattern was more common.

Batik cap work, in contrast, was done almost entirely by male laborers, villagers as well as urban dwellers. Although their work tended to be reimbursed on a piecework basis, as was true for *batik tulis*, it was usually done not part-time in the home but more or less full-time during a regular workday in an urban workshop.[27] *Batik cap* production usually required a larger workspace than *batik tulis*, not only for the process of stamping the designs in wax on cloth, which required a separate table for each worker, but also for dyeing and other stages of the process, since the scale of production was much larger. With the adoption of the *cap*, then, batik production became far more centralized than it had been before; it became, in short, a full-blown industry. *Batik cap* did not eliminate the market for the hand-decorated *batik tulis*, however, for there continued to be a demand for the higher-quality (and more prestigious) *batik tulis* from those who could afford to wear it on a daily basis and from others who purchased it to wear at weddings and for other ceremonial occasions.[28] The two forms of production thus coexisted, sometimes even under the same roof when an entrepreneur decided to produce batik for both markets.

The development of the batik industry came at a time when Solo and the rest of the Principalities (Vorstenlanden), as the Dutch called this region of Java,[29] were experiencing an expansion of the cash economy through the investment of private Dutch capital and the rapid growth of the plantation economy (Shiraishi 1990, chap. 1). Takashi Shiraishi, who calls this period "the Age of Capital" in the Principalities, notes that the Dutch plantations brought cash to the peasant economy in the form of wages and rent, while at the same time depriving them of time through the exploitation of their labor. As a result, they looked to the market to fill their everyday needs, including clothing. Manufacturers of cheap batik cloth therefore found a ready market for their product beginning in the 1850s and 1860s, and batik production rose at a rapid rate (23–24). The intense population growth in Java in this period further heightened the demand for clothing; from the late eighteenth to the late nineteenth century there was roughly an eight-fold increase in the island's population, from about three million in 1795 to nearly twenty-four million in 1890 (Ricklefs 1981, 116).

In the 1870s a national market for Solonese batik began to develop, thanks at least in part to the construction of the railways, which linked Solo to other parts of Java and made it possible for large quantities of cloth to be transported quickly and easily to cities like Surabaya in East Java and Batavia (Jakarta) and Bandung in West Java (Shiraishi 1990, 24), and from those cities to other parts of the Indies and beyond. The railroads also facilitated batik manufacturers' access to the raw materials they needed, particularly the imported cotton fabrics that were widely used in batik production.[30] By the early 1900s batik was considered almost a primary necessity by people in Java, Kalimantan, Sumatra, and other islands of the Indonesian archipelago (Economic Research Bureau 1958, 352). Solonese batik was appreciated for its fine designs and for the richness of its natural golden-brown dyes (soga); it may also have been popular among Javanese because of the association of Solonese batik with the high culture of Solo's palaces. Even the copper stamps crafted in Solo for making batik cap were sought after all over Java for their designs and high quality (Koperberg 1922, 150). Solo became one of the largest centers of batik production in Java, although it soon encountered significant competition from Yogyakarta (the other court city in the Principalities), Pekalongan on the north coast, and other batik centers scattered throughout Java.[31] Solonese batik was marketed throughout the islands of the Netherlands East Indies, and even outside the colony to such places as Singapore, Penang, Ceylon, and Suriname (where there were many Javanese contract workers).

Along with Javanese producers and merchants, local Chinese and Arabs as well as a few Europeans were also actively involved in the batik industry and trade.[32] Javanese firms dominated production of batik in Solo, but there were also a number of firms owned by Chinese and Arabs; to my knowledge, all of the labor was Javanese, however, regardless of the ethnic identity of the owner.[33] In general, Chinese and Arab merchants exercised their influence on the industry more in trade than in production. Almost all Javanese entrepreneurs relied on Chinese (and, to a lesser extent, Arab) wholesalers for their raw materials (Soerachman 1927, 30, 40). Many also depended on Chinese and Arab merchants to market their batik outside Solo, although Javanese controlled a large portion of the local batik trade and some of the trade to nearby cities like Yogyakarta and Semarang.[34] The importing of raw materials from Europe and elsewhere—undyed cloth, paraffin, and eventually synthetic dyestuffs and other chemicals used in the batiking process—was monopolized by a few large Dutch-owned

3. The *pendopo*, or sitting area, of a Laweyan home dating from the 1880s.

import-export houses, which then sold their goods to Chinese middlemen, who in turn sold them to retailers and batik manufacturers. Only a handful of the largest batik producers obtained their materials directly from the European importers; most bought on credit from local Chinese suppliers. Even the trade in beeswax and natural dyestuffs that were used in Solonese batik production was dominated by Chinese and some Arabs.

The control of the wholesale trade in raw materials by Chinese in the batik industry fit with the broader economic scheme of colonial Java, in which Europeans monopolized the large import and export trade in most products; Chinese and other "Foreign Orientals" (*Vreemde Oosterlingen*, D., a category that also included Arabs and Indians), as they were classified under the colonial system, dominated the field of intermediate wholesale trade; and Javanese and other "Natives" (*Inlanders*, D.), who were at the bottom of both the social and the economic hierarchies, were active primarily in the smaller, less lucrative local spheres of trade.[35] In the ethnically stratified colonial economy, where the majority of the indigenous population was rural and poor, Javanese were largely assigned the role of providing labor for the cultivation and processing of crops for export; those who engaged in trade were mostly involved with petty local trade in agricultural products or household necessities (Alexander and Alexander 1991). In the late nineteenth and early twentieth centuries, when few opportunities were open to Javanese for earning more than a subsistence living, batik manufacturing and trade were among the small number of fields in which Javanese were able to build sizable businesses. In the Netherlands East Indies there was no indigenous capitalist class of any significance; the batik industry in Java was one of the only commercial sectors to be controlled, at least in part, by indigenous entrepreneurs (see Ingleson 1986, 7).

Batik workshops appeared in many quarters of Solo.[36] During the mid-1800s, batik production was concentrated in the neighborhoods of the Kauman, Pasar Kliwon, and Keprabon, all located in the densely populated central part of the city (Shiraishi 1990, 24). The Kauman and Pasar Kliwon are near the Kraton, while Keprabon is close to Solo's minor palace, the Mangkunagaran; it is likely that batik production as a commercial venture in these neighborhoods grew out of the batik making of noblewomen and court retainers associated with the two palaces. After 1870 new firms were established in the less-populated southwestern outskirts of the city, in the neighborhoods of Tegalsari, Kabangan, and Laweyan.[37] Batik firms in the eastern and central parts of the city tended to specialize in *batik tulis* and high-quality *batik cap*, while the western neighborhoods, including Laweyan, concentrated on producing the cheaper, mass-produced *batik cap* (Soerachman 1927, 31).

The advantage enjoyed by entrepreneurs in the latter neighborhoods was that land there was relatively cheap and undeveloped, which enabled them to build workshops and homes on a scale much larger than was possible in the central parts of the city, where there was little room for expansion. In addition, the streams running through these neighborhoods provided an ample supply of water, which is essential for the batik-making process. Furthermore, because they were at a remove both geographically and culturally from the Solo's palaces, the entrepreneurs in these neighborhoods felt little obligation to uphold the standards of refined batik making associated with the courts; this enabled them to concentrate more on large-scale production than on aesthetics. Although they took care to maintain the quality of their batik, they nonetheless produced it not for the highly discriminating buyer but for the average villager or urban laborer, for whom low price rather than refinement was key.

LAWEYAN IN THE LATE COLONIAL PERIOD

Solo, then, was a major center of the batik industry in Java, and by the first decades of this century Laweyan had come to dominate the batik industry in Solo. One source estimated that during times of normal economic activity in the 1920s there were some 30,000 workers employed in Solo's batik industry—the city's major industry and a mainstay of the local economy—

with the largest number of firms concentrated in Laweyan (Kat Angelino 1930–31, 2:103).[38] The scale of production in Laweyan was also unrivaled by other batik-producing neighborhoods. By manufacturing a commodity aimed at the mass market, both for local and national consumption, Laweyan had managed to catapult itself into a position of supremacy in the industry. Laweyan was, moreover, almost purely Javanese; there were no Chinese or Arab batik entrepreneurs in the area. It was a neighborhood of affluent indigenous batik entrepreneurs and merchants, its concentration of wealth rivaled by only a small number of Javanese communities elsewhere on the island.[39]

The average batik firm of Laweyan, like many others in Solo, consisted of a large enclosed or semienclosed workshop attached to the back or side of the owner's house, which contained a number of small tables for doing *cap* work and several large vats for dyeing and removing wax from the batik. Most had a large loft and a yard with bamboo rods for hanging wet cloths to dry. A firm might employ as few as four or five workers or as many as several hundred.[40] The lucrativeness of such businesses, at least by local standards, should not be underestimated. In the 1920s and 1930s, when most Javanese were living in simple cottages with woven bamboo or wooden walls, many Laweyan entrepreneurs owned one or more large, lavishly appointed houses that were built to last for generations.

They kept their own horses and carriages, and some even owned American cars. Several sent their children to Holland for higher education, while a number made the very costly pilgrimage to Mecca. The women bought large gold and diamond earrings, bracelets, and necklaces; besides serving as personal adornment, these items simultaneously advertised the success of their businesses, enhanced their social standing in the community, and served as a form of savings. Although the wealth of Laweyan entrepreneurs paled in comparison with the wealth of large Dutch importers or the Chinese revenue farmers of the nineteenth century, it was, for indigenous Indonesians of the colonial period, still considerable.[41] In a political and economic system that discriminated against the indigenous population, keeping the majority poor while enriching many Europeans and Chinese, prosperous Javanese communities like Laweyan were a departure from the norm, to say the least.

At times, the batik industry seemed a source of nearly limitless wealth. As long as the economy was healthy, the firms generated enough money to keep entrepreneurs happy and many workers employed, although there were slow periods every year as a result of local seasonal influences, when firms would temporarily lay off some or all of their workers. An elderly retired *batik cap* worker from Banaran, a village just south of Laweyan that supplied many laborers for Laweyan firms, recalled for me that during the boom days of the early 1920s, wages had been so good for workers in the batik industry relative to what they could earn in other sectors, including farming, that "some Banaran people wouldn't have wanted rice fields even if they'd been given them [for free]."

But the batik industry was from the very start subject to the fluctuations of the global as well as the local economy, because of its reliance on imported materials and because the buying power of the Indies' population was also intimately tied to shifts in the world economy. The dependence of the batik industry on the global economy was felt, for instance, during World War I, when the imported cloth and synthetic dyestuffs used in making batik were scarce. One author noted, "The scanty supply caused the necessary raw materials to go up in price in such a way that the population, which had already been impoverished by the war, could seldom buy new batik goods" (Koperberg 1922, 148). Many batik firms slowed down production considerably during this period, and some were forced out of business altogether (149). An event as seemingly remote as a labor dispute in a textile-manufacturing region of the Netherlands could result in higher prices of imported cotton cloth, and therefore of batik in the Indies; this occurred in 1924, for example, when a labor lockout in Twente, a textile center in the eastern part of Holland, led to a fear of diminished exports to the Indies, driving up the price of batik (Kat Angelino 1930–31, 2:100). The recession of the 1920s and global economic depression that began in 1929 also sharply affected the industry: workers were laid off, stocks went unsold, and many firms closed down for good.[42]

By the end of the nineteenth century, the colonial government had started to pay careful attention to batik making as an art and as an industry. Dutch bureaucrats began to express concern over the economics and aesthetics of batik production.[43] By the first quarter of the twentieth century, Dutch writers were decrying the "corruption" of the batik industry brought about by the importation of "characterless" European designs and dyes (Fock 1904, 108–9) and bemoaning "the decline of this ancient handicraft with its astounding techniques" (Koperberg 1922, 152). These critics called for the government to take steps to help the industry by providing business assistance and at the same time protecting the artistic aspects of batik making. An American admirer of batik reported in 1918 that "the Dutch have at last realized the beauty and art of this ancient handicraft and are doing everything they can to encourage it."[44] One such concerned Dutchman was S. Koperberg, who wrote in 1922 that "it has been insisted upon from various sides—the indigenous as well as the European side— that the Government do everything possible in order to offer help to this native business. How far is it possible to help the indigenous batik makers through guidance and support, so that the decline of the batik industry can be countered?" (147).

In response to his and other voices, the government established the Batik Research Station at Yogyakarta in 1929 to provide technical, business, and artistic assistance to batik manufacturers (Kat Angelino 1930–31, 2:102–3). The station collected old batik designs and created new ones; it also worked to improve dyeing methods. The station's employees invented batik motifs based on designs taken, for instance, from old Javanese temples and New Guinea bamboo work (Furnivall 1936, 375). Interest in the economic status of the industry and concern over labor conditions and wages also led to government-sponsored investigations of the batik industry. This culminated in the publication of the exhaustive, three-volume *Batikrapport* (Batik report) in the early 1930s, authored by the colonial official P. de Kat Angelino (1930–31), which provided extraordinarily detailed information on wages, the division of labor, and economic conditions in the batik industry in cities and towns throughout Java and Madura. Batik making in Java may have been a "typical self-reliant industry of the native population . . . with an old, very interesting history" (Fock 1904, 108) and an "ancient handicraft" (Sams 1918, 510; Koperberg 1922, 152), but as a commercial venture the batik industry was inextricably bound up with the colonial state and the world economy. Entrepreneurs in communities like Laweyan saw the economic effects of this integration with the colonial and global economies in the sharp price fluctuations of imported cambric cloth, paraffin, and dyestuffs from the local Chinese suppliers, as well as in the slow sales of batik during times of global recession.

Given the economic significance of the batik industry to Indonesians and Europeans alike, the government's efforts to prop up the industry are not surprising. One source estimated the value of Netherlands East Indies' imports of cotton goods (a substantial portion of which were used for batik production) by 1925 to be between forty and fifty million U.S. dollars annually (George 1925); most of this cloth was produced in Holland, England, and Japan. The money earned from sales of cloth to the Indies was obviously an important source of revenue for the Netherlands and for Dutch importers in the Indies, which may help to explain why the colonial government came to take such an interest in the batik industry.[45] With a population of some forty million by 1930, Java was a very attractive market.[46] Wertheim, for instance, notes that the industrialists of Twente advocated a colonial policy of improving the purchasing power of the Javanese peasantry in the early twentieth century (1956, 66); it is surely no coincidence that Twente was a major source of cloth for the Javanese batik industry. As one casual observer put it, "batick is scarcely less a necessity of life to the Javanese than is his daily rice; and, apart from the extremely improbable contingency of a widespread national impoverishment driving him back to a state of nature, he will doubtless continue to 'do his bit' in keeping the mills of Manchester going" (Banner 1927, 103)—*and* those of Twente, the writer might have added.

The economic dependence of Laweyan and other batik-manufacturing communities on the colonial economy also linked them to the development of political movements throughout Java and beyond. The 1910s and 1920s witnessed an upsurge of political activity in Laweyan as well as in other parts of Solo, Java, and the Netherlands East Indies.[47] The first mass political movement in the Indies, Sarekat Islam (Islamic Union, also known in its early years as Sarekat Dagang Islam, Islamic Commercial Union), was founded in 1912. It grew out of a mutual aid and neighborhood watch association that had been established shortly before that time in Laweyan; the founder of the association and its first president was Haji Samanhoedi, a very successful Laweyan batik entrepreneur and merchant.[48] Initially most of the organization's members were from Laweyan, but it soon expanded outside the neighborhood and then outside Solo to many parts of the Indies.

One of the earliest goals of Sarekat Islam was to enable indigenous entrepreneurs and merchants in the batik industry to loosen the stranglehold of the ethnic Chinese middlemen on whom they depended so heavily for raw materials and for marketing their batik, and generally to fight business practices of the Chinese that they perceived as unfair. The technique of the boycott was introduced in Solo by Sarekat Islam leaders in 1912; the first boycott was organized against a large Chinese-owned trading house after it attempted to beat down the price of the batik that it purchased wholesale from Laweyan batik manufacturers. Javanese resentment of the Chinese was also heightened by their perception that local Chinese were assuming airs of superiority following the success of the Chinese Revolution in 1911. By dressing and behaving as equals of the Europeans, the Chinese were seen as asserting their higher position in the Indies' social hierarchy relative to the Javanese (Noer 1973; Shiraishi 1990).

Within a matter of months after its founding, Sarekat Islam had become immensely popular in Solo; Shiraishi observes that almost every adult Muslim male in the city joined the organization, with the exception of high-ranking officials and princes of the royal houses (1990, 47). Branches soon sprung up all over the Indies. With the broadening of its base, the goals of the movement also broadened, aiming at more general social justice and political representation for the indigenous people of the Indies who had long suffered under colonial rule. Within a relatively short period of time, Sarekat Islam became a major nationalist movement that profoundly influenced the course of Indonesian politics.[49]

Although Sarekat Islam lost its popular base in Laweyan and Solo within a few years—during World War I, Laweyan batik entrepreneurs were more concerned with keeping their businesses afloat than with engaging in politics (Koperberg 1922; Shiraishi 1990, 80)—other movements followed, for this was, as Shiraishi puts it, "an age in motion" in the Indies, and the tide of political sentiment was swelling. The 1920s saw in particular the rise of popular communist-linked organizations in Solo and elsewhere in the Indies.[50] Laweyan, Keprabon, and the Kauman, three neighborhoods of Solo that were all heavily involved in batik production, were the major centers of communist activity in Solo at this time. The leaders and participants in leftist organizations included batik entrepreneurs and traders as well as batik workers (Shiraishi 1990, 318). In the mid-1920s a communist-linked trade union, Sarekat Buruh Batik (Union of Batik Workers) agitated in Laweyan and other batik-manufacturing neighborhoods of Solo (318–19). De Kat Angelino reports that during the recession of that period, when many batik firms were shut down temporarily or permanently for lack of business, "many people in the industry are now without a livelihood, and form good material for the communist action. Almost all *cap* workers were already members of communist unions, but aspire to the job of recruiter for the union in these slack times. They often then forget to hand over the dues of 40 cents per member to the union" (1930–31, 2:101).

Although the communist movement in Java was crushed by colonial authorities in late 1926 and early 1927, and popular political movements did not rise again until after World War II (McVey 1965; Shiraishi 1990), de Kat Angelino comments that when an inquiry into the conditions of the batik industry in Laweyan was held in 1930, the labor inspectors were frequently assumed to be political investigators sent by the government in search of communist elements, "for Laweyan has always been a hotbed of extremism" (1930–31, 2:130). His remark, although referring to the preceding two decades, was also prescient, because communism was to reassert itself strongly in Laweyan some three decades later, after Indonesian independence—only to be brutally suppressed once again in the widespread anticommunist arrests and massacres of 1965–66.

THE CREATION OF A COMMUNITY: TURNING INWARD

Laweyan, then, could hardly have been called an isolated community. Whether directly or indirectly, those who earned a living from the batik industry—which meant the entire community, essentially—were in constant contact with the outside world, in both a local and a global sense. The life of the community during its formative years was profoundly affected by its involvement with the economics and politics of colonialism, for the developments of late colonial society were what enabled Laweyan to ac-

4. The *pendopo* of a Laweyan home built between the 1920s and the 1930s.

quire its distinctive character as an enclave of successful entrepreneurs and merchants. These circumstances were not incidental to Laweyan's formation and identity as an entrepreneurial community, for many members of the community had moved to Laweyan from villages outside Solo precisely to take advantage of the burgeoning opportunities for earning money in commercial ventures that were afforded by the social and economic conditions of Java beginning in the mid–nineteenth century.

Modernity was, in short, the midwife of this community. The ability of Laweyan's residents to produce batik for the mass market depended on the uninterrupted supply of cloth and chemicals from abroad, and their ability to sell it in large quantities depended on the expanding cash economy in the Indies. For obtaining raw materials as well as marketing their finished products widely they also relied on modern transportation provided by the railroad and the steamship. Through their regular interactions with Chinese and Arab merchants they were fully integrated into the plural society of the Netherlands East Indies (see Furnivall 1944). And by participating in, or at least witnessing firsthand, the political ferment of the 1910s and 1920s, they were thrust into the emerging nationalist consciousness of what Benedict Anderson has called the "embryonic Indonesian 'imagined community'" (1991, 32). During this age in motion, Laweyan, too, was in motion. It was a thriving community that had been launched headlong into the modern era.

This modern orientation, as I have already suggested, was reflected in the architectural style and interior design of the entrepreneurs' homes, which by the late 1920s had come to reflect Western as much as Javanese sensibilities. The homes were decorated with European tilework and light fixtures, stained-glass windows depicting pastoral (Western) scenes or modern art deco designs, and ornate mirrors imported from Belgium. A number of the homes were designed by Dutch architects or by Indonesians who had apprenticed themselves to Dutch architects or builders (Naniek Widayati 1992). In the Indies at this time, "modernness" was more or less synonymous with "Westernness," and vice versa; as Kenji Tsuchiya remarks of the language that was current in Java during the first decades of the twentieth century, "the phenomena, ideas, and feelings that characterize the new age are all expressed in Dutch loanwords, such as *modérn*" (1990, 77). The choice of Laweyan's entrepreneurs to build their houses in a modified European style reflected not only their aesthetic preferences but also their receptiveness to the modern age—as well as, perhaps, their acknowledgment of its personal significance to them and their community.

I want to highlight Laweyan's status as a fundamentally modern community in the first half of the twentieth century because it stands in such sharp contrast to what the community was to become in later years: a stronghold of tradition that continually erected barriers, consciously or unconsciously, to further modernization. The question that remains to be answered, of course, is why a modern, affluent community would permit itself to be transformed over time into an anachronism, especially during a period when the state was forging ahead with its plans to turn Indonesia into a modernized, "developed," and industrialized nation. It is this question that I will attempt to answer in the subsequent chapters of this book.

I should mention here that even when the community was flourishing in the early twentieth century, there were already some limits to its willingness to embrace the outside world. For all its exposure to the tastes, ideas, products, economics, and politics of people and places that existed outside the neighborhood's immediate purview, Laweyan remained a curiously provincial enclave in certain ways. Although the community was open to the economic, political, and aesthetic influences of outsiders, socially it looked inward, earning it a reputation in the wider society for being insular, parochial, and more than a little mysterious. It is notable that even Haji Samanhoedi, the wealthy and influential founder of Sarekat Islam who had made the pilgrimage to Mecca and had traveled widely in the colony for political and business purposes, was nevertheless accused in 1915 by a Dutch official, R. A. Rinkes, of being "practically uneducated in both the Mohammedan as well as modern sense, [and] narrow-minded on anything outside his everyday Lawean environment."[51] That such a remark could have been made about Samanhoedi, who was presumably one of the more worldly members of the community, suggests that Laweyan by that time had already begun the process of turning in on itself, giving it the reputation for being "closed" (*tertutup*, I.) that it still has today.

Why was Laweyan, which was tied in so many ways to the outside world, perceived as such an insular community? To begin with, the entrepreneurs showed little interest in providing any education to their children beyond what they needed for business purposes. Rinkes's remark about Haji Samanhoedi's lack of education reflects the environment in which Samanhoedi was raised: most children received no more than a primary or middle school education, although some of their parents did send them to the more elite and expensive Dutch-language schools for indigenous students rather than to the cheaper schools for "ordinary" Javanese, where instruction was in local languages.[52] Even some of the richest entrepreneurs in the community saw no point in sending their children to high school or beyond. One of the most successful merchants in Laweyan's history is rumored to have said, "Why should I let my children get too educated? Then they won't want to listen to their parents anymore!" This woman and others believed that higher education was for the *ambtenaren* (D.), bureaucrats and civil servants, not for merchants and entrepreneurs.

Both boys and girls were groomed from an early age to become batik entrepreneurs like their parents; therefore their practical education in the workshop and the marketplace was deemed far more important than any formal education. In the frank words of one aging Laweyan man, "In the old days parents in Laweyan never wanted to think about their children's schooling, because they didn't need a diploma for the success and wealth that they got from their businesses" (quoted in Soedarmono 1987, 71). Even after Indonesian independence, relatively few Laweyan children attended high school, let alone college. Only in the 1970s and 1980s, when it became clear that the batik industry was in a state of permanent decline, did parents put greater value on educating their children in the hope that it would lead to alternative (and more profitable) careers.

Religious education, too, was often neglected, even though the merchants professed their faith in Islam and had a reputation among outsiders—undeserved, for the most part—for being very devout practitioners of the religion. Unlike the batik merchants of the Kauman, the neighborhood adjoining Solo's Great Mosque (Mesjid Agung) where the sunan's religious officials lived, many Laweyan entrepreneurs, with some exceptions, did not trouble themselves or their children with Islamic learning beyond what they needed for common prayers. Even those who made the *haj*, the pilgrimage to Mecca, were often unable to read Arabic and had only a basic knowledge of Islam, although some devoted themselves more to the study of religion while they were on the pilgrimage and upon returning home— usually when they were well along in years and contemplating what might lie ahead in the afterlife. The appeal of modernist Islam, which had taken hold of a number of other Javanese merchant enclaves as early as the 1910s (see C. Geertz 1963; Castles 1967; M. Nakamura 1983) and which emphasized Islamic education, was apparently also lost on most people in Laweyan, who preferred more traditional forms of Javanese Islam.

Lack of education, then, contributed to a certain insularity in the community. Equally significant, however, was the strong preference of Laweyan's entrepreneurs for marrying their children off to others from the neighborhood. Although endogamy was not a hard-and-fast rule, until the mid- to late 1960s most marriages in the community were contracted between two children of Laweyan entrepreneurs. Some of those who married were relatives, as close as first cousins; others were not related at all—although after decades of in-marrying, almost everyone in the community was related, if only distantly, to everyone else in a tangled web of familial connections that would have confounded even the most patient genealogist.[53] In the occasional marriages that did take place between a child of Laweyan entrepreneurs and an outsider, the outside party was usually the child of a batik entrepreneur of the Kauman, Tegalsari, Keprabon, or another center of batik production.

Since almost all marriages were arranged by parents for their children until the 1960s—some marriages are still arranged by parents today, although usually with both children's consent—there was little chance that a son or daughter would attempt to find his or her own spouse from outside the community. Those few who did insist on marrying outsiders of whom their parents disapproved were likely to receive a stern warning that they were "on their own" as far as financial help and other assistance from their parents were concerned. However, until secondary and higher education became more common for the sons and daughters of the neighborhood, there were few opportunities for those of marriageable age to become acquainted with outsiders of the opposite sex. Parents were very strict about overseeing their children's activities—"It was like being in a cage," one woman recalled about her youth.

The prescription of endogamous marriage within a single local community is uncommon, although not unheard of, in Javanese society.[54] One of the main reasons that endogamy was preferred by the merchants of Laweyan was, as several outspoken residents of the neighborhood informed me, "so that their money wouldn't go anywhere"—in other words, so that it would not be lost to the family or to the community. With very few exceptions, the son of Laweyan batik entrepreneurs would marry the daughter of other Laweyan batik entrepreneurs; the couple would then settle in a new home in the neighborhood shortly after marriage and go into the batik business themselves, with start-up capital from both sets of parents.[55] When a wealthy couple married their child off into a family of the same occupational and economic status, they felt assured that the extended family of their son- or daughter-in-law would sap neither their own financial resources nor those of their child. "The strong with the strong," they said, meaning that there should be social and economic parity between two families contracting a marriage. Ultimately their goal was to see their wealth passed on to their grandchildren, and since the batik business was one of the most profitable fields open to Javanese, they believed that the likelihood of their wealth being perpetuated was greatest when both families were involved in the industry.

Another factor encouraging marriage within the community was that few men could manage a batik firm without the help of a wife who was knowledgeable about the business, for women played the dominant roles as batik entrepreneurs and traders among Javanese in Solo, as in Yogyakarta. The majority of firms in Laweyan were run by a husband-and-wife team; men were often active in the production end of the business, but as a general rule most of the crucial business decisions were made by the women. Women were also felt to have a better understanding of the aesthetic subtleties of batik than men—subtleties that were key to determining quality and price in a competitive market. The position of women in the industry is nicely summarized in a passage written by a Dutch-educated Javanese in 1927:

> In the discussion of the commercial aspect of the batik firm, one should not neglect to point out the role that is played by the woman [or wife; *vrouw*] in the life of the Javanese business. She is really the soul of the firm; she buys the raw materials, sells the cloths, and sees, in a word, that the business keeps going. The influence of the woman is so strong that she is never left out of negotiations over supplies, especially not on the part of the suppliers, because they know all too well that in the last instance she makes the decision and, if necesssary, can cancel a decision that has already been made. (Soerachman 1927, 39)

In order to ensure that a son would be successful in the batik business, parents had to find him a wife with the requisite background and skills, and Laweyan was certainly one of the best places to find such a woman. The reverse did not necessarily hold true—many women from batik families were quite capable of running a business on their own, and they frequently did, in fact—but a team of husband and wife was considered ideal for managing the family firm. The central role of women in Laweyan firms is a point to which I will be returning, because this is a pivotal issue for understanding both the community's position vis-à-vis the wider society and the transformations that it was to undergo over time.

Finally, although the Javanese system of descent is reckoned bilaterally and a newly married couple may settle near either set of parents (or in a new location if they wish), ties between mothers and daughters tend to be especially close (see H. Geertz 1961), and there was some preference in Laweyan for daughters in particular to settle near their parents' homes. This further discouraged their parents from seeking prospective spouses for them outside the community. Because women were often the principal moneymakers in the batik community, and daughters acquired business contacts and learned the skills of batik making and marketing from their mothers, the mother-daughter bond had economic as well as emotional significance. Daughters, like sons, also stood to inherit substantial property from both their mothers and their fathers. It is understandable, then, that a daughter would have wanted to remain close to her mother, and that a mother would have wished to keep her daughters nearby. But it was not uncommon for parents to want both daughters *and* sons to settle near them. Marrying one's child off to another from the neighborhood was the best guarantee that he or she would remain there after marriage.

The desire to keep children, especially daughters, close at hand was exemplified by one extended family that I knew. Bu Rachman, an elderly widow, lived in a large house on the main road in Laweyan. Flanking her house on both sides were the homes of her four daughters and their families, which she and her husband had built for each of them when they had married. As Bu Rachman explained to me, chuckling, when I asked her how many children she had, "I have eight children—four daughters and four sons. When a Chinese has four daughters, they all leave when they get married [i.e., they move away to settle near the husband's family]. With the Javanese, though, sometimes the man comes to live with his wife (*nèk wong Jawa, sing lanang sok mèlu nyonyaé*)." Bu Rachman epitomized an old Laweyan ideal: a successful entrepreneur surrounded—literally, in this case—by her children and grandchildren. Somehow the word "matrifocal," which I had seen used to describe Javanese families, seemed inadequate to describe this matriarch and her domain (see H. Geertz 1961; Tanner 1974).

What we will see in the chapters that follow is how crucial this "woman-centeredness" was to Laweyan's identity. It is no exaggeration to say that women were the heart and soul of the community, as they were of the family firm, and that women's centrality here defined in critical ways the community's internal social relations as well as its connections with the outside world. We will also see how gender itself came to figure prominently in the transformation of Laweyan from a locus of modernity to a site of nostalgia. While many factors were involved in this transformation, gender forms a key piece of the puzzle, and if this piece is missing, the picture is incomplete. I would argue as well that "the family," both as a "real" social entity *and* as an ideological construct, has played a fundamental role in processes of social transformation in Java, but that this role has not been given the recognition it deserves. Far from being peripheral to the workings of "contemporary" societies, the family is deeply enmeshed with the politics, economics, and social forces of modern life.

But the specific configurations of family or gender in any given locale can never be assumed: they are knowable only in their concrete details. So I return, in the next chapter, to Laweyan's history, and to its relationship with the centers of power—political as well as cultural—that stood outside it, for only in its historical and cultural contexts can we begin to grasp the importance of women, gender, and the family in this particular corner of Javanese society. Within a relatively short time—only a few decades, it would seem—Laweyan was transformed through occupational specialization, endogamy, and wealth from a neighborhood of new entrepreneurs in a young industry to a well-established merchant community, with clearly marked boundaries, which was increasingly closing in on itself. But in order to fully appreciate the reasons for Laweyan's transformation, we first need a more complete image of where it was situated in the social hierarchies of colonial Java, and how this shaped the ideologies that defined Laweyan's place in the larger society. In this chapter I have given an overview of where Laweyan stood in the political economy of late colonial Java; in the next chapter, my aim will be to place it in what might be called Java's *cultural* economy, mapped onto a social landscape that was irrevocably shaped by the colonial experience.

Chapter Two

HIERARCHY AND CONTRADICTION

MERCHANTS AND ARISTOCRATS IN COLONIAL JAVA

T HE EIGHTH MONTH of the Javanese Islamic lunar calendar is called Ruwah, derived from the Arabic *ruh*, meaning "spirit" or "soul."[1] During this month, which directly precedes the Muslim fasting month (Ramadan, or Pasa in Javanese), Javanese villagers and city folk alike make individual and group visits to the grave sites of ancestors and other relatives, venerated Islamic teachers, mystics, legendary rulers, the first settlers of their villages, and any others from whom they wish to request blessings (*nyuwun pangèstu, nyuwun berkah*), or for whose souls they wish to offer prayers. Ruwah is the time when people return to their natal or ancestral villages to make offerings at the graves of their forebears; they make pilgrimages to grave sites too distant for a casual weekly visit on a Thursday night or Friday morning, the usual times to "send" (*ngirim*) flowers, prayers, and incense to the spirits of the dead.

Toward the end of one Ruwah, I was invited to accompany several neighbors on a day trip to Kotagede, just southeast of Yogyakarta. Early on a Monday morning several of us piled into a chauffeur-driven passenger van belonging to the wealthy merchant couple that had organized the trip, the Sapardis, who were in their late sixties. About two hours later, we arrived at the royal cemetery of Kotagede, established in the late sixteenth century. This is the burial place of the founders of the kingdom of Mataram, ancestors to the present-day royal houses of Solo and Yogyakarta.[2]

Upon entering the high-walled complex, which had only a few other visitors, we removed our shoes as a sign of respect, and changed our clothes in a room designated for that purpose. The one man in our group, Pak Sapardi, changed his Western-style clothing for full formal Javanese attire, donning a high-collared white jacket, a Solonese batik sarong, and a stiff batik headdress. The women, who were already wearing batik sarongs, replaced their usual long-sleeved *kebayas* with a simple wraparound breast cloth (*kemben*) that leaves the shoulders bare, in the style worn in the palaces by female servants and courtiers. Having been warned beforehand that I would also be expected to dress in that style if I wished to see the interior of the complex where the graves were located, I followed suit. Before entering the inner courtyard, a gatekeeper wearing the regalia of a palace retainer (*abdi dalem*) asked me politely to remove my necklace, bracelet, and watch; the other women, I noticed, had already taken off their jewelry. The reason, I was told by a member of my party, was so that we would not appear to be "trying to put ourselves on the same level" with the royalty buried there: in the presence of royal graves one dressed the same way that one would dress for a formal audience if their inhabitants were still alive. So, barefoot and dressed in the unadorned style of courtiers, we proceeded to *sowan*—to pay a visit to someone of superior status—to the tombs of the royal personages interred in the inner sanctum of the cemetery.

Walking past the more minor graves, which were outdoors, we stopped at the doorway of a large mausoleum. Each member of the party sat cross-legged outside the door for a few minutes, without speaking, once again in the respectful manner of a courtier. Before going inside, everyone performed a *sembah*, an obeisant gesture made by holding the hands before the face, palms pressed together and thumbs approaching the nose.

The inside of the mausoleum was dimly lit, illuminated only by occasional thin rays of sunlight that streamed through a few glass roof tiles and beveled glass windows emblazoned with the insignia of Sunan Paku-buwana X of Solo (r. 1893–1939). The damp air was heavy with incense and the smell of fresh and decaying rose petals strewn liberally over all the tombstones. Members of the group greeted several male caretakers in formal Javanese clothing, who wore the yellow sash around their necks that indicated their status as court retainers.

As we approached the tombs of the most senior figures, which were on a raised dais above the level of the other graves, each person dropped to his or her knees and moved forward in a humble, half-crouching posture (*laku dhodhok*) used in the palaces for approaching someone of high rank. We sat cross-legged in front of the most important tombs. Two of the women burned incense in a small brazier and scattered flower petals over the tombstones. Pak Sapardi made a short introductory speech in very high Javanese, mentioning the names of the members of the party (excluding the anthropologist) who had come to pay respects to the dead buried there, and to pray that the souls of the deceased would be accepted by God and given a place in heaven. He asked forgiveness from the spirits of the dead for any mistakes or offenses the members of the group might commit in their presence.

After he stopped speaking, the three men whose services he had enlisted sat down before the tombs on the raised platform and chanted Arabic prayers for the souls of the dead. When these prayers were finished, Pak Sapardi, followed by the other members of the party in turn, inched forward in the same crouching walk until he was directly in front of one of the tombstones, uttered a prayer under his breath, then wiped his face afterward with both hands in the gesture that follows an Islamic prayer. After this he moved even closer to the tombstone. With one hand touching the base of the stone, he knelt deeply in front of it, almost prostrate, his forehead and nose also touching the base. He moved his lips in a whisper for several minutes while remaining in that position. Upon completing this part of the ritual, he made the respectful gesture of the *sembah* before the tomb, then moved on to the next grave, where he repeated the whole routine. This went on at about ten tombs, which were arranged in tiers according to rank and seniority. The progression of the ritual was from the tombs of the most senior figures to those of lower rank.

Having gone around to each of the major tombs, the members of the group left the chamber, turned around, knelt, and performed a final *sembah* before departing the graveyard. After a brief chat with a few of the court retainers, a stroll around the rest of the grounds, and a photo session just inside the main gates, we changed back into our street clothes and exited the complex. On the way out, Pak Sapardi distributed small coins from a plastic bag to women and children beggars who sat at the outer gates.

As we left the cemetery, I asked Bu Sapardi what she had whispered at each grave. The first part, she told me, was a prayer to God that the sins of the dead would be forgiven and their soul (*arwah*) accepted in heaven; this was the Arabic prayer that ended in the face-wiping gesture. The second part, when she "kissed" the base of the tombstone, was a prayer offered up directly in high Javanese to the spirit of the person buried there and consisted of requests for various blessings. The other members of the group had followed the same routine, it turned out. I asked her husband what favors he had requested from the spirits of the dead. "Health, lots of good fortune, and great profits," he answered without hesitation.

This was only one of many cemeteries that were visited by the Sapardis during the month of Ruwah; during that day alone we went to three other grave sites in the Kotagede area, and Bu Sapardi let me know that during a typical Ruwah she might visit well over fifty cemeteries. "It's better than just sitting around at home, isn't it?" she asked rhetorically. What was striking about this particular ritual at the Kotagede cemetery, however, was that it involved an open, completely unabashed display of obeisance and supplication to royalty—or at least, to the spirits of royalty—by people who on other occasions adamantly declared their absolute independence from, and disdain for, the hierarchies and values of the palaces.

The Sapardis were the consummate representatives of the prosperous Laweyan merchant couple: both had been born into well-established entrepreneurial families that had enjoyed uninterrupted prestige in the community for several generations, not a small accomplishment considering the wild swings in fortune that many other families had experienced. The Sapardis' own textile business, which they had started in 1938, had continued to thrive through times when most Laweyan businesses were foundering or had gone totally bankrupt. Their opulent home and gardens, situated behind a high wall crowned with barbed wire and impeccably maintained by a large house staff, were extraordinary by any standards. Their wealth, acumen in business, and family heritage gave them a degree of status in the Laweyan community that few others could match. Their female servants were expected to kneel while serving them and to avert their eyes submissively while speaking to them. The Sapardis had the self-assured air of people who had reached the pinnacle of success, at least by local standards. When they walked down the street, those of lesser status would move aside deferentially to let them pass.

Only a few days after arriving in Laweyan I had been escorted to the Sapardis' home by Pak Wiyono. It soon became clear to me that this was a couple that commanded great respect, and not a little envy, serving as exemplars for the rest of the community. During the course of our conversation, Pak Sapardi stated proudly and in no uncertain terms, "The people of Laweyan have always had the spirit of entrepreneurs. Since the time of our ancestors, we haven't liked people telling us what to do. We don't like serving people. Our souls are the souls of entrepreneurs—we work for ourselves." He made no effort to hide his scorn for those whose livelihood depended on catering to the will of others, especially those who served the palaces and the government bureaucracy. His wife indicated her full agreement, and I was to hear this sentiment expressed by many other residents of the neighborhood in the months to come.

Given their own almost "royal" stature in the Laweyan community, and their vehement declaration of independence from the true Solonese royalty and the values that they espoused, it was, then, most remarkable to see the Sapardis on their knees in Kotagede, nearly prostrate before the tombs of the ancestors of that same royalty. Their willingness to humble themselves in this way was directly related, no doubt, to their expectation that they would receive the blessings of the dead in return. Implicitly, however, it was also an acknowledgment of their acceptance, if only partial, of the ideologies of the Javanese *priyayi* (aristocratic and bureaucratic) elite—the very ideologies that they claimed to disdain. Even when they made offerings at the graves of their own ancestors to ask for blessings of health and prosperity, they never performed the gesture of the *sembah*, a sign of deference to those of high rank, since their own forebears were, after all, only commoners. When the Sapardis crawled on their knees in Kotagede to invoke blessings of good fortune and good profits from the ancestral spirits of Java's royalty, it was a sign of their willingness to enter into the aristocratic hierarchies of Javanese society, at least temporarily, in order to secure a respected place in the hierarchies of their own, more marginal sector of society.

This ritual made me keenly aware that although I had situated myself at a remove from the palaces, in a community that had long resisted their social and cultural hegemony, I could not ignore their lingering influence on local society. While the colonial era had drawn to a close more than forty years earlier, bringing to an end the protracted fiction that the nobility were still, in some sense, the "rulers" of Javanese society, the legacies of that period remained a very real presence in Solo. What I witnessed in Kotagede were the residual effects of an era in which the Javanese nobility had stood at the apex of Javanese society, enjoying great prestige and imbued with a sacrosanct aura of power and privilege.

Although Laweyan's merchants had established an identity that was self-consciously independent of the palaces, neither they nor anyone else in Solo had been able to avoid the deeply entrenched social hierarchies that emanated from the palaces and the elite *priyayi* class associated with them, hierarchies that were shored up by the support of Java's Dutch overlords. During the colonial period, the merchants had been compelled to come to terms with *priyayi* ideologies that denied members of the merchant class the right to hold truly high status in Javanese society. The nobility and other members of the *priyayi* elite had looked down on the merchant's vocation and lifestyle, and Laweyan, as the epitome of the merchant community, stood in many ways as the antithesis of the palaces and the aristocratic way of life associated with them. The palaces represented something that all of Laweyan's wealth could not bring to its merchants: an exalted position in the dominant hierarchies of Javanese society.

Understanding the historical relationship between the *priyayi*, the elite class of aristocrats and officials of the Javanese palaces and state bureaucracy, and the merchant or *sudagar* (*saudagar*, I.) class, two small but at one time very influential groups in Solo, is important for what it reveals about the cultural and political bases for the construction of hierarchy in Javanese society. It is a relationship that has been fraught with tensions and rivalries since at least the early nineteenth century, with reverberations continuing to the present. The story of this relationship also provides another part of the historical background that we need in order to make sense of Laweyan's resistance to the New Order state's ambitious efforts to promote development both locally and nationally. Without this historical depth, Laweyan's rejection of the state's modernizing agendas could be dismissed as a quaint but fairly meaningless conservatism, a phenomenon of no real significance within the nation's more sweeping movements toward modernization.

What I want to suggest is that Laweyan's ambivalent relationship to the state and to modernity itself can be traced in part to the peculiar configuration of power, wealth, and hierarchy that characterized colonial Javanese society in the nineteenth and early twentieth centuries. Knowledge of this uneasy relationship also helps explain Laweyan's gradual process of social involution and its embracing of "tradition" in New Order Indonesia. Finally, it sets the stage for an exploration of women's pivotal roles in the community, which I will explore in detail in the chapters to come.

Systemic conflicts between merchants and political elites are not unusual, especially in agrarian-based societies like inland Java, where access to power and material wealth typically depends on control over land and labor rather than on control over commerce. In Java, where large-scale trade has been predominantly in the hands of people of foreign origin or descent since the latter part of the seventeenth century, one is also not surprised to find the qualities generally associated with foreign trading minorities—avarice, a lack of social concern, a calculating rationalism and selfishness in place of a spirit of cooperation—attributed to the indigenous merchant class as well. During the colonial period, Javanese merchants were at odds with the elites of their society, but they were also marginal to the mainstream, perhaps even more marginal than the nonindigenous merchants with whom they competed. Unlike the ethnic Chinese, for example, who had a well-defined position as middlemen, no clear niche was allotted to them in the colonial order. This marginality has continued into the postcolonial period, despite sporadic (and relatively ineffective) efforts of the postindependence regimes to strengthen the position of indigenous entrepreneurs and merchants relative to nonindigenous groups.

Scholars of Javanese society have sometimes seen this social marginalization as a sign of a radical disjuncture between the values of the indigenous merchant class and those of both the *priyayi* and the wider population. In *Peddlers and Princes*, for example, Clifford Geertz writes of the "historically persistent tension between the value system of the general society and that of the interstitial bazaar culture, and between the peasant and gentleman on the one hand and trader on the other" (1963, 44). While I would not deny that such tensions have existed in Solo, what I observed of the merchant class there would perhaps be better described as a process in which the merchant class alternately resisted, accommodated, and appropriated the dominant values and hierarchies of the *priyayi* elite. While the merchants refused to accept the hegemony of *priyayi* ideologies that placed them toward the bottom of Java's social hierarchies, they did not reject the notion of hierarchy itself but rather refigured the criteria on which status was determined, in effect turning hierarchy on its head.

Members of the merchant class created their own hierarchies on the basis of something that is, from the perspective of *priyayi* ideology, outside the sphere of culture altogether: money, the universal equivalent of exchange. In the merchant community money, not rank, was what generated status; it was the source of authority and of the ability to command deference. In *priyayi* ideologies, however, wealth is a sign, but *not* the source, of authority, power, or the right to expect deferential language and behavior. Wealth should follow from power, not power from wealth. The possibility that wealth could be translated to status challenged *priyayi* ideologies of power, all the more so when *real* political power in the Indies lay in the hands of the Dutch colonial authorities.

"Power" and the Contradiction of Wealth

Many scholars have found an intense concern with status and hierarchy to be one of the most distinctive features of Javanese language and society (see, e.g., C. Geertz 1960; Siegel 1986; Keeler 1987; J. Errington 1988). Status is determined through a complex but somewhat fluid system of social hierarchy based on rank, class, age and seniority, occupation, education, and other considerations, such as whether one is a villager or an urbanite. Ideas about hierarchy operate not merely as a simple principle of social ranking but also as a way of conceptualizing the broader sociocultural order and the place of everything in it.

Hierarchy in Java is often linked to the notion of cultural refinement, which encodes ideas about ethics, aesthetics, and cultural value. This conceptualization of refinement revolves around a basic opposition of two terms, *alus* and *kasar* (see C. Geertz 1960; J. Errington 1984, 1988; Siegel 1986). *Alus* can be glossed as "refined," "civilized," or "smooth" and carries the added connotation of "high status." *Kasar* means "unrefined," "uncivilized," "crude," or "coarse" and is associated with low status. Javanese tend to evaluate everyone and everything according to relative standards of refinement, including linguistic and behavioral styles, occupations, and the arts. People, too, can be characterized as generally *alus*, refined, or *kasar*, coarse. High Javanese (*basa* or *krama*), the polite, respectful, and sometimes deferential register of the Javanese language, is considered to be the more *alus* level of the language, whereas low Javanese (*ngoko*), the familiar form of the language often used to address children, servants, close friends, and junior relatives, is seen as more *kasar*.

Javanese children are immersed in status distinctions as soon as they enter the world. They quickly learn that completely different sets of vocabulary items and speech styles are used in the Javanese language to indicate fine gradations of status, and their parents, siblings, and others in their environment teach them from an early age to recognize these differences and to make use of them in their own speech.[3] Javanese is said to exhibit "the most highly elaborated speech levels of any language in the world" (Keeler 1987, 19). To speak Javanese one must ascertain where one stands socially (or thinks one stands) relative to the interlocutor, as well as relative to any third person about whom one speaks, regardless of whether he or she is present. This means that the issue of status can never really be put out of mind, for to the extent that language shapes one's apprehension of the world and is in turn shaped by it, to speak or even to think in Javanese establishes the world as an intrinsically hierarchical place.[4]

The preoccupation with matters of status and refinement is especially pronounced in the cities of Solo and Yogyakarta, where the palaces, with their intricate internal hierarchies, set the tone for the rest of the population. This concern is reflected and reproduced in the dialect of the Javanese language that is spoken in and around these cities, which exhibits the most elaborately hierarchical speech styles found anywhere in Java, and in the forms of behavioral politesse that accompany it.[5] However, because there are no formal castes in Java—even the hereditary nobility quickly decline in rank over successive generations—determining relative status can be a subtle and often tricky matter. Social status may change over the course of an individual's lifetime, as he or she rises or falls in social position through education, marriage, parenthood, acquisition or loss of wealth, promotion or demotion, and other achievements or changes in fortune. Because status is never fixed, always relative, and constantly renegotiated, there are inevitably contradictions in the ways that hierarchy is established and subjectively understood. It is at these points of contradiction that slippages occur in the system of hierarchy itself, allowing room for contestation of the means by which status is produced and deference elicited.

One of these points of contradiction, which hinges on the role of wealth in producing status, is key to understanding the relationship between two groups that vied for status in late colonial Java: the merchant or *sudagar* class and the *priyayi* class of aristocratic and bureaucratic elites. Laweyan's marginality and its ambivalent relationship to power was largely attributable to one specific contradiction in the system of Javanese hierarchy. Its source was the conflict between the *priyayi* belief that status should be determined mainly on the basis of rank or title, cultural authority, and personal refinement and the reality of late-nineteenth- and early-twentieth-century Java, in which there emerged a small, independent Javanese bourgeoisie that took wealth as a key determinant of status and as the basis, moreover, of much of its subculture.

The traditional *priyayi* elite consisted of hereditary nobility as well as others who served either the palaces or, in the colonial period, the Dutch government. In late colonial and postcolonial Java the term *priyayi* gradually came to include other Javanese who were not necessarily associated with the aristocracy or the government but who were considered to belong to the elite professional, clerical, or managerial class, such as doctors, teachers, and those employed in white-collar positions in private firms. The historian Heather Sutherland offers a useful description of the *priyayi*, especially of the more traditional, idealized type:

> Originally the term was *para yayi*, meaning "younger brothers" (of the king), and by extension it came to include the governing aristocracy. Nobles and officials, court-based administrators and local chiefs could all be classed as *priyayi*. Ideally speaking, a *priyayi* was a well-born Javanese holding high government office, thoroughly versed in the aristocratic culture of the courts. He should be familiar with classical literature, music and dance, the *wayang kulit* (puppet shadow play), and with the subtleties of philosophy, ethics and mysticism. He should have mastered the nuances of polite behavior, language and dress and, until well into the late nineteenth century, he was expected to be at home in the arts of war, skilled in the handling of horses and weapons. (1975, 57–58)

As she points out, this was a model tied to particular political and social interests that was not always followed in practice. However, it remained the prevailing model of the *priyayi* in nineteenth-century Java, based largely on an idealized image of the Mataram court, and it was given considerable weight by local Javanese elites as well as the Dutch.

The *priyayi*, who continued to set cultural standards for the Javanese population long after they had lost their political power to the colonial regime, appointed themselves the guardians of "authentic" Javanese traditions, a role that was fully endorsed by the Dutch and generally accepted by the wider population. The notion of cultural authenticity, based on a certain understanding of the relationship between history and the present, was central to the legitimation of *priyayi* claims to status and cultural authority in Javanese society. In *priyayi* thought, which had a widespread influence in Javanese society more generally, cultural value and authenticity are historically produced. The greatest value is accorded to those things that are believed to have originated in a golden age of the past, at a time when Javanese civilization was at its full glory, and that have been passed down to the present as treasured inheritances, preserved in the form truest to their origins. The ancient courts in particular were seen as a source of valuable cultural inheritances, and the *priyayi* considered themselves the heirs to the knowledge and traditions of the great precolonial kingdoms of Java.

As suggested earlier, the Dutch were almost as concerned with the preservation of authentic Javanese traditions as the *priyayi* were—and sometimes more so. They designated the courts of Solo and Yogyakarta, scions of the kingdom of Mataram, as the repositories of the purest and highest of Javanese traditions. They also supported *priyayi* claims to be the inheritors of those traditions and to be the arbiters—along with Dutch experts in "Javanology"—of cultural authenticity and value. By this logic of authenticity, the rightful place of the *priyayi* was at the top of the Javanese social hierarchy, with the paramount status reserved for the royalty, who were the most direct heirs to sanctified Javanese traditions. By this logic, too, the rest of the Javanese population, the commoners (*wong cilik*: literally, "little people") were expected to defer to the *priyayi*'s supremacy without question, because the great wisdom and hallowed traditions of the ancestral past, and the potent spiritual forces that had generated them, were assumed to flow through the palaces and the *priyayi* elite down to the broader population. The established hierarchical structure of Javanese society, then, had the appearance of a natural system that was legitimated in history itself. Virtually everything that had a presumed link to the high culture of the past was associated with the *alus*, for refinement and high status themselves were often thought to be generated through the preservation of tradition.

The *priyayi* did enjoy elevated status in Javanese society, bolstered by Dutch support. But the rise of the Javanese bourgeoisie conflicted with the ideological premises on which *priyayi* authority were based. *Priyayi* ideologies were spawned from the marriage of Javanese aristocratic values with nineteenth-century codes of proper conduct for Javanese employees of the colonial bureaucracy, and they were legitimated by reference to Javanese tradition. But members of the merchant class were, for the most part, of humble origins. Unlike the *priyayi*, they could not claim to be the conservators of high Javanese culture. Money earned through trade had no roots in history, no noble lineage, no connection to ancestral Javanese traditions—in short, it had no cultural value or authenticity.

The *priyayi* disparaged the merchants' attempts to gain prestige through wealth. They considered a lifestyle based on the overt pursuit of money to be *kasar*, coarse and unrefined. An elderly grandson of Sunan Pakubuwana X scoffed when I inquired whether the royalty had been resentful toward the rich merchants of Laweyan in his grandfather's day, or jealous of their wealth: "What was there to be jealous about? To be *priyayi* is to be honored. The people in Laweyan were just workers. Traders are lower than *priyayi*." Yet through the accumulation and conspicuous show of riches, members of the *sudagar* class rivaled *priyayi* displays of grandeur, thereby pitting their own hierarchies based on wealth against those of the *priyayi*. Their efforts to gain prestige on the basis of wealth, and their ability to command deference from others as a result of that wealth, directly confronted the system of hierarchy that, in theory, accorded status only on the basis of inviolable claims to cultural and historical legitimacy.

In an influential essay about Javanese conceptions of power, Benedict Anderson (1990c)[6] observes that the *priyayi* set themselves off from the rest of the Javanese population not only by rank and occupation, but also by lifestyle and the self-conscious adoption of a distinctive and highly elabo-

rated system of ethical values and philosophical beliefs. Within this philosophical system, the power of the ruler and other persons of high status is
understood to be based on their accumulation of a powerful spiritual force
or substance ("Power," in Anderson's terminology). According to *priyayi*
ideologies of spiritual potency, the active quest for material gain that is
characteristic of the merchant is a sign of personal indulgence and lack of
refinement, which in turn indicate low status and a corresponding lack of
spiritual power:

> This judgment should not be taken to suggest that the typical high-status Java
> nese is not a man of wealth or that the Javanese tradition does not conceive of
> riches as an important attribute of the ruler and his closest associates. But money
> in itself should never be the object of active pursuit. Wealth should flow to the
> holder of Power as a consequence of that Power, in the same way that pusaka
> [sacred objects or heirlooms], large populations, wives, neighboring kingdoms
> or states flow toward the ruler, as it were, magnetically attracted to the center.
> The vast wealth that the great rulers of the Javanese past are described as pos
> sessing is always an attribute of Power, not the means for acquiring it. Thus in
> the Javanese political tradition wealth necessarily follows Power, not Power
> wealth. (Anderson 1990c, 53)[7]

The impact of these ideologies was far-reaching in colonial Javanese
society, not only among the *priyayi* but also among common people. Service to the palaces and the state was considered a much loftier occupation
than trade, and excessive outward concern with matters of money was generally scorned. The Javanese merchant class, however—which emerged,
significantly, at a time when the economic power and social prestige of the
priyayi were waning as a result of colonial policies limiting their rights over
land and labor (M. Nakamura 1983; Shiraishi 1990)—defied these cultural
ideologies by claiming its own right to high status based on wealth rather
than title. It thus set itself up as an alternative elite, indirectly challenging
the social and cultural hegemony of the *priyayi*.

One of the central focuses of life in Laweyan, as elsewhere in Solo, was
the attainment of status. The crucial distinction was that here, the "aristocracy" consisted of those who had the greatest riches—and especially those
who could pass down their riches from generation to generation. If this
basis for acquiring status was more flexible than that of aristocratic rank or
title, it was also more tenuous, for even the richest of merchant families
could not be assured of holding onto their money for long. Everyone in
Laweyan knew families that had fallen from great prosperity to near destitution in the space of one generation or less. The higher the status a merchant family attained in the community, the more it became obsessed with
maintaining and reproducing that status. This obsession was still very
much in evidence when I lived in Laweyan; the Sapardis' numerous excur-

sions to cemeteries to request the blessings of the dead demonstrated the lengths to which members of the merchant class would go to ensure their own prosperity and that of their descendants.

But the social divide between the *priyayi* and the merchant class was real, even if the two groups did not occupy such different cultural universes as has sometimes been assumed. How then did this division come to be so sharp? This question is not simply one of vague historical interest, because it has implications for understanding the impact of colonialism on social categories and cultural ideologies over an extended period of time, long past the period of colonial rule itself. Knowing about the historical development of the rift between these two classes of competing elites sheds light on basic issues that will emerge in the discussion of Java in the New Order in the chapters to come. The salience of these historical issues to my explorations of gender in particular will also become apparent.

A Legend of Defiance: Pakubuwana II's Misadventures in Laweyan

In the context of modern Indonesia under the New Order regime, both Laweyan and the Kraton, the sunan's palace and one of the symbolic centers of *priyayi* culture in Java, stand today as vestiges of a bygone era. Behind the imposing whitewashed walls surrounding the Kraton compound one expects to find the inherited riches of a 250-year-old history. Instead, one finds timeworn buildings, sparsely furnished and inhabited, filled with little more than the lassitude of a dissolute and somewhat impoverished aristocracy. To speak of any real political power on the part of the sunan and his family would be absurd, since this descendant house of the once-preeminent kingdom of Mataram had come completely under the control of the colonial regime by the end of the Java War (1825–30), which enabled the Dutch to consolidate their power in Java.[8] Moreover, unlike the sultan of Yogyakarta, the sunan of Solo lost his claim to special political status after Indonesian independence, and therefore had no official right to participate in the governance of the republic.[9]

Although the sunan and his entourage had lost almost all of their effective power by the mid–nineteenth century, they nevertheless continued to envision themselves—and were in turn envisioned by much of the population—as standing at the pinnacle of the Javanese social hierarchy for the duration of the colonial period. The symbiotic relationship between Dutch suzerain and local nobility that characterized colonial rule in Java enabled the house of the sunan (like the other royal houses of the Principalities) to maintain symbolic power in Javanese society at the same time that its actual power to govern the populace became increasingly limited.

Even as the functionaries of an alien regime, the royalty continued to dominate Solo's social and cultural landscape. However, the lack of education, gradual impoverishment, and self-absorption of the royal family after independence led to a marked decline in the respect that the sunan and his followers were able to command from the population. While many people in present-day Solo still consider it prestigious to hold a title from the Kraton, there is at the same time a good deal of cynicism toward the royalty and a widespread belief that a noble title can be purchased by anyone who has the money and inclination to do so.

The neighborhood of Laweyan, like the Kraton, has an anachronistic and debilitated air about it. Many of its batik workshops and immense homes are empty and decaying, hollow reminders of an earlier, more prosperous time in the neighborhood's history. There are exceptions to this overall decline, such as the well-kept homes of the few people, like the Sapardis, who continue to operate profitable businesses. But in Solo, the name "Laweyan" itself has become associated with a rapidly fading mercantile ethos and an obsolete way of life. In this latter sense as well it may be compared to the Kraton, which is seen as the locus of Javanese tradition in Solo and throughout much of Java, but which is essentially irrelevant to the workings of the modern Indonesian political, social, and economic order—another site of nostalgia in a modernizing city.

To speak of the relationship between Laweyan and the Kraton is to speak of the past, then, for although sentiments of mutual suspicion and disaffection continue to be voiced on both sides late in the twentieth century, the sources of tension between them date back to an earlier period. According to local legend, the strained relationship began just prior to the establishment of the Kraton at Solo by Sunan Pakubuwana II in 1745. A story that is told today in Solo, most commonly in Kraton circles, dates the inception of the antagonism between Laweyan and the Kraton to Pakubuwana II's flight from Kartasura after his palace had been overtaken by rebel forces. Although there are quite a few variations on the story, I offer here an abridged translation of one popular version, which was written down in modern Javanese by Samsudjin Probohardjono, a titled courtier of the Kraton, in 1981:

> Three hundred years ago, the village of Laweyan was already famous as the home of wealthy merchants who dealt in thread (lawé), woven cloth, and batik. Their large walled houses loomed up everywhere. Their vast yards were surrounded by brick walls that were as thick and high and strong as the walls of the palace.
>
> There are some who hold the opinion that the people of Laweyan were by nature strongly inclined toward trade, working only for themselves, and being entrepreneurs. This was a far cry from the honor and prestige of serving the

King or the State. The greatness of their rank, the loftiness of their status, what was good and bad, were all determined by wealth and worldly riches.

The story is told that on A.D. June 30, 1742, the Palace at Kartasura was ravaged by Chinese soldiers. His Royal Highness Pakubuwana the Second, together with his son the Crown Prince and his entourage, all of whom had just fled from the palace, were traveling east on horseback. Passing Pajang, they reached the eastern side of the Premulung River, where they rested for a spell to put all their things in order, as well as to rest their tired horses, which had not been tended to for several days because of the battle that raged, and because the Chinese soldiers were hot in pursuit.

While they rested there, His Highness sent a retainer to the village of Laweyan to borrow fresh horses that could be used to ride and to carry their supplies for the remainder of the journey. But none of the people of Laweyan were willing to offer their horses, since all were being used to transport their wares, trade being very brisk at the time.

His Highness Pakubuwana the Second received this report with a heavy heart, thinking of how bad his luck was, facing the trials that the Almighty God was setting him. But then, calming himself, he said to himself clearly and firmly: "The people of Laweyan are not of the stature of *priyayi*, but are by nature traders who calculate profits and losses, who strive for wealth and treasures. May God the Almighty grant them these things."

The words of his Royal Highness Pakubuwana the Second have been true to this day. Many of the people of Laweyan have been successful in trade and in their firms. Many have become large-scale traders and entrepreneurs, very wealthy, their property and riches overflowing. But few have become *priyayi* or servants of Court and State with distinguished rank. (Samsudjin 1981, 5–7)

This rendition of the story places the uppity people of Laweyan within the symbolic sphere of Kraton control by attributing their long-lasting success as merchants to the charity of Pakubuwana II and to the power and efficacy of his word (*sabda*). In spite of their refusal to serve the sunan, he proves his own spiritual potency and the superiority of the aristocratic ethos by forgiving them for their transgressions and by acting as an intermediary with God to secure blessings for them.

In other versions of the story, though, Pakubuwana is not quite so generous. Several people told me that when the sunan's request to borrow horses was turned down, he *cursed* the people of Laweyan, swearing that none of their descendants would ever be permitted to marry his descendants, and that thenceforth the people of Laweyan would be barred from attaining high rank in the Kraton, doomed forever to be low-status traders instead of honored aristocrats or courtiers.[10] In fact, there does seem to be an informal rule in the Kraton, still in effect today, that enjoins high-ranking members of the royalty from marrying residents of Laweyan. Those who told me of this prohibition invariably cited the unfortunate experiences of Pakubuwana II in Laweyan as the reason for it.

This legend was understandably more popular in Kraton circles than in Laweyan; many people in Laweyan seemed not to know the story or, if they had heard it, gave it little credence. However, an older Laweyan woman, Bu Sudibyo, and her daughter related a version of the story that was similar to the others, but which differed in one significant respect. I had asked Bu Sudibyo whether any member of the royalty had ever married into a Laweyan family, to her knowledge. "No," she answered simply, "That wasn't allowed by the Kraton. It was the word (*sabda*) of the sunan." Her daughter explained further: "People say that a woman from Laweyan was going to be made a wife (*selir*, a minor wife or concubine) of the sunan, but she refused. The sunan was angry, and swore that from that time on, from generation to generation, the people of Laweyan would always be far from the king, but they would be blessed with abundance" (*Sa'turunturuné wong Laweyan bakal adoh karo raja, nanging diparingi keluwihan*). The older woman added that the name "Laweyan" came from *luwih sembarang*, meaning "more of everything." "More riches (*luwih bandha-bandha*), for instance," she explained.

This version of the story is especially telling, since it points to the unwillingness of the independent-minded merchant women of Laweyan to be placed under the control of aristocratic men. Whereas many Javanese women would have considered it an honor and a privilege to be made a wife or concubine of the sunan, Laweyan women were in general agreement that it was preferable to be a common but autonomous trader than to be kept as a royal consort, pampered but confined like a bird in a gilded cage, and forced to compete with co-wives and mistresses for the attentions and favors of the men of the court. They found the idea of being dependent on men for everything—their image of what it meant to be a woman of the noble classes—to be particularly unappealing, because most were accustomed to earning, saving, and spending their own money, with the freedom that provided. On several occasions I heard Laweyan women remark disapprovingly that the ladies of the palace were little more than "vessels" (*si wadhah*) for bearing aristocratic children (see Carey and Houben 1987, 15 n. 5).

Underlying this version of the legend is a central but often overlooked point of distinction between the aristocracy and the merchant class in Solo. I will argue presently that the different positions of women—or at least, the imagined differences—and their relationships with men in these two groups accentuated, and in certain ways even defined, the gap between them. For now, however, I merely observe that while this variant of the story highlights an important factor in the schism between aristocrat and merchant, which hinges on the contrasting roles of women in the two communities (with the contrasts sometimes exaggerated, as we will see), it does not stray from the basic theme that runs through all of the other versions. It, too, points to the aversion of the people of Laweyan to recognizing Kraton hegemony, as indicated by their refusal to acquiesce to the sunan's wishes. We should take note, though, that even in this rendering of the story by two Laweyan merchants, it is ultimately the sunan who seals Laweyan's fate. He forbids the merchants and their descendants to attempt any rapprochement with the Kraton through marriage alliances or through direct service to the court, yet provides them with perpetual abundance by means of the magical potency of his word.

This legend expresses the palpable friction between the Javanese merchant class and the *priyayi*. Indeed, the relationship between the *sudagar* class and the *priyayi* in Solo under colonial rule was marked by mutual suspicion and condescension, but also by a certain mutual envy. To the members of the nobility and colonial bureaucracy, the qualities of the merchant class epitomized character traits that they claimed to despise: greediness, cultural boorishness, devotion to material rather than spiritual pursuits, and the valuation of personal profit over loyal service to palace and state. The *priyayi* saw themselves as the inheritors and protectors of a venerable, refined (*alus*) cultural tradition, while the merchants, in their eyes, were ostentatious bumpkins in gaudy clothes and jewelry, with no taste, no culture, and no sense of proper etiquette. They were, in short, coarse and unrefined (*kasar*). Their wealth, which came to them through commercial activity rather than through service to the state, was wealth that refused to be assimilated to the dominant hierarchies of colonial Javanese society. While the merchants had considerable financial capital at their disposal, the circulation of symbolic capital (see Bourdieu 1977) in Javanese society remained foremost in the control of the *priyayi*.

Sharpening the *priyayi*'s negative views of the *sudagar* class was the fact that many merchants were wealthier than the less-affluent *priyayi* themselves—and flaunted it. No doubt the impressive diamond ornaments worn by female merchants and the bejeweled daggers (*keris*) sported by their husbands, visible indicators of success in business, were a constant, irritating reminder to the nobility and other *priyayi* that jewels did not necessarily go hand in hand with blue blood. In *Student Hidjo*, a novel written by a Javanese in 1919, the author evokes the rivalry of merchant and *priyayi* in his description of a nighttime scene at an amusement park in Solo: "At that time in the King's Garden the light of the electric lamps was like the radiance of the sun, especially because the lighting was enhanced by the brilliance of the diamonds that were worn by nobles and merchants alike" (Marco 1919, 13).

The irritation and disdain of the nobility toward the merchant class is still evident today, although its expression is often couched in aesthetic terms, as a matter of refinement (or lack thereof). A woman from a high-born Mangkunagaran family, Bu Kartika, who herself ran a small dyeworks for high-quality batik, wrinkled her nose in distaste as she recalled the styles worn by merchant women in the past: "*We* never wore *selèndang* (a long scarf worn over one shoulder), because that was what all those traders in Laweyan wore. And then, they always went around showing off those big diamond earrings of theirs." Even the spirits of the dead could be annoyed by a display of jewelry, as I discovered at the Kotagede cemetery, where visitors were asked to remove their jewelry in the presence of the royal tombs. And at a Solo batik shop run by another aristocratic woman of the Mangkunagaran clan, the owner took out two pieces of batik from her display case, unprompted, to show me the differences between what she called "*priyayi*-style batik" (*batik priyayèn*) and "merchant-style batik" (*batik sudagaran*). After first pointing out what she perceived as the refined motifs and tastefully subdued dyes of the *priyayi*-style batik, she then showed me a few examples of "the kind of batik they make in Laweyan," which, she informed me, were too cluttered in design and yellow in hue to be aesthetically pleasing. (To my eye, the differences between the two styles were so subtle as to hardly be noticeable.) She stressed that the batik made in *priyayi* workshops used *traditional* designs and dyes, unlike the batik produced in Laweyan and other *sudagar* workshops, which were corrupted by modern fashion. Significantly, although these two Mangkunagaran women were both proprietors of businesses, they clearly identified themselves as *priyayi* gentlewomen rather than as members of the disesteemed merchant class.

The merchants were no less harsh in their judgments of the *priyayi* than the *priyayi* were of them. Criticisms that I heard in Laweyan about the nobility and civil servants of the Indonesian state (who are considered modern-day *priyayi*) echoed complaints about the *priyayi* that had apparently resounded for generations in the merchant community. The merchants accused the *priyayi* of being lazy, decadent, corrupt, arrogant, and perpetually dependent on the good graces of their superiors in what was perceived as an endless chain of patronage and sycophancy. Members of the merchant class deliberately contrasted themselves with the *priyayi*, asserting their autonomy and taking pride in their willingness to work hard for a living, something that most *priyayi* were incapable of, they said. One of my neighbors summed up this attitude rather bluntly: "People here [in Laweyan] aren't 'yes men' [she used the English term even though she was speaking Indonesian]. We don't like to be told what to do. We have the spirit of traders, we work for ourselves. We don't like to receive wages from others. And we don't like to suck up to people" (*ndak suka menjilat*, I.: literally, "don't like to lick"; she stuck out her tongue to emphasize the point).

The contempt, mixed with envy and defensiveness, that the merchants held for the *priyayi* as a class was reflected during the colonial era in their responses to local representatives of the Kraton and the colonial bureau-cracy. Although the merchants were likely to act respectfully in personal encounters with the *priyayi*, they were privately scornful of them, especially those who had no wealth to show for their position.[11] A number of my acquaintances in Laweyan expressed sentiments that continued to reflect the merchants' lack of respect for those who were in the employ of the palaces, for there remains even today a small but loyal corps of people who continue to offer their services at court. Some of Laweyan's residents were puzzled, even amused, at the notion that anyone would want to become a palace retainer when the wages were so low, particularly at a time when the palaces had lost so much of their traditional status in Javanese society. Most saw service to the courts as a rather foolish waste of time, time that could be better spent pursuing more remunerative activities.

The apparent disdain of the *sudagar* for the *priyayi* frequently gave way to a more active rivalry, however, through displays of wealth reminiscent of those of the royalty, which few lower-ranked *priyayi* could match. Mer-chant weddings and other ritual celebrations were extravagant exhibitions modeled after court ceremonial,[12] and the luxurious homes built by the *sudagar* rivaled those of the high nobility in scale and grandeur. Further-more, the wealthier and more established the merchants became, the more they seemed to emulate the *priyayi* in certain aspects of their lifestyles, while continuing to voice their contempt for *priyayi* values. This was ap-parent, for instance, in their sharply asymmetrical relations with their em-ployees; like the *abdi dalem*, servants of the palaces, the servants and batik workers of well-to-do Laweyan employers were expected to speak to them in high Javanese and be answered in low Javanese, to come at their beck and call, and to serve them deferentially. One Laweyan woman of fairly modest means summed up a common attitude in the community when she remarked, "It's nice to be an employer. You can tell people what to do." Although most *sudagar* found the notion of serving others distasteful, this did not mean that they disliked having others serve them, or that they were any more egalitarian than the *priyayi* in their outlook.

COLONIAL FICTIONS OF POWER

It is difficult to pinpoint precisely when the fissure between merchant and *priyayi* occurred; to what extent these tensions already existed in inland Java during the precolonial period is not entirely clear.[13] What *is* certain, however, is that colonialism created a situation that severely restricted Ja-vanese participation in trade, and that also gave rise to an insurmountable ideological gap between aristocrats and merchants in Javanese society. The colonial economy was geared primarily toward the production and processing of agricultural commodities for export, and the Dutch themselves monopolized the huge export trade to Europe and the plantation and banking sectors, as well as the large import trade in commodities like cloth, as we have already seen. Only petty trade and small-scale commodity production were left in Javanese hands (Robison 1992, 68).

The Dutch encouraged the Chinese, members of an immigrant minority group who were politically powerless but very active in commerce, to take control of the large-scale intermediate trade in Java and other islands of the Indies. They also facilitated Chinese control of local and regional commerce by leasing them the rights to government-held monopolies over such lucrative fields of business as the opium trade and pawnshops, as well as the rights to collect various tolls and taxes (Furnivall 1944; Alexander and Alexander 1991; Rush 1990, 1991). Javanese, in contrast, rarely had the access to the cash or government facilities that would enable them to compete successfully with members of the other groups. Javanese lack of success in business, however, was usually attributed by Dutch observers to poor business skills rather than to the structural constraints placed upon them by the system of colonial rule and the economic exploitation of the indigenous population on which it was based (see Alexander and Alexander 1991).

At the same time that they effectively limited Javanese participation in commerce, the Dutch also ensured that the indigenous aristocracy was largely dependent on the colonial regime for its access to wealth. While Solo's palaces commanded substantial economic resources, including extensive agricultural lands and profitable sugar factories, the gradual erosion of their power during the nineteenth and twentieth centuries made it evident just how dependent they were on the colonial government for their well-being. Beginning in the early to mid–eighteenth century, Dutch subsidies were what really sustained the courts of Central Java (Ricklefs 1974; Kumar 1980a, 1980b). This was all the more apparent after the colonial government instituted the agrarian reorganization of the Principalities in the 1910s and 1920s, including the abolition of the long-standing appanage system, through which palace officials had been assigned rights over the produce of particular lands as well as to corvée labor from the peasants who worked the land. The replacement of land endowments with cash salaries led to a serious reduction of power, prestige, and wealth on the part of the sunan and the Solonese *priyayi* as a whole.[14]

Colonial policy and practice in Java, then, kept independent access to wealth out of the hands of those (besides the Dutch themselves) who had prestige and power—even if it was only the largely symbolic power of the Javanese nobility under colonial rule. The Dutch also kept political power away from those categories of people, such as local Chinese, who could readily obtain wealth through commerce. The Chinese often became rich as traders, but they did not have access to the prestige or political influence of colonial service, and thus they remained members of an ethnic minority who were alternately courted and praised for their financial skills and despised for their sharp business practices and "foreignness" by Europeans and Indonesians alike. Politically vulnerable and dependent upon the colonial regime, the Chinese were an asset to the Dutch in their economic exploitation of the Indies.

A side effect of colonial policy in Java, which kept trade and political power separate for all categories of people except Europeans, was the rigidification of the ideological division between the merchant class and the *priyayi*. The Dutch fostered *priyayi* ideologies that stressed service and self-sacrifice on behalf of the state (including the palaces, which also served the colonial state) as the noblest profession for a Javanese.[15] For Javanese the main route to power and prestige was to serve the colonial bureaucracy. The Dutch identified the *priyayi*, particularly those of the courts of Central Java, as the standard-bearers of high Javanese culture who were deserving of respect from their fellow Javanese. Although the *priyayi* remained politically subordinate to the Dutch, the Dutch also relied on them to maintain order and control over the Javanese population, as well as to extract the products of the population's labor. In this relationship of mutual dependency, the colonial regime rewarded the loyal service of Javanese *priyayi* to the state both materially and symbolically, by providing them with subsidies and by allowing them to maintain an illusion of power long after their real power to govern had waned.

By providing subsidies that permitted those in the upper echelons of the Javanese aristocracy to enjoy lavish lifestyles, the Dutch reinforced *priyayi* assertions that wealth should flow naturally to the holders of power, even at a time when the "power" of the Javanese nobility had come to depend entirely upon Dutch support. The wealth of the nobility remained ideologically legitimate because it continued to be linked to the symbolic centers of power, both Dutch and Javanese. In keeping with these same ideologies, however, the wealth of the Javanese merchant was problematic because it neither emanated from nor flowed toward the center of power, and therefore ran counter to the established hierarchies of Javanese society. The legend of Pakubuwana II's encounter with the merchants of Laweyan reaffirms the ideology that wealth should flow to or from the holder of power. By attributing Laweyan's riches to the all-powerful word of the sunan, the story suggests that even those intractable merchants, who refused the great honor of serving the king because they were more concerned with making money, ultimately owed their wealth to the sunan's formidable concentration of spiritual potency and his beneficent nature. In reality, the Javanese merchant owed little or nothing of his or her wealth to the "powerful center," whether that center be identified with the palaces or with the colonial state (the distinction is, in fact, an artificial one for the period in which full colonial control had been established in Java). The merchant's accumulation of wealth challenged the assumed linkage between wealth and power, but the tale of Pakubuwana II brings the merchants of Laweyan back into the conceptual sphere of the palaces, which restores the linkage once again.

THE FEMINIZATION OF JAVANESE TRADE

We have seen that the increasing penetration of capital into the Principalities in the mid– to late nineteenth century was accompanied by the emergence of a small indigenous bourgeoisie in the batik industry (and to a lesser extent in a few other spheres of petty commodity production and trade). This occurred at the same time that the economic power and social prestige of the *priyayi* were declining as a result of colonial policies limiting their rights over land and labor (Shiraishi 1990). Colonial policy and *priyayi* ideology combined, however, to effectively limit the size, influence, and social status of the Javanese merchant class. The indigenous bourgeoisie remained marginal to the Javanese mainstream, never becoming a large, powerful, or cohesive enough group to alter the basic shape of colonial society. The marginalization of the Javanese merchant class guaranteed that it could not create a serious challenge to the colonial state or to the hegemony of *priyayi* ideologies. And as long as the *priyayi*, thoroughly coopted by the colonial regime, retained their place at the apex of Javanese society and continued to look down on the activities of the merchant, the wealth held by members of this numerically insignificant class could not pose a genuine threat to the social hierarchies or ideological system that had been firmly established and maintained through colonial rule. Dutch colonial policy was invested in the artificial preservation of a static, semi-traditional, *priyayi*-dominated social order in Java; this precluded the possible rise of a large, independent Javanese bourgeoisie of the sort that, in Europe, had successfully challenged the hegemony of the traditional landed aristocracy and ushered in fundamental changes to society (see Wertheim 1964, esp. chap. 10).

A further, important element must be considered in understanding the peripheralization of the merchant class in colonial Javanese society and its confinement to a position of relatively low status: the attitude of the Dutch themselves toward Javanese traders. At the same time that the Dutch were supporting *priyayi* claims to high status, they were also declaring emphatically that the Javanese people were unfit to engage seriously in commerce.

In 1904, for example, C. Th. van Deventer, a major figure in Dutch colonial affairs, contrasted the financial acumen of local Chinese with the seemingly "natural" inability of the Javanese to manage money:

> Real thrift is foreign to the modern-day Javanese; money rolls through their fingers, or burns in their hands; the Chinese is thrifty, frugal, cautious at the same time. In the matter of free will, of the spirit of enterprise, the Native of Java has not come far either; his nature is rather docile. . . . Carefree too is the nature of the ordinary Javanese; they live from hand to mouth, and would rather think as little as possible about tomorrow; this source of a cheerful outlook on life, however, stands in sharp contrast with the inborn notion of the Chinese that people, as much as possible through material appearances, must uphold the sacred honor of their ancestors. Already in this one cardinal notion the Chinese possesses a mighty incentive to drive him to work, while the spirit of the Javanese knows nothing of this sort. (1904, 100–101)

Van Deventer himself was known as a strong advocate for the improvement of native welfare, one of the leading promoters of what became known as the Ethical Policy of colonial rule in the Indies (Furnivall 1944, 231), and his remarks were part of his larger effort to expose the indigenous Indonesians' economic and social plight after their long period of exploitation by Dutch and Chinese. However, when read in another light, such assessments of "the Javanese character" also appeared to explain and even legitimate the privileged position in commerce that was held by foreign minorities, including the Dutch themselves. For those less concerned than van Deventer with native welfare, these evaluations of the Javanese also seemed to justify their relegation to the roles of happy peasant, carefree laborer, or obedient government functionary. Javanese were portrayed as people who were by nature childlike and irresponsible; it thus fell to the Dutch to manage them as they saw fit. Hence, in a popular account of Java, H. W. Ponder wrote in 1934 that

> The roemah gadean (pawnshop) is an indispensable feature of Javanese life. The native is always in financial difficulties of some sort: every cent he earns is heavily mortgaged beforehand; he is an inveterate gambler; and to deny himself anything that he wants, unless it is manifestly unobtainable, is entirely foreign to his nature. So, with this shrewd knowledge in their possession, the Dutch wisely made the pawnshops a government monopoly, and a very valuable one they are. ([1934] 1988, 73)

As Jennifer and Paul Alexander note, the Dutch continually emphasized the ineptitude of Javanese as traders during the course of colonial rule. They did this, in part, by stressing that trade among Javanese was conducted primarily by women, and on a petty scale. A declaration of the Dutch East India Company in 1658, Alexander and Alexander suggest, reflects the general attitude that was to prevail throughout colonial rule, which was that Javanese trade was inefficient and insignificant in scale, "a mere sideline activity in a subsistence-oriented agricultural economy" (1991, 372). The 1658 text describes Javanese traders as "Women who, instead of taking up some honest business by which to earn a living decently, seek to make a little money by sitting all day by the road-side selling a few vegetables and other little things of small value, and do this in such multitudes that they jostle each other and create great disorder in the market place, beside depriving one another of profit and the possibility of obtaining a sufficient living from this trafficking" (Vries and Cohen 1938, 364; cited in Alexander and Alexander 1991, 372).[16]

Other observations by Europeans about women's prominent role in trade were to follow. In 1817 Thomas Stamford Raffles, who had held the top administrative post in the colony during the brief period of British rule, wrote of Java that "In the transaction of money concerns, the women are universally considered superior to the men, and from the common labourer to the chief of a province, it is usual for the husband to entrust his pecuniary affairs entirely to his wife. The women alone attend the markets, and conduct all the business of buying and selling. It is proverbial to say the Javan men are fools in money concerns" ([1817] 1965, 353). Nearly a century later van Deventer, who pegged "the modern-day Javanese" as carefree, docile, and unenterprising, nevertheless gave some (rather patronizing) credit to Javanese women by observing that "The Javanese woman especially is small trader to the marrow." He added that it is "the Javanese village woman who by far conducts most of the retail trade. Her talent for looking after every last penny in buying or selling is, of its kind, unsurpassable. The rice trade, the *warung* trade—the offering of all kinds of foodstuffs for sale in stalls—the retail salt trade, the trade in fruits or vegetables, rest almost completely in her dependable hands" (1904, 98).

Alexander and Alexander make a persuasive case that European comments about women's skill in trade were intended to express less an appreciation of Javanese women than a disparagement of Javanese men. Trade in women's hands tended to be portrayed as traditional in character, economically inefficient, and small in scale: proof that indigenous trade did not need to be taken seriously, and that the Javanese truly were not suited to commercial ventures. This rhetoric served in the legitimation of colonial policies that helped confine the Javanese to the subsistence economy rather than permitting them to participate in the lucrative fields of trade that were dominated by Dutch and "Foreign Orientals" (Alexander and Alexander 1991). I would add that it also contributed to the more general denigration of Javanese men in colonial discourse; they were often portrayed as weak, undisciplined, lacking in ambition, and inferior even to their own wives in handling financial matters—a far cry from the enterprising, hard-working,

Calvinist Dutchman or Chinese immigrant.[17] The subtext is transparent: one could not expect men of such weak character to be able to hold their own in business against the more capable Europeans or Chinese—let alone to govern themselves without "guidance" from those who were more fit to rule their country. If Javanese men were bettered by their own women in managing financial affairs, then they surely could not be entrusted with the financial and political affairs of the nation.

The colonial dismissal of Javanese trade as trivial women's work reinforced the *priyayi*'s deprecation of merchants as well. The *priyayi* had little respect for *sudagar* men, both because they had no official rank and because they were overly concerned with the pursuit of money, which was seen in *priyayi* ideology as especially demeaning for males. It would appear that the *priyayi* also saw *sudagar* men as men who could not control their women. Members of the *priyayi* class looked askance at the involvement of women traders in the market, a place that they associated with things *kasar*: coarse language and behavior, lust for money, and unrestrained association between the sexes. To permit one's wife to trade in the marketplace was to expose her knowingly to the dangers of uncontrolled desires. As the self-appointed custodians of the *alus*, the *priyayi* declared the market a place inappropriate for women of high rank to work. Female traders were also viewed by members of the high nobility as unsuitable partners for marriage; I once heard a local scholar, who was also the granddaughter of a former sunan, state in a public forum that Javanese kings had always refused to marry traders because of their reputation for being "loose." I will return to this association of unrestrained female sexuality with the marketplace in chapter 4, when I discuss the relationship of women, money, and the control of desire in contemporary Solo.

Given the prominent role of women in Solo's merchant class, we can see why the prohibition of marriage between members of the nobility and the people of Laweyan both signaled and reinforced a fundamental point of distinction between them. The different positions of women in these two classes of competing elites—the *sudagar* class, in which women occupied pivotal economic and social roles both inside and outside the home, and the class of high-ranked nobility, in which women's activities were largely confined to the home—accentuated the rift between the two groups. While it was true that the nobility did not want their daughters or wives engaging in "coarse" work or exposed to the seductive desires of the marketplace, it was also true that the entrepreneurial families of Laweyan had no use for women who were unwilling to work for a living, because a work ethic for women was a basic feature of the community's identity. They were therefore disinclined to seek *priyayi* women as prospective brides for their sons. As one Laweyan merchant stated straightforwardly, "In Laweyan, the word *ndara* [a term of address for a person of high rank] means someone who doesn't want to work." She said this in a tone of moral condemnation, indicating just how central the value placed on work was in the community's ethical and economic system.

Nor were the people of Laweyan particularly eager to arrange unions with *priyayi* men for their own daughters; as I mentioned earlier in connection with the legend of Pakubuwana II's cool reception in Laweyan, *sudagar* women did not relish the thought of being dependent on aristocratic men. In Laweyan, women valued their autonomy, which went hand in hand with their economic independence. The most feared consequence of marrying a *priyayi* was being made a co-wife, possibly one among several wives. Although polygyny was not unknown in the merchant community—Islam permits men to take as many as four wives, and both the colonial and postcolonial regimes allowed this for Muslim men—it seems to have been less common than among the *priyayi*, perhaps because the typical *sudagar* man relied so heavily on his wife to manage the family business that he could not afford the possibility of incurring her wrath, which might lead to her demanding a divorce. Divorce was considered by some women a preferable alternative to being made a co-wife in a polygamous marriage, but it was a rather dire prospect for a *sudagar* man of Solo, because it would mean losing access to his wife's business skills and property, which could be a considerable loss indeed.[18] The merchants also feared that contracting a marriage with a *priyayi* would lead to a constant drain on their own resources, since as well-heeled in-laws, they would likely be called upon to make "contributions" to the lavish upkeep of the *priyayi* household in which their daughter lived; such demands could be financially ruinous for a merchant family.

In the merchant community, women's value was intimately linked to their economic productivity, which depended on their ability and willingness to engage in trade. Among the aristocracy, in contrast, female value was tied much more to their domestic roles, and to men's control over women's sexuality and fertility. Daughters were most valuable insofar as they could be used to forge politically expedient marriage alliances (Carey and Houben 1987), while wives were assigned the basic tasks of serving their husbands, regenerating their husbands' descent lines, and maintaining the household. The place of the noblewoman was in the home, her movement in public increasingly restricted the higher her father's or husband's rank.[19] The marketplace was the antithesis of the aristocratic home, in that it was a place where men could not control women—a point that I will explore in greater depth in chapter 4.

Between these two ends of the *priyayi-sudagar* spectrum, however, was a gray area in which the distinction was blurred: while the conceptual divide between merchant and *priyayi* stood firm, in actual practice the division was not always as sharp as either group would claim. For example, it was common during the late colonial period for the wives of lower-and middle-ranked *priyayi* to help support their families as batik entrepreneurs or merchants while their husbands worked in prestigious but often low-paying jobs. In the Kauman, for instance, which was the religious hub of the city, many women supported their households through the batik trade while their husbands served as Islamic officials (*penghulu*) at the Kraton or as religious teachers in the community.[20] From a practical standpoint, many *priyayi* men could not financially afford the luxury of keeping their wives confined to the home. In the case of those who had polygamous marriages, small salaries had to be stretched even further to meet the needs of several wives and their children.

Furthermore, wealth contributed in important ways to prestige. Even for the *priyayi*, there was no honor to be gained in living on a pittance; to support his claims to high status and spiritual potency, a man of rank needed the material accoutrements of rank, which he might not be able to afford on his own salary. A *priyayi* man on a limited salary might look to his wife to augment the income that he brought to the family. Thus, although *priyayi* ideology devalued trade, *priyayi* practice was not always in line with ideology. Because a family's status was defined more by the social position of the husband than of the wife (which made it possible, for instance, for a male member of the royalty to marry a commoner and still sire royal children), the wife of a *priyayi* could engage in trade without her family being "demoted" from *priyayi* to *sudagar* status as a result. This held true provided that neither her rank by birth nor her husband's rank were so high as to make trade out of the question.

Not all fields of trade were equally acceptable, though. It would have been unseemly for the wife of a *priyayi* to engage in the *kasar* work of peddling fruit, for example, or opening up a roadside food stall at night. Since commodities and arenas of trade, too, were evaluated hierarchically, it is no accident that batik production and trade were among the few areas of business that were considered acceptable for *priyayi* women.[21] Batik cloth, especially that which is crafted by hand, is considered an *alus* object through its historical connections to Javanese court culture. One might say that the commodity itself brings an element of respectability to the field of trade that surrounds it. Women of high rank were expected to craft their own batik at home during their spare time; this was a sign of cultivation and a refined leisure-time activity for a gentlewoman, and those who were especially skilled batik makers often became known for the quality of their workmanship. As J. S. Furnivall wrote, "By tradition batik work is the normal occupation and pastime of all ladies of good birth" (1936, 373).[22]

The association of batik with palace culture often made it possible for
priyayi women to subtly circumvent the restrictions on trade for members
of their class; some inconspicuously sold the batik that they crafted at
home to earn extra money for their families. Bu Kartika, a *priyayi* woman
whose father had been a high-ranked official of the Mangkunagaran
court during the final decades of colonial rule, recalled how her aristocratic mother had quietly supplemented her father's income: "Even as a
regent (*bupati*), my father didn't earn enough to support the family. He
would turn his salary over to my mother, and say to her, 'Here—if this
isn't enough, you'll just have to make do somehow.' So she made money
by selling her batik. But she wouldn't sell it to just anyone, and she *never*
sold her batik in the marketplace. There were prohibitions on work for
ladies of high status—their work had to be something that could be done
at home, something that didn't stand out too much." A *priyayi* woman
could unobtrusively sell the batik cloth she made to friends and acquaintances without being subjected to criticism; for a "gift" of batik to be reciprocated with a "gift" of money was quite in keeping with *priyayi* standards of propriety, as long as the transaction was not blatantly conceived
of as an exchange of commodities. Among the lower *priyayi*, a woman
might participate more openly in the batik trade without her or her family being stigmatized for it, since the shift from selling one's own batik to
buying and selling other people's batik did not require a great conceptual
leap.

Many families of the Kauman and other neighborhoods of Solo were
neither purely "*priyayi*" nor purely "*sudagar*"—they were hybrids. Here,
priyayi and merchant lived under one roof as husband and wife, but the
husband's *priyayi* status defined the household as a *priyayi* household. Some
of these families had ties of blood to the Kraton or the Mangkunagaran, as
indicated by their noble titles.[23] This suggests that the boundary between
priyayi and merchant was not as impermeable as it seemed: it was an imagined divide that could be crossed under numerous circumstances. Even
inside the palaces of Central Java, there was a long history of women managing court finances and engaging in certain types of trade (Carey and
Houben 1987).[24] The general rule that women controlled the family purse
held true in aristocratic families as well as among commoners; Bu Kartika,
for example, remembered that her high-ranked father had commonly
asked his wife for "pocket money" when he left the house.

The Laweyan stereotype that women of the nobility "would not work"
was not entirely accurate, for even those women who would not trade in
the marketplace often earned money through other kinds of activities. In
the palaces, as in the wider society, women, unlike men, could handle
money without significant loss of prestige. In the early nineteenth century,
it was usual for one of the high-ranked ladies of the Kraton to manage the

A man meditates at the grave of Kyai Ageng Anis at the royal cemetery in Laweyan.

household expenses and to look after all the contents of the inner court, including the sunan's gold and jewels. "All this stood in marked contrast," write Carey and Houben, "to what was expected from the male members of the court, both relations of the ruler and senior officials, who were not supposed to soil their hands with business ventures" (1987, 23).

Being labeled as *priyayi* or *sudagar*, then, was not solely a matter of occupation, since a woman could be a full-time entrepreneur and still be identified as *priyayi* by association with her *priyayi* husband. It was *his* social standing that fixed the family's identity more or less irrevocably. The categories of *sudagar* and *priyayi* remained meaningful, however, because of their social and cultural connotations. The term *sudagar* not only signified "merchant"; it also implied "those who are removed from the hierarchies of palace and state." A peripheral neighborhood on the outskirts of town, Laweyan, unlike the Kauman, was a true *sudagar* community, for it identified itself precisely in opposition to the Kraton and to the *priyayi* more broadly—even with Kyai Ageng Anis, venerated ancestor to the royal families of Solo and Yogyakarta, buried in its midst. Virtually none of Laweyan's residents, with the exception of the few people who were caretakers at the royal cemetery, had any claims to *priyayi* status. A *bécak* driver, looking around at the grand homes that dominated the neighborhood, put it most succinctly: "This is a place of kings. But the kings are all women. It's a place of rich people, but none of the men have any rank."

THE POLITICS OF THE DOMESTIC SPHERE

We can conclude, then, that when Laweyan rose to prominence during the late colonial period, being a member of the merchant class meant defining oneself in opposition to, or at least apart from, the centers of power. A "proper" occupation for a Javanese male who wished to advance in social standing was to serve the palaces or the colonial bureaucracy; being an entrepreneur or a merchant was not respectable by the standards of the *priyayi* elite, even if it was lucrative. The response of Laweyan's entrepreneurial families, and of their counterparts elsewhere in Java, was to reject those standards and to create their own independent social hierarchies and sources of legitimacy.

The cornerstone of Laweyan's identity rested on the ideal of autonomy—an ideal that accorded well with an entrepreneurial ethos. If elsewhere in Solo the ideal was to serve the palaces or the government bureaucracy, in Laweyan the goal was to serve no one at all. To be a *juragan*, an owner of an enterprise, was greatly valued because it meant that one was autonomous; a *juragan* was, above all, one who told others what to do instead of being told what to do. Along with wealth, this was crucial in determining an individual's social standing in the community. Even a struggling batik producer with only a few employees could be called a *juragan*, with the right to be treated deferentially by her workers and to be accorded respect in the community, as long as she continued to control the means of production and the labor power of other people. Notably, the few people in Laweyan who had managed to elevate themselves from low-status laborers to successful batik entrepreneurs were treated much the same as those who had been born into wealthy *sudagar* families. Among merchants, "the social representatives of unfettered equivalence" (Appadurai 1986, 33), one could find a former household servant and her husband, who together had built up a lucrative business through skill and luck, being treated as the social equals of the established elites of the community. Everyone knew of their humble origins, but once they had established themselves as successful entrepreneurs who had other people working for them, their new status as *juragan* superseded the old; they were, moreover, widely admired for their ability to improve their lot in life so dramatically.

Within the community, the emphasis on autonomy influenced the organization of business as well as interpersonal relationships. Although husbands and wives did cooperate regularly in business, long-term business cooperation between siblings, or even between parents and children, was quite rare. Family members saw close cooperation in business as a recipe for either financial or familial disaster, or both: it wasn't "businesslike" (*saklek*, from *zakelijk*, D.), people agreed. In the few instances when relatives *had* attempted a business partnership, most had reportedly broken down before long, leaving a residue of hard feelings on all sides. The consensus in the community was that partnership in business with anyone besides a spouse would lead to an undesirable loss of independence and to inevitable conflict. Brothers and sisters, even parents and children, frequently eyed each other as business rivals rather than as potential business partners. Marriage signified a break with one's natal household, the time to form a new household and a new business. Parents felt strongly that their children should "learn to live on their own" shortly after marrying; the majority did not encourage their children to join them in business. Most firms were not corporate, and they rarely lasted for more than one generation. This has historically been a common pattern in Javanese businesses throughout the island.

The high value placed on autonomy and independence shaped Laweyan's interactions with the outside world as well as its internal social relations. Laweyan's entrepreneurs were notably reluctant to interact, curry favor, or collaborate with representatives of the colonial regime, Dutch or Javanese. This set them apart from many of their Chinese counterparts, who often relied on their contacts with government officials for advancing their businesses—what James Rush calls the "dance of collaboration" between Chinese businessmen and colonial bureaucrats (1990, 1991). The tendency of Laweyan *sudagar* to distance themselves from the centers of political power is not surprising, given the categorical disrespect that Javanese merchants received from both Dutch bureaucrats and the Javanese *priyayi* who collaborated with them.

Furthermore, there were sound practical reasons for wanting to avoid too much contact with bureaucrats. When a government representative came around to Laweyan, it was usually to assess or collect taxes, to conduct a labor inspection, or to evaluate the political situation among entrepreneurs or workers during times of heightened political activity—and no such visits were likely to turn out to the entrepreneur's advantage. In a 1927 study of the batik industry in central Java, Soerachman comments on the strong reluctance of batik entrepreneurs, Javanese, Chinese, and Arab alike, to discuss their financial affairs with strangers. Any interested questions about the condition of their businesses, he writes, they "immediately distrust and identify as efforts to assess their taxes at a higher rate. The fear of the tax man appears to be universal" (39).[25]

The deep-seated distrust of Laweyan entrepreneurs toward government officials was also observed by de Kat Angelino; he makes a point of noting the cold response that colonial representatives received in Laweyan. As evidence of this great distrust, he writes that two bureaucrats on a mission to investigate wages in the batik industry were summarily denied entry to the workplace of one of the largest batik firms of Laweyan. "It needs no further explanation," he adds, "that the Labor Inspector expected a very difficult task here [in conducting his investigation in Laweyan], and that much discretion and patience was required of him in order to break a path into this ground, which was almost closed through distrust" (*dit door wantrouwen bijna afgesloten terrein*, D.) (1930–31, 2:130). The suspicion that Laweyan entrepreneurs harbored toward the government was still obvious in the 1980s. Any stranger with even a remotely official look about him was immediately branded as "tax collector," or the unwelcome equivalent thereof, regardless of his real occupation. An Indonesian anthropologist described to me the frustrating experience of attempting to collect data in Laweyan for a study on Javanese family life: "It was hard to get anyone to talk to us," he recalled ruefully. "They would peer at us through the little windows in their huge front gates, but they wouldn't let us in." Another scholar from a public university told me that his efforts to conduct a survey in Laweyan had failed as well; I witnessed the distinct discomfort of one local couple as he interviewed them while wearing his civil servant's uniform.

The mistrust and avoidance of government representatives certainly had its rationale in the *sudagar* community: tax collectors and labor inspectors were the bane of the entrepreneur's business. But efforts to avoid dealing with the government in Laweyan were rooted in something deeper than the desire to escape heavier taxation or having to cope with labor inspectors. De Kat Angelino's pointed description of the difficulties that bureaucrats encountered in Laweyan makes it apparent that even among the ranks of batik entrepreneurs all over Java, Laweyan's distrust of the government in the late 1920s was rather extreme. The attitude in the community that I saw seemed to have changed little from what he had observed some sixty years earlier. Laweyan's concerted efforts to avoid authority were not merely practical: they were also ideological. In the process of establishing themselves as a collective of independent bourgeois during the late colonial period, the merchants of Laweyan developed a self-conscious ideology that proclaimed their autonomy from the centers of political and cultural power. At times this desire for autonomy manifested itself in the form of open political action—for instance, in the Sarekat Islam movement. More often, though, it was expressed in the types of quiet individual resistance mentioned by de Kat Angelino.

The independent-mindedness of some sectors of the Javanese bourgeoisie, combined with their amassed riches, did at times seem to openly defy established authority, Dutch as well as Javanese, during the colonial era. Mitsuo Nakamura relates a story about a merchant family of Kotagede that is illustrative in this regard. The family belonged to a very wealthy but marginal community of pawnbrokers and moneylenders, the Kalang (or Galgendu) people, who had much in common with the people of Laweyan:

> A local tradition says that sometime around World War I, a Kalang family obtained such great wealth that they wanted to cover the floor of the open reception hall (*pendapa*) of their house with thousands of rix-dollar coins. Hearing

about this plan, the Dutch Resident of Yogyakarta was annoyed by the possibility that the face of Queen Wilhelmina on the coins would be repeatedly stepped on by the "natives." However, lacking any proper legal means with which to halt this attempt, he "suggested" that the coins be placed in an upright position rather than flat as originally intended. The family, immensely rich as they were, did not have enough coins to comply with the Resident's "suggestion" and were eventually forced to give up their plan. (1983, 40)

I heard nearly identical versions of this story on a few occasions, but in connection with several rich entrepreneurs who were not of the Kalang group mentioned by Nakamura. The alternative protagonists included Nitisemito, the famous clove cigarette "king" of Kudus, as well as an extremely wealthy Laweyan batik entrepreneur, Tjokrosoemarto, who was known for his dislike of the Dutch.[26] The fact that this story has been variously associated with Javanese entrepreneurs of Kotagede, Kudus, and Laweyan, three strongholds of the Javanese bourgeoisie in the nineteenth and early twentieth centuries, shows that there was something in the nature of indigenous entrepreneurship itself, and the wealth associated with it, which was seen as a challenge to colonial authority. The story of the Dutch coins became a generic tale of the subtle threat to power, obviously more symbolic than real, that money posed when it was in the hands of those who neither served the colonial state nor depended on being in its favor for their livelihood. The thought that such wealth could give the owner an opportunity to step repeatedly on Queen Wilhelmina's face must have been a disquieting one indeed to the colonial representatives of Her Majesty's government.

Perhaps the most patent sign of the Laweyan merchants' sense of independence, and hence the most provocative, if indirect, challenge to those who would govern them, surrounded their homes. The great whitewashed walls that hid the houses, workshops, and inhabitants of Laweyan from view appeared both as a challenge to the symbolic authority of Solo's two walled palaces (see Soedarmono 1987) and as a silent act of defiance toward the authority of the colonial regime that supported the palaces' continued existence. The walls were a sign of wealth uncontrolled, wealth that did not emanate from the center of power and that seemed to flout that power. They served as a sign of the merchants' autonomy. Moreover, like the walls surrounding the two palaces, the high walls of Laweyan marked the neighborhood as a seemingly self-contained, impregnable fortress, which piqued the curiosity of outsiders about the secrets that might be concealed within. One could only imagine what lay behind them. In both cases, the walls were an allusion to wealth, mystery, and the differences that separated the inhabitants inside from those who lived outside.[27]

The key to Laweyan's "difference" was that people in this sector of society, which had come into being in the nineteenth century through a particular conjunction of economic, social, and political factors, were seen by the broader population as both Javanese and not Javanese, because they simultaneously denied and accepted the established hierarchies and ethical codes of Javanese society. Laweyan and other merchant enclaves like it were, for this reason, culturally problematic. At the root of this problem was an object that had been known to the Javanese for centuries, but that had also come to take a new place of prominence in the social life of the Indies from the nineteenth century on: money. Money disrupted hierarchy because it enabled its holders to deny *priyayi* assertions that wealth and status should follow from power, title, noble descent, and the accumulation of spiritual potency. With their conspicuous displays of wealth, Javanese bourgeois defied the cultural authority of the *priyayi* and, indirectly, the political authority of the Europeans who upheld *priyayi* claims to supremacy in Javanese society. It was on the basis of money that Laweyan developed its own distinctive social and moral order and closed itself off from the incursions and moral condemnations of the wider society and the authorities that governed it.

But there was another, related "problem" in Laweyan, which removed it even farther from the centers of power: the problem of gender. If *sudagar* men were alienated from the political center, then their wives were even more distant from colonial sources of power. No matter how successful they were in business, merchant women usually preferred that their husbands represent them in unavoidable dealings with officials of the colonial bureaucracy; they avoided dealing with the government as much as possible. In this sense, the otherwise independent and outgoing *sudagar* women did not directly challenge the system of gender that prevailed in the Indies, which placed official power in the hands of men, not women. However, Laweyan's quiet resistance of colonial and royal officialdom was undoubtedly strengthened by the position of the female "rulers" of the community, already at a remove structurally from the colonial centers of power on the basis of their sex alone.

Laweyan's politics of resistance toward the colonial state cannot be separated from the politics of gender. Because none of Laweyan's merchants, female or male, could gain access to power or cultural prestige in the public arenas of colonial society, they chose an alternative path by turning inward, shutting out the reigning powers (as much as they could) and establishing their own, localized forms of power. The main site for their resistance to the colonial order was what we often refer to as the "domestic sphere," a place that, in modern Western ideology, is usually conceived of as a haven from the heartless world of politics and the market, as the locus of familial affect and nurturance, and as the primary domain of women (see Armstrong 1987). In Laweyan the household was indeed a site of sentiment and nurturance, and a place for the social and biological reproduction of the family, but it was also much more than this. Because the family firm was almost always located on the same premises as the home, the domestic sphere was also a site of material production, a place where wealth was generated in the form of commodities for the market. Furthermore, as we will see in subsequent chapters, it was also a locus of cultural production, and a place where wealth could be converted to status through its conversion to the signs of cultural value.

The domestic sphere was, in contrast to its usual representation in modern Western discourse, an intrinsically *political* domain: it was the source of the *sudagar* family's power and prestige in the community, if not always in the wider society, and the site of the merchants' struggle to appropriate the signs of cultural value that were denied them by the ruling elites of colonial society. It was, moreover, a place where merchants could resist the penetrating surveillance of the state, as suggested by de Kat Angelino's rather irritated account of Laweyan's recalcitrance. The merchants saw "home" as an autonomous domain, intended to be as impervious as possible to outside sources of authority. This autonomy was signified by the walls that fortified their homes and workshops. Everything inside those walls was conceived as inviolable; the walls encapsulated a private and sovereign sphere. But the *sudagar* household, while envisioned by its inhabitants as an autonomous realm, was not truly independent of the world outside it, for the dynamics of family and family firm were both shaped by and constitutive of a larger social dynamic that extended well beyond the confines of the domestic sphere itself.

There was little distinction between household and family firm in Laweyan; the prosperity of one was closely bound to the other, and the workshop and the house were usually physically adjacent. The firm was an extension of the household physically, economically, and conceptually. Almost always, the key figure binding them together was the woman who managed both the household and the family firm, the female *juragan*. She ruled the home, but she was by no means confined to it; the meaning of what we might call the domestic sphere and her role in it was, I will argue, quite different from its modern discursive construction in the West as well as in the ideologies promoted in recent years by the New Order Indonesian state. As much as her husband, she resisted the intrusions of the state into her private domain, but she, too, engaged in a politics of culture, class, and gender that was ultimately enacted both on private and public ground.

Similar political struggles, quiet though they were, were still being waged more than four decades after the end of colonial rule. There were changes, of course, among the players—the Dutch having long since departed the scene, the traditional aristocracy now reduced to a caricature of its former self—but the grounds of contestation in the New Order had a surprisingly strong resonance with what they had been under Dutch rule. Contrary to the expectations and hopes of some people after the Revolution, members of the old *sudagar* class had not, by and large, been transformed into the economic elites of Indonesia, ready to step into the niche that had been vacated by the Dutch. While they might have seemed relatively well positioned after independence to take over the lucrative sectors of the economy that were formerly in Dutch hands and, as some thought possible, to serve as the motors of economic development in a newly emancipated nation (see C. Geertz 1963), members of the Javanese merchant enclaves, such as those of Laweyan, Kudus, or Kotagede, remained distinctly peripheral to the modern Indonesian economy after independence.[28] They were members of a declining class of petty commodity producers and merchants rather than a rising capitalist bourgeoisie (Robison 1986, chap. 1).

Curiously enough, while the old colonial political and social hierarchies had been dismantled, making it possible for Javanese and other Indonesians to hold the greatest political power and highest status in their own society, members of the *sudagar* class also continued to suffer from some of the same social stigmas that had long been associated with their class. Officials of the government bureaucracy, many of whom were ethnic Javanese, kept alive the *priyayi* disdain for those who earned a living from business, including indigenous Indonesians (*pribumi*) as well as Chinese (MacIntyre 1991, 45). By the 1980s the old merchant class was suffering an additional stigma: that of being an anachronism in a society bent on modernization. As in the past, they remained outside the mainstream of society and alienated from the centers of power—power that was now in Indonesian, not European, hands.

What I found in Laweyan were the remnants of a lifestyle and an ethos that, while certainly affected by the changes taking place in and around the community, bore the unmistakable marks of the old colonial order. The merchants continued to assert their autonomy and to resist the penetration of the state. And they remained concerned, above all, with gaining and maintaining status in a society that was as obsessed with hierarchy in the New Order as it had been under colonial rule. Ironically, at a time when the disjuncture between wealth, power, and status was diminishing in Indonesia, wealth was now in short supply in Laweyan. But with the dwindling inheritances of an affluent past, its families did their best to maintain an image of prosperity—and of the status that they hoped would accompany it.

Chapter Three

THE SPECTER OF PAST MODERNITIES

B Y THE LATE 1980s and early 1990s, a number of articles had begun to appear in Indonesian newspapers and magazines lamenting the decline of the batik industry in Java. Quite a few of these articles focused on Laweyan, whose spectral quality made it appealing to journalists seeking to portray the loss of a venerable industry and a distinctive way of life:

> Everything was quiet. The hands of a clock showed that it was already 3:30 P.M. Even the narrow alleys hemmed in by high walls, which served as dividers between the small "palaces" that were so numerous, were deserted. Only the voice of Makiah Nurdiniyah, the youngest daughter of the owner of the house who was learning how to recite from the Qur'an, broke the stillness. The young girl was accompanied by a *santri* [a student at a traditional Islamic school] who had been brought there from Solo's Al-Muayat Islamic School.
>
> For a moment the distinctive smell of batik wax stung the nose. Three men drenched in sweat, their chests bare, carefully applied their *caps* [copper stamps] to white cloth in a wooden building in front of the main house. No longer could the strains of *Dandanggula* be heard.[1] Nor could one hear any longer the sound of jokes provoking laughter.
>
> Laweyan was like a dead city. Its residents could not be seen roaming the streets. This was understandable, because various activities were taking place behind walls that, on average, towered as high as four meters.
>
> All that was visible were small doors shut tight. Or roofs that were blackened with age. This was the atmosphere in Kampong Laweyan, Solo, late one afternoon. . . .
>
> Laweyan is part of a bygone era.[2]

This passage comes from the article "Laweyan, the Story of Your Past," which appears in a slick Indonesian magazine called *Matra* (Dimension), billing itself as "The Magazine of Trends for Men" (*Majalah Trend Pria*, I.). The same issue of the magazine, which is published in metropolitan Jakarta, also features a discussion of "Taoism, Tantra, and Ecstasy," an article about the "disastrous" marriage of Prince Andrew and Sarah Ferguson, a piece on a Japanese fashion designer in Paris, and an article on Solo's sex trade. The magazine also includes flashy advertisements with English slogans for Guy Laroche watches ("Appearances may change over time; Value and style remain constant"), Levi's jeans ("Quality never goes out of style"), and Lucky Strike cigarettes ("An American Original").

Unlike each of these commodities, whose slogans all assert their timeless, enduring value, Laweyan is portrayed as a place whose time has definitely passed. The tone of the article is one of vague nostalgia for a receding era in Indonesia's history. Laweyan serves here as the marker of a lifestyle that is distinctly remote from that of the average *Matra* reader, assumed to be a modern, worldly urbanite for whom the married life of the English royalty is at least as interesting a subject (and probably more so, given the number of pages dedicated to it) as the fading glory of an old neighborhood in Central Java. While attempting to evoke the sentiment of nostalgia through a vivid description of Laweyan's sights, sounds, and smells, the journalist writes not from the perspective of those who live inside the community but from the distanced perspective of someone who views Laweyan as a passing, and slightly exotic, curiosity, just one of many sites in the country that have been "left behind" (*ketinggalan*, I.) by modernization. The article's tone attests to the self-awareness possessed by the author and by *Matra*'s readers of their own modernness relative to that of Laweyan's inhabitants—not to mention the many millions of Indonesians who live in conditions far less "modern" than those of Laweyan.

This "historical consciousness of modernity" (Habermas 1987, 6), in which the modern is always imagined as a break with the past and a simultaneous transcendence of it, is, as both Habermas and Osborne (1995) point out, a defining characteristic of "modernity" itself. Although this form of historical self-consciousness always envisions the contemporary era as a wholly new, modern age, the process by which the present is imagined to supersede the past occurs, in fact, again and again. This is the process by which modernity is itself perpetually re-created. In Java, such self-awareness of being part of the modern age has been repeatedly in evidence since at least the turn of the twentieth century.[3] That the idiom of the modern can be used over and over again attests to its enduring power as a signifier of historical transformation.

In this chapter, we will look at how Laweyan's own sense of progress gave way over time to an increasing identification with the past, as it became a place in which the self-confidently modern readers of *Matra* could see the reflection of a "bygone era." The chapter begins with a brief discussion of the political and economic conditions that hastened the decline of the batik industry and the Javanese merchant community associated with it after the mid-1960s. Although these conditions certainly contributed to Laweyan's demodernization, they do not, in my opinion, fully explain it. The remainder of this book explores why many of the community's merchants responded as they did to a situation that, while unfavorable for continuing along the path that they had followed in the past, could have allowed them to take part in the rapid capitalist expansion that began in Indonesia in the 1970s and continues through the present.

Through a description of life in Solo's merchant community as I saw it in the 1980s, including a discussion of the relationship between entrepreneurs and their workers, this chapter also investigates the ways in which distinctly Javanese forms of hierarchy and social relations became thoroughly interwoven with a way of life that centered on the production of commodities for the market. This engendered a local social system and mode of production that, while oriented toward an urban, market economy, were neither strictly capitalist—itself often conflated with "modern"—nor, by any stretch of the imagination, "traditional" (whatever that might mean in a society subjected to colonial rule for as long as Java was). In the 1980s and 1990s, the community's orientation toward the past gave it a feeling of in-betweenness—not of evolving from a "traditional" way of life toward a "modern" one, but of being stuck, somehow, between two worlds—what Mary Steedly describes for Karo of North Sumatra as a feeling of "being trapped between a past that was no longer tenable and a present to which they were, at best, only marginally relevant" (1993, 11).

THE DECLINE OF LAWEYAN

By the mid-1980s it was amply clear to the residents of Laweyan that the batik industry was not just experiencing one of the temporary slumps that had plagued it periodically from its inception. It was in an irreversible tailspin caused, most people said (with much sad shaking of the head), by competition from the mass-produced imitation batik, called *batik printing* or just *printing* in Indonesian, that was flooding the market. The subtext of this complaint was that the batik industry and other labor-intensive, often undercapitalized fields of manufacture that remained in the hands of ethnic Javanese were being put out of business by the growing number of highly capitalized and more technologically sophisticated businesses that were owned primarily by Chinese Indonesians or, sometimes, by Javanese and other *pribumi* (indigenous Indonesians) who had access to political power and the benefits that went along with it.[4]

It is remarkable that the demise of the batik industry did not come sooner, for the technology of batik production had undergone no significant change since the innovation of *batik cap* in the mid-1800s and the introduction of chemical dyestuffs at the beginning of this century. Quite possibly, the downturn of the industry would have come earlier had it not been for a series of measures taken under the Sukarno regime that aimed at protecting the indigenous bourgeoisie in general and the batik industry in particular.

The years of the Japanese occupation (1942–45) and the war for Indonesian independence (1945–50) had been disastrous for the batik industry throughout Java. During the occupation, the raw materials needed for batik production—white cloth, dyestuffs, and paraffin, most of which were imported—were practically unavailable, and the population was so impoverished that most people could not have afforded to buy new batik even if it had been abundant.[5] During the years of revolution, the batik industry ground to a standstill. But beginning in 1950 in newly independent Indonesia, the batik business boomed as a result of the pent-up demand for new clothing that had accumulated during the lean years of the 1940s. Between 1950 and 1956, the number of batik firms in Java doubled, totaling about 10,000 by the end of that period. In October 1956 there were 1,191 batik enterprises registered in Solo; one study estimates that in the city and its environs, there were roughly 13,500 full-time workers (male and female) and 30,000 part-time workers (all female) employed in the industry.[6] This great expansion in the number of firms, however, was not brought about only by the increased demand for batik. Many of the new firms were being founded by the children and grandchildren of batik entrepreneurs. With each successive generation, the family's wealth was subdivided and new enterprises begun: the larger firms owned by entrepreneurs in the 1920s and 1930s spawned the more numerous and competitive firms of their descendants.[7]

At the same time, the Sukarno-Hatta government, as part of its larger program to promote economic indigenism, began to provide subsidies to non-Chinese batik entrepreneurs in the form of allocations of raw materials, sold at artificially low prices, which were distributed through the many batik manufacturers' cooperatives all over Java that were united under the powerful umbrella organization GKBI (*Gabungan Koperasi Batik Indonesia*, I., or Indonesian Federation of Batik Cooperatives).[8] The price of cambric and other undyed cotton cloth (*mori*) allocated through the cooperatives was so far below market price that many batik entrepreneurs found it much more lucrative to resell their allotments illegally on the black market than to actually make batik with them.[9] It was so profitable to be a member of a batik cooperative during this period, which people fondly remember as the "Cloth Allotment Era" (*Jaman Jatah Mori*, I.), that for the first time in decades, significant numbers of new firms were also established by people who were *not* from batik families, in order that they, too, could join the cooperatives.[10] Some were founded by former batik workers who had either managed to scrape together the capital to actually start a small *batik cap* enterprise, or else had simply borrowed the equipment needed to pass the initial inspection that was required to qualify for membership in the local cooperative. People in Solo tell stories of equipment being transferred secretly from one workshop to another in the middle of the night, just before the inspection was to take place; after passing the inspection, the newly certified "entrepreneur" would return the equipment to its rightful owner.[11]

An additional measure taken by the government to protect the batik industry was an import restriction on imitation batik, which at that time was produced mainly in Japan (Economic Research Bureau 1958, 177). I was also told that there had been a ban in Indonesia during the Sukarno era on printing imitation batik. President Sukarno himself is said to have taken a personal interest in the welfare of the batik industry; toward this end he combined protectionist policies with active efforts to promote batik as a form of national culture (see chapter 5).

For many people, then, the mid-1950s to the early 1960s were the halcyon years of the batik industry (although some older people recalled that they had fared better in the 1930s, when there was less competition in the industry). Virtually every household in Laweyan had a batik firm attached to it, and the smell of hot wax that hung in the air was also the smell of money. The maze of narrow alleys in the kampongs teemed with activity— as did the batik cooperatives themselves, which were the ground for fierce political battles in the early to mid-1960s between those members who affiliated themselves with the increasingly powerful Indonesian Communist Party (PKI) and those who belonged to Muslim or nationalist factions.[12] But neither the prosperity nor the politics were to last for long. The Sukarno government was overthrown in 1965–66 amid a bloodbath of political violence; this was an extremely painful period in Laweyan as in many other parts of Indonesia, where hundreds of thousands of people suspected or known to be communists or communist sympathizers were killed or arrested.[13] Backed by the military, General Suharto and his supporters seized control of the government at this time, bringing to power the self-proclaimed "New Order" regime.

After the fall of the Sukarno government, GKBI and its member cooperatives lost their monopoly on importing, producing, and distributing the raw materials for batik production. The allocations of heavily subsidized materials to individual batik producers abruptly stopped, and the price of white cloth and other materials rose sharply on the open market. The bans on manufacturing or selling imitation batik in Indonesia also ceased to be enforced. A steep decline in the industry began as soon as the government's protectionist policies were ended in the early years of the New Order. A large number of batik entrepreneurs went bankrupt almost immediately: after years of operating under artificially advantageous conditions, smaller firms especially were unable to stay afloat with the sudden return to normal market conditions and the swift rise in the cost of raw materials.

On top of that, mass-produced, printed imitation batiks began to flood the market beginning in the late 1960s and early 1970s. The ability of genuine batik cloth to maintain a share of the market at all after that point appears to have been due to the strong attachment of some people to certain aesthetic properties of real batik lacking in the printed imitations; such considerations had also shaped the market in the nineteenth century. As the quality of the imitations got better and better, however—and cheaper and cheaper relative to the price of real batik—the only batik that could ultimately hold its own in the market was expensive, high-quality *batik tulis*, which gained in prestige value as genuine batik increasingly became once again an item worn primarily by the elite.[14]

The producers of the printed imitations went to great lengths to make their product resemble genuine batik, even to the point of including the uneven edges and cracks in the design that would normally result from the wax-resist process, and printing the words *motif batik tulis halus* (I., fine hand-drawn batik motif) on the edges of the cloth. Whether or not people were actually fooled by these imitations, they purchased them in great number because they were cheaper than *batik cap* and indeed closely resembled the most refined hand-drawn batiks, which previously only the wealthiest members of the population could afford. By the late 1980s the markets for *batik cap* and coarse styles of *batik tulis* had shrunk to a tiny fraction of what they had once been. Communities like Laweyan, which had focused on the production of the inexpensive stamped batik, were badly hurt by the shift of the market to printed imitations.

Another factor leading to the batik industry's decline was that more and more women, especially in the cities, switched from Javanese dress to Western-style or modern "Muslim-style" clothing, which only occasionally used batik fabric. (Urban men had begun to wear Western clothing on a regular basis decades earlier, although they often wear dress shirts made of batik cloth for special occasions.) In the past girls and young women had often worn Western dress, but once they reached marriageable age they considered it an improper style and had changed to the Javanese ensemble of sarong and *kebaya*. During the course of the New Order, though, a growing number of women continued to wear Western dresses after marriage, donning Javanese garb only for formal or ceremonial occasions.[15]

The batik producers of Laweyan (and elsewhere in Solo) failed to turn quickly to other, more lucrative businesses even when they saw the writing on the wall in the late 1960s and early 1970s. One Kauman batik entrepreneur, Pak Usman, described his reaction when he first realized in 1970 that the batik industry was doomed: "My nephew worked at a factory that made printed textiles. I gave him a batik design with several colors on it, and told him that I wanted a number of sarongs printed with that motif. My nephew asked me how many thousands of *kodi* [1 kodi = 20 pieces] I wanted them to make in a day. After that, I didn't want to make batik anymore." In Laweyan, with a few exceptions, those firms that had not been put out of business immediately when the cooperatives' subsidies were withdrawn continued to operate for diminishing profits; a few new batik firms even started up during the 1970s and early 1980s. For some of the firms that had survived the initial crisis of the New Order, it was business as usual, although under ever more unfavorable terms.

To switch from producing genuine batik to producing "batik printing" would have been an obvious choice, had these entrepreneurs decided to change businesses. Although the techniques of production were completely different, the basic technology for making imitation batik was not terribly complicated. Much of the imitation batik manufactured in smaller firms was made by silkscreening, which, while requiring somewhat more fixed and working capital than traditional batik and a certain amount of technical know-how, would by no means have been beyond the resources of many Laweyan entrepreneurs, particularly if they had made the transition fairly early, before their batik businesses failed completely. Their intimate knowledge of batik designs and marketing procedures would have been an advantage in the textile printing business. But only a few Javanese entrepreneurs made this switch. In Solo imitation batik was made predominantly by ethnic Chinese (on the largest, most capital-intensive scale) and by people in the Arab community (on a smaller scale). Only a handful of Javanese followed suit, most of them well after Chinese and Arabs had gained the lion's share of the market.[16]

A number of Laweyan entrepreneurs and former entrepreneurs told me that they had not gone over to batik printing because they lacked the capital to do so. This may have been true in some cases. The unwillingness of family members to pool their resources made it difficult for Laweyan entrepreneurs to accumulate sufficient capital to expand their businesses beyond the scale of petty commodity production (see also Weix 1990, 56), especially after the batik industry went into decline. Lasting partnerships were rare not only among relatives but also among those not kin.[17] Although Javanese entrepreneurs recognized that one of the business advantages of ethnic Chinese was their willingness to join their resources together, they seemed to feel that this kind of successful collaboration was beyond the capacity of most Javanese. (It is telling that the term Javanese use for "business partnership" is the Chinese-derived *kongsi*.) The desire for independence apparently outweighed even the motivation to be successful in business.

Still, the wealth that many Laweyan entrepreneurs had inherited from their parents could have been used as capital to expand their businesses, and government bank loans were also available to them had they truly wanted to switch to batik printing. But the comment of an Arab batik trader was, I think, more to the point: "Laweyan people don't switch to printing," he said, "because they still hold strongly to custom (*masih pegang*

kuat pada adat, I.). Their ancestors made traditional batik, so they do, too."
In chapter 5, I will examine in greater depth the origins of this conservatism, and the resulting paradox—that the desire to conserve their ancestral
inheritance was what led to its dissipation. Economic factors alone were
not enough to persuade most people to abandon the batik business, which
had been passed down for decades in the community, for a new and unfamiliar technology.

Laweyan's failure as an entrepreneurial community, I should also point
out, was not an isolated phenomenon, nor was it entirely attributable either to factors internal to the community or to the competition from
printed textiles. During the Sukarno era, the indigenous Indonesian merchant class (which had never been a very robust group during the colonial
period) did not succeed in taking over the sectors of the economy that had
been controlled by foreign (mostly Dutch) and nonindigenous (especially
local Chinese) capital, despite the state's implementation of various policies that were supposedly aimed at that end. As Richard Robison (1986)
remarks, the growth of the indigenous bourgeoisie in the decades following independence was not impressive; most members of this group were
unable to expand beyond small-scale trade and petty commodity production. Indonesia of the 1950s and 1960s lacked a cohesive, substantial capi-
tal-owning class (Robison 1992, 68). The use of politically secured economic privileges proved a necessary precondition for successful capital
accumulation. Robison notes, "Increasingly there developed a polarisation
within the indigenous bourgeoisie, between those able to gain access to
state facilities and political patronage and able to secure access to the
finance and distribution networks of foreign and Chinese capital, and
those who remained within the confines of a declining petty trade and
commodity production sector" (1986, 57).

While the decline of the indigenous merchant class began under the
Sukarno regime (despite the deceptive prosperity that some entrepreneurs
enjoyed temporarily through government subsidies and credit), the New
Order hastened its demise, for the pattern of "bureaucratic capitalism"
(Robison 1986) that had developed under the Sukarno regime became
firmly entrenched in the post-1965 period. Without political power or
access to political favor, it became extremely difficult for members of the
old indigenous merchant class to survive in business, let alone to compete
with the highly capitalized enterprises that were increasingly dominating
the Indonesian economy. The new corporate groups that emerged in Indonesia during the 1970s and after relied heavily on the political patronage
of the state for credit, licenses, contracts, and concessions. Most of the
successful corporate capitalists were either businessmen, often ethnic Chinese, who had close relationships with bureaucrats or military officers, or
else political powerholders themselves (or their family members), who

took full advantage of their positions of power to enrich themselves and their families (see Robison 1986, 1992).

As I discussed in chapter 2, not only was there no tradition of collaborating with bureaucrats in Laweyan, but from its earliest days the community had scrupulously avoided contact with them out of deep mistrust as well as for ideological reasons. The "Cloth Allotment Era" during the Sukarno period was probably the closest the entrepreneurs of Laweyan ever came to a rapprochement with political power, but even here the relationship was indirect, mediated institutionally through the batik cooperatives; it was not an arrangement involving direct political patronage. The pattern of collaborating with government officials and petty bureaucrats that had been ingrained in the Chinese business community from the colonial period on, which had in some ways been necessary for the success of the politically vulnerable Chinese as a foreign trading minority, was never internalized in Laweyan, nor, it would seem, in most other comparable Javanese merchant communities. In Laweyan every effort was made to keep the state at a distance—outside the walls, as it were.

It is important to keep in mind the issue of gender here as well. In Laweyan, even though men generally acted as the representatives of their families in dealings with the bureaucracy (men had also been more active in the batik cooperatives than women), women took a more active role in the business and social life of the community than did men. Among the *priyayi* elite in colonial and postcolonial Solo, men drew their power from their involvement with the royal and state bureaucracies, whereas the men of Laweyan had no such source of power or protection. The "center" for the *sudagar* class was the marketplace, not the government. Women avoided dealing with the government more than their husbands did, and were consequently even more distant from the centers of political power than the men. It would have been more difficult for them, both psychologically and logistically, to attempt to further their own business interests by currying favor with those holding political power—the same people whom they had always tried to keep at arm's length. The distrust of government officials that had been handed down to them from their parents and grandparents was not easily overcome. As a result, with the rise of bureaucratic capitalism, the old *sudagar* class became more and more marginalized, dispossessed of even the small niche that it had occupied in colonial society.

When I moved to Laweyan in 1986, only a relatively small number of batik firms were still functioning, and quite a few of these were to close down before I left. Some formerly wealthy *juragan* were reduced to trading a little batik here and there for minimal profits. There were also batik entrepreneurs who had made the transition to other businesses, but only a handful were successful, and by the standards of New Order capitalism their businesses were still small-scale. The community that had grown up around the batik industry was more or less intact, however, although aging noticeably as many of its younger members moved away to pursue higher education or other lines of work. It is to a description of this community that I now turn.

"COMMUNITY" AND STATUS

According to a government survey conducted in 1987, Laweyan, the smallest ward in Solo, had a population of slightly over two thousand, a substantial (but unrecorded) number of whom were temporary residents—mostly laborers who considered their real homes to be the villages that they had left in search of work.[18] These workers, even the ones who had spent many years employed as servants or batik workers in the homes and workshops of the wealthier members of the community, did not consider themselves to be true "Laweyan people" (*wong Laweyan*), nor were they considered as such by other Solonese. The "real" Laweyan people, many fewer in number than the official population figures would indicate, were those who had been born and raised in the community, most of them second-, third-, and fourth-generation residents of the neighborhood. Just how many of Laweyan's residents were migrants from the villages was most apparent during Lebaran (Idul Fitri), the big holiday celebrating the end of the Muslim fasting month of Ramadan, when almost everyone goes home to their natal village or town to be with their family. The streets of Laweyan (along with the rest of the city) became eerily empty for several days each year at this time.

There were sharp social divisions within the community, based largely on wealth and occupation. Elsewhere in Solo, title often figures prominently in determining social status: a noble title affixed to one's name is still prestigious, as is a title indicating high rank in the government bureaucracy or a university degree. In Laweyan, however, where aristocratic and bureaucratic titles were almost nonexistent and university degrees few and far between (although increasing steadily among the younger generation), what really mattered was wealth and whether one was counted as an employer (*juragan*) or a worker (*buruh*). The elites of the community were the well-heeled merchants and entrepreneurs, many of whom were already retired or in semiretirement, but who retained their status as entrepreneurs in the community's collective consciousness.[19] The nonelites—often referred to as the "kampong people" (*wong kampung*)—included those who were employed by the entrepreneurs as laborers or domestic servants, and others who worked as petty traders, *bécak* drivers, construction workers, or artisans, with limited income and resources.

Between the merchant elites and those who ranked lowest on the social scale were a few assorted others: small entrepreneurs with only a few employees, as well as people who worked in low- and middle-ranking positions as civil servants or employees of private firms. A number of these people were the descendants of batik entrepreneurs whose families had moved downward in the local status hierarchy, an inevitable occurrence given the number of businesses that failed over time. Although it was a largely Javanese enclave, the neighborhood also included a handful of Chinese Indonesians, most of whom were proprietors of small businesses on the main thoroughfare, Laweyan Street. Relations between the Chinese and Javanese in the neighborhood were cordial but were limited almost entirely to business transactions. The Chinese were not assimilated to the tightly knit, core community of Laweyan elites, nor did they participate in the everyday life of the Javanese kampongs in Laweyan. Socially they were almost invisible in the community, rarely invited to attend the rituals and other gatherings that often brought local Javanese together.

When those from inside as well as outside the community spoke of "Laweyan people," they almost always meant the members of the Javanese merchant class and their families, including those who were no longer active in business but who still had property and a claim to high status. These were the people who lived in the large, walled-in homes right on Laweyan Street or on the side streets and alleys just off the main road.[20] The farther one went from Laweyan Street down the maze of narrow streets and alleys that lay behind it, the deeper one penetrated the world of the kampong people. The difference that traversing only a few back alleys made was startling. From the spacious houses made of brick and cement that lined the main road, built around large courtyards and decorated with heavy carved teak furniture, beveled glass windows, and inlaid tile floors, one quickly found oneself amid clusters of small, windowless one- or two-room dwellings, with thin walls of woven bamboo or wood, dimly lit and sparsely furnished. Here lived people who were barely making ends meet; many of them worked as the laundresses, handymen, *bécak* drivers, or batik workers of the neighborhood's elites, while others worked outside the neighborhood. Some were self-employed: they ran tiny food stalls from the side of the road, made all sorts of sweets or fried snacks to sell to individuals and local shops, or vended cigarettes, drinks, and other small items from little stands in front of their homes for minuscule profits.

The kampong people provided essential services to Laweyan's elites, not only in their daily wage labor but also in helping to prepare and serve food and to clean up for hundreds of guests at the endless cycle of lavish ritual occasions hosted by local elites to commemorate weddings, engagements, circumcisions, birthdays, first pregnancies, or death-day anniversaries. Although the poorer people were neighbors to the elites, they were rarely invited to their ceremonies as guests but were often expected to offer hours or days of their labor in exchange for minimal payment—sometimes little more than a decent meal or two. And whenever the local government called for "voluntary" service (*kerja bakti*, I.) in the neighborhood, such as keeping the night watch or cleaning up local streets, the burden was always on the kampong people to make their labor available, for the elites often considered such work to be beneath their dignity.

The merchants also distinguished themselves from the poorer people of the kampongs by claiming themselves the rightful heirs of the neighborhood by descent. It was customary among them to make weekly visits to their parents', grandparents', and other relatives' graves in Laweyan on Fridays, the Muslim holy day, to ask for blessings, to recite Arabic prayers for the souls of the dead, and to make offerings of incense and flower petals (*nyekar*). Although this practice was not confined to Laweyan or to the merchant class alone—the custom of visiting the graves of one's forebears and other spiritually powerful figures is widespread in Java—the frequency and faithfulness with which the merchants visited the graves was out of the ordinary. Given the risky nature of business and the rapid rise and fall of fortunes in the merchant community, merchants felt the need more than most others, apparently, to call for the blessings of their close ancestors and to offer thanks for all past favors received.

When I asked one of the wealthy women of the community, Bu Sukanto, why the kampong people were usually not in the habit of visiting their parents' graves each week as the merchants did, she replied in a tone that suggested the foolishness of my question, "Well, where do they come from? (*asalnya dari mana*, I.; 'where are their origins?'). Are their parents' graves in Laweyan?" Her rhetorical questions referred partly to the fact that many of the poorer people in Laweyan were migrants from villages outside Solo. Their parents and grandparents were buried elsewhere, which made it difficult or impossible to visit their graves every week. However, the question "Where do they come from?" also implied that the poorer people, unlike the merchants, did not have "ancestral" roots in Laweyan, and therefore could not legitimately claim Laweyan as their true home.

Bu Sukanto's answer was reminiscent of the comment of the Javanese author whom I cited earlier (Samsudjin 1981; see chapter 1), to the effect that Laweyan had no history before the time of Kyai Ageng Anis because its inhabitants had been "just ordinary people" who had "left no traces" of their existence. The issues of descent and inheritance are very important in Java, especially among the elite: to be able to give evidence of one's origins, and especially to establish a direct line of descent from a powerful ancestor, confers legitimacy—the right to claim a place, property, or a position of power as one's own. Those who do not make their mark on history, however, even local history, are soon forgotten; their "traces" disappear. The merchants of Laweyan saw themselves rather than the kampong people as the legitimate inhabitants of the community because they could look to their ancestors' graves there as proof that they themselves *belonged* in Laweyan, and that Laweyan, in turn, belonged to them. Their wealth, moreover, was taken as a sign that their ancestors had passed something of value down to them and were continuing to look after them even from the grave.

The elites also saw the large homes and plots of land that they had inherited as indications that their forebears had staked a claim to the neighborhood. An elderly female *juragan* recalled that as the earlier entrepreneurs of the neighborhood had raised children and those children themselves had married, many of the poorer people had "moved aside" (*minggir*) to make room for the large, new houses that the entrepreneurs built for their children and their families. Extended merchant families had taken over entire kampongs close to Laweyan Street, pushing the workers to the peripheries of the neighborhood.

The "community," then, was defined as much by social class as by bounded space; there were, in reality, separate communities of elites and nonelites that cross-cut the neighborhood. Only a few marginal people straddled the boundaries between the elite and nonelite communities— these were mostly the less wealthy, but not-quite impoverished descendants of former entrepreneurs, many of whom were the relatives of Laweyan's contemporary elites. Most of the kampong people, however, were completely outside the social world and, I believe, the awareness of the merchants and their families. One former *batik cap* worker I knew, Pak Djohari, lived with his wife in a cramped, two-room house almost directly opposite the large, walled home of Bu Sukanto and her family. Now in their seventies, they had been renting their tiny house in Laweyan, which stood surrounded by the gated homes of Laweyan's elites, since 1945. To illustrate the great social barrier that divided rich and poor in Laweyan, Pak Djohari pointed to Bu Sukanto's house, commenting, "Now, take Bu Sukanto, for instance. I've been to a few of her ceremonies, and my wife goes there sometimes to help out if there's a ritual. But if I go over to her house, she still has no idea who I am. 'Where are you from?' she asks me. We've lived across the street from each other for years." Gesturing toward another imposing home nearby, he said, "Those people over there—in the old days that man's father used to invite us if they held a ceremony, but now he and his wife never do. That's the way rich people are. They don't want to invite me (*Kaya ngoten tiyang sugih. Mboten gelem ngundang kula*)."

The ideologies of mutual cooperation and neighborly exchange that have often been emphasized in discussions of Javanese society really only applied to members of one's own social group in Laweyan; the elites carried on exchanges of food and ritual labor primarily with each other, leaving the less-affluent kampong people to carry on their own exchanges among themselves. Although some of Laweyan's kampong people were kin to the neighborhood's elites, the latter rarely acknowledged these blood ties when they were far enough removed to be easily put out of mind. Even when the ties were recognized, they were always subordinated to the social and economic hierarchies that underlaid all interactions in the community.

This was made clear in the case of Bu Suharni, a woman in her late sixties who was the poor second cousin of some of the wealthiest people in Laweyan. Her husband had been imprisoned in the sweeping anticommunist arrests and bloody massacres of 1965 and had died a broken man not long afterward. Bu Suharni had struggled to support herself and her family since that time. In order to earn a little money, she would bring small pancakes made of rice flour and bananas to sell at the weekly neighborhood gatherings of an elite women's *arisan* (rotating savings club). Some of the women were her relatives, and she had known all of the others for many years. Never joining the group inside the house, she would sit patiently alone on the veranda, waiting for individual women to come outside to buy her pancakes for a little over a penny each and to chat with her for a few minutes. Although the women were friendly to her, and she to them, there was no effort to make Bu Suharni feel that she was a member of the group; as a poor neighbor and relative who could not afford the weekly contribution to the *arisan*, she did not expect to be treated as an equal of the others. What respect she did receive from them she earned mostly through her age and generational seniority.

Some relatives of Laweyan's elites lived in such different worlds from them, even within the same neighborhood, that it was hard to believe that they had shared common roots only two or three generations back. One of the more poignant examples that I saw was the situation of Endang, a young woman who lived on the edge of a kampong that had once been home to some of the richest entrepreneurs in the community. The kampong still contained their walled dwellings, some now empty and dilapidated but impressive even in their decay. Endang's own home, however, was tucked away in a narrow alley where little shanties were squeezed together like chicken coops. This sector of Laweyan society was marginal in every sense of the word. Her house consisted of one room enclosed by thin, woven bamboo walls—dingy, filled with mosquitoes, and lit by a single dim bulb. It was furnished with two cheap metal chairs and a metal settee with red vinyl cushions, a couple of small tables, and a bed with a well-worn mattress. There was no indoor plumbing, and the cooking was done outside. Like most Javanese hosts, Endang was gracious, serving me a glass of tea and offering the usual apologies for the "dirtiness" of her place. Three small children, two girls and a boy, wandered in and out as we talked, the smallest one eventually perching in her mother's lap. Endang's grandmother also sat quietly in a corner, interjecting a word here and there.

Endang worked as a helper at a small *warung*, a roadside food stall, where she earned about eight dollars a week for six nights of work. Her husband, a *bécak* driver, was estranged from the family and never gave her any money for herself or her children. After her second child was born, she explained, her husband had started to act strangely; she attributed this to the fact that he had begun studying magical arts (*ngèlmu*) around that time but "wasn't strong enough" to bear the weight of the mystical knowledge that he was being taught. Endang was left to support herself and her three children on her small weekly wage. She was embarrassed to ask her family for help because they had initially opposed her marriage to this man when she was in her late teens. She had then deliberately become pregnant, knowing that her parents would have no choice but to allow the couple to marry—a fairly common tactic used by some young people when their parents are otherwise unwilling to accept their choice for a spouse. "I was *nékad* (willful, stubbornly persistent)," she told me regretfully. "Now I know, it's not good to be *nékad*."

It turned out that Endang's great-grandparents on her father's side had been the founders of a Laweyan batik "dynasty"; the couple were still venerated as the ancestors of a number of well-to-do Laweyan entrepreneurs. Endang's father, however, had had four legal wives, several mistresses, and a large number of children, so Endang had grown up with very little money. Although she was a cousin to some of Laweyan's most prominent merchants, they would have nothing to do with her, she said, because she was so poor. She admitted that she was also shy and uncomfortable in their company, preferring to avoid them because she felt inferior. They shared the same ancestors, but unlike her affluent relatives, she had lost her place in the community's history, becoming just another poor woman in the kampong. It did not mean much to her that she was descended from one of Laweyan's founding merchant couples—her grandmother had to remind her of their names, which she had forgotten—because, without wealth or property, her bloodline was irrelevant. Her destiny, like that of so many others, was to disappear into the crevices of the kampong, remembered as no one's descendant and, most likely, as no one's ancestor. Her traces would quickly fade from Laweyan's collective memory; as far as local elites were concerned, they already had.

THE FETISHIZATION OF DEFERENCE

The strongly hierarchical character of Solonese society was as evident in Laweyan as it was in any other quarter of the city. Laweyan employers expected their workers to exhibit the degree of obseqiousness in their presence that has come to be associated in Java with the "feudal" (*féodal*) social relations of the palaces. These asymmetrical relations were made sharply apparent by the use in daily speech of the full range of the language levels indicating relative status, respect, social distance, and politeness that mark the elaborately hierarchical dialect of Javanese spoken in Solo. Domestic helpers, batik workers, and other nonelites spoke to the elites of the community in deferential high Javanese, with the appropriately submissive bodily postures and averted eyes to accompany it. Members of the merchant class spoke low Javanese (*ngoko*, or, at best, a very low *madya*, the middle level of Javanese) to the workers in return, indicating their own higher social status.

There was no pretense of egalitarianism here: if they watched television in the same room, household workers would sit on the floor at a respectful distance while their employers and employers' families sat on chairs. A female worker asking her employer for a favor was likely to get down on her knees to do so, and some employers insisted that their female domestic workers serve them from a kneeling or crouching position. Batik workers and domestic servants alike were expected to make their labor available day and night if their employer made a wedding or other ritual celebration, and to attend in numerous other ways to the needs of the employer and her family. Wages were extremely low even by local standards, and the turnover in such jobs was frequent, but Java's severe state of overpopulation meant that there was a steady supply of cheap labor from the villages, as people who could not earn an adequate living from farming migrated to the cities in search of work.

Like many other Americans I knew in Java, I was always somewhat uncomfortable with the open acknowledgment of such dramatic status differences. Even Indonesians from outside Central Java often find these extreme hierarchies hard to accept. But there was a certain resignation to many Javanese people's acceptance of these differences—"everyone has their own luck" (*begjané wong dhèwé-dhèwé*), they would say. It was not that they saw their position in the hierarchy as being carved in stone, for one's luck could, after all, change. Those at the bottom often dreamed of being elsewhere in the hierarchy (the brisk trade in lottery tickets among *bécak* drivers and other kampong people being just one indication of this) and those at the top knew well that they, or their children or grandchildren, might not always enjoy such an enviable position. As one man told me, "there are two things that determine the course of people's lives: luck (or 'fate'; *nasib*) and status (*drajad*). Even if someone is born into a high-status family, if his luck isn't good then he can end up poor. On the other hand, even if someone is born with low status, if he has good luck then he can end up rich."

To be sure, there were plenty of examples in the community's history of people who had slipped from great wealth to utter bankruptcy or, less commonly, who had turned themselves from low-status villagers or urban workers to prosperous entrepreneurs. But the inevitability of hierarchy *itself* was not really questioned—certainly not in Solo, where it was so integral a part of the local social order. Perpetually reenacted through everyday linguistic and social interactions, hierarchy was a fact of life: it was taken for granted that there would always be a few people at the top and many people at the bottom, and those at the top invested a great deal of effort in trying to stay where they were.

In most circumstances social class overrode other bases of difference, such as sex: while men might ultimately receive more respect than women in the overall scheme of things, a high-status woman had the right to absolute deference from all of her employees, male or female. Men of low status were as respectful in their language and behavior to high-status women as they were to high-status men, if not more so. Almost always, women were defined not merely as women, but as women of a certain class; their access to power and respect in the community had everything to do with their social position. The wealthier women in the community saw themselves as having little in common with the poorer women, and vice versa: the fact of being female alone was not a strong basis of identification. The same was also true for the men. Men of different social classes rarely mixed with one another, except for those who went to the mosque for Friday prayers, one of the few contexts in which the hierarchies would be temporarily, and superficially, suspended.

While there was little social intercourse among people of different classes outside of work, Laweyan's elites relied in a very real way on the nonelites for their status in the community. The entrepreneurs' profits had depended upon the availability of cheap labor over the decades, and female entrepreneurs were also freed by their domestic servants of many of the tasks involved with caring for children, cooking, and keeping up the household, which enabled them to devote more of their time and energy to their businesses. Besides providing cheap labor, however, the kampong people also (and just as significantly) supplied members of the *juragan* class with the deferential behavior that reinforced the entrepreneurs' claims to high status in the community. The maintenance of a strong social hierarchy depended on the participation of all classes in an economy of deference and respect in which everyone knew their place and knew precisely how much—or how little—deference they should pay to others.

Because the Javanese merchant class commanded comparatively little respect in the hierarchies of the wider society, it was all the more important for them to receive the respect of others in their own community. Outside Laweyan the merchants had no titles, but inside the community their employees and other nonelites addressed them with the respectful titles *Mbok Mas* (for the women) and *Mas Ngantèn* (for the men), which have a meaning in this context similar to that of *juragan*, with its dual connotations of "entrepreneur" and "employer." Merchants often used these terms to refer to each other as well, especially when speaking to people of low status ("Here, take this to Mbok Mas Haryo's house"), thereby reaffirming each other's elite positions in the community.

In Laweyan being a merchant was similar to being a *priyayi* elsewhere in Solo: it was the type of work that commanded the most respect in the community. But, like the *priyayi*, a sign of the merchants' respectability was not only the deference that they could elicit *from* others, but also their ability to exhibit their own refinement and civility by showing respect *to* others. An illustration of this came from Pak Djohari, who over the course of his life had earned a living in many different trades, including *batik cap* work. He and his wife now earned a little cash by selling small household items from a stall in front of their home. While we were chatting one morning, I asked him what he had liked the most of all the various kinds of work that he had done in his life. Without hesitation he answered, "I like trading (*dagang*) the most." His reasoning was that "trading is work that involves respect" (*urmat*). He explained further: what he meant was not just that traders get other people's respect, but that people who trade for a living must also show respect for others. They must be friendly, polite, and dignified. "My wife and I may be having an argument in the back room, but if someone comes to our place to buy something, I'll come out to the front of the house with a smile on my face, and greet them pleasantly, as if nothing had been happening. Because who wants to buy from a person who isn't friendly or polite?"

As for the other kinds of work that he had done—mostly different types of manual labor—none of these had involved respect, Pak Djohari said. "Take doing *batik cap* work, for instance. The clothes you wear are just undershirts and shorts. The clothes themselves aren't respectful, especially when you consider that most of the time it's the lady [the female *juragan*] who you're dealing with. It's not polite to wear shorts, especially in the presence of a lady. No, there's no respect there." It is important never to abandon etiquette, he stressed, especially if you are someone without money (*Wong sing mboten nduwé dhuwit, nèk ninggalaké tatakrama, wah . . .*).

He added that if he had enough capital to have a bigger business, he would put on a tie and pay someone to work for him. "But I only make about a thousand *rupiah* a day" (about sixty cents), he told me, gesturing to the few shelves containing his wares, "so how could I afford to pay anyone? I just don't have any capital."

The constant preoccupation with status and respect, then, was a basic feature of life in Laweyan. This was not unusual in Java, especially in the environs of the courts of Central Java. What *was* unusual in Laweyan were the distinctive ways in which local economies of hierarchy and respect were intertwined with the material economies of commodity production and exchange. Subjectivity and sociality were deeply enmeshed with the logics of an incipient (or, more accurately, arrested) capitalism. The logic of capitalism was not fully developed here—its maturation would have been contingent on the subordination of other social and cultural logics to its relentless demands, a subordination that never really took place in Laweyan. However, the modern forms of commercial economy that made possible Laweyan's establishment as an entrepreneurial community in the nineteenth and twentieth centuries proved to be compatible with a whole range of practices and interests that were neither strictly economically motivated nor necessarily "rationalized" in a Weberian sense—nor, as the term is generally deployed in the West, entirely "modern." If anything, economic interests in Laweyan were often secondary to other sorts of social and cultural preoccupations, such as the obsessive concern with status and the related concern with cultural legitimacy.

The relationship between worker and entrepreneur, as I have suggested, was not simply an economic one; it was also a social relationship of great consequence for maintaining the hierarchies that were so basic a part of daily life. James Siegel has pointed out, for example, that the payment of wages to workers in Javanese batik firms in Solo is understood less as the payment of a wage in return for labor than as a "gift" bestowed upon a subordinate in return for that person's deference to the employer. Workers' labor itself is seen as a form of respect to those of higher status (1986, 176–77). My conversations with some entrepreneurs and my observation of the interactions between workers and their bosses seemed to confirm this. A female *juragan* in her late forties spoke to me yearningly of "the old days, when workers were satisfied just to be fed and to be given whatever small wage the employer wanted to give them." She contrasted this with present conditions, in which employees "expect to be paid a set wage for each day or piece of work." She also complained that nowadays workers expect to receive a certain amount of bonus pay for the Lebaran holiday, and will ask for it if it is not given to them, whereas in the past "they were happy to be given anything at all." It was easier for an entrepreneur to make money under the old system than under the current one, she said, in which many entrepreneurs go out of business because they cannot afford the cost of labor.

While I am not convinced that her reconstruction of "the old days" was entirely accurate—de Kat Angelino's (1930–31) detailed discussion of labor in Solonese batik firms, at least, suggests a fairly rationalized system of wages that varied predictably according to market conditions—this woman's nostalgia reflected an obvious longing for a time, real or (more likely) imagined, when workers would be properly deferential to their employers, and employers could return the deference with a "gift" of as little or as much money as they saw fit.

Another woman grumbled about the string of would-be servants who had come to her house, worked for two or three days, and then left because they weren't comfortable there. "In the past, people who wanted to work for you would truly put themselves at your service (*ngawula*). But now they don't do that anymore—they're more advanced (*sekarang lebih maju*, I.)," she added. She also complained that one of her most recent hires, a young woman who had left after only two days, "didn't even wait to find out what her wages would be; she didn't stay a whole month." The worker, especially someone in as low a position as a domestic servant, often dares not ask her employer beforehand what she will be paid, but waits to see how much she will be given.

The imagined assimilation of the relationship between employer and wage laborer to that of patron and client, which is implied by the notion of employer as benefactor and employee as one who offers grateful and unconditional deference and loyalty, obscures the fact that the labor of workers was fully commodified under the production system that had reigned in Laweyan for a century. Workers were rarely given any personal protection from prevailing market conditions or the whims of the employer, either of which could result in their wages being reduced or in their being laid off at a moment's notice without compensation (see Kat Angelino 1930–31). Workers, in turn, often left their employers for others who were willing to pay them more, sometimes taking their bosses' production secrets with them. I saw no evidence that things had ever been different, either in the reports of Dutch bureaucrats or in the personal accounts of older workers. As far as I could tell, the ties between *juragan* and their workers had never been akin to a genuine patron-client relationship. Pak Djohari, whose parents had both been batik workers, scoffed at the idea when I inquired whether, in his memory (which extended back to the 1920s), the entrepreneurs had ever looked after the welfare of the workers by providing them with anything more than their basic wage, such as paying for doctors' fees when they were ill. "The only people they would help out were their relatives," he retorted. "For anyone else, it was, 'If they're gonna die they're gonna die' (*Nèk arep mati ya mati*)."

Not only did workers rarely expect their employers to behave like true patrons, but they were actually suspicious of employers who treated them too well. A common fear expressed among workers who felt that their employer was being unusually kind or generous with them was that the employer had entered into a secret pact with a demonic being, referred to generically as *pasugihan* (from the root word *sugih*, "rich"), and had agreed to exchange the life of the worker or a member of the worker's family for the promise of guaranteed wealth.[21] I heard stories of workers who had left their employers simply because the *juragan* had given them unanticipated gifts or extra pay, or had been "suspiciously" kind to them in other ways. The workers worried that they were being set up as "bait" (*umpan*) for the *pasugihan*, the malevolent creature that they believed would soon take their lives, or that of their child, through an accident or a sudden illness if they continued on in the same person's employ. The *pasugihan*, which is believed to "eat" the victim in exchange for giving the entrepreneur abundant riches, might take one of a number of fantastic forms that are well known in Javanese folklore: a green giant or a white tortoise, for instance, or a *thuyul*, a little bald-headed creature resembling a child, which nurses from its owner, is invisible to most people, and steals money or other forms of wealth to bring home to its master.[22]

A *batik tulis* worker informed me that an indication of someone having a *pasugihan* is that "their work is simple but they have a lot of money." A sure sign that a wealthy batik entrepreneur used a *pasugihan*, according to this young woman, would be, for example, if the entrepreneur gave one of her workers more money than was usual; when the worker arrived at home, she would discover that her child had died suddenly. Although most members of the merchant class dismissed such stories as the superstitions of ignorant folk, many kampong people believed them to be true and were always on the lookout for the telltale signs that a *juragan* had entered into a diabolical pact, especially one that might turn out to be at their own expense. Laweyan was rumored to be a hotbed of *pasugihan*, especially in its more prosperous past—one of the factors that, some believed, had contributed to the neighborhood's dense concentration of wealthy merchants.

Michael Taussig and Aihwa Ong have viewed South American and Malaysian workers' stories of falling prey to the devil or various other evil spirits as fetishized expressions of the alienation and strain that people experience as they move from rural, precapitalist economic and social relations to the full proletarianization of modern capitalism. Caught between "noncapitalist morality and capitalist discipline" (Ong 1987, xiv) or between "the sense of organic unity between persons and their products" in precapitalist economies and "the subordination of men to the things they produce" in capitalist economies (Taussig 1980, 37), neophyte proletarians, they argue, express their radical sense of social, moral, and psychological dislocation through episodes of spirit possession or through stories of contracts with the devil.

Although there are some notable similarities between workers' stories of demonic spirits in South America and Malaysia with those told in Java, it would be difficult to apply Taussig's or Ong's theoretical frameworks directly to Java, given the long history of capitalist relations, commodified labor, and production for global markets under Dutch colonialism and subsequent regimes. Javanese workers, both rural and urban, have had their labor alienated from them for quite some time; they are not aptly characterized as naive peasants suddenly thrust into the grips of capitalism.[23] Java's batik workshops, for example, have been operating under essentially the same relations of production since the nineteenth century, and proletarianization took place at that time in many other enterprises as well: sugar factories, railroads, cigarette factories, and so on. Worker mobilization, unionization, and strikes were already well underway in Java by the first decades of the twentieth century (see Ingleson 1986).

Indeed, one could argue that the commodification and exploitation of labor are so entrenched in Java that, significantly, workers seem to be afraid that there is evil afoot only when they are being treated uncommonly *well* by their employers, not when they feel that they are being exploited or subjected to harsh discipline in the workplace. I should also point out that fears about diabolical pacts were held not only by workers in firms but also by domestic servants, who were not directly involved in commodity production. The conditions under which these domestic workers labored were frequently as oppressive as those faced by workers in firms, if not more so. The psychological and physical demands placed on them were often intensified rather than mitigated by the "personal" relationship that existed between worker and employer, which required that they be at their employers' service twenty-four hours a day and isolated them from their families and peers.

Still, workers' fears about their bosses' motives for treating them well clearly do represent a fetishization of the relationship between worker and *juragan*. The asymmetrical nature of the relationship requires that the worker offer both her labor and her deference to her employer in exchange for only a minimal wage. She must attend closely to her employer's needs and desires, but her employer need not reciprocate in any significant way. A worker becomes anxious when the *juragan* seems overly attentive to *her* needs or pays her more money than she would ordinarily expect; it suggests an imbalance in the usual relationship between *juragan* and worker, and thus an unfulfilled debt on the part of the worker that is accrued as a result of the entrepreneur's excessive generosity, which the worker cannot adequately repay through her labor or deference alone. Such stories reflect the power and hierarchy built into worker-employer relationships, as well as a more general principle of debt and exchange that many Javanese take quite seriously (see Keeler 1987). Any unpaid debt, people believe, will eventually come back to haunt the debtor; failure to complete an act of exchange initiated by another party puts the debtor at risk of personal or cosmic retribution. The *juragan's* excessive "gift" to the worker demands a return, and the worker's anxiety that she may have to repay her debt to the *juragan* with her life (or the life of her child) causes her to leave her employer rather than to await whatever unpleasant fate she fears might be in store for her.

WORKERS AND ENTREPRENEURS

The conditions of production in the few batik firms that were still operating in the 1980s stood in stark contrast to those of the large, modern textile factories that had been built on Solo's outskirts since the 1970s. Batik workshops, although commonly referred to as "factories" (*pabrik*, from the Dutch *fabriek*), were little more than cavernous rooms with cement floors and a loft (*lotèng*) where the newly dyed cloths were hung to dry; less commonly, a workshop might be a roofed, open-air space attached to the back of the house. There were vats, sinks, and troughs for preparing the cloth with a chemical bath, dyeing it, and boiling away the wax to reveal the design. *Batik cap* workshops had rows of small tables at which the individual workers, all men, would stand to stamp lengths of cloth with designs in hot wax; in a corner there were usually shelves full of copper stamps, dark and discolored from use, often covered with a thick layer of dust if their designs were no longer in demand. *Batik tulis* workshops were even sparser than those for *batik cap*, because they used no tables; women sat on thin mats or on little wooden stools on the floor, just a few inches off the ground, with a bamboo frame in front of them to hold the piece of cloth on which they were working. A group of four to six women would cluster around a small, iron pot of molten wax set over a burner, into which from time to time they would dip the tool of their trade, the delicate, copper-spouted *canting*, before applying designs lightly to the cloth. The indoor workshops were usually poorly ventilated and illuminated with only a few bare lightbulbs. Respiratory ailments from the stinging smoke of hot wax were common, and the older workers often wore thick glasses after years of doing finely detailed work in dimly lit spaces.

Teenage girls and young women from the villages who worked in Solo's *batik tulis* workshops often stayed in the workshop for weeks or even

6. A *batik cap* worker applying wax to cloth with a copper stamp.

months at a time, going home to the village only occasionally to contribute
their labor at harvesttime or to help with the preparations for a family
wedding or other ritual event. Some lived too far from the workshop to
make daily commuting practical, and their wages were so slim that the cost
of transportation home, even if they did not live far away, would leave
them with almost nothing. Eventually many of these young women would
return to the village to get married themselves, after which they often remained in the village permanently, sometimes continuing to do batik work
from their homes on a putting-out basis. Female workers who stayed at the
workplace usually slept on mats in the workshops. When they were paid on
a piecework basis (*borongan*), which was common, they worked whenever
they felt like doing so, even in the middle of the night; in the heat of the
afternoon they sometimes napped or went outside for a stroll. Their food
might or might not be provided by the employer; when it was not, they
frequently bought their meals from cheap sidewalk food stalls. In contrast
to the female workers, men who worked in batik firms seemed rarely, if
ever, to sleep in the workshop. Although many of them also hailed from
the villages, they often lived close enough to Solo to ride their bikes or take
a minibus to work, or else they had taken up residence in urban kampongs
on a temporary or long-term basis.[24]

Laweyan had once had several thousand workers like these, especially
those who produced *batik cap*, the specialty of the neighborhood. Now very

7. Young women in a *batik tulis* workshop in Solo.

few workers were still employed in the batik industry here, although batik workshops were scattered in other parts of the city, most notably in the neighborhood of Pasar Kliwon, where a number of people from the local Arab Indonesian community still ran batik firms. Many former batik workers who remained in Laweyan and its bordering neighborhoods were unemployed or underemployed, trying to scrape out a living as *bécak* drivers or occasional day laborers. As hard as the decline of the batik industry had hit the local entrepreneurs, the workers were in far more difficult straits.

The ideal work relationship between *juragan* and worker often seemed to be envisioned—at least by the employer—as one in which the will of the *juragan* was executed through the "hand" of the worker, a sign of the worker's deference for the employer. In such images of work, the worker is accorded a kind of negative subjectivity; she should be able to suppress her own desires and replace them with the desires of the *juragan*, which figuratively flow through her to create the final product of labor. This conceptualization of labor was strongest in people's comments on female workers, including batik workers as well as domestic servants; they seemed to be thought better at suppressing their own egos than male laborers. In workshops where *batik tulis*, hand-drawn batik, was produced, the *juragan* would speak of the more skilled female batik workers as having "a good hand," but this was never attributed to their talent or creativity. Rather, they were invariably said to be *tlatèn*, patient and persevering in a tedious task: in other words, able to restrain their own desires and to give themselves over completely to the painstaking work of drawing exquisitely fine designs on cloth with molten wax—which meant, at the same time, giving themselves over to the will of the *juragan* who was directing their work. The worker's willingness to efface her own ego and to allow herself to serve as a vehicle for the *juragan's* desires was a sign of her respect for her employer's superior status.

The full commodification of workers' labor was made clear by the frequent references to the batik worker's "hand" as a synecdochic replacement for the worker herself. Entrepreneurs would often complain about the lack of uniformity that resulted from different hands working on the same piece of batik, creating in my mind a rather jarring image of disembodied appendages applying themselves to cloth. It was acceptable, and in fact usual, for different hands to work on the same cloth at different stages of the batik-making process, because the procedure for making *batik tulis* is broken down into a number of steps, each of which is often carried out by a different worker.[25] But each step of the waxing—drawing the outline, for instance, or filling it in with tiny dots or other design elements—is usually done by only one person, lest the design appear uneven, for each worker has her own style. As people, batik workers were considered more or less interchangeable—a worker who went home to the village was often asked to send back a sister or cousin to replace her in the workshop—but their "hands" were unique, so the worker was usually asked to complete the piece of batik that she was working on before she left.

Domestic servants were also sometimes viewed as, essentially, manual extensions of the *juragan*. In my early months of research, I was always puzzled when women in the neighborhood or marketplace would ask about my host, as a way of making polite conversation, "What did Bu Wiyono cook today?" even though they knew perfectly well that Bu Wiyono, like most of the wealthier people of the neighborhood, had a housekeeper who did almost all of the cooking for the family. I soon came to realize that my literal interpretation of this question was off the mark; the woman who did the actual cooking was again seen as the hand that carried out her employer's will. A *juragan* could then acceptably say, "I cooked everything myself," even if she had never actually touched any of the food. If it was prepared in her kitchen, even nominally under her supervision, then it was "her" cooking—especially if she was pleased with the results.

These sorts of workers—domestic servants and *batik tulis* workers—were among the lowest-paid and lowest-status laborers I encountered. A housekeeper might be paid only ten or fifteen dollars a month, plus room and board, for work that started before dawn and ended late at night; a female batik worker also earned as little as thirty-five or forty cents a day.

8. A batik worker buys *jamu* (herbal tonics) from a local peddler.

Although *batik tulis* was quite expensive by local standards, far more so than stamped batik, *batik cap* workers, who were always male, were paid a significantly higher wage than female *batik tulis* workers. The labor of women who made batik in someone else's workshop was never accorded much value; the value of their work, no matter how good it was, was considered to be roughly equivalent to the work of a domestic servant. I even met women who doubled as servant and batik worker for the same employer, cooking, cleaning, or crafting batik as the *juragan* demanded. As poor females, mostly from the villages and often quite young, their status in the social hierarchy was very low, and the monetary value of their labor was calculated accordingly.

In contrast, a member of the Solonese nobility who made fine pieces of *batik tulis* in her home and sold them herself was treated as a skilled craftswoman whose labor was valuable in its own right. The fact that she, rather than someone else, had the right to sell the final products of her labor gave it an entirely different value, especially because of her respected social position, and she was usually paid handsomely for her batiks. High-quality *batik tulis* exemplifies a Javanese art form that is *alus*, refined and of high status. The noblewoman's high rank by birth or marriage adds to the evaluation of the batik as *alus*, even as it is transformed from classical art form to commodity. Noblewomen who make *batik tulis* take great pride in the quality of their craftsmanship, boasting about the fineness of the detail, the beauty of the design, and the overall "*alus*ness" of their work. *Batik tulis* workers, in contrast, rarely show any outward pride in work that is sometimes just as good. Although the commodity that they produce might also be called *alus*, as poorly paid wage laborers they themselves are categorized with that which is *kasar*, coarse and of low status. The association of *batik tulis* with high culture enables the commodity to retain its aura of refinement even when it is crafted by women of low status, but the refinement itself is not seen as emanating from the workers who make it. It comes, rather, from the long tradition of batik making and its historical linkages with court culture.

Parmi was a clever, nineteen-year-old woman with a sardonic sense of humor who made *batik tulis* in a workshop that specialized in very high quality batik. She had begun doing batik work after school in her village when she was ten years old, learning the craft from her mother and sisters, and had worked in the same workshop in Solo since she was thirteen. She downplayed her own skill at batik making and seemed to take no particular satisfaction in the fine quality of her work. "Making batik is the easiest thing in the world," she insisted when I commented on her deftness and patience at decorating lengths of white cloth with intricate designs. Paid about thirty-five cents a day plus meals, she saw herself not as an artist, nor even as a skilled artisan, but as a low-status laborer (*buruh*) who worked just to eke out a living. Sometimes she was asked to help cook for or serve the *juragan* and her family in addition to making batik. She slept at the workshop, only returning to her village for special occasions.

Parmi told me that if she had money, she would "not have to do this kind of work anymore." As workers who were required to suppress their own wills in order to defer to the will of the *juragan*, women like Parmi could not feel genuine pride in work that was conceptualized as their employers' rather than their own, and that was remunerated so poorly. The notion of "pride" assumes that there is an active subject at work with a strong ego, but the *batik tulis* worker's job requires that she divest herself of her ego. The fact that multiple workers usually worked on a single piece of cloth meant that workers had even less pride invested in their work; from the point of view of the *juragan* they were simply the various "hands" that the cloth passed through before it was sold as a commodity. Many batik workers did not even see the finished product of their labor after it was dyed and ready for the market.

Another reason that the patience and docility of female workers were not well rewarded financially was that these were considered to be "natural" female traits, especially among lower-class women. Batik work, like cooking, cleaning, or doing laundry, was seen as something that took no particular talent; instead, it was part of a village girl's ordinary upbringing (even though not all village women actually learn how to make batik). Batik work was also regarded as something that village women did in their spare time, not as the major source of income for their families—a generalization that continues to be used in urban batik workshops to justify paying female workers low wages but that is, in many cases, simply untrue: many women do support their families by making batik. Parmi's mother, her sisters, and her brothers all earned a living this way; her father, she said, was unemployed—not an unusual state of affairs in this part of Java.

The labor of male batik workers, while also not highly paid, was accorded more value. In some batik workshops, there were a few young, male workers who painted large, abstract designs in wax on cloth with a brush to make modern styles of batik fabric for dresses or men's shirts. It was usually also a man who drew the broad outlines of designs on cloth with a pencil that would eventually be used as a very rough guideline for women making *batik tulis*. I rarely saw women workers doing freehand brushwork or penciling the outlines of a design. When I asked the entrepreneurs why, I was told repeatedly that "women aren't capable of being creative in this way." The *juragan*, male or female, usually believed that female workers were neither freethinking nor bold enough to do designing or abstract batik work. Female workers were good at doing fine, detailed work because they were patient and persevering, employers commented, but not at doing work that required imagination or flexibility. They had to be explicitly shown or told what batik patterns to make and where to place them on the cloth. Not surprisingly, wages reflected these stereotypes: in one workshop, the female batik workers were paid an average of 750–800 *rupiah* per day (about fifty–sixty cents at that time), while the young men who worked freestyle with brushes earned more than 3,000 *rupiah* a day—a living wage, unlike the women's—for work that, to my eyes, looked much easier than traditional *batik tulis* work, and certainly less tedious. I inquired whether the men who worked freehand on the cloth had had any training in schools or art academies, but was told no, that they just had "talent"—something that female workers were never said to possess.

These gender stereotypes were largely class-specific. In contrast, among the ranks of textile merchants and entrepreneurs, people often remarked that women rather than men had the aesthetic sensibilities, motivation, and adaptability to succeed in business. Some of these women merchants, particularly the older ones, had not had much more schooling than their workers from the villages, so they had not necessarily acquired these positive traits through formal education. The difference was that female batik workers, because of their very low status as well as their sex, were expected to empty themselves of precisely those qualities that were encouraged and valued in the *juragan* and, to a much more limited extent, in some male workers: initiative, creativity, and independent-mindedness. The personal qualities that were most desired in female workers were docility and willingness to defer to the *juragan*. Even those workers who were spunky by nature, like Parmi, were always very submissive in the presence of the *juragan*—usually, though not always, another woman. Female entrepreneurs themselves were anything but passive and docile: they were typically strong-willed, demanding, and energetic.

A successful *juragan* who lived in a neighborhood close to the Kraton was remarkably frank in describing what traits he looked for in a batik worker, and how he treated those who worked for him. Mas Budiono,[26] thirty-four, was smooth, urbane, and college educated; in addition to his high-end *batik tulis* business he also manufactured printed imitation batiks for the mass market. He lived in a beautiful old Javanese-style home filled with antiques, where he had been raised; his parents had also been batik entrepreneurs. In the context of a more general explanation of his formula for making money, he said that he preferred having village women do batik work for him on a putting-out basis rather than having them work for him in an urban workshop, because he could pay them less and make greater profits. He would pay them a small wage to wax the designs on cloth, then have the cloths dyed in a workshop in Solo, and finally market them in Jakarta. His rationalization for paying the women such a small amount was that village women who make batik are not supporting their families through their batik work; "they do it in their spare time when they're not working in the fields or around the house, instead of just sitting around doing nothing." Some are "housewives" (*ibu rumah tangga*, I.), he said, who are mostly supported by their husbands; these women are "happy if they can buy a bowl of sweet rice porridge in the morning for twenty-five *rupiah*" (less than two cents). Their needs and wants are simple—they haven't been ruined by exposure to the city, which makes people want to have things that they can't afford, he added.

"Most of the women who make batik in the villages are ignorant (*bodoh*, I.)—they don't know the real value of batik, so they sell their work very cheaply," Mas Budiono continued, smiling. He admitted to paying these villagers as little as he could for their labor. "I don't think this is a sin," he remarked confidently. "The workers sell their work to me voluntarily, without being forced, so it's not exploitation to buy from them cheaply." In Mas Budiono's view, women living in the city were spoiled—they were no longer so ignorant about the value of their work, and they wanted to consume more and more because their desires had been awakened by the city and all the material pleasures that it has to offer. So they demanded higher wages.[27]

The batik he dealt in, he confided, was of good quality, but not the best: "Its value is between 6 and 8 on a scale of 10. I don't like to deal in batik that's really fine, a '9,' because that would already be 'art' (*sudah seni*, I.).

And artists are bold (*berani*, I., which also means 'defiant'); they don't want to get down on their knees. I want batik workers who are willing to get down on their knees, to be told what to do. Someone who does batik work that reaches 9 on a scale of 10 won't be willing to put herself in that position." The key to making money in the batik business, he had concluded, "is to buy [batik work] from women who are ignorant and to sell [the finished product] to people who are ignorant"—in the latter case rich Jakartans who, like the villagers, do not understand the true value of the commodity.

He had figured out a way to sell goods for more than their actual worth. "Money won't just fall into your lap," he reasoned. "You have to use 'human relations'" (he used the English term "human relations" in the midst of speaking Indonesian). Mas Budiono marketed his batik in Jakarta instead of Solo because "people in Solo are too smart about the price of batik—they know too well what it's worth, so they can't be fooled into thinking that a '6' is a '7.'" He took full advantage of the wide gap between village and metropole, using his position as a cultural broker between the two to his own profit. Mediating between the "ignorance" of villagers, in their simplicity, with the "ignorance" of those living in metropolitan Jakarta who, for all their urban sophistication, lacked the cultural knowledge to understand the subtle aesthetics of batik, he could use his understanding of both worlds to make money.

THE LOGIC OF THE COMMODITY, THE FAILURE OF CAPITAL

Not all entrepreneurs were as coldly calculating as Mas Budiono—nor were many as successful in business. But the general principles on which he operated were widely applied by entrepreneurs in the batik industry, particularly in their relations with workers. By using their relative power and status to their advantage, they could convince workers, especially village women, to sell their labor for very little money. The workers, usually poor and quite desperate for work, had little choice but to accept what the entrepreneurs offered them. Bu Sugiarto was a Laweyan entrepreneur whose batik business had once been large, but she was now reduced to doing only a little trading here and there. She had a few village women doing putting-out work for her; she would then send the waxed cloths out to be dyed and sell them at a small profit. I was at her home one day when one of her "regulars" arrived by bus from Sukoharjo, a rural district just southwest of Solo. Bu Sugiarto sat in a chair while the worker, a woman about thirty years old, sat on the floor in front of her. Bu Sugiarto looked at all six pieces of waxed cloth that the woman had brought to sell, selecting only two of them for purchase. Speaking low Javanese to the woman (who replied in high Javanese, but said very little), she made mildly disparaging remarks about the designs and execution of the batik work. She acted as if she were doing the woman a favor by accepting any of the pieces at all. She paid her eight thousand *rupiah* each, a little more than five dollars, for two waxed sarongs, each of which had probably taken the woman about a week to make. The woman had paid for the cost of the raw materials herself, significantly reducing the amount that she received as a return on her labor.

Bu Sugiarto gave the woman some rather gruff suggestions as to how she might improve her work the next time around: how the designs could be made more appealing, what batik motifs were currently in fashion, and so on. She pointed to one simple, classic pattern and said, "City people don't like this sort of thing." Before the woman left, Bu Sugiarto gestured to one of the pieces that she had purchased and uttered with an air of impatience, "You can make another one like this" (*Gawé manèh ya kena*). Everything in the two women's body postures, the levels of speech used, and their tone of voice, in addition to what they actually said, served to reinforce the *juragan's* hierarchical superiority to the worker. As soon as the woman politely excused herself and left, Bu Sugiarto's tone and demeanor changed, becoming light and relaxed. Her daughter-in-law remarked on how nice one of the pieces was, and Bu Sugiarto agreed. She would never have admitted this to the worker, of course, because that would have removed her advantage in bargaining. As in the case of Mas Budiono, it was in the *juragan's* interest to keep the worker from knowing what her work was worth; the value of her labor was always deprecated so that she would not ask for a higher payment. Bu Sugiarto was not a mean-spirited person, nor was she unusually stingy. She merely behaved as all entrepreneurs did in order to turn a profit—and her margin of profit was actually quite slim on pieces of batik like these. I have no doubt that later, when she went to sell the finished batik sarongs wholesale to a trader in the marketplace, the tables were turned: in order to get the best price possible, Bu Sugiarto surely argued that the work was of superior quality, and the market trader probably disparaged it so as to keep the price down.

Like all forms of wage labor, the commodification of labor in Solo's batik industry encoded in mystified form a social relationship between worker and entrepreneur (see Marx [1867] 1977) that appeared to be derived from the "natural" relationships between entrepreneur, worker, and the products of labor themselves. Mas Budiono's description of his entrepreneurial philosophy illustrated this perfectly: his insistence that his workers be willing to get down on their knees before him "proved" that he was justified in paying villagers very low returns on their labor, for as poor village women, they had neither the need nor the right to be paid more, as far as he was concerned. By using "human relations," as he put it, and obscuring to both the worker and the consumer the true value of the labor that went into making the batik, he could extract a higher profit from the sale of his commodities.

But we also see from this example that the commodification of labor here, and the mystified forms that it took, had a significance that was peculiar to the Javanese context: it both reinforced and was shaped by local ideologies and social hierarchies that extended beyond the realm of commodity production and exchange. These hierarchies were defined neither solely by the relations of production nor by the demands of capitalism more broadly. The logic of capital was not so far advanced in Laweyan and other Javanese merchant communities that it could shape all social relations to fit its inexorable requirements. What was striking here, on the contrary, was how capitalism itself was molded, and ultimately impeded, by other kinds of cultural considerations, and by a history that continued to exert its force on the present. While life had revolved around commodity production and trade for the better part of a century, this had not been enough to ensure that the community would continue on in an upward spiral toward full capitalist development. The logic of the commodity was not the logic of a full-blown capitalism.

A number of authors have pointed out the problems inherent in conflating economies based on money or on commodity production and exchange with those based on capitalism (e.g., Appadurai 1986; Parry and Bloch 1989b; Kahn 1993).[28] Marx, however, is quite clear about the difference between two forms of the circulation of commodities, only one of which constitutes capitalism proper: on the one hand, the transformation of commodities into money and the reconversion of money into commodities ("selling in order to buy"); on the other hand, the transformation of money into commodities, and the reconversion of commodities into money ("buying in order to sell"), which is the formula for capital (Marx [1867] 1977, 247–48). The final goal of the first type of circulation is consumption, or the appropriation of use values; it is not a fully developed capitalism. True capitalism aims not at the consumption of money in the form of use values, but at keeping it in circulation as capital: the capitalist's aim is "the unceasing movement of profit-making," the "boundless drive for enrichment" (254).[29]

Had the ceaseless quest for profit—profit for its own sake—been a primary motive of Javanese merchants and entrepreneurs in Solo, then they might have become bona fide capitalists. But, as I have already stated, the overriding logic here was not that of capitalism; it was a logic of status and hierarchy. As social actors whose behavior was guided, if not entirely contained, by that logic, they could not simultaneously fulfill all the requirements of capitalist accumulation and investment. Their engagement in the market was subsumed by their engagement in the cultural politics of status.

Instead of using their profits from the batik trade, then, as capital to expand their businesses, they often used them as investments in prestige, mostly through conspicuous displays of wealth in the form of large homes, jewelry, and other luxury items, as well as in lavish ritual celebrations. That this had been the case for at least half a century, and probably longer, is suggested by de Kat Angelino's observation about Javanese batik entrepreneurs in Solo: "A considerable part of the funds required for their firm is put into fine houses and valuables; hereby the outward appearance of prosperity is created and the creditworthiness shall be judged by it, but in the end, these unwise merchants are unable to hold their own in the great struggle against the hundreds of competitors elsewhere" (1930–31, 2:97). A similar comment was made about batik entrepreneurs in Central Java in the 1950s: "Entrepreneurs prefer to spend their increased income for consumption purposes (buying new cars, jewelry, building new houses, etc.) rather than for expanding their business. Non-economic considerations are here playing the more decisive role" (Economic Research Bureau 1958, 388).[30]

Even more indicative of capitalism's arrest in Laweyan and similar Javanese communities is that the entrepreneurs often behaved less and less "entrepreneurially" as time went on. If the quest for profit had indeed been their foremost aim, then most batik producers would have abandoned this field of business as soon as it began to decline and switched to more lucrative arenas of manufacturing or trade, as many Chinese Indonesians did. That they did not do so (with some exceptions) is a sign that the profit motive was in competition with other motivations that did not fit well with the stringent demands of capitalism.

One should be skeptical of any notion that communities like Laweyan were following a capitalist trajectory, but were "not quite there yet"—that they had merely reached an intermediate stage on the road toward capitalism, and were slowly wending their way in that direction. Such an evolutionary model of capitalist development cannot account for the irreversible decline that every prominent Javanese merchant community experienced from the mid– to late twentieth century, from the cigarette manufacturers of Kudus, to the pawnbrokers and moneylenders of Kotagede, to the batik manufacturers and traders of Solo, Yogyakarta, and Pekalongan. Even as these communities were declining, the goals of capitalist development were being hailed by the New Order regime as a cure for all that ailed the nation, the key to a prosperous, modern future. Indonesia, like so many other "developing" countries, was increasingly drawn into the arena of global capitalism after the mid-1960s, its schemes for economic development engineered largely by Western-trained technocrats. Communities like Laweyan, however, had become distinctly marginal to this arena, and many people in these merchant enclaves attributed their marginalization to the very processes of capitalist development that were rapidly advancing in other quarters.

NARRATIVES OF PROGRESS

There were many criteria for establishing social hierarchies in Laweyan, as in Solo and Java more broadly. Wealth was an important factor, but not the only one, that figured in the determination of status. Another very basic division that encoded a hierarchy was that of village (*désa*) versus city (*kutha*, *kota*, I.), a hierarchy that we have seen played out in the dynamics between urban entrepreneurs like Mas Budiono and Bu Sugiarto and their village workers. Villagers and urbanites alike saw the city as a place that was more modern, more "advanced" (*maju*) or "developed" than the countryside, although villagers and recent migrants to the city tended to be more ambivalent in their views of city life than longtime urbanites were. Newcomers were attracted by the city's wealth, opportunities, and sophistication, but also wary of the unfettered desires that it seemed to arouse in its inhabitants and its lack of humanity compared with village life. Most people agreed that the city was a place where modern individualism had supplanted the village spirit of cooperation, and where relationships based on money had replaced those of neighborliness and social interdependence.

A group of kampong women explained the differences between city and village by reference to two neighborhoods, Laweyan and Banaran. Laweyan was "city," while Banaran, just to the south, was "village," and there was a noticeable difference between them even though they were adjacent. In Banaran, the women claimed, if someone built a house or sponsored a ritual event, all of the labor would be donated by friends and neighbors. But in Laweyan, contractors and wage laborers would be hired to build a house, and caterers called in to provide the food for a ceremony (this was sometimes, but not always, true). The moral of their story, one that was already quite familiar to me from other people's accounts, was that the march of progress in the city could only be accomplished at the expense of social harmony and mutual aid: what the city gained in progress, it lost in human decency and communal spirit.

The romance of the village, however, had limited appeal for most people who had been raised in the city: very few would have been willing to trade their "individualistic" urban lives for the simpler and supposedly more cooperative lifestyle of the village. To do so, as they saw it, would be taking a step in the wrong direction, for the transformation from "backwardness" to "modernity" was imagined not only as a progression over time but also as a synchronous movement through space. Backwardness and modernity were seen as coexisting only a short distance from one another, in rural periphery and urban center. I use the term "backwardness" here in place of "tradition," because what city dwellers perceived in the villages was not the lofty tradition of the courts, the venerable, *alus* tradition of Javanese history. Rather, it was the unenlightened traditionalism of simple folk, the "ignorant" villagers of whom Mas Budiono had spoken so patronizingly: people who aspired, in his view, to nothing more in life than to be able to eat a bowl of sweet porridge in the morning. "Progress" and "development" could be mapped onto the landscape, revealing an uneven topography of modernity.

Those who lived comfortably in the city—though there were many impoverished people who did not—usually felt fortunate to have left village life behind, certain that the movement out of the village had simultaneously been a movement up the ladder of status and civilization. Urbanites distinguished themselves from villagers by their dress, mannerisms, and styles of speech. In Pasar Klewer, Solo's sprawling textile bazaar, the market traders could size up their customers' origins and social class with a glance, and they tended to speak a lower (but still polite) level of Javanese to buyers from the village, in part because villagers themselves were often uncomfortable with the florid speech styles of the high Javanese spoken in Solo. Most of the traders who catered specifically to village tastes and purses had their stalls at the rear of the marketplace, which spatially demarcated a position of secondary status where wealthier urban patrons would be less inclined to venture. In a nation in which the large majority of the population is still rural, being an urbanite is often considered to be a marker of status and privilege, especially if one has the material accoutrements to bolster one's position—nice clothes, a large house, or a motorcycle or automobile, for instance. The city is where villagers go to try to improve their lot in life, although not always with great success.

Most members of Laweyan's merchant community had very few ties to the villages, save for a yearly outing during the month of Ruwah to make offerings at the graves of their more remote ancestors. They considered themselves true urbanites, envisioning themselves and their community as the end products of a journey from village to city that had immeasurably improved their station in life and enabled them to rise above the humble roots of their village-born ancestors. Although many of their parents, grandparents, or great-grandparents had come to Laweyan from villages outside Solo, the merchants expressed little nostalgia for village life. On the contrary, some of them seemed to shudder at the thought of what their lives would have been like had their forebears remained in the village. "Village" represented stagnation, underdevelopment, boredom, lack of material comforts—all things that they were glad to have left behind. "City," on the other hand, meant opportunity, prosperity, progress, and modernity. Although Laweyan itself had been considered "village," *désa*, in its earlier history, it was now fully incorporated into the city of Solo, and its merchants had long since dissociated themselves from village life.

One *juragan*'s narrative of her father's migration from village to city was a triumphant tale of progress against tough odds, a theme that recurred frequently in other peoples' family histories. Bu Harjanto, an affluent and still active entrepreneur in her forties, recounted the story of her father's struggle to improve his status in life, and that of his descendants, by leaving the village behind. He had been born into a well-to-do family in a village not far from Laweyan, where his father owned a large stretch of wet rice lands. But his father had had two wives, and his mother (the second wife) decided to move to Laweyan with her children to distance herself from the first wife. When his father died, he inherited little property because his father had left almost all of it to the first wife and her children. So Bu Harjanto's father quickly went from being the son of a wealthy landowner to being a poor young man in Laweyan.

At first he had supported himself by working as a servant in someone's home. Then he had apprenticed himself to a craftsman of copper stamps (*cap*) for making batik. After that he became a *batik cap* worker, and eventually he became the right-hand man (*carik*) to a batik entrepreneur. In the long run he managed to go into batik production himself, becoming a full-fledged *juragan* and marrying the daughter of a Laweyan merchant couple. Bu Harjanto said that it touched her to think of the struggles (*perjuangan*, I.) that her father had waged, and also to think of where his offspring would have been today if he had remained in the village as a poor man: they might have been selling *tèmpé* (a cheap food made of fermented soybeans) or doing other such lowly work. By moving to the city from the village, she concluded with a hint of emotion in her voice, her father was able to elevate the status of the family to where it was today (*bisa menjunjung derajat keluarganya*, I.). As she spoke of the hardships that her father had endured for the sake of his descendants, she seemed to forget the reason that his mother had moved to Laweyan in the first place—to escape the discomforts of a polygamous marriage. Instead, her story focused on her father's determination to raise his family's status against the odds, and on his having done so by forging a path in the city, where there were opportunities for advancement unknown in the countryside.

In Bu Harjanto's narrative, Laweyan figured as a site of the modern, of progress and upward mobility from the village. Yet compared to the cosmopolitan world of Jakarta, or even to some other sectors of Solonese society, Laweyan was, in truth, quite provincial. While thoroughly modern by some standards—few elite homes lacked a television or a telephone, items that were unattainable luxuries for most villagers—it still seemed to inhabit an interstitial position in the world of late-twentieth-century Indonesia. Solo itself, a fairly quiet inland city removed from the coastal hubs of commerce like Jakarta and Surabaya, seemed reluctant to plunge headlong into the maelstrom of modernization, although the pace of change was quickening in the 1980s, and it was to move even faster in the 1990s. Stuck somewhere in the vast gray area between village Java and metropolitan Jakarta, Solo occupied an intermediate point between the two worlds, strongly influenced by both but resembling neither. Although people like Mas Budiono were able to grasp and use this intermediacy to their own advantage, for others the negotiation between these very different worlds was more difficult. In Laweyan the failure of so many businesses and the decline of the community more generally seemed symptomatic of its having become entangled in the webs of modernization, but without completely embracing modernity in all of its aspects. Modernity, like capitalism, appeared to have been arrested midstream in this corner of society.

The Making of the Unmodern

Although Laweyan had developed its distinctive character mainly in the first half of the twentieth century, it may be compared in certain ways to Europe and America in the nineteenth century, in what is frequently seen as a period of transition. In his exploration of "the dialectics of modernization and modernism" (1988, 16), Marshall Berman writes of this period that "the nineteenth-century modern public can remember what it is like to live, materially and spiritually, in worlds that are not modern at all. From this inner dichotomy, this sense of living in two worlds simultaneously, the ideas of modernization and modernism emerge and unfold" (17). A similar sense of in-betweenness, it seems, has been part of every nation's and locality's experiences of modernization. The stories of older people in Solo's merchant community made it clear that from early on they had identified with the modern world in some aspects of their lives, but that they had also experienced the sense of being part of two worlds that Berman describes.

One wealthy entrepreneur who was born in the Kauman around 1912, Bu Hamzuri, told me a story that exemplified this experience. Her story showed as well how closely modernness was identified with the West in late colonial Java. As a child, Bu Hamzuri's parents, who were also merchants, had sent her to an Islamic school. But one day while she was in her teens she heard a very attractive woman speaking Dutch, and she was impressed. She decided that she, too, would like to learn Dutch. With a note of modest pride in her voice, she told me, "I liked hearing people speak Dutch. I was rather modern." (*Aku seneng krungu wong omong cara Landa.*

Aku rada modhèren.) But her father was old-fashioned (*kolot*), and forbade her to go to a modern school. She was determined, though, and with some savings of her own from her part-time trading she secretly went to a Dutch school (HIS) for a while. One night, she muttered some Dutch in her sleep, including the phrase, "I don't know" (*Ik weet 't niet*). Her father, convinced that she was possessed (*kesurupan*) by a Dutch-speaking spirit, shook her to wake her up and free her of its hold on her. As Bu Hamzuri recounted the story I was amused to think of the zeitgeist of modernity, the spirit of the age, almost literally being embodied in this woman as her old-fashioned father tried to exorcise it. The story is a nice metaphor for the sometimes unintended effects of encounters with the modern, which at times took the form of a casually borrowed Dutchness that could be put on or taken off at will like a hat or a pair of shoes.

This active and self-conscious participation in the modern world, fitful though it sometimes was, was what set these merchants apart from the village lifestyle that most Javanese still followed. As first- and second-generation city dwellers, they were not so far removed from the village that it was outside their consciousness altogether; they could still imagine what it would have been like to live as poor villagers, mired in what they perceived as the backwater of Indonesian society, a place that was not yet modern. Their understanding of progress was shaped deeply by their parents' and grandparents' experiences. "Progress" was what their forebears had achieved by leaving the village and becoming entrepreneurs in Laweyan. In doing so they had set a new course for themselves and their descendants, "elevating their status," as Bu Harjanto put it, and pushing them toward a modern life.

But the modernizing process had been partly stifled by the community's tendency toward insularity and its halfheartedness in pursuing its own agendas of progress. Bu Harjanto herself, who struck me as one of the more forward-looking people in the entrepreneurial community, was somewhat bitter about how Laweyan's traditionalism had hindered her in her efforts to seize fully the opportunities offered by the modern world, the same world that had been opened up to her by her father's efforts to transcend the confines of the village. She had wanted to go to college in the early 1960s, at a time when most Laweyan people still thought that higher education was wasted on a woman. Although her parents had strongly resisted the idea, she had finally persuaded them to allow her to attend a prestigious university in another city. "I told them, 'You can take whatever jewelry you were planning to pass down to me, and sell it off to pay for my education.' That's how determined (*nékad*) I was." But after only a short time her parents had pulled her out of the university. "In those days, Laweyan was a little old-fashioned," she explained with resignation. "Almost everyone from Laweyan had to marry someone else from Laweyan, and my parents had decided it was time for me to get married. So I had to come home. We got married and moved in with my in-laws. Then my husband and I began to make batik."

The memory of the limitations of the past (as exemplified in the figure of the village) and how they were overcome was what made Bu Harjanto and others self-aware of their own status as "modern" people. But new constraints had replaced the old ones as Laweyan had turned in on itself and transformed the novelty of modern life into the safe comfort of well-worn habits and conventions. The question remains: what had stifled the process of modernization in the community, ultimately bringing about its stagnation?

Laweyan's traditionalism did not result from a desire to turn back the clock on all that the founders of the community had achieved, nor from a rejection of modernity per se. On the contrary, I would venture that it was due in part to what might best be understood as an overidentification with the modernizing moment, the moment of progress as the earlier generations had experienced it and as it was remembered in the community's individual and collective memories. It has been argued that traditionalism itself is a distinctly modern phenomenon, often produced, paradoxically, by processes of modernization.[31] Laweyan's origin stories were modern narratives of progress from the turn of the twentieth century; its ancestral inheritances were the secrets of commodity production and trade that had been passed down from the community's first entrepreneurs. So successful had the earlier generations of Laweyan entrepreneurs been in improving their own fortunes that they had assumed that their children needed only to imitate them in order to regenerate their wealth and positions of high status in the community. And for a while, this formula had worked for many people. The second and third generations of Laweyan merchants had imitated these past models not by forging a pioneering path, as their ancestors did, but by following carefully in their footsteps: marrying within the same circles, manufacturing the same goods using exactly the same techniques of production, and so on.

One sees other alternatives in the course followed by Solo's Chinese Indonesian community. A large number of ethnic Chinese in Java earned a living as entrepreneurs and traders in the twentieth century, and many had been involved in batik production in the industry's years of expansion. But when the batik industry began to decline, the majority quickly switched over to more profitable fields of business. There was a dynamic quality to the Chinese entrepreneurial community that was lacking in Laweyan and other Javanese merchant circles, a willingness to let go of the past and to embrace the future, with all of the risks and opportunities that it might hold. Most Javanese entrepreneurs did not follow the Chinese example, which was readily available to them, but chose instead to prepare for the future by orienting themselves toward the past, clinging to all that had been bestowed on them. While this was certainly a form of conservatism, it should by now be apparent that any traditionalism in merchant enclaves like Laweyan can only be understood with reference to the modern conditions under which they developed. The reasons for their dedication to preserving the status quo will become clearer in the following chapters—it demands a more involved explanation than can be conveyed in a few lines, or even a few pages.

It is worth taking a moment, however, to consider how a relatively modern, urban community might become so attached to its past as to hinder its own future—a situation that, in its general form, is unique neither to Laweyan nor to Indonesia more generally. Nietzsche ([1874] 1980) addressed this condition in nineteenth-century Germany; his more global thoughts on "the advantage and disadvantage of history for life," although written with a very different context in mind, are nonetheless suggestive for twentieth-century Java. While a certain amount of history and historical consciousness are useful (and indeed essential) for the well-being of any society, he proposes, a surfeit of history has the effect of stifling the present and hindering the future—becoming, in short, a threat to life itself. All human action requires a certain forgetting of the past, a willingness to cut loose the memory and bonds of history and to move, unfettered, through the present and into the future. But the attraction of history and the sense of authority, awe, and security that it evokes are not easy to cast off:

> history belongs to the preserving and revering soul—to him who with loyalty and love looks back on his origins; through this reverence he, as it were, gives thanks for his existence. By tending with loving hands what has long survived he intends to preserve the conditions in which he grew up for those who will come after him—and so he serves life. The possession of ancestral furniture changes its meaning in such a soul: for the soul is rather possessed by the furniture. The small and limited, the decayed and obsolete receives its dignity and inviolability in that the preserving and revering soul of the antiquarian moves into these things and makes itself at home in the nest it builds there. The history of his city becomes for him the history of his self.... And so ... he looks beyond the ephemeral, curious, individual life and feels like the spirit of the house, the generation, and the city. (Nietzsche [1874] 1980, 19)

The hazard of this strong pull of history, Nietzsche believes, is that instead of putting the past at the service of life, the situation is reversed and life comes to serve the past, resulting in a withering of spirit and a paralysis of action. An excess of history thus leads to the extinguishing of the will or capacity for action; such a dedication to history "merely understands how to preserve life, not how to generate it" (21). And so it was in Laweyan. An exaggerated deference for the past, for local history itself, had a stultifying

9. A retired batik entrepreneur (left) at home with her family and neighbors.

effect on the present; the desire to immortalize the past foreclosed the possibilities of the future. The houses, the furniture, even the pictures on the wall became the unchanging signs of the past-in-the-present, objects that possessed their current owners as much as they were possessed by them. This is what I called earlier the making of the "unmodern." Although this state can be found in many settings and historical moments, the conditions under which any particular "unmodernity" is produced are unique and must be explained according to their own distinct social and historical circumstances. Laweyan's conservatism, its state of unmodernity, should not be taken for granted; in the chapters to come I will describe as best I can their genealogy.

Nowhere did I feel the hold of the past on the present as strongly as I did during my occasional visits to Bu Dinar's house in the kampong. One of the oldest homes still standing in Laweyan, it had been built in the 1880s in an old, ornate Javanese style, with a steeply arched, tiled roof. I liked walking the short distance to Bu Dinar's at sunset, *magrib*, when all of the nearby mosques and prayer halls would broadcast the call to prayer through loudspeakers, the Arabic chants rising and falling on the air in a strangely soothing cacaphony. As I slipped past the gates of the outer wall that hid the home from curious eyes, the house was enveloped in twilight shadow. Everything within it—the old Delft plates that adorned the wall, a tapestry that someone long dead had brought back as a souvenir from Mecca, two intricately carved wooden chests—seemed to have been left just as it had been for decades, undisturbed by the changes that had rippled through the kampong over the years. The house appeared as a cenotaph to its builders, Bu Dinar's great-grandparents on her father's side, batik entrepreneurs who were the ancestors of a number of prominent Laweyan merchants (Bu Dinar, however, was not one of them). Their portraits were displayed on the wall of the enclosed *pendhapa* (*pendopo*, I.), the main sitting area of the house where guests are received. Looking at the dignified, sepia-tinted photographs of this patriarch and matriarch, I could well imagine that their descendants had been constantly aware of living beneath their unblinking gaze—and, fearful of their disapproval, had dared not make any changes to this home-turned-museum.

On cool evenings during the wet season, as I listened to the rain beat down on the roof of the *pendhapa* and to Bu Dinar's stories about her childhood in that house, I shivered, half expecting to turn around and see her father, who had died years before, sitting quietly in a chair in the *pendhapa*, reading by the light of a dim lamp, or to see her strict mother in the inner room of the house (*dalem*), teaching her young daughters how to recite from the Qur'an. Bu Dinar had told me several times that she was thinking of moving to a smaller, more modern house on Laweyan Street: the kampong was too quiet at night, she complained, and the house too big and hard to take care of without the help of servants, which she could not afford. I was not convinced, though, that she would really have the heart to leave that house, where she had been raised and which echoed with the memories of the past. When I last visited her in 1996 she was still living there, and seemed to have abandoned her plan to leave the house behind.

Bu Dinar was one of those people who seemed, as in Berman's formulation, to live between worlds both modern and not-modern. Significantly, given her surroundings, Bu Dinar often made a point of identifying herself as a citizen of the modern world, someone more progressive in her outlook than most Laweyan people were. Whenever I came to visit she would send her daughter to the kitchen to bring out slices of Kraft cheese and white bread, an unusual snack to be served in a Javanese home (many Indonesians find the smell and taste of cheese offensive). She explained that she had "learned" to eat cheese from her older brother, who had gone to an elite Dutch high school in the late colonial period and boarded with a Dutch family, who had taught him European table manners and eating habits. He in turn had insisted that his sister also learn these things, which she had eventually taught to her own children (once a week they ate bread and cheese for breakfast instead of rice). Bu Dinar was obviously pleased to be able to share her "Western" habits with me. The Kraft cheese was her way of demonstrating that she and her family had from early on rejected local insularity and opened themselves up to a modern way of life.

And indeed they had, more than most Laweyan families. A number of her siblings had moved away from Solo and become high-ranked military officers or government bureaucrats. Hers had been the only old Laweyan family to go into the civil service or the military, she told me proudly. She herself had married an army officer of high rank, and had lived with him on another island of Indonesia. But her excursions into the modern world had ultimately failed her. She related how, after living comfortably as the wife of an officer, she had suddenly found herself a widow when someone had killed her husband by means of black magic (*guna-guna*), the signs of which she described in great detail: snakes that appeared in their house and car; a pressure lantern flying by itself across a room; a friend's discovery of burning incense and other strange objects behind their house; and a large tumor in her husband's stomach that revealed itself through a sudden, wrenching pain, "as if someone was grabbing hold of his stomach and twisting it." The tumor was removed surgically, but he died two weeks later. Left alone with two children and a small army pension, she had re-turned to Laweyan to live, once again, in the old house in the kampong.

Bu Dinar had a sharp sense of the contradictions between, as she put it, "modern times" (*jaman sekarang*, I.) and "the old days" (*jaman kuno, jaman dulu*, I.). The first time I had visited her, after meeting her at a wedding, she had taken me on a tour of her home. Explaining to me that this was an "old-fashioned Javanese house" (*rumah Jawa kuno*, I.), she had enthusiasti-cally described the various parts of the house and their ritual functions, encouraging me to take notes. Pausing before the ritual center of the house, which included a small chamber where a bride-to-be used to sleep the night before her wedding, she explained solemnly how "in the old days, young women would fast for forty days before their wedding, eating only a little bit at night. They had to be thin when they married. But in those days, women were strong. Even though they fasted, they didn't faint or feel weak. Nowadays women aren't that strong." She would often talk about the differences between "people in the old days" and "people nowadays." In the past, she informed me, many of the illnesses that plague people now, such as cancer, did not exist. This is because people drank *jamu*, herbal tonics, every day. And most ailments that did trouble people could be treated with traditional medicines, which really worked in those days. But the strange thing, she reflected, is that what worked in those days usually isn't effective anymore.

Bu Dinar sometimes felt trapped between the demands of "tradition" (*tradisi*, I.) and those of "modern times." For instance, when her mother died, most people in the community had assumed that she would hold the usual series of memorial *slametan*, ritual meals, during which neighbors, friends, and relatives gather to eat and chant Islamic prayers for the soul of the deceased (*tahlilan*).[32] These rites are held three, seven, forty, and one hundred days after the death, and then one year, two years, and finally, one thousand days after the death (in practice, the third-day rite is often omitted). On the advice of her brother in Jakarta, however, who was an ardent follower of a reformist Islamic organization, she had decided not to hold the seventh-day *slametan* after her mother's death. Reformist Islam condemns the *slametan* as being rooted in Javanese tradition rather than Islamic doctrine and, according to her brother, to hold such a ceremony would be sinful. So she called in seven young *santri* to recite prayers for her mother instead, and donated the money that she would have spent on the *slametan* to an orphanage. When neighbors showed up of their own accord seven days after her mother's death to help with the preparations for the ceremony that they assumed would take place that day, they were surprised and critical of her decision not to hold it. They took her decision as an abandonment of venerable Javanese traditions. Not liking the gossip that ensued, Bu Dinar succumbed to collective pressure and decided to hold the next *slametan* in the series, forty days after her mother's death.

To better grasp why the people of Laweyan had become so attached to their own past, weighed down by an ancestral heritage that owed much of its existence to the forces of modernization and the demands of the market, we need to return once again to the question of how money is related to status and hierarchy. In chapter 2 I argued that during the late colonial period, the wealth of the emergent Javanese bourgeoisie posed a challenge to the prevailing system of hierarchy as it had been fostered by the Dutch and the *priyayi*. According to the hegemonic ideologies of the *priyayi* elite, the possession of wealth should be intimately connected to the possession of power. The often substantial wealth of the Javanese merchant class disrupted the linkage between wealth and power, but not enough to negate the influence of these ideologies in Javanese society. To have money did not guarantee one a place of high status in colonial Java, because money and the market were considered to lie outside the sphere of *alus* Javanese culture, the site where high status was produced. Cultural value and authenticity, I suggested, were understood to be generated in the historical process itself. In order for money, a quintessentially acultural and ahistorical object, to be assimilated to the hierarchies of Javanese society and to generate status, it had to undergo a process of transformation to culturally recognizable signs of status.

To earn money, then, was never the final goal of Javanese merchants, because money alone could not engender status. This was made all too apparent by the categorical disparagement of the ethnic Chinese, a generally well-to-do minority group, by the Javanese majority: their wealth did not translate to status and respect in Javanese terms. Money was the means to an end, not an end in itself. However, the pressure to emulate the *priyayi* by making heavy investments in status—the way that money becomes valuable in Java—posed certain problems for members of the Javanese bourgeoisie, the nature of which will become clearer in the chapters to come. It also prevented them from accumulating the capital that would have enabled them to move beyond the sphere of petty commodity production and trade; in some cases, it prevented them even from keeping their businesses afloat.

The end of colonial rule did not bring about a radical dissolution of Javanese hierarchies or the dominance of *priyayi* values. Although the two decades after independence under the Sukarno regime are known as a relatively populist period in Indonesia's history, hierarchy was too deeply ingrained in Javanese society to be erased in such a short time.[33] Suharto's New Order regime, which brought a rapid end to almost all forms of populism, led to the rise of a system in which the bureaucratic elite took over many of the functions, privileges, and ideologies of the old colonial regime, effectively becoming a neo-*priyayi* class without the Dutch overlords. Concerns of status were again paramount, and the invocation of *tradisi*, tradition, to legitimate a conservative vision of social order seemed to repeat the efforts of the colonial *priyayi* class and Dutch administrators to shore up the *priyayi's* place at the apex of Javanese society (see Pemberton 1994).

Among members of the *sudagar* class, the means of generating status that had begun in the colonial period also continued through the Sukarno years and into the era of the New Order. In the latter period, "tradition" came to acquire a new and revitalized significance, especially after the rapid decline of so many businesses threatened the livelihood, and the very way of life, of this class. As in the colonial era, though, most Javanese merchants did not attempt to ally themselves economically or otherwise with those in power, but chose to remain independent. Money continued to occupy a crucial place in the social imaginary of the *sudagar* community, even though it was becoming an increasingly scarce commodity. The need to generate status through the conspicuous display of wealth was all the more important in the New Order, given the tenuousnesss of most people's economic (and therefore social) positions, as well as the rise of capitalist culture and conspicuous consumption in Indonesia more generally during this period.

As in the past, however, status did not follow automatically from the possession of wealth, but wealth *could* be symbolically converted to status through its "domestication," or transformation to the signs of cultural value. What we will next examine is how this conversion takes place, and how women serve as the prime agents of this domestication. To do this, we will need to peer once again behind the walls of Laweyan, into the homes usually so carefully guarded from public scrutiny. It will be necessary as well to venture into the marketplace, an intensely public space that is nevertheless intimately tied to the affairs of the *sudagar* household. In order to build a bridge between these domains, I will turn, as promised, to the issue of gender—a topic that almost always emerges when one speaks of the relationship between public and private spheres. And we will discover, finally, how important this issue is to understanding the workings of status and hierarchy in Java.

But ideas about gender are inextricably bound up with the politics of culture, and are therefore always subject to change. What remained in Solo were the traces of a particular configuration of gender, subjectivity, and economy that clearly predated the New Order, but that was slowly being eroded by powerful new ideologies of gender tied to the projects of modernization and development. In the next two chapters, however, I will speak of the older patterns of gender in the present tense, because they are still alive despite the gradual penetration of New Order ideals. We will see, then, how women act as domesticators—of money, desire, and men, among other things—in order to produce status for themselves and their families in the wider hierarchies of Javanese society.

Chapter Four

GENDER AND THE DOMESTICATION OF DESIRE

IN THE ENERVATING heat and humidity of midafternoon, the normally crowded streets of Solo become quiet as the city's residents retreat into the relative cool of their homes, to nap or simply to await the relief that evening, and a refreshing bath, will bring. Most shopkeepers close their establishments from 2:00 till 5:00 P.M., children come home from school, and government offices end their working day. At about three o'clock, just as a feeling of lethargy has overcome all but the most energetic of the city's inhabitants, the door to one of the many large homes of Laweyan opens and a well-dressed, amply endowed matron wearing a dark brown and blue batik sarong, a long-sleeved, flowered polyester *kebaya*, and flashing diamond earrings emerges into the hot sun, then climbs into the passenger seat of the *bécak* whose driver has been waiting for her. The *bécak* driver places her neatly tied bundle of batik cloth next to her on the seat and sets off down the dusty thoroughfare toward the center of town.

This scene is repeated at a number of points along the road. One by one, Laweyan women leave their houses, step into a *bécak*, and head east, in the direction of Pasar Klewer (Klewer Market), the enormous, two-story emporium specializing in textiles and clothing that covers more than a city block. One of the hubs of Solo's economy, its traders range from roving village women hawking garlic and onions from a basket, to petty retailers selling cheap clothing and accessories, to wealthy wholesalers of batiks and other textiles, some of whom even have telephones in their well-stocked stalls. Located right outside the main gates leading to the town square (*alun-alun*) and the Kraton, with a recent addition to the market intruding just inside the gates, Pasar Klewer seems to flout the quietism and supposed refinement of the palace with its brash, noisy, and openly materialistic atmosphere.

Approaching the marketplace, the narrow road becomes increasingly congested with *bécaks* that converge from all directions, jockeying for space with bicycles, cars, minivans, and motorcycles. When the woman arrives at her destination, she delicately disembarks, hands the driver a 500-*rupiah* note, and pushes her way through the tangle of food vendors who cluster at the entrance to the marketplace, selling everything from tangerines to bowls of steaming meatball soup. Once inside, she wends her way intently through the vast labyrinth of more than two thousand stalls. Knowing exactly where her clients, usually longtime acquaintances, have their stalls,

10. Pasar Klewer, Solo's large bazaar specializing in the sale of batik and other textiles.

she makes the rounds from one stall to another, occasionally stopping to greet friends or to buy snacks from peddlers roaming the aisles. At various stalls, she offers samples of batik cloth that she has brought to sell, or tries—often unsuccessfully—to collect payment on debts. And at each stopping point, she exchanges business information, pleasantries, and gossip with the market trader, which, if it is a slow time, may be the only transaction that takes place between them. Still, it is the hope of bringing back money that makes the Laweyan *juragan* leave the comfort of her home in the afternoon heat, since she knows that late in the day is when the market traders are likely to have the greatest amount of cash at their disposal.

The majority of the faces that one sees in Pasar Klewer, buyers as well as sellers, are female. Indeed, the Solonese say that the market is a woman's world (*donyané wong wédok*). Among the ethnic Javanese of Solo, there is no question that women control the marketplace, although there are a number of male traders of Chinese and Arab descent.[1] The prevailing stereotype is that while the Solonese woman goes to the marketplace to earn a living, her husband stays at home, amusing himself by whistling to his songbirds.[2] Solonese men of the middle classes are masters of what has been called "conspicuous leisure" (Veblen [1899] 1979). This leisurely image is perfectly in keeping with the *priyayi* emphasis on cultivating the art of quiet contemplation and on keeping a refined distance from worldly affairs.

It is considered a notorious truth that batik firms or market stalls entrusted to the control of men are doomed to failure, a point that the Solo-born author Arswendo Atmowiloto highlights in a section of dialogue from his novel *Canting:*[3] "Pasar Klewer is a woman's market. Just look, where do you see a husband-and-wife team that's successful in Pasar Klewer? Count them! If there are more than ten, cut my throat. Cut it just like that. A team like that will never work. Because it'll always be the woman who runs the show. A husband in Pasar Klewer just sits at his wife's ass. That's not good for a man" (1986, 89). Even those men who accompany their wives or mothers to the market to trade generally prefer not to take too active a role in business transactions, as one would gather from the passage just cited. "Here the men usually just help us out a little," women traders in Pasar Klewer say. I witnessed a typical example of this one day when a Klewer trader went off to the mosque across the street for midday prayers, leaving her husband to mind the stall. While she was gone, another trader came to collect payment on a debt. The moment he saw her approaching the stall, the man shook his head, saying, "She's off at the mosque. Come back in fifteen minutes." The woman nodded in understanding and moved on. No further explanation was needed; this was women's business, and it would have been a waste of her time to insist that the man take responsibility for financial transactions that were obviously in his wife's domain.

In this sense, the relationship of men and women to money at the marketplace closely parallels the situation often found in Javanese homes. In most families, regardless of social standing or occupation, it is the wife who handles household finances. Javanese women often voice the opinion that men are incompetent in managing money, and many men seem to agree (see H. Geertz 1961; Jay 1969). Husbands are expected to turn over most or all of their income to their wives, who in turn allocate it as they see fit for household expenditures, sometimes giving their husbands only pocket money with which to buy cigarettes or snacks. Although one hears complaints on both sides—the wife grumbling that her husband keeps more for himself than he should, while the husband feels that his wife demands too much from him—this financial arrangement is widely accepted as the proper one between husband and wife.

The obligation for a man to hand over his wages to his wife has almost the force of law in Java. At a wedding that I attended in a village not far from Solo, the village headman delivered a typical lecture of fatherly advice to the bride and groom, amplified through the public address system for all the guests to hear, during the course of which he drew attention to "the notion that we Javanese have of 'female money' (*dhuwité wédok*)." "This means," he instructed the young couple, "that the husband should set aside a portion of his wage every month to turn over to his wife." Many people—women in particular—would argue that a man should give his entire salary to his wife, not just a portion of it.

A number of scholars have remarked on the prominent economic roles of Javanese women and their central position in the household.[4] These scholars almost always link women's dominance in the household to their economic clout, particularly inside the home. In *The Javanese Family*, for example, Hildred Geertz finds that within the domestic domain, "The wife makes most of the decisions; she controls all family finances, and although she gives her husband formal deference and consults with him on major matters, it is usually she who is dominant" (1961, 46). The issue of who, really, is the "head" of the household remains unresolved, however. As Geertz suggests, men frequently receive the deference of other family members, including that of their wives, which could be taken to indicate their dominance in the household. In formal dealings with the outside world, such as matters concerning the state bureaucracy, men are also usually considered the heads of their households. However, the fact that most decisions about the daily running of the household are left to the wife, and that she almost always holds the family's purse strings, leads one to suspect that in many households men may serve more as figureheads than anything else.

A small ritual that is included in many Javanese wedding ceremonies seems to encapsulate the ambivalence with which the gendered division of domestic power is viewed in Java. At a certain point in the ceremony, the bride and groom approach each other. When a few paces still remain between them, each one takes up a small packet of betel (*sirih*) and throws it at the other, the idea being that the one whose betel hits the other person first will be the dominant partner in the marriage. It is often said that the bride should make sure that she loses the contest, but apparently the outcome is not always predictable. In a tone of mild amusement, Augusta de Wit describes this nuptial ritual as she observed it in the early twentieth century:

> With measured steps, the two advanced towards each other; and whilst yet at some distance paused. Two small bags of sirih-leaves containing chalk and betel-nuts were handed them; and with a quick movement each threw his at the other's head. The bride's little bag struck the groom full in the face. "It is she that will rule the roost," said one of the women, chuckling. And I fancied I saw a gleam of satisfaction pass over the bride's demure little face, half hidden though it was by the strings of beads and jessamine flowers dependent from her head dress. The next moment, however, she had humbly knelt down on the floor. One of the bridesmaids handed her a basin full of water and a towel; and she proceeded to wash her husband's feet, in token of loyalty and loving submission. ([1912] 1984, 306–7)

The dominant gender ideologies of Javanese society dictate that the wife should defer to her husband's greater prestige and authority as the head of the household; thus, the bride is (in theory) supposed to make sure that the groom wins the betel battle, and she washes his foot "in token of loyalty and loving submission." However, the reality of the situation is that in many Javanese households, women enjoy a de facto power which out-weighs that of their husbands. Consequently, no one is too surprised if the bride's betel strikes the groom first. Indeed, some Javanese grooms seem to fear this possible outcome. One man described to me a wedding he had attended where the groom had ducked out of the way when the bride threw her betel. Then, grasping his chance, he took careful aim at his wife-to-be and flung his betel at her as hard as he could! A comment made by Robert Jay may shed light on why men are afraid to lose the contest to their brides: men in Java, he writes, are "probably among the most henpecked lot of husbands anywhere in the world" (1969, 92).

On a number of levels, Javanese women do seem to fare quite well rela-tive to their spouses. This can be seen, for example, in prevalent patterns of inheritance and property ownership. Both descent and inheritance are reckoned bilaterally in Java. Javanese custom prescribes that daughters and sons should inherit equal shares of property from their parents; this can include land, houses, jewelry, money, and other valuables.[5] Although some strict Muslims prefer to follow Islamic rules of inheritance, whereby a brother receives two shares for every single share that his sister receives, my impression in Solo was that more people followed the prescription of "Javanese custom" (*adat Jawa*)—that is, equal inheritance for males and females—than that of "Islamic law" (*hukum Islam*), which some people felt was unfair to women.

Women often own property separately from their husbands, especially property that they have brought with them into the marriage or inherited from their parents, and they may dispose of it as they please. Husbands have no claim over their wives' property and, in the event of divorce, a woman may take with her whatever she inherited or otherwise owned apart from her husband. (The reverse is also true: women do not have a claim over their husbands' property.) Property that has been acquired during the marriage and owned jointly by both partners (*gana-gini*) is usually divided evenly between them if they are divorced.

I found that husbands and wives were often remarkably independent, even businesslike, in their financial affairs. Bu Hartati, a young *juragan* and devout Muslim who was rather old-fashioned in her outlook for someone of her age, informed me that she and her husband kept their money sepa-rately. She ran the *batik tulis* side of their business while he managed the *batik cap* business, and they considered the money that each earned from their respective ends of the business to be their own. "I don't like to have to ask for money," she told me. "That's why I have my own money. If I want to buy clothes for myself, I use my own money. If I happen to be short of cash, sometimes I'll borrow some from my husband, though once in a while he tells me I don't need to pay him back. But usually we keep track of who pays for what, and try to keep things even." This independent attitude toward managing money does not appear to be a recent development; some of the elderly women I knew had also been raised to regard this approach as customary.

That Javanese women are very important economic contributors to their households in their own right holds true not only for women of the merchant class. Women's income through agricultural or other wage labor, craft manufacture, business, or employment in the civil service or other professions frequently equals or exceeds their husbands' financial contributions to the family. In fact, it is not uncommon in Solo and its environs for a woman to be the main or even the sole breadwinner for her family. This is certainly the case in households where men are absent (some households are headed by women alone, partly because of the high divorce rate in Java), but it is also sometimes true in households where both spouses are present. "It's an Islamic obligation for a husband to support his wife (*mencukupi nafkah*, I.)," an administrator of an Islamic university informed me, "but in Solo, women don't insist on that. Wives don't make all sorts of demands of their husbands here, but they're still loyal to them." Although Solo does have a reputation in Java for having especially independent women who contribute more than their share to the family financially, the pattern of women earning a substantial portion of their households' incomes is not limited to this city alone.

In Solo's merchant community, women are commonly the major providers for their families as textile entrepreneurs or market traders, while their husbands take a back seat to them in running the family business and in managing household finances. What Raffles observed in the early nineteenth century continues to be the rule in Solo today: among Javanese, women dominate the markets, from petty retail trade up to the lucrative large-scale wholesale trade in agricultural products, textiles, and other commodities. In the batik community this is particularly true. In Laweyan, women often play the crucial roles in running their businesses as well as their households. Their influence in the family and the community is, as a result, quite extraordinary. From what I could determine, this has always been the case. Reminiscing about past generations, Bu Dinar once summed up local women's roles quite succinctly: "The women ran almost everything. They ran the household and looked after the kids, they supervised the batik making and dyeing, and they paid the workers their wages. If their husbands wanted money, they would ask their wives for it, and get mad if it wasn't enough. A Laweyan woman who was left by her husband wouldn't be afraid. But a man who was left by his wife wouldn't know what to do."

STATUS, STYLE, AND MONEY

The dominance of women in their households, combined with their economic strength and autonomy, would seem to suggest a degree of social and economic status for Javanese women comparable to that of men. To the extent that status can be measured by financial independence, influence in the family, and the freedom to make one's own decisions, many women do enjoy, at least in some respects, nearly equal standing to men.

Yet the notion of "status" is a very complex one in Java, not reducible to economic position or to any other simple factor. As we have seen, status is measured not only on the basis of factors like wealth, occupation, education, and descent line, but also according to somewhat less tangible qualities, such as degree of cultural refinement, mastery of elaborate linguistic etiquette and social skills, and the reputed possession of spiritual potency. Scholars of Javanese society are generally quick to point out that while women have economic power and considerable control over household affairs, in the realm of prestige they fall far short of men.[6] This seems to detract from society's overall evaluation of their status. According to key gender ideologies, women have certain character traits that doom them to an inferior station in life no matter how much money they earn or how much power they wield in the household (Hatley 1990; Keeler 1987, 1990).

What is it about women that relegates them to this (ideologically, at least) inferior position? Ironically, one of the very characteristics that appears to give women so much autonomy and power in the household—their economic prowess—is also one of the main factors detracting from their prestige. In the central ideologies of Javanese society, particularly those that are associated with the *priyayi* class, there is an undeniable devaluation of the economic activities for which women and traders are known. Excessive attention to financial matters and to the pursuit of wealth, as I discussed earlier, is said to be a sign of low status, lack of refinement, and a corresponding lack of spiritual potency.[7] Matters of money, especially where bargaining or the open pursuit of profit are involved, are considered *kasar*. Individuals who are mindful of their prestige must be careful never to show too much concern with money, lest they be seen as *kasar*, too.

The idea that a preoccupation with money points to low status—an idea that is strongest among traditional *priyayi* elites but that is also held, to some extent, by nonelites—shows how deeply ingrained *priyayi* ideologies are in Javanese society. The influence of *priyayi* values has continued into the New Order, in a process that has been referred to as "priyayization," whereby *priyayi* norms and values are adopted by other elements of the population (see Djajadiningrat-Nieuwenhuis 1987). While Javanese men are increasingly involved in business, especially in the more modern sectors of the economy, and although wealth is, in practice, a very important source of status in contemporary Indonesia, there remains a certain taint to business matters and to the handling of money, as well as a continued association of the less savory aspects of monetary and mercantile pursuits with women and ethnic minorities.

Women, then, appear to be destined to inhabit the low-status, "coarse" realm of Javanese social and cultural hierarchies. Their firm obligation as wives and mothers is to attend to financial matters: they are supposed to see to it that every last *rupiah* of the family's money is wisely spent. Those who are traders must bargain and calculate shrewdly in order to compete successfully in the overcrowded marketplace, where acting refined is out of the question. Other aspects of women's conduct also seem to support the conclusion that women are more *kasar*, and therefore of lower status, than men. Women are quicker to use low, or *kasar*, forms of Javanese language than men are, and to behave without embarrassment in ways that many men would feel to be beneath their dignity. In the marketplace, wealthy women traders can be seen slapping each other on the arm in a gesture of friendliness, or hurling pieces of cloth across the aisles to each other. They loll about on the counters in front of their stalls and climb over them in a rather undignified manner when they want to enter or leave the stall, toss garbage into the aisles, and call out loudly to attract the attention of potential customers ("What are you looking for, ma'am?") or passing food vendors ("Hey, iced tea! Over here!"). Few men of similar socioeconomic status would be willing to comport themselves this way in a public setting; they would consider such behavior demeaning and damaging to their prestige.

It is not only in the marketplace that women can be found conducting themselves in a manner that some might think indelicate. At a weekly *arisan* meeting attended by well-heeled, middle-aged Laweyan women, someone announced that the son of one of the members present, Bu Susanto, had just passed his university examination to become an engineer. This created a stir of excitement among the ladies, and, quite spontaneously, one of them picked up a piece of starfruit that was lying on a tray nearby and flung it across the room at Bu Susanto, exclaiming warmly, "Why didn't you tell us sooner?!" Nor was it unusual to find the same ladies, the elites of the neighborhood, throwing wads of money at one another during the *arisan* rather than going to the trouble of getting up from the mats upon which they sat in order to tender the money by hand.

It would be difficult to imagine the husbands of these women behaving so, or even to imagine the women themselves being willing to act this freely if there were men around. However, this, like their willingness to handle money, should not be taken as an indication that women are considered to be *kasar*, or of low status, in any absolute sense. Rather, in many situations, Javanese women have a broader range of social and linguistic styles available to them than do men (see Keeler 1990). To the extent that their comportment and speech are accorded less weight than men's, women have the freedom to engage with relative impunity in behavior that would be compromising to men's status. Women are not thought incapable of behaving in an *alus* manner—indeed, it is primarily women, not men, who are given the task of educating their male and female children in linguistic and behavioral politesse—but the wider range of social styles deemed acceptable for women gives them the reputation for behaving erratically, and not always in accordance with standards of refined behavior.

Men's interactions with each other tend to be stiff and formal, marked by an attention to social and linguistic decorum that is almost painful to watch when one has become accustomed to the earthier, more relaxed styles of women (see H. Geertz 1961). The higher a man's social standing, the more circumscribed his range of behavioral and speech styles must be in order to protect and regenerate his status, for style is a critical element of an individual's status image (see J. Errington 1988; Keeler 1987, 1990). Although this is also true for women, the latter are not expected to control their language and conduct to the same degree as men.[8] One reason for this, as Ward Keeler explains, is that a woman's status is defined in many situations by that of her husband; therefore a woman who marries a high-status man will automatically be respected. "Her style, as long as it isn't really outrageous, will not be thought to undermine the family's status. A man's status is of course also defined by wealth and means of livelihood, not just style. But he is expected to present himself to the world fairly carefully, the more carefully the higher his status" (1990, 144–45; see also Hatley 1990, 184).

As the head of the household, in name if not necessarily in terms of actual power to control day-to-day affairs, the husband and father represents his family to the wider society.[9] The members of his family draw their status from *his* status, at least in theory. A woman not only takes on her husband's name at the time of marriage; she also acquires his rank. Thus, a trader in Pasar Klewer whose husband was the headman (*lurah*) in a village outside Solo was addressed respectfully by people in the market as "Mrs. Headman" (Bu Lurah), even though she maintained a separate household in the city and rarely spent time in her husband's village.

If we consider the case of the Javanese merchant family, though, a paradox seems to arise. On the one hand, as is true for families from other social groups, the status of the wife and children may be said to derive in large measure from that of the husband. On the other hand, in the regions of Solo and Yogyakarta in particular, in many instances it is the wife, not the husband, who is active in running the family business. Bearing in mind that wealth is the most important determinant of status for the merchant family, and that it is the wife who produces wealth, then we are faced with the thorny question: is it the wife or the husband who is generating status for the family? The matter is complicated further by *priyayi* ideologies, which hold that to devote oneself openly to the pursuit of economic gain is itself indicative of low status. This would appear to put the entrepreneur or trader in a double bind: at the same time that she accumulates wealth, which is intended to *produce* status, she is also engaging in behavior that is *detrimental* to status.

This paradox can never be completely resolved. However, given the symbolic dominance of the husband in the family, coupled with the relative freedom that women have to conduct themselves in ways typically marked as "low-status," a woman can engage in trade without her family's status (including her own) suffering as a result. By insulating her husband from trade and, more broadly, from most matters having to do with money, a wife protects her husband's status, and by extension protects her entire family's position in the social hierarchy. Yet her active role in economic production is critical to the production of her family's status.

As I have pointed out, high status does not follow automatically from wealth. In order for wealth to lead to heightened status, it must first undergo a process of symbolic conversion to the cultural signs of status. By accumulating wealth, the merchant does not immediately produce status for her family; rather, it is more appropriate to say that she produces the *means* by which status is produced. This distinction turns out to be important for understanding the relationships of wealth, status, and gender in Java. In generating status for the family, a woman's latitude to disregard some of the conventions that constrain behavior in Javanese society is as essential as a man's cautiousness in adhering to those conventions. Husbands and wives play complementary roles in the process of converting wealth to status.

Arswendo Atmowiloto's novel *Canting* (1986) concerns the family of a titled member of the Solonese *priyayi* elite, Pak Bei Sestrokusuma, and his wife, a former batik worker who runs a batik firm at home and a stall at Pasar Klewer. Exploring the internal social contradictions in this family, the author shows how Pak Bei Sestro(kusuma), who considers himself a true upholder of *priyayi* values, tries to dissociate himself from his wife's mercantile activities. In a scene that takes place in 1962, Pak Bei Sestro is attending a nighttime gathering of male scions of the Kraton, when a drunken member of the group confronts him: "Where's Bei Sestro? Bei Sestro is a capitalist." But Bei Sestro retorts quickly, "No. I'm not a capitalist. It's my wife who's the capitalist. She's the one with the workers, the one who sells batik at Pasar Klewer, the one who shops. It's my wife who's a capitalist. I've never had anything to do with it" (23).[10] By refusing any connection with his wife's "ignoble" occupation, Pak Bei Sestro manages to protect his *priyayi* image, while still availing himself freely of the money earned by his wife in order to boost his social position. At the same time, his wife, formerly a lower-class laborer, enjoys the prestige of having the aristocratic title "Bu Bei" attached to her name, which elevates her to a social position superior to that of a mere merchant.

GENDER, DESIRE, AND SELF-CONTROL

Among Solonese, even those men who do not properly qualify as *priyayi* through rank or title often prefer to avoid trade or other dealings with money as much as possible. Amazingly, this includes men of the merchant class. Most men find bargaining, which is a key component of many business transactions in Java, to be particularly embarrassing. One example of this was presented to me by Pak Usman, a Kauman man in his seventies who was of high status because of his prominent position in Solo's Muslim community and by virtue of the considerable wealth that he and his wife had accumulated in the batik business. He remarked that even at his age, he preferred riding a motorcycle to taking a *bécak* for traveling short distances. The reason, he admitted, was that "sometimes when you try to bargain with the *bécak* drivers, they get mad at you," a remark that might seem a bit odd, considering that Pak Usman had earned his living in business. In contrast, his wife, who was certainly of high status as well, never hesitated a moment to haggle over a fare with a *bécak* driver (nor did she have any qualms about trying to sell a piece of batik to a visiting American anthropologist at a price significantly higher than its market value). Bargaining and other dealings with money are not tainted for women as they are for men.

Women attribute men's reluctance to bargain to its making them feel socially awkward or ill at ease. Bu Hartati, who was eight months pregnant, told me rather proudly that despite her condition, she was still going to Pasar Klewer almost every day to market the textiles that she and her husband produced in their small firm. For a while, her husband had tried to take over the marketing, but this had resulted in shrinking profits for their business. The reason, she said, was that her husband was too uncomfortable to bargain with the shrewd traders at the market for a better price than what they initially offered. "If someone offers him 3,500 *rupiah* for a piece of cloth, he's too embarrassed to ask for 5,000. Most men are like that. In Solo everything has to be *alus*. . . . But *I* know how to bargain without feeling awkward about it: 'I'm sorry, ma'am, but 3,500 isn't quite enough' (*Nyuwun pangapunten, Bu, tiga setengah dèrèng saged*)," she intoned in high Javanese, demonstrating her own firm but polite style of bargaining. She added that most women are capable of bargaining effectively without embarrassment, whereas few men have this ability.

Just as it is a matter of honor for a man not to bargain, it is a matter of pride for a woman not to pay a penny more for an item than it is worth, or to sell for too little profit. Women constantly compare notes on how much they have paid for things or at what price they have sold their goods, and a woman who has overpaid or sold too cheaply will be informed of this in no uncertain terms by her female friends and relatives. (I personally experienced this mild shaming on a number of occasions.) In other words, while a man believes that bargaining will cause him to lose face, a woman loses face by *not* bargaining.

At the root of men's reluctance to bargain is the fear of loss of control, either on their own part or on the part of their "opponent." One is often struck by the bland, stilted quality of conversations between elite men in Java, even between men who have known each other for many years. Men are more likely than women to speak to each other in high Javanese, an elaborate, controlled form of the language that allows the speaker to spend a great deal of time saying almost nothing at all. (This is considered a real art in Java.) Affect and communicativeness are readily sacrificed for the sake of maintaining impeccable linguistic propriety, *alus* behavior, and smooth social relations, all of which are essential to the preservation of status, men's status in particular. The nature of bargaining, however, makes it impossible for those involved to preserve an image of being *ikhlas*—detached, controlled, in a state of equanimity, without desire or emotional investment—and thus able to adhere to the codes of behavior that preserve status. As James Siegel remarks, "Ordinarily the purpose of speaking Javanese is to leave one's desires behind, outside of speech. But there can be no disguise of the purpose of bargaining: it is a frank acknowledgment of wants" (1986, 165).

Normally a man of high status like Pak Usman would expect deferential, or at very least polite, behavior from a low-status *bécak* driver. His discomfort with bargaining was that it sometimes led to a situation in which social hierarchy and balance were disturbed, which was the case (at least from his perspective) whenever a *bécak* driver became "angry" with him. This inability to command deference was in itself compromising to Pak Usman's status. Even more distasteful to Pak Usman was the possibility that he himself might lose control, becoming angry in response to the *bécak* driver. This would detract from his status even further, not only because losing control is something that a person of high status should not do under any circumstance, but especially because it would mean losing his temper over a trivial matter of money, and in response to a person of lower status than himself, someone whom he ordinarily would not consider deserving of much attention. Pak Usman's response was to remove himself from this potentially compromising situation altogether by choosing to ride a motorcycle instead of hiring a *bécak*.

It is this feeling of discomfort that leads men to leave the business of bargaining to their wives, something upon which Siegel also comments: "One sees here why men, more protective of their status than women, avoid the market. They are addressed in a language lower than they often feel they deserve. But perhaps worse than that is having to attend to the mental calculations of someone whom they could otherwise disregard, and in the process, having to respond with language they would prefer to keep to themselves" (1986, 166). Even though it is possible to bargain using the polite and respectful forms of high Javanese, given that all the necessary lexical items are present, to do so, in fact, is usually not to one's economic benefit. Each party to a round of bargaining hopes that the outcome will be in his or her own favor, either by maximizing profit or minimizing expenditure. Paying too much attention to linguistic amenities reduces the possibility of turning the bargaining to one's advantage, since it implies that one is willing to sacrifice personal economic gain for the sake of preserving dignity and social decorum. To speak high Javanese is to offer deference, and at the same time to suppress one's own desires (Siegel 1986). This utterly contradicts the purpose of bargaining, which is, most basically, to gain at another's expense. However, to put aside the protective veneer of high Javanese and the polite behavior that must accompany it is to run the risk of allowing one's emotions and behavior to escape from control. We can see, then, why Javanese men in Solo usually steer clear of the marketplace. Although they often claim disdain for the market and dislike of its *kasar* atmosphere (in keeping with *priyayi* ideologies denigrating the pursuit of wealth), it appears that what they fear most is the possibility of losing the image of self-control, equanimity, and disinterest in personal gain that is so important for maintaining men's status.

While visiting Pasar Klewer one day, I witnessed a particularly amusing bout of bargaining between two experienced traders, which brought home to me the difference between women's and men's styles of interaction, especially with regard to the notion of self-control. One of the traders, Bu Sita, was a friendly woman, quite successful in business, who had owned a stall in the market for a number of years. The other was a self-assured woman who wanted to buy a quantity of batik wholesale from Bu Sita to sell again elsewhere. The pace of their bargaining was fast and furious, and the language used by the women, all low Javanese, was rough, their tone almost a growl. The buyer was pointing out imperfections in the cloth and making low offers, while the seller, Bu Sita, kept refusing, insisting on a higher price. The bargaining became more and more intense, and the two of them seemed to be getting angrier and angrier with each other, to the point where I was beginning to wonder if they would actually come to blows. All of a sudden, before I knew what was happening, they both broke into broad grins, slapped each other on the arm jovially, and the sale was made, with sounds of disgust and exasperation, obviously exaggerated, coming from the buyer as she looked at the prices on the receipt that Bu Sita was writing for her. They chuckled together, chatted amicably and inquired about each other's families, the tone of their conversation changing dramatically from what it had been just moments earlier. It was only at that point that I realized the women were old friends who had been doing business together for years.

The hostility that I had witnessed between these two traders was not genuine, it turned out. As professional traders, they had temporarily put aside their friendship so that each could bargain effectively, to her own advantage. Had they been forced by concerns of etiquette to treat each other as old friends from the outset, it would have been difficult for them to bargain at all. As women, they had the flexibility to shift registers abruptly without fearing loss of face, or even loss of friendship. Two Javanese men would be much less apt to put on such a display, however, since even a semblance of strong emotion like anger would be construed as lack of control. Their status would be threatened, as would be their friendship.

Sudden shifts in language and behavior are fairly common in the marketplace, and in women's interactions more generally. Keeler (1990) notes that women's lability in style is considered by some Javanese as a sign that women are by their very nature lacking in self-control. Dominated by their impulses and emotions, their behavior is never fully predictable. This categorization of women, he adds, has certain implications for their social status relative to men. Building on an argument first proposed by Benedict Anderson (1990c), which ties the notion of spiritual potency to status in Javanese culture, Keeler argues that generalizations about women's lack of self-control ultimately point to their lack of spiritual potency and consequent lower status with regard to men.

It is useful to recall here Anderson's exploration of Javanese ideologies of spiritual potency ("Power"). To grossly simplify his more elaborate explanation: this form of Power goes beyond ordinary worldly power as it generally understood in the West. It is a kind of divine energy and mystical inner strength that enables an individual to control himself, other people, and his environment without the use of crude physical, political, or material force. This Power is said to be accumulated and concentrated through ascetic exercise and through other forms of self-discipline that involve sustained control over one's personal passions, instincts, and desires. The more self-discipline an individual has, the more spiritual power he amasses, which in turn leads to further self-control as well as the ability to master supernatural forces and the wills of other human beings.

A calm, *alus* demeanor is taken to indicate that an individual possesses a large store of personal Power. Achieving high status is contingent on having this Power, and consequently, on projecting an image of having total but effortless mastery over the inner passions. Powerful persons can thus be recognized from their poise, restraint, and equanimity in all situations. Conversely, those who are unable to control their emotions, speech, or behavior demonstrate their lack of spiritual potency (Anderson 1990c; see also Keeler 1987; Hatley 1990). Excessive attention to the pursuit of personal gain, including economic profit, is seen as a sign of greed and self-interest, betokening lack of Power and low status.

Anderson does not directly address the issue of gender, intending primarily, as he writes in a later retrospective piece, to offer an alternative, culturally unique perspective on Weber's concept of charisma (Anderson 1990b). Whether this model of Power might apply differently to women or men is beyond the scope and intent of the article: the relationship of women to Power is not specifically discussed (see Djajadiningrat-Nieuwenhuis 1987, 46). The argument does clearly link male sexual potency and spiritual potency, however, and the examples cited of Powerful figures are all male.

Later studies of gender in Java have been more explicit in revealing the male-centered focus of the ideology of spiritual potency (see Hatley 1990; Djajadiningrat-Nieuwenhuis 1987). These gender ideologies present an unproblematic image of men as potent, self-controlled, and in possession of the higher mental and spiritual faculties that allow them to maintain order in their own lives and in the social and supernatural world. Women, in contrast, are depicted as spiritually impotent, less rational than men, and lacking in self-control. Such categorical statements about the nature of the sexes are well in keeping with an ideological system that places men at the center of the social, moral, and political order. These ideologies have been generated and reinforced not only by the values of the *priyayi* but also by the patriarchal tendencies of Dutch colonial rule, by Islamic gender ideologies asserting men's superior capacity for self-control,[11] and by the policies of the Indonesian state and the representations of the mass media.

Almost everyone I knew in Java, men and women alike, gave lip service to the notion that the husband/father is the head of the household, and therefore deserving of deferential behavior from every other member of the family. Men also dominate the political order, from the community level up to the national level, and serve as the representatives of their households in most matters concerning the local and state bureaucracies. It is hardly surprising, then, to find gender stereotypes that associate women with low-status behavior—capriciousness, lack of control, emotionality—and men with the positive, high-status qualities of behavioral stability and self-control.

A CONTRARY VIEW: THE DANGER OF MEN'S DESIRE

I stress the *ideological* nature of these constructs, because in many situations one finds an entirely different conceptualization of human nature in Java. The alternative view is also formulaic, but it contradicts the dominant ideological premise that to be male is to have greater self-control, whereas to be female is to be lacking in control. According to this vision of male and female nature, *men* find it much more difficult to restrain their innate passions and desires (*nafsu* or *nepsu*) than do women. While both men and women are subject to the sometimes overwhelming influence of their own desires, it is *women*, not men, who are believed to have more ability to control themselves. Although this idea is expressed more openly and more often by women than by men, as one might expect, it is *not* a view held exclusively by women; men, too, often make statements or engage in actions that support this belief. I would argue, in fact, that this conception of the nature of the sexes underlies key roles that men and women play in the household, and that it forms the basis for their practices in many other spheres of social life.

By underscoring this alternative understanding of gender and self-control, I do not intend to offer it as a "female countercultural" model that undermines male views. Nor do I propose that this is the "true" Javanese model, to be accorded absolute primacy over competing models. Rather, this is a view of human nature that is invoked in specific contexts by men as well as women, *priyayi* and non-*priyayi*, devout Muslims and non-Muslims. It contradicts dominant gender ideologies, yet its proponents include people who in other situations would uphold the dominant ideology of male potency without hesitation. Even to characterize this contradiction as a conflict between ideology and practice misses the mark, because these two conflicting representations of gender and self-control are both verbalized as axiomatic truths *and* expressed implicitly in people's actions. The key to understanding these contradictory views of gender is to see them as alternative paradigms that can be called on to legitimate and to interpret the actions of men and women in different contexts. In formal discourse the hegemonic view of male potency and self-control is more likely to be emphasized, while the view that men have less self-control than women often comes to the fore in casual discourse when there is less is at stake ideologically.

At the heart of these competing ideas about instinctual self-control are culturally specific understandings of gendered subjectivity that people constantly call on in order to explain, anticipate, criticize, or justify behavior, their own as well as others'. In particular, it is important to look at the ways that the concept of desire, *nafsu*, is figured in a specifically Javanese sense. Many Javanese believe that to experience desire is normal to the human condition, but to be governed by desire is dangerous, not only to the individual but also to the family and to society. Here, one should distinguish between ordinary desires and those that are excessive and therefore potentially disturbing both to an individual's internal equilbrium and to the social relationships in which he or she participates. *Nafsu* often connotes ardent longing or passionate desire that, if left totally uncontrolled, causes people to behave in an unbalanced, irrational, or socially unacceptable manner.[12]

Nafsu may take many forms, but the most powerful, and therefore potentially most dangerous, desires are those for sex and money—lust and greed, which are sometimes seen as intrinsically related. Many Javanese men and women seem to take as a given that men have an innately greater desire for sex than women, and that this desire is extremely difficult for them to suppress. Although this notion runs counter to both Javanese and Islamic ideologies that hold males to have greater control of their instincts and emotions than females, I encountered it often enough to be convinced that it was not just the idiosyncratic opinion of a few individuals. The degree to which it actually contradicts the ideology of male potency is debatable, however, since it reaffirms male sexual potency—a concomitant of male spiritual potency (Anderson 1990c)—even as it challenges men's ability to master their passions.[13]

In relation to economic practices, this view of the inherent differences between men and women leads Javanese people in Solo to conclude that women are "naturally" better suited to managing domestic finances, the family firm, or the marketplace, drawing a clear connection between controlling money and controlling one's passions. Pak Djohari, who was an unusually candid man, summed it up quite frankly for me one day: "Women make better traders and entrepreneurs than men, because men have greater lust (*syahwat*) than women. Men can never hold onto money for long, because if you give them money, they'll spend it on getting women. Give 'em enough money, and they'll have more than one wife, either out in the open or on the sly. Men have greater desires than women (*Nafsuné niku, gedhé wong lanang*). It's always men who spend money on women, who 'buy' women. Who ever heard of a woman buying a man?" He paused for a moment, then continued, "You know, if I were to say these things to most Javanese, they would tell me it was indecent (*saru*), that I was *kasar*. But maybe these are things that you need to know."

Pak Djohari's views were actually shared by many people. A female merchant once remarked to me that among Javanese in Solo, women dominate trade because they are careful with money, they do not squander it. "When men get ahold of money, they use it to take another wife, or to gamble," she said. Another woman observed along the same lines that "men can't hold onto money—as soon as they get their hands on it they just go out and buy whatever they feel like. But women usually think first: 'Do I really need this or not?'" Men were frequently willing to admit that they were not well suited to financial management; they seemed, in fact, to take a certain pride in this. Most characterized their own incompetence in handling money in terms of their unwillingness to pay attention to such petty material matters, which, they believed, were best left to women. (This was still in keeping with the ideology of spiritual potency, of course.) However, a few men, like Pak Djohari, were more open about the inability of those of their sex to control their passions.

Many people take it for granted that uncontrolled desire is detrimental to the welfare of the family, especially when it leads to the dissipation of money that should properly be used for investments in the status and material well-being of family members. Since men are often thought unable to restrain their desire for sex, however, many women tolerate, and even expect, a certain amount of sexual infidelity from their husbands, although they certainly do not encourage it. Here, my own observations echo those made by Hildred Geertz in her study of Javanese family life, which she carried out in East Java in the 1950s:

> Javanese women are generally more deeply committed than men to the social and economic welfare of the family and therefore rarely overstep the marital boundaries. They are tolerant of their husbands' irregularities because men are considered to be by nature irresponsible. Their sexual promiscuity is called being *nakal* (naughty), which is the same term applied to disobedient or unruly children, there being no connotation of adult misdemeanor; and they are expected to be *nakal* both during their bachelorhood and after marriage. When a woman is young, her injured pride makes her angry upon discovery of her husband's infidelity, but, as she grows older and there are children, she is more concerned with the loss of money that might otherwise be spent in the family's interests. (1961, 131)

What seemed really intolerable to some of the women I knew was not their husbands' unfaithfulness in itself, which they appeared resigned to, but rather, as Geertz also discovered, the draining of family resources to support their extramarital affairs. Women are often presumed to put the needs of the family above all else. The personal affront of their husbands' sexual infidelity is considered a relatively minor offense compared to the perceived threat to the security of the household, and especially to their children's interests. A man's "playing around" is marginally acceptable, provided that he does not squander the family's money in the process. However, most of the women I knew found the idea of polygyny utterly repugnant, even though the practice is not uncommon in Solo, since it means that both the co-wife (or wives) and any children that she might produce are in competition with the first wife and her children for the husband's property.[14] A middle-aged woman I knew explained Javanese women's disapproval as follows: "If a man takes more than one wife, he's going to neglect his first wife and the children from the first marriage, and concentrate on his new wife. You can tell if a man is keeping a woman on the side—eventually he gets found out because he's spending money too quickly."

Bu Anggit, a *juragan* in her early forties from the central part of Solo, told me that she had divorced her husband because he had wanted to take another wife. Bu Anggit and her husband had been married for eighteen years without her becoming pregnant, but they had adopted a son several years earlier. It came out after some time that her husband was having an affair with another woman; she was able to accept that, she said, because it's normal for a man to "snack" (*jajan*). But when her husband announced that he wanted to marry the other woman in order to have children of his own, Bu Anggit flatly refused to be made a co-wife. So she demanded a divorce. A male friend who heard this story responded by quoting a Javanese expression that again makes use of the "snacking" metaphor for extramarital sex: "It's okay to eat out, but don't bring your leftovers home" (*Yèn jajan ya jajan, ning pincuké aja digawa mulih*).[15] In other words, fooling around is one thing, marrying again quite another. Women tacitly grant men considerable sexual license, as long as their promiscuity does not interfere too much with the interests of the household.

For men, sexual desire and the desire for money, two manifestations of *nafsu*, are often seen as two sides of the same coin; it is assumed that a man must have money in order to find satisfaction for his lust. The obverse of this is the assumption that a woman will not agree to have extramarital sexual relations with a man unless there is some palpable benefit to be gained from it, preferably of an economic sort. Men are driven by lust, it is believed, but women are not, at least not to the extent that they will risk their reputations without insisting on some material return for doing so. As Pak Djohari remarked to me, "If you're in love you've gotta have money" (*Nèk nduwé asmara kudu nduwé dhuwit*).[16] It is a commonplace that a man with cash to spare will spend it on womanizing; one sees here the danger to the family that may result from entrusting a man with too much money.

A classic instance of this was related to me by an American couple who lived with a family in a village in Central Java. After the father of the household told them that he urgently needed money to help his son find a job in the city, the couple offered to pay him three months' room and board money in advance. While they ordinarily would have paid the rent to his wife rather than to him, because women usually take charge of domestic finances, they assumed that he would turn the money over to his wife, or at least let her know that they had paid it. Meanwhile two or three months went by, and nothing further was mentioned, but the couple noticed that the food that they were being served was becoming simpler and simpler. Finally, it came out in a conversation with the wife that she had never received the money from her husband, nor even known that the couple had paid it, and that she had been feeding them for several months by drawing on her own hard-earned money. Dismayed to learn that they had turned over three months' rent to her husband, she admitted to them that her husband kept a mistress in the same hamlet, to whom she was sure he had given most or all of the money. When she told her teenage children what had happened they were indignant, and went immediately to their father to demand the money. Thus confronted, he pulled one-third of the original sum from a drawer and said that he had just been holding onto it for "safekeeping." No one mentioned the other two-thirds of the money—they seemed relieved to have him return any of it at all.

One often hears lower-class women in particular, such as household servants or batik workers, complain about the financial drain that their husbands' sexual indulgence, gambling, and general irresponsibility create for them and their children. Stories of husbands who abandon their wives and children to run off with other women are everyday fare in Solo, but many women feel that this is still preferable to having a husband who sticks around and continues to sap the family's already strained resources, without contributing anything in return.

Inem, a village woman who worked as a servant for a family in Solo, often grumbled about the problems that her husband's womanizing caused for her and her two children. Not untypically, it was Inem, not her husband, who supported the family; her husband only worked about one month in ten, she figured, but he continued to come to her for money when he needed it. He spent most of his time with another woman in a nearby village, only making an appearance at home once every week or so. Fed up with the situation, Inem asked her husband for a divorce, but he refused, as did the local village authorities, who had the final say in the matter. She told me that she would have been happy to divorce him and would not have wanted to marry again. She already had two children, lived close to her mother, and got along well with her mother-in-law, with whom she and her children shared a house. What did she need a husband for? She was better off without one, she declared. That way, she could devote herself and her limited money exclusively to her two children.

Although anecdotes and warnings about men's lack of self-control frequently focus on their lust, men are also accused of (and sometimes admit their own guilt over) uncontrolled gambling, extravagant consumption, and other spendthrift practices. Since lust is considered one of the most potent forms of *nafsu*, though, it seems to stand as a figure for all forms of desire, representing the power of base passions over the will to be self-disciplined. Money tempts men to various forms of profligacy, but lust serves as the ultimate symbol of human—especially male—weakness. Money is thus seen as the gateway to the fulfillment of desire, and sex comes to represent all the desires that money can fulfill, which may explain why discussions of men's inability to handle money so commonly refer to their lustfulness.

The desire for money and the things that money can buy exerts a powerful influence on both women and men, but women are expected (by men and women alike) to be able to keep their desires under control for the sake of the family. While such self-discipline is certainly an ideal for men as well, the belief that a man's passion-ridden nature sorely taxes his ability to exercise restraint is widespread, and becomes a self-fulfilling prophecy. Although this flies in the face of the ideology of superior male self-control, it is notable that many men appear to take a perverse pride in the unquenchable lust and "naughtiness" of those of their sex—suggesting, once again, that the positive associations of sexual potency and of generally "manly" behavior offset any shame that might accompany their inability to exercise self-control. From the perspective of many women, though, men's lack of control is a sign of masculine weakness, not strength. I was surprised at how much agreement there was on this point from women of all different social classes—workers, merchants, even members of the Solonese royalty.

The potential for the arousal of *nafsu* exists everywhere, but the possibility for its satisfaction is limited when the object of desire—frequently money, or something that can only be had with money—is scarce. It is understandable, then, that the presence of money or other valuables should provoke desire, especially in situations in which such goods are normally hard to come by. *Nafsu* is most likely to rear its head in situations where money or other objects of value have been introduced onto the scene suddenly, creating a temptation that even someone of normally strong character might find difficult to withstand.

A friend related the story of a young village man who had made off with all the gold jewelry that his wife, who was expecting a child, had borrowed from his mother to wear for a ritual ceremony that is held during the seventh month of a woman's first pregnancy (*mitoni*). Several months after abandoning his wife and unborn child, he showed up destitute on his sister's doorstep in the city, having spent all the money from the sale of the jewelry, everyone assumed, on gambling and prostitutes. His parents came to pick him up and brought him back to the village, where he resumed life in their home with his wife and new baby. The young man, who had never had much money of his own, was unable to overcome the temptation that was presented when he suddenly had access to a considerable amount of wealth in the form of his mother's jewelry. However, it is not too surprising that his parents and wife were willing to accept their prodigal son and husband back into their home, since his behavior, although certainly reproachable, was in keeping with common Javanese beliefs about men's nature. From infancy on, males are expected to be "naughty," as Hildred Geertz noted, and the attainment of adult status does nothing to change this expectation.

Women's control over their own desires serves to compensate for men's lack of control (or so many people believe), in the process preserving the assets that should properly be used to ensure the family's security. It is the wife's responsibility to do her utmost to make sure that her husband's desires do not drain the family's resources, at the same time that she does everything in her means to *increase* those resources, thereby contributing to the improvement of her family's social status. By taking charge of the family's financial affairs and keeping her husband away from matters of money, the wife prevents her husband from squandering the family's wealth. She also protects her husband's dignity and status, which by association (since he is considered the main representative of the family) protects her own status and that of her children.

In accepting control of the family's finances, a woman is entrusted, in a sense, with her husband's desires, his *nafsu*. In other words, she must control not only her *own* passions, but also, to whatever extent possible, those of her husband. A number of women told me that men cannot be trusted to keep the best interests of the family in mind at all times, but most women can, so it is the wife who must take it upon herself to secure the family's welfare. "It's just not possible for a man to think about his children 100 percent of the time," Bu Sri, a young *juragan* and a mother of two, told me. Bu Hartati, her sister, nodded in agreement, adding, "The burden of raising children, of thinking about their future, is on the mother, not the father. If a man is bored at home, he can just go out. Can a mother do that? Of course not. She has to look after her children no matter what." Women realize that there are limits to how far they can restrain their husbands' desires, but by controlling the family purse, they do what they can to keep in check the major source of temptation, money.

The standard view that has been emphasized in the ethnographic literature is that men are too concerned with their prestige to bother themselves with petty and demeaning monetary matters. They turn their wages over to their wives and leave all of the marketing to their wives as well. This is consistent with the ideology of male potency, for undue concern with financial gain is considered to be detrimental to an individual's spiritual power and social standing. But the view that men cannot hold onto money because they cannot control their desires suggests that the accepted "official" line is not sufficient to explain why women take charge of financial affairs while men tend to avoid them. The alternative view is invoked often enough to take on an authority of its own, encouraging as well as explaining certain types of behavior for men and women.

By turning matters of money over to his wife, a man acknowledges her role as the guardian of the family's welfare and as the keeper of his *nafsu*. He identifies her interests with his own, and with those of the family, by assuming that she can resist temptation better than he can. In return, a woman acknowledges her husband as the head of the household, the source of authority (in theory if not always in practice) and the symbolic generator of status for the family. In the home she serves him and attends to his needs before her own. The relationship of husband and wife is complementary, then, in terms of their roles in producing and reproducing the family's status in the wider society. One might say that he *performs* status while she *accumulates* it. Each is involved in the conversion of the family's resources, symbolic as well as material, to status.

One of the local scandals that occurred while I was living in Solo concerned a shy young woman, Yanti, who worked as a secretary. Yanti had agreed to marry a man whom her parents, a wealthy merchant couple, had found for her. Only one month before the wedding was to be held, and long after the couple had formally exchanged rings before several hundred guests in an elaborate engagement ceremony, Yanti suddenly ran off with her boss, a divorced man with children, causing her parents great embarrassment and distress. Rumors of black magic immediately began to circulate in the neighborhood—many people assumed that Yanti would not have done something so disrespectful to her parents and damaging to her own reputation unless her employer or someone else had put a spell on her. Her father, while not denying the possibility of black magic, suggested that the man had ultimately won her over by allowing her to handle the large sums of money that came through the office. I took his remark to mean that by entrusting her with that much cash, Yanti's boss appeared to identify her concerns with those of the business, and therefore with his own concerns as head of the office. Yanti's father, I believe, was drawing an implicit parallel with the family, where the husband/father, another figure of authority, entrusts his wife with control of the household's money, thereby linking her interest in the family's prosperity with his own. As an unmarried woman who had never before been given responsibility for managing money, Yanti was thus flattered into imagining herself for the first time in the position of a wife. Yanti's father attributed her elopement with her employer to the fact that he allowed her to handle money, rather than to any other means of seduction. This was consistent with the popular notion that women's interests lie primarily in domesticity, and only secondarily in passion.

GENDERED SPACES

Women's assigned role as guardian of both money and the domestic sphere is inscribed spatially in the setup of Javanese batik firms. Among the Javanese batik families of Solo, there is usually no clear separation between the household and the family firm. In most cases, the batik workshop is located on the same premises as the home, and the *juragan* moves freely between the house and the workshop. In the morning she distributes cloth, chunks of wax, and other materials to the batik workers, giving them their tasks for the day. Then she returns to the house to give money and instructions to the servant who will shop for food at the local market and cook the day's meals for the household, sometimes for the workers as well. The *juragan* alternately supervises the batik workers (sometimes with help from her husband) as they wax and dye the cloth, and assigns new tasks to the servants who cook, clean, and run errands for the family.

I found an interesting contrast to this arrangement in the batik firms of Pasar Kliwon, an old quarter of the city where most of Solo's Arab Indonesian families are concentrated. Many of the workshops of the Arab-run firms are located in a separate location from the entrepreneur's home, on a different street or even in another neighborhood. The difference between the setup of Javanese and Arab firms seems to be related to their distinct organization along gender lines and the way that the firm is imagined vis-à-vis the home and the family. Javanese batik firms are run primarily by women, and a woman's role in running the business is tied closely to her running of the household. In most Arab firms, however, it is men, not women, who run the business; most Arab women do not involve themselves in the family firm at all. The firm is conceptually as well as physically distinct from the household, and only the latter is typically considered the proper domain of the wife. (Significantly, in the very few Arab batik firms that I saw where the wife *was* active in the business, the workshop was attached to the house.) An Arab entrepreneur, Pak Harun, explained to me that he liked to maintain some distance between his home and his place of work because he did not like to mix the affairs of the household with those of the firm; when he came home at night to his wife and children, he liked to leave his business concerns behind. And he did not expect his wife to worry herself about the business at all; it was enough for her just to run the household. "We're different from the Javanese," Pak Harun and his wife agreed. "The [Arab] women take care of the household and educate the kids. The wife stays at home—it's a pity for the children if they don't."

In Javanese batik circles, in contrast, both the business and the household revolve around women. Servants and batik workers answer most directly to the same figure of authority: the female head of the household and firm. Although the husband might claim ultimate authority within the family, he considers it beneath his dignity to bother about the daily routine of running the household, usually preferring to leave such mundane matters to his wife. Her roles as wife, mother, and *juragan* are all intimately linked to each other, with no absolute boundaries drawn between them. In Laweyan a woman entrepreneur's position in the family and community is always identified with her status as *juragan*. Solonese women take charge of the family firm, then, just as they manage the household, since the family business is, in effect, an extension of the household.

In this merchant enclave, the family's prosperity is closely bound to the vitality of its business. In her all-important role in the firm as well as the family, the wife assumes responsibility for the well-being of both. The size of the gold and diamond earrings that she wears as she makes her rounds through Pasar Klewer are taken as an indication of both the soundness of her business and the fortunes of her family, the two being essentially inseparable. It is she rather than her husband who occupies the central position that defines the household as well as the business. Most people in the Javanese community agree that a woman can manage a batik business quite well on her own, but that few men can get by in the business without a wife's help. As a general rule, the family business has no corporate existence apart from that of the woman who runs it; when she retires or dies, it simply shuts down, unless there is a child who has been groomed to take it over.

While the connections between the household and the marketplace are not as immediately obvious as those between the household and the adjacent firm, the same principles apply among market traders and batik producers when it comes to the sexual division of responsibilites. This is why most market stalls are run by a woman. By keeping her husband away from money, a woman guards his prestige and, by association, that of his family. At the same time, she protects her family and business from the threat posed by his *nafsu*.

I might mention here that the practice of seclusion of women that has been common in some Muslim societies was never adopted in this sector (or most others) of Javanese society.[17] Again, one sees a contrast with the local Arab community. I was told by women and men of Arab descent that in generations past, the seclusion or near-seclusion of Arab women (almost all of whom were actually of mixed Arab Indonesian ancestry) had been common in Solo. Even in the Kauman, however, the most devout Javanese Muslim quarter of Solo, women were traditionally very active outside the home as batik manufacturers and traders. Some of their husbands served as religious officials in the Kraton, a position that brought prestige to the family but generally did not pay well. In many cases the women effectively supported their families while their husbands devoted themselves to their religious pursuits.

Among Javanese merchants in Solo, then, the success of the family firm was and is predicated, in most cases, on the willingness of the wife to leave her home daily for the marketplace. There, women sell their goods, collect on debts, and gather information on current fashions, prices, terms of credit, and potential trading partners. They also trade information of a more social nature: who has a son or daughter eligible for marriage, for instance; whose husband has secretly taken a second wife; or who is going to make the *haj* to Mecca this year (an important sign of wealth and status). The public sphere of the marketplace is as much their domain as the private space of the household.

Conversely, men of the *sudagar* class characteristically stay clear of the marketplace, preferring to remain at home while their wives go out to do business. I would suggest, in fact, that if a prescription for "seclusion" can be said to exist at all within this class, it is for men, not women. Some men do play an active role in running the family business, but in most instances they restrict themselves to overseeing production, leaving marketing and the purchase of raw materials to their wives. Because the vast majority of workshops in Javanese batik firms are attached to the house, the husband tends to be "confined" to the home and the workshop while his wife goes out to the marketplace. We have seen that a man's separation from bargaining and the management of domestic finances protects his own status as well as his family's. Because mercantile activity is detrimental to a man's status in Solo, and is increasingly so the higher the family climbs on the social scale, there is a tendency for a man of this class to avoid too much public exposure as a merchant. By staying at home, away from the marketplace, he projects the cultivated air of a man of leisure rather than appearing to be someone who is unduly concerned with matters of money. His seclusion in itself, far from being a source of embarrassment or shame, actually preserves his status.

In a less literal sense, though, when a man stays out of circulation, he and his family are protected from the ever-present threat posed by his *nafsu*. In the home, his desires are more easily domesticated, kept under control. Once he has entered the public sphere, he is no longer fully accountable for his actions. ("My mother used to say to me, 'When he's at home, he's your husband, but when he's outside, think of him as someone else,'" recalled one matron.) It is the *possibility* of a man's loss of control, whether or not it actually occurs—the imagination of what he would do if he gave in to his desires—that suggests the need for restraint. His willingness to restrain his own passions also establishes his strength of character and personal potency. Of course, there have always been limits on how much men's *nafsu* could be contained, and to what extent they could actually be confined to the home. A comment made by Bu Dinar about prior generations in Laweyan is telling: "Women hardly ever stayed up till late at night, because they'd be up at the crack of dawn. At 5:00 P.M., the gates would be shut and the women of Laweyan would be inside for the night. But the men would go out to gamble, play around with women, and go to cockfights."

Men's tendency to avoid the marketplace, which scholars have often attributed to their deep concern with prestige and spiritual potency, can also be understood in terms of this alternative model of gender and self-control. As a prime site for the accumulation of money and the acquisition of commodities, the marketplace seems to incite desire and at the same time advertise the potential for its satisfaction. The priority of an economic logic of commodity exchange in the marketplace, moreover, leads to a partial breakdown of the hierarchies and boundaries that conventionally order and circumscribe social relations in Java, creating a situation in which the social mechanisms for the suppression of desire are weak. Women believe that they are better able than men to restrain themselves from giving in to the desires of the marketplace, and many men seem to concur, whether tacitly or explicitly. Most women and men believe that aside from concerns of prestige, Javanese men are ill suited to trading in the marketplace because they lack the self-discipline needed to bring money home at the end of the day instead of squandering it.

In Pasar Klewer, few Javanese men were to be found, either as consumers or traders. One notable exception, however, was a Javanese transvestite (*banci*) who ran one of the largest rotating cooperative credit associations (*arisan*) among the traders in the market.[18] Every day Pak Hardjo—some people called him *Bu* Hardjo because of his inclination to cross-dress—perambulated the marketplace collecting money from participating traders, and he was responsible for picking the winners of that day's jackpot and distributing their shares to them. This was a job that the traders felt required tremendous self-discipline, because handling several million *rupiah* (well over a thousand dollars) each day was a source of temptation that even those of the strongest character might find difficult to resist. My sense was that as far as the women traders were concerned, Pak Hardjo's ambiguous gender made him an acceptable person to fill the role of *arisan* coordinator (from what I could tell, all of the other *arisan* managers among Javanese in the market were women). His femaleness suggested trustworthiness, a self-control of which an unambiguously gendered male would probably not have been assumed capable. By taking on the mannerisms and clothing of a woman, Pak Hardjo also acquired the reputation that women have for being able to control their desires.

THE DANGER OF AUTONOMOUS WOMEN

The "circulation of women," not as objects of exchange in the classic anthropological sense (see Lévi-Strauss 1969; Rubin 1975), but as the *agents* of exchange, has historically served as one of the distinguishing features of the *pribumi* merchant class in the Solo-Yogyakarta region, setting it apart from the nobility as well as from comparable communities of Javanese traders on the more heavily Islamicized north coast and in the western part of the island. In the past (through the 1960s, and even into the 1970s), daughters born into this class learned to circulate themselves from an early age, beginning in primary or middle school, by accompanying their mothers to the marketplace every afternoon.[19] In this way they gradually mastered their mothers' techniques of bargaining, negotiating credit, and collecting information, eventually acquiring enough savvy and personal contacts to go into business on their own when they got married. The daughters of textile manufacturers learned how to sell their goods wholesale to market traders, as well as to collect on debts and to purchase raw materials on credit, while the daughters of market traders observed the ways in which their mothers attracted customers, persuaded them to buy their wares, and bargained for a suitable price.

This training was not always easy for the shyer girls, some of whom would have been much happier to stay at home. One exceptionally prosperous trader, a flamboyant *hajjah* (a woman who has made the *haj*) named Bu Hadi, recalled her first unhappy days as a teenager in Pasar Klewer, when her mother insisted that she come to the market to help out. "My mother was a trader, and in those days that meant that *I* had to become a trader, too. But I hated going to the market. I used to cry every day. My mother made me call out to people all the time to try to get them to buy things. I was still young then, and it was so embarrassing. Besides, the language of the market was so *kasar*, even though the language used by people in Solo is usually *alus*."

Circulating in the public sphere implies exposing oneself, making oneself vulnerable, which is what Bu Hadi objected to as a timid teenager. Indeed, one can hardly imagine a place more open and exposed than the marketplace, which stands in sharp contrast to the privacy of the walled-in homes of affluent Solonese entrepreneurs and merchants. People, like the goods they sell or buy, are nakedly displayed for public scrutiny. The intermingling of all kinds of people—with each other as well as with their commodities—that characterizes the marketplace is unparalleled in other spheres of Javanese life. Pulsating with energy, the marketplace has a kind of sensuousness and vibrancy that one rarely finds elsewhere.

Women's circulation in the market puts them into a position of exposure where they, like the goods in which they traffic, may become the objects of the *nafsu* that is rampant there. Since passion for sex is often conflated with passion for money and other objects of desire, it is perhaps not surprising that the marketplace, Pasar Klewer in particular, is sometimes associated with sexuality. Women in Pasar Klewer say that one of the keys to attracting customers and to keeping them coming back as regular clients (*langganan*) is to be friendly and charming—another skill that daughters learn from their mothers. Women traders are said to use their femininity to sell their goods, particularly when the buyers are men (as are many non-Javanese traders who buy from them wholesale). By doing so, they embody the famous—or infamous—image of the *putri Solo*, which literally means "Solonese lady," but with the underlying connotation of femme fatale. The women of Solo are so well known in Java for their dangerous powers of attraction that a journalist from Banten, West Java, told me that before he left Banten for Solo, his grandfather warned him to "watch out for those Solonese women."

Beyond this, however, women traders have a reputation in the wider society for being willing to sell more than just their wares. The journalist from Banten recounted an anecdote to illustrate the allure of female traders in Solo: "A man was on his way to Solo from another city, when he ran into a friend. When his friend found out where he was going, he said that *he* would like to go along, too, so that he could visit the marketplace in Solo. 'I'll go to a batik trader there, and ask to see all of her goods,' said the man. 'After she's laid out the last sarong in stock for me, I'll ask her for the *very* last one—the one she's wearing.'" Using a similar metaphor, a woman of royal descent quoted an expression that was well known in Solo: "What people say about women traders is that their 'sarongs are loose' (*tapihé kendho*)—in other words, they come off easily (*gampang dicopot*)."

It appears, then, that the relationships of gender, desire, and economic practices that I have discussed so far are complicated by the ambivalence with which women's self-control and their control over money are viewed. On the one hand, women are considered to be ever mindful of their families and less lustful than men, which keeps them in control of their desires. These are some of the factors that are said to make them "naturally" better traders than men. On the other hand, the more money a woman controls, the more autonomous she is, and an autonomous woman is always somewhat suspect. Self-control over one's desires is evaluated positively in Java, but a woman who is not subject to any *man's* control is potentially threatening to the male-dominated social order. Widows and divorcées, for example, are frequently the objects of gossip and suspicion regarding their sexual activities because they are no longer under the supervision or control of fathers or husbands (see also Ong 1987, 89).

The "danger" of the Solonese market trader, it seems, stems from the imagined power of an uncontained female sexuality combined with money and independence. The connections between women's economic independence and sexual license are often made explicit. Featuring the front-page headline "Hunting for Satisfaction: Sex among the Ranks of Javanese Women," a newspaper article published in the provincial capital of Semarang reported that "sexual freedom" was widespread among women traders in "one of the centers of trade in Solo" (possibly Pasar Klewer):

> At 8:30 in the morning, Hartini, 27, a tall, slender, beautiful woman, steps supplely. Her hips sway, fully confident. "There's a diamond deal in Tawang-mangu," she remarks as she says goodbye to her husband and children and makes for the Mazda 323 Trendynamic that's ready to go.
>
> The metallic black Mazda hits the road without a moment's hesitation. And, at a plush villa, the car comes to a stop. Soon the attractive woman who was driving it gets out, and, as if quite at home, enters the villa. A man with the air of a big shot, who appears to have been waiting for some time, greets her, "Hello dear."
>
> How intimately this man takes Ms. Hartini by the shoulder. And as if by plan, they jokingly go into a bedroom. Ah . . . must a diamond deal take place inside a closed room between two human beings of different sex?
>
> The above illustration is one incident that was recorded during a field study (*grondit*) conducted for almost a year among women traders between the ages of 25 and 40, in one center of trade in Solo.
>
> The conclusions from that study were truly startling: "The higher the degree of a woman trader's economic independence, the greater her degree of sexual freedom." Might there be something amiss in the study, for instance, that the respondents were chosen incorrectly?[20]

This "field study" merely seemed to support the rumors about female market traders that were already rife in Solo. There were stories, for instance, that some traders participated in a magical practice that requires having sexual relations with someone other than one's own spouse as a means of ensuring success in business. Others said that a few Pasar Klewer traders were actually prostitutes or madams who used their stalls in the market in order to find clients from among out-of-town male traders or customers, especially when sales of textiles and other goods were slow. One man mentioned that there are ways that a potential client can tell whether a market trader will let a man "bring her" with him or not—"you can tell from her eyes, and the way that she throws her smile at you. It's hard to describe exactly—you just know from looking at her."

When I questioned Bu Hartati, the young *juragan*, about whether she was aware of the stereotypes surrounding women traders in Solo, she assured me that she was. "Oh, it's been that way for generations (literally, 'since our ancestors'). It was already like that in the days when my mother-in-law used to go to the market. It doesn't shock me anymore to hear these things," she informed me with a knowing air. "Sometimes it's passed down from mother to daughter—the apple doesn't fall far from the tree, you know (*kacang ora ninggal lanjarané*; literally, 'the bean doesn't leave the pole'). I never mentioned all this to you before just because I figured you already knew." She went on to relate that not long after marrying, she had suggested to her husband that she should open a stall in Pasar Klewer to sell batik. He had been adamantly opposed to the idea because of the reputation that the women there had, fearful that she would be enticed into following their immoral ways. Hoping to change her husband's mind, Bu Hartati had pointed out that not all of the women in the market were "that way." But her husband would not be convinced. "Those male traders are too clever at seducing women," he insisted, closing the argument.

To call such "sexual freedom" for Solonese market women the norm would certainly be an exaggeration. Like most stereotypes, this one was blown out of proportion. What is significant, however, is the extent to which such generalizations prevail, and what their implications are for understanding the cultural logics of gender in Java. These stories suggest that the marketplace, a domain controlled by women, is also a place where women cannot be controlled by men. But can market women control *themselves?* At first glance, these stories about the "looseness" of women traders seem to contradict the notion that women have more control over their desires than men, making them better suited to handling matters of money. For if it is indeed the case that the women who have the most dealings with money are also perceived as being the most widely involved in illicit sexual affairs, then it would appear that there is no clear connection between the control of money and the control of desire.

I should point out, however, that I never heard anyone in Solo attribute women's engagement in extramarital affairs to their uncontrollable desires. Sometimes it was blamed on women's dissatisfaction or boredom with their husbands, the wish to "get even" with husbands who had been unfaithful, or even "the need for recreation." More commonly, though, women's infidelity was imputed to economic need or ambition; for instance, a way to increase sales of merchandise or to compensate for a slow period in the market. There was a general belief that few women would be willing to have adulterous relations if there were not some financial gain to be had in the bargain. When Bu Hartati told me about a married woman she knew who was driven by economic hardship to seek out liaisons with men, for example, I asked her if she was sure that the woman was being paid by the men she was seeing. "Well, if they didn't give her money, do you think she'd do it? Of course not," she answered matter-of-factly. Since the possible consequences for a woman having an affair may be far more dire than they are for a man who does the same—for instance, the threat of being divorced—it is felt that women will not engage in such activities lightly.[21] Furthermore, as one man explained to me, men will usually give some money to a woman with whom they sleep illicitly, whether or not she is not a prostitute, in order to rid themselves of any feelings of guilt or responsibility: "It's like eating *pecel* (a snack often purchased from street vendors)—you have to pay for it before you can throw away the container it's served in."

Prevalent beliefs about the dissimilar natures of men and women often lead people to conclude that whereas men are driven by their great lust to seek out extramarital relationships, women are more apt to be motivated by other factors, including concern for the family's financial welfare. Women may be the objects of *men's* sexual desire, but they are not thought likely to succumb to their *own* sexual desires. This notion contradicts dominant gender ideologies that hold men to be ruled by reason and women by their passions, but it should not be taken at face value, for it, too, constitutes a prescription for, rather than a description of, reality. I stress the formulaic nature of both the dominant and alternative conceptions of gender and self-control lest one or the other be taken as a statement of "fact" or "practice." Nonetheless, it should be kept in mind as well that these normative prescriptions often do have a real effect on individuals' everyday practices and their reactions to the behavior of others. In my observation, the belief that women have more self-control than men in matters of sex and money leads women and men to have very different expectations of themselves and of each other, and frequently to fulfill those expectations through particular courses of action.

It is worth noting here that "snacking" (*jajan*) metaphors for illicit sex typically focus on the image of men buying street food (which is cheap), eating it on the spot for their own immediate enjoyment, and then throwing away the container before returning home. The conventional portrayal of women purchasing snacks, in contrast, is never a wry comment on adultery, as it is for men. Rather, the picture is one of women buying snacks at the market or on the street as *olèh-olèh*, small gifts for their families. It is a token that a mother brings home at the end of the day to show that she has been thinking of her husband and children while she has been away from the house.

Although categorical pronouncements about gender and self-control are usually made with a sweeping assertiveness, the stories about the sexual activities of market traders point to the underlying *ambivalence* with which the notion of self-control itself, in all of its aspects, is viewed in Java. When a man controls his desires, it is commonly believed, he makes himself potent. When he lets his self-control lapse, he is a danger to the family, but his sexual potency may also be linked to a more spiritual kind of potency. When a woman controls *her* desires, she accumulates economic and spiritual value for the family, more than personal potency. But a woman with too much control over her own person, it appears, is considered a threat to society. Bridging the gap between public (the marketplace) and private (the household) spheres, the woman merchant occupies an ambiguous position. She is thought better able than a man to suppress her own passions, but she is also seen as manipulating the desires of others toward her own ends. At home, she is entrusted with the safekeeping of her husband's *nafsu* for the sake of her family, yet her success in business depends on her capacity to *arouse* the desires of her customers, to make them willing to spend money. It is this ambiguity that is reflected in the stories about the "sexual freedom" of women traders. Their "danger" lies in their ability to control their own passions, even as they awaken those of others.

Reconsidering Ideologies of Gender

We can see, then, that a one-sided approach to the relationships of gender, self-control, and potency obscures the ambiguities, paradoxes, and multiple layers of meaning that attach to ideas about maleness and femaleness in Java. While describing and analyzing the impact of dominant gender ideologies is worthwhile, to grant them too central a position in analysis may obscure subtler but equally important ways that people think and talk about gender. Attention to peripheral discourses may reveal fundamental views of women's and men's natures that bypass or reconfigure the idioms of potency and prestige. I am here advocating what Gayatri Spivak refers to as "an espousal of, and an attention to, marginality—a suspicion that what is at the center often hides a repression" (1988, 104). It is clear that both men and women in Java make pronouncements and engage in practices that support as well as contradict the dominant ideologies of spiritual potency and self-control. We cannot assume that any of the viewpoints offered here represent "the male point of view" or "the female point of view" (see Yanagisako and Coller 1987), even if one perspective seems to privilege men over women (or vice versa), or is voiced more often by men or by women. Javanese discourses and practices of gender embody contradictory representations that sometimes confound the ideological association of males with a higher degree of self-control, potency, and morality than females.

Discourses of gender, complex and contradictory though they may be, also guide and give meaning to social action; in this sense, too, they deserve attention. The key is to avoid giving so much weight to one set of discourses that one overlooks others because they are not voiced as formally or as insistently. As Jane Flax writes, "Perhaps reality can have 'a' structure only from the falsely universalizing perspective of the dominant group. That is, only to the extent that one person or group can dominate the whole will reality appear to be governed by one set of rules or be constituted by one privileged set of social relations" (1990, 49). The "rules" that are frequently invoked for Javanese society only represent "reality" as it exists within the limited framework of a particular ideological system—one that grants superior status to men and their domains of activity.

Javanese women give tacit approval to ideologies of superior male potency and status by deferring to their husbands in both private and public contexts, and by helping them avoid situations in which their prestige might be compromised (see Keeler 1990, 134-45, for a nice illustration of this point). At the same time, women freely express the opinion that most men have uncontrollable passions and childlike dispositions that prevent them from acting in the best interests of their families. Women, they believe, must rely on their own superior strength of will in order to compensate for their husbands' lack of control. Many Javanese men also admit openly that members of their sex are less capable than women of controlling their base desires (especially lust), even while they make categorical statements about women's inability to manage their emotions and behavior. In formal or public interactions, where male dominance and prestige tend to be highlighted, men attempt to project an image of equanimity and total self-mastery, but in private, they may give rein to their passions, thereby fulfilling other cultural expectations for male behavior. Conversely, in public situations Javanese women sometimes appear cheerfully unconcerned with conveying a dignified, self-controlled image (though they are every bit as capable as men of assuming an air of refinement when the situation requires it), but at home they take the injunction to be self-controlled quite seriously in order to accumulate economic and spiritual resources for themselves and their families.

Writing about traditional gender ideologies in Java, Barbara Hatley comments, "Women's economic activities outside the home, in market trade particularly, are seen as an extension of the natural female household concern with money matters. The association of women with money brings more disparagement than esteem, as men complain of their wives' tightfistedness and rather contemptuously attribute to women a *jiwa dagang*, 'soul of a trader'" (1990, 182). But women's dealings with money can also be viewed in a different, more positive light: as a means by which they domesticate the antisocial forces of desire so as to ensure the prosperity and status of their families. By accumulating wealth and investing it in the material and social welfare of the family, they generate prestige for themselves, their husbands, and their children.

Dominant gender ideologies in Java—like those in the West—often regard as unprestigious those activities that are associated with the "domestic sphere." But in the alternative configuration of gender relations that I have outlined here, the "domestic sphere" acquires a new meaning, as does the close association of women with the household. Here, women take on the role, at least in some contexts, of domesticator—of men, money, and desire, among other things—rather than domesticated. Seen from this light, the domestic sphere itself becomes a crucially important site of cultural production and social reproduction.

Yet the linkage between women and the domestic sphere, I wish to emphasize, is by no means absolute. Since many Javanese women work outside the home, they move easily between private and public domains. As I have shown, in the case of Javanese merchants, it is a woman's freedom to move between the home and the public sphere—in particular, her willingness to expose herself to the desires of the marketplace while controlling her own desires—that enables her to accumulate wealth for the family. Even in their forays outside the conjugal bond, women are thought to keep the best interests of their families in mind; they therefore retain their status as domesticators. Whereas men's extramarital sexual activity is associated with uncontrolled *nafsu* and the dispersion of family resources, female sexuality remains conceptually bound to economic accumulation and to the production of status for the family. A shift away from the ideologies of the center reveals that women do not only participate tangentially in the status systems of men—they themselves play a central role in defining the status hierarchies of Javanese society.

To the extent that it is identified with unbridled desire and the breakdown of social boundaries in the marketplace, money lies in the realm of the *kasar*, representing that which has not yet been brought under control and which is therefore uncivilized and devalued, even dangerous. But money can be domesticated—that is, brought into the domain of culture and the *alus*, which converts it from something devalued to something valuable in a specifically Javanese sense.[22] Javanese women play a key role in transforming money from the *kasar* to the *alus*, from the untamed to the civilized. They do this by taking money out of circulation—in particular, out of the sphere of *nafsu*—and bringing it home. Once removed from circulation, it can be used toward producing status for the family and, even more important, for reproducing the family's ability to produce status for itself (as economic and symbolic capital).

Money, then, is "domesticated" in a double sense: it is brought under social control *and* it is converted into something of cultural value in the domestic sphere. Women make money in the undomesticated marketplace and transform it to something valuable in the home. Women's role is to *conserve* money, to keep it in reserve. Through their ability to control *nafsu*, women domesticate money, and attempt to domesticate men as well, though with varying degrees of success.

By now it should be clearer why women have figured so centrally in the life of Solo's merchant enclaves. Earlier, I discussed some of the historical reasons for women's domination of trade among Javanese in this region, linking it to the cultural politics and ideologies of colonial rule. In this chapter, I have explored some of the cultural justifications for women's prominent economic positions in the household and in the marketplace, which challenge the common assumption that Javanese women manage money simply because they are unconcerned with their status and are therefore willing to involve themselves in financial matters that men would find demeaning. On the contrary, I have tried to show that women are fundamentally concerned with status, their own as well as their families', and it is precisely this concern which leads them to take such an active role in managing the financial affairs of the household and the family business.

What I have not yet discussed, however, is the relationship between the gender arrangements that prevailed in Laweyan and similar Javanese communities and their demodernization in the New Order. There is no simple causal connection between women's domination of trade and the process of Laweyan's demodernization; I do not want the reader to conclude that women are somehow more traditional or conservative by nature than men, and that this has brought about the state of affairs that exists in Laweyan today. The connections are much subtler than such a simple explanation could account for, and gender is by no means the sole factor in Laweyan's rejection of its own modernity. In the next chapter, I will argue that the domestication of both money and desire is conceived of as an ongoing process that links the present with the past, a process in which women also play a most important part. In attempting to shed light on the nature of this process, I will suggest that if we continue to pay attention to the issue of gender and subjectivity, certain stubborn divisions that anthropology has long preserved—such as that between gifts and commodities, the public sphere and the domestic sphere, or spiritual life and economic life—tend to break down. By understanding how these would-be opposites are actually deeply implicated with one another, we can then begin to make sense of Laweyan's demodernization—and domestication—in the New Order.

Chapter Five

THE VALUE OF THE BEQUEST

SPIRITUAL ECONOMIES AND ANCESTRAL COMMODITIES

> In order that gold may be held as money, and made to form a
> hoard, it must be prevented from circulating, or from dissolving
> into the means of purchasing enjoyment. The hoarder there-
> fore sacrifices the lusts of his flesh to the fetish of gold. He takes
> the gospel of abstinence very seriously.
> *(Karl Marx,* Capital *([1867] 1977), vol. 1)*

THE PROCESS of generating and conserving value through the control of *nafsu* has both an economic and spiritual aspect to it. Many Javanese believe that by mastering their desires they can accumulate both material wealth and spiritual merit: both forms of value are understood as an excess that is created through a sacrifice. In Solo, just as women are called on to restrain their passions for the sake of the family's economic welfare, they are also involved in the production of a more spiritual type of value for themselves, their families, and others. The most potent sacrifices are seen as those that can regenerate value over an extended period of time; thus the most valuable objects are those that have been passed down as an ancestral bequest, a sign of the sacrifices of past generations for their descendants.

In this chapter I analyze how wealth acquires cultural value through its conversion to such objects of value. The batik industry itself came to be seen as such an ancestral inheritance that should ideally have been able to regenerate value for many generations. Paradoxically, the very process of designating the batik industry as something of ancestral value led to its ossification and decline as its inheritors became unwilling or unable to adjust to the changing economic and political climate of New Order Indonesia.

In *The Religion of Java* (1960), a remarkable ethnography that has deeply influenced subsequent studies of Java, Clifford Geertz opens with a description of the *slametan*, an "undramatic, almost furtive, little ritual" that lies at the core of the entire Javanese religious system. A communal feast that "symbolizes the mystic and social unity of those participating in it," the *slametan* "can be given in response to almost any occurrence one wishes to celebrate, ameliorate, or sanctify"—birth, death, marriage, pregnancy, circumcision, illness, opening a new factory, changing one's name, and so on (11). Elsewhere, Geertz remarks that these rituals "are intended to be both offerings to the spirits and commensal mechanisms of social integration for the living" (1973, 147). He describes the usual pattern of the *slametan* as follows:

> The meal, which consists of specially prepared dishes, each symbolic of a particular religious concept, is cooked by the female members of one nuclear family household and set out on mats in the middle of the living room. The male head of the household invites the male heads of the eight or ten contiguous households to attend; no closer neighbor is ignored in favor of one farther away. After a speech by the host explaining the spiritual purpose of the feast and a short Arabic chant, each man takes a few hurried, almost furtive, gulps of food, wraps the remainder of the meal in a banana-leaf basket, and returns home to share it with his family. It is said that the spirits draw their sustenance from the odor of the food, the incense which is burned, and the Moslem prayer; the human participants draw theirs from the material substance of the food and from their social interaction. The result of this quiet, undramatic little ritual is twofold: the spirits are appeased and neighborhood solidarity is strengthened. (147)

Of the sexual division of ritual responsibilities, he observes that women's role is to cook the food, while only men participate in the actual ceremony; the women remain in the kitchen, peeking through the bamboo walls at the men who are performing the ritual (1960, 12). Geertz's observations on the division of male and female roles are confirmed in other studies of Java (see, e.g., Keeler 1987), which find the same general pattern of men serving as the ritual representatives of their households and women remaining behind the scenes, cooking and serving the food.

One of the first ritual events that I attended in Solo was a large *slametan* marking the one-year anniversary of Pak Wiyono's father's death, which was held at the spacious home of Pak Wiyono's sister, who lived outside Laweyan. Upon arriving at the site where the ceremony was to be held, I was immediately whisked off to the back of the house, where I joined a crew of women who were busily dishing out food for the guests. Being asked to help with the food seemed natural, for by all accounts that I had read, this was what women in Java were supposed to do. After the ceremony had started, I excused myself and tiptoed out front to see what was going on. There, much to my surprise, were about two hundred women and only a dozen or so men, all seated in rows of metal folding chairs, chanting Arabic prayers on behalf of the soul of the deceased. The chanting was led by a group of devout Muslim women who sat on a raised platform in the front room. The handful of men attending the ceremony sat unobtrusively in the corner, far away from the center of the action. After it was over, I asked my hosts where all the men were. "Oh, this is a *slametan* especially for women (*khusus putri*)," they told me. The only men who had been invited were from the immediate family of the deceased.

I was convinced that this ritual had to be out of the ordinary; it was especially perplexing to me that this mostly female *slametan* was being held to commemorate the death of a high-status *man*, not a woman. I received only vague answers to my questions about why this particular ritual had been designated "especially for women"; I was assured that others in this series of death *slametan* for Pak Wiyono's father would be "especially for men." Ultimately I decided that it must be an aberration. But a few weeks later I witnessed another event which made me question that assumption.

Shortly after I moved to Laweyan, I began attending a weekly meeting of a neighborhood *arisan*, which is usually glossed as a "rotating credit [or savings] association" (see C. Geertz 1962), but which was rather like a group of matrons getting together for a weekly card game, where the opportunity for socializing is at least as important as the financial stakes involved. Like most *arisan*, the members were all women.[1] Every Wednesday morning the same group of women gathered for about an hour in the home of one of the members. The *arisan* was a sort of rotating lottery: each woman would contribute five thousand *rupiah* to the kitty, and every week a different woman's name was drawn to win the money. This continued until each woman had had her turn winning the pot, at which point the whole cycle would begin again. Additionally, a portion of the money was set aside to make short-term loans to members of the group who were in need of a little extra cash.

In practice, the financial aspect of the gathering was downplayed (although it was not unimportant) and the social side emphasized: the women obviously looked forward to the chance for friendly gossip in the company of old friends, neighbors, and relatives. They also used the *arisan* as an opportunity to plan upcoming ritual events that one of the members might be planning; it was common for the members of an *arisan* to help each other out when any of them sponsored such an event. At weddings or other ceremonies hosted by a member of the group, the women liked to wear matching *kebayas*, or "uniforms" (*seragam*) as they called them, to show that they belonged to the same *arisan*.

This particular *arisan* actually looked rather like a female version of the all-male *slametan* that Geertz had described. About twenty middle-aged women, most in Javanese dress and all with bare feet (having politely left their sandals outside the door), sat in a circle on floor mats in one woman's living room, which had been cleared of furniture for the occasion. Each participant was served a glass of hot tea and a small package of food wrapped in banana leaves, to eat on the spot or to take home as she pleased. But the stiff formalities, the "polite, embarrassed, muted manner," and the high Javanese language that Geertz describes for the *slametan* (1960, 11–12) were almost completely absent here. This *arisan* consisted of some of the elite women of the community, but their behavior, although not improper for such a setting, did occasionally border on the indecorous. The ladies chatted and laughed among themselves (mostly in low Javanese), sometimes half shouting to each other across the room. Some of them ate their snacks with great relish, commenting on the tastiness of the food—behavior that would be taboo at a formal ritual event, where guests are expected to consume their food in an *alus* manner, without obvious desire or interest. Occasionally one of the women would belch loudly. When money had to change hands, the women would often throw it to each other, yelling "*Nyoh!*" (Here, take it!). All of this was an exemplary display of the *kasar* behavioral style that men often associate with women in Java. The women at the *arisan* were clearly unconcerned with appearing refined. Indeed, on the rare occasions when one of the older women would use high Javanese to make an announcement to the group, it was usually in a humorous, exaggeratedly refined tone that mocked the grandiloquent styles of formal (typically male) speech; this would be greeted by the appreciative chuckles of the other women.

But in the middle of one otherwise ordinary meeting of the *arisan*, boxes of neatly arranged *slametan*-type food (provided by a caterer) were distributed to each of the women present, and the jovial atmosphere in the room suddenly changed. On cue, all of the women fell silent, while one of them made a brief, formal speech in very high Javanese, this time completely in earnest. She explained that this was a ritual of thanks (a *syukuran*, which is a variation on the *slametan*) that was being sponsored by another member of the *arisan* whose recent wedding for her daughter had gone off smoothly (despite the fact that the bride was already a few months pregnant; this, of course, was not mentioned, although undoubtedly everyone in the room knew about it). After her introductory speech, the woman led all the participants in chanting Arabic prayers for a few minutes, and then the short ritual was over, although additional boxes of food were later sent off to a number of other households that were not represented at the *arisan*. Everyone relaxed again, and the women resumed their casual chatting.

I was taken off guard when, only a few minutes later, *more* boxes of food were passed around, with slightly different contents, and a new round of high Javanese preliminaries and Arabic prayers were led by another woman. This time the occasion was the thousand-day anniversary of the death of another member's father, the last in the series of death-anniversary *slametan* that are intended to ensure the lasting peace of the deceased person's soul. Once again, everyone was absolutely serious during the ritual. But as soon as the prayers were over, the women immediately resumed their joking and gossiping again, as if nothing had happened.

To me, this combined *arisan-slametan* was a very strange event, for I could hardly imagine a more unlikely mixing of sacred and profane spheres. The *arisan* was a kind of sociable neighborhood lottery, the climax of which was the drawing of names for the weekly pot. The two *slametan*, in contrast, had all the markings of "religious" or "ritual" events. It seemed incongruous, to say the least, that one could literally throw money around one minute, and then pray to God to forgive the sins of a dead relative the next. Could the "core ritual" of Javanese society really be carried out in such a setting? But clearly I was the only one present who saw anything odd about this sudden switching of gears. The other women seemed perfectly at ease with dispatching these ritual duties quickly and efficiently in the context of the *arisan*. This turned out to be a common occurrence, and I was to witness many similar rituals held in the midst of an *arisan*.

It was equally striking, given the ethnographic record, that women, not men, were carrying out the rites as the representatives of their households. These were not unimportant rituals: in one of them a man's soul was at stake, and whether or not God would spare him from the eternal tortures of hell depended partly upon the efficacy of the women's prayers. While I was in Solo, I attended countless ritual affairs—weddings, death *slametan*, engagement ceremonies, circumcisions, and so on. Almost invariably, women outnumbered the men by a significant margin. In the merchant community, at least, it was unusual, although not unheard of, for an affair to be designated as "all-male" (it was well known that a ceremony so designated was likely to have a poor turnout), but there were plenty of "all-female" ceremonies, always well attended. At first I attributed the larger numbers of women at ritual events to the fact that I was working mostly in Solo's merchant community, where women were unusually dominant socially as well as economically. But I discovered that even at rituals held outside merchant circles, including some hosted by Solo's royalty, women were often more in evidence than men.

Yet there was an unconscious complicity among women, it seemed, in trying to cover up for men's frequent neglect of ritual. Again and again, I received a stock set of answers to my repeated questions about why so few men were present. If an event was held in the morning, someone would say, "Sometimes the men don't like to get up early." In the middle of the day, the standard excuse was "The men are at the office." (I even heard this in Laweyan, where most men did not work in offices.) At a ceremony sponsored by the Mangkunagaran clan at their royal cemetery in Girilayu, seven days after the death of Prince Mangkunagara VIII, I turned to a woman next to me and asked her why so few men were present. She offered me the excuse that I had heard so many times before: that the ritual was being held during working hours, so the men were "at the office." But then she paused for a moment. Looking slightly befuddled, as if she had caught herself in her own flawed logic, she added, "*I* work at an office too, but I took the day off."

The power of ideologies that assert male dominance, I believe, is what leads women to search for excuses for men's conspicuous absence at ritual and social events. Women often seemed a bit embarrassed when I pressed them on this point; although men's scarceness was as plain as day, they treated it almost like a family secret that should not be publicly aired. If one subscribes to the idea of male spiritual potency, then one might conclude that men's ritual action is more effective than women's—and presumably, no one would want to entrust the delicate matter of ritual efficacy to persons of inferior status or spiritual power. In addition, there is still a fairly strong notion that men, as the heads of their households, ought to represent their families in formal, public settings. The gap between ideology and practice, however, was apparently unsettling to women only when I asked them to account for the men's absence. Otherwise, they simply took it for granted that it was *their* obligation to carry out the endless cycle of ritual duties that were demanded of them, whether or not their husbands were in attendance.

These scenes—of two hundred women chanting Arabic prayers for the soul of a dead man; or of the *slametan*, the core Javanese ritual, being carried out in the midst of the Javanese equivalent of a ladies' kaffeeklatsch—seemed peculiarly out of sync with the images of Javanese ritual that had come down to me through the ethnographic canon. I cannot fully account for the discrepancy: it may reflect contemporary, urban developments in ritual practice, or regional differences—Solo is famous in Java for its strong-minded, financially independent women, and this may be mirrored in their unusually prominent role in ritual events. However, I am less interested in explaining (or explaining away) the difference with other regions or with other anthropologists' accounts of Javanese society than I am in making sense of the logics that might allow for such a thorough intermixing of what would ordinarily be seen (by anthropologists, at least) as unmixable events, the *arisan* and the *slametan*. Furthermore, I want to explore the question of what discourses of gender would place both sorts of events, ostensibly "secular" and "religious," "modern" and "traditional," "economic" and "spiritual," "*kasar*" and "*alus*," in the hands of women. How are we to account for the fact that in a city which has long had a reputation for being *the* center of high Javanese culture and tradition, women are entrusted more than men with matters of ritual efficacy, as well as with matters of money?

To address these questions, it is necessary to return to the topic of money and its transformation to an object of cultural value. I will propose that the act of conserving wealth through the control of desire, which is primarily in women's hands, operates as part of an economy of value that is at once material and spiritual. Seen in this light, the immediate juxtaposition of *arisan* and *slametan* is not a bizarre shift from the profane to the sacred, or from the "economic" to the "cultural," because these sharp dichotomies ultimately dissolve under close scrutiny. A Javanese man might say that this curious conjunction is just one more example of women's erratic and unpredictable behavior, another sign of their lack of self-control. Viewed from another angle, however, the *arisan* and the *slametan* are merely two moments in the ongoing process of producing and conserving value, a process in which women play a central role.

THE CONSERVATION OF WEALTH: GIFTS AND LEGACIES

The act of conserving money for the family is not finished when the Laweyan merchant brings it home from the marketplace at the end of the day. Many Javanese believe that wealth and status have little value if they cannot be conserved and reproduced over successive generations. It is the fervent wish of all parents to leave a bequest, *warisan*, to their descendants, in the form of jewelry, land, houses, and other property, especially things that will not depreciate significantly in economic value over time. Objects that have been passed down from past generations are often treated as treasured inheritances. The value of such objects lies in their ability to serve as a conduit of ancestral blessings (*pangèstu*) and as a sign of intergenerational continuity, as much as in their potential market value (although the latter is always kept in mind).

By passing down property that will appreciate, or at least will not decline, in economic value, parents feel that they will be providing for the security of their children and future descendants even when they themselves are no longer living. The term *warisan* conveys not only the sense of some*thing* passed down, but also that of some*one* leaving a part of themselves, through their blessings, to future generations. The *warisan* falls into the category of what Annette Weiner calls "inalienable possessions"—"possessions that are imbued with the intrinsic and ineffable identities of their owners which are not easy to give away." Ideally, she notes, such objects should be kept within the family or descent group, passed down from generation to generation. The loss of an inalienable possession "diminishes the self and by extension the group to which the person belongs" (1992, 6).

The *warisan* can also be understood as a form of "gift" in the Maussian sense. According to Marcel Mauss (1990), in the so-called gift economy the objects that are exchanged are never completely separated from the people who exchange them. Because the bonds that seem to be created by things are in fact bonds between persons, to give something to another person is, in fact, to give a part of oneself. As a form of gift, the *warisan* creates a bond between giver and receiver. This is a vertical bond rather than a horizontal one, however, which extends beyond the life span of individuals. The *warisan* ties together ancestors (*leluhur; nènèk moyang*, I.) and descendants (*turunan* or *anak-putu; keturunan*, I.) in an unbroken chain of descent. The links that forge this chain between past and future generations are both material and spiritual; indeed, as I will show in this chapter, the boundary between the "material" and the "spiritual" is not always clearly drawn.

The capacity to provide for one's descendants is not limited to bequeathing them material wealth accumulated during one's lifetime. Some Javanese believe—although this is hotly contested by the adherents of reformist Islam, ever growing in number—that the spirits of the dead are in a position to look after the well-being of the living. There is a close spiritual connection between ancestors and their descendants, particularly those who actually knew each other in life. People often expect that those individuals who took care of them while they were still alive, especially parents and grandparents, will continue to guard their welfare after they have died. But this gift, like all gifts, demands a return: descendants incur the obligation to "feed" their close ancestors and to provide for the comfort of their souls through prayer and rites of propitiation, such as the scattering of flowers and burning of incense at the grave site. The actual power of ancestors to provide for the welfare of their descendants is ultimately only "proven," however, by the perpetual transmission of the inheritance and by the continued prosperity of their descendants over time.

Money is widely viewed as something inherently unstable, which has a tendency to dry up regardless of any efforts to preserve it. Because of this, money in its raw form does not make for a very suitable *warisan*. Considering the frequent devaluations of the Indonesian *rupiah*, the constant outlays for ritual expenses and children's education, and the unavoidable requests for "contributions" from relatives and government officials alike, it is not surprising that people do not expect money to last long. Furthermore, anyone with money in his or her possession is particularly vulnerable to the influence of *nafsu*, for money is all too readily gambled away (a favorite pastime of some people, especially men) or spent on sensual satisfaction of one kind or another. Being so quickly dissipated, money is not easily passed down to future generations.

This perception of money's instability leads most women to convert at least a portion of whatever cash they manage to put aside into gold jewelry, which they consider to be one of the few "safe" forms of savings.[2] The large numbers of gold shops in every town of Java, most run by Chinese Indonesians, indicate just how widespread this practice is. In Solo a long line of gold jewelry stores is found on Coyudan Street, starting at Pasar Klewer and extending several blocks westward. These shops always seem to be busy, at any time of the year. An acquaintance of mine explained to me why wealthy Solonese women, unlike women in Jakarta, rarely buy expensive batik sarongs or other high-priced clothing, preferring to frequent the gold shops instead: "It's a pity to spend a lot of money on something like batik. Women in Solo would rather put their money into jewelry, which never loses its value. If there's a need for cash, it can be resold. An expensive sarong, though, after it's been worn once or twice, won't be worth more than half its original value."

Anyone who purchases gold jewelry knows that it can be reconverted to money at any time; seated at small tables amid the sellers of mangoes and plaited straw mats on the busy sidewalks of Coyudan Street are women and men with nothing on hand but a balance scale and a few small bottles of chemicals, ready to offer quick cash for gold once they have determined its purity and weight. But when jewelry has been acquired, whether through purchase or inheritance, the ideal—one that is often difficult to realize, given the constant drain on resources—is not to sell it, but to keep it in the form of jewelry so that it can be passed down as a *warisan*. Women of all classes wear earrings of real gold, if only small ones. Even baby girls wear tiny gold hoops in their ears, which suggests that their role as guardian of the family's wealth begins, symbolically at least, at an early age. As an object of condensed value that literally and figuratively attaches to women, jewelry generates prestige for the wearer and her family, representing her ability to preserve something of value for her children. Usually in the possession of women, it is one form of wealth that is generally secure from men's *nafsu*. A woman's obligation to protect the welfare of her family cannot be separated from her central role in maintaining continuity between the generations; the act of conservation is an ongoing one.

While people are fully aware of the economic value of inherited property, they normally prefer not to sell those objects that have been received as a *warisan* if they can avoid doing so. To sell off an inheritance is not only an act of disrespect to one's ancestors, it also means failing in one's obligations to descendants by not providing them with those things that should be theirs by birthright. The *warisan* is a gift put into reserve, passed down to the future. Each generation has the obligation to perpetuate what it received from preceding generations. Selling off the inheritance breaks the chain of continuity with past generations, and by so doing cuts off a source of ancestral blessings. A man I knew, Pak Tridjono, once explained to me that for Javanese, one of the most important things—perhaps *the* most important thing—is to maintain honor, *njaga praja* (literally, "to guard the kingdom"), which he defined as "upholding the name of your family, and the name of those who gave issue to you." The dyadic relationship between ancestors and descendants implies mutual obligation: first, the responsibility of progenitors to provide for their progeny; and second, the responsibility of descendants to bring honor, if only retroactively, to their forebears. To fail to maintain one's good name or social standing is simultaneously to bring shame upon oneself, one's immediate family, and one's ancestors, while also suggesting an inability to fulfill one's responsibilities as an ancestor to future generations.

No individual is more highly regarded than one who has been able to provide something everlasting (*langgeng*) for his or her descendants—although this can really only be determined in retrospect. To reserve material wealth for one's descendants it is necessary to overcome the temptation to consume it in the pursuit of one's own pleasures. This involves the sustained control of *nafsu*: it is a sacrifice that leads to accumulation and conservation. The value of the *warisan* as a wellspring of ancestral blessings stems from its having been set aside through repeated acts of self-denial and designated for the benefit of future generations. This serves to indicate the spiritual strength of each successive generation of benefactors and the depth of their concern for their descendants.

The Economy of Sacrifice

The deliberate act of denying oneself some pleasure or elemental comfort is often designated by the word *prihatin*, which in some contexts means "concerned," "anxious," or "prayerful" but which can also imply "to undergo hardship." In some usages, including the one that I will explore here, it corresponds to our own concept of asceticism. Perhaps the most suitable gloss in this context is "to make a sacrifice." The notion of *prihatin* is based on a kind of law of conservation that is deeply ingrained in Javanese discourse and practice, which might be summed up as "sacrifice now in order to gain later." Or, as Ward Keeler succinctly puts it, "One resists desire in order to see one's desires fulfilled" (1987, 47). This sacrifice, as he notes, is essentially understood as a form of exchange.[3] While sometimes envisioned by Javanese as an "exchange" with God, the assumption of its effectiveness frequently seems to lie less in an individual's direct relationship with an omnipotent deity than in the nature of the cosmic order itself, where every deed, positive or negative, has its corresponding return.

Any conscious effort toward self-denial may be considered a form of *prihatin*; such an act may be dedicated toward the attainment of a specific goal, or it may simply be done in the general conviction that something good is bound to come of it. A rich man who eats cassava instead of rice as his staple food is said to be *prihatin*, since he can afford to eat rice (the preferred staple) but chooses to forgo it for the cheaper and less desirable food. A poor man who eats cassava because he cannot afford rice, however, is never said to be *prihatin*—he is just poor, which, alas, affords no merit.

People believe that to voluntarily give up something that satisfies basic desires will always have its rewards in the long run. Such actions include depriving oneself of the comforts of sleep by staying awake all night or sleeping sitting upright, or forgoing sex or the foods that one likes best. Pak Tridjono remembered that in his youth, older people used to praise him when he would eat nothing but white rice with salt, telling him that when he grew older he would surely become an important man. "Though when you think about it, food like that isn't at all nutritious, and will make you stupid in school," he reflected half-jokingly. Elderly Bu Hamzuri recalled that on reaching puberty, her parents had encouraged her to fast on Mondays and Thursdays, the preferred days of the week for optional fasting, as well as during Ramadan.[4] She was also forbidden to laugh loudly or to behave in other improper ways. "They told me that I had to be *prihatin*, so that I would find a good husband and have a bright future," she said.

What becomes apparent in examining the concept of *prihatin* is that its material dimension is virtually inseparable from its spiritual aspect. To ask someone whether his well-to-do parents ate cassava rather than rice in order to be thrifty or to be *prihatin* was, I soon discovered, to pose a meaningless question. The two are not clearly distinguished in most people's minds, since they merely represent different aspects of a more generalized logic of economy that runs throughout Javanese discourse. The ability to control *nafsu* is seen as an integral part both of economic accumulation, as I discussed in the last chapter, and of the production of the more abstract benefits that accrue through ascetic exercise. What really counts is the act of conservation through self-denial; this is how value, whether economic or spiritual, is produced. Being thrifty may in itself be identified with being *prihatin*, since it requires the ability to deny, or at least delay, gratification. All immediate economic benefits aside, Javanese praise this ability, which is taken as an indication of strong character. One who is able to forgo gratification now will definitely reap the rewards later, many people assured me.

The emphasis on self-sacrifice as a means of accumulating value can be seen in the popularity of various sorts of ascetic practices—*laku*—in Java.[5] Many Javanese seem to feel that withstanding desire through self-discipline or self-denial strengthens an individual's inner self (*batin*), thereby leading to greater spiritual potency (*kakuwatan batin*; see C. Geertz 1960; Anderson 1990c; Keeler 1987). However, asceticism is more than just a character-building exercise. In most cases it is carried out as an instrumental activity aimed at achieving a tangible, often material, goal, such as increased wealth, status, or political power. People engage in *laku* because they want to be successful in business, pass their university examinations, get a promotion, gain access to the spirit world, or win the lottery, among many other possibilities. Ascetic practices, like other forms of being *prihatin*, may also have broader aims, like good health, prosperity, tranquillity of spirit, invulnerability to harm, and a long and peaceful life for oneself and one's family. Some people fast when they are feeling unhappy or out of sorts, as a way of regaining their mental composure.

The scholarly literature on Java has tended to portray ascetic exercise as a predominantly male activity that is closely associated with men's efforts to attain spiritual potency. As Madelon Djajadiningrat-Nieuwenhuis writes, "According to the Javanese idea of the woman's role, she is more bound to her social and material context and consequently less suited for asceticism, which after all means distancing oneself from one's social environment. Only in exceptional cases can women muster sufficient kekuwatan batin (mental strength) to acquire Power" (1987, 47; see also C. Geertz 1960, 329; Keeler 1987, 42 n. 6; Hatley 1990, 182). Once again, there appears to be a gap between ideologies asserting male potency—which usually carry with them a notion of female impotency—and the actual practices of Javanese men and women.

I found that in Solo, both women and men believed in the effectiveness of asceticism as a means of reaching a desired end. Among the people I knew, women were far more likely than men to fast or to rouse themselves from a deep sleep in the middle of the night to pray, two common forms of ascetic practice. On the whole, *laku* is associated less with men than with women in the *sudagar* community, although there are some men who engage in it regularly. One other difference that I noticed between women's and men's ascetic acts is that women are more inclined to dedicate their efforts to the welfare of their children and grandchildren than are men, whose aims tend to be of a more personal nature. There is a widespread belief that engaging in ascetic exercise and other forms of self-discipline can benefit not only the individual who actually carries out the practice but also his or her offspring. Women seem to believe, however, that their ascetic efforts on their childrens' behalf are more effective than their husbands'; some women I knew thought it unlikely that a man would engage in asceticism for his children at all. As Bu Wiyono explained to me, "It's usually women who do *laku*. You see, the one who has feelings, who can feel for her child, is the mother. Fathers just aren't the same." The five or six other women sitting nearby all nodded in agreement, as if they found this point quite obvious.

It is common for women to fast on the days that their children have examinations in school, in the hope that the benefits accrued from controlling their own desires will help their children to do well on their exams. A guest who was visiting the Wiyonos' house turned down the cup of tea that was offered her, informing Bu Wiyono that she was fasting for her son's college exams. To refuse such basic hospitality would normally be a breach of social etiquette, but Bu Wiyono immediately accepted her reason for doing so. "My son isn't so smart," the guest said, smiling apologetically, "so I do it to help him out." One woman who sold textiles in Pasar Klewer even fasted regularly for a son who was studying engineering at a university in Holland. "He always writes to let me know the date of his exams, and asks for my prayers. Each time, when the day comes around, I stay up all night, fast, and pray for his success." Her husband, she admitted, never fasted on their son's behalf: "Fathers don't fast for their children. It's the fasting and prayers of a mother that are the most effective." In general, when a child is ill or in any sort of trouble, it is usually his or her mother who fasts or gets up in the middle of the night to pray in order to bring about a speedy recovery.

I encountered many women who fasted, sometimes twice a week, or engaged in other ascetic acts on a regular basis. These practices were not confined to the circles of the elite. So many women fasted in Laweyan on Mondays and Thursdays that a woman who ran a food stall in the kampong did not bother to open it on those days for lack of business. Men were less inclined to fast, it seemed; several women even told me point-blank that most men did not have the willpower to carry out ascetic practices, drawing into question the ethnographic commonplace that asceticism is mostly a male undertaking in Java.

Bu Sapardi, who was in her sixties, remarked that she, like many other women she knew, woke up automatically at about three o'clock every morning to do *sholat hajat*, a type of optional Islamic prayer that is done when one hopes that a particular wish will be granted by God. It required one hundred movements and took her nearly a quarter of an hour to complete. "Most people here do *laku*," she said.[6] "This is important to us. We do it for our descendants (*anak-putu*; literally, 'children and grandchildren'), to make sure that they're protected (*slamet*—safe, secure, free from trouble) and get rewards from God. We think a lot about our descendants. That's why you're not supposed to fritter away money, or buy lots of things that you don't really need. It's better to put it into the form of savings, like jewelry, for future generations." Like many others, Bu Sapardi did not make an absolute distinction between the material and incorporeal legacies that she intended to leave to those who would follow her. She believed that the spiritual merit that she accumulated through ascetic practices would be passed down to her children and their children, just like the glittering diamond and gold bracelets, earrings, necklaces, and brooches that she kept locked in a safe in her bedroom, many of which she had inherited from her own mother.

Bu Dinar similarly related that when her mother was approaching marriageable age, she would sleep outside on the veranda—also a form of ascetic exercise, since it involves the discomfort of exposing oneself to the elements and unknown spirits of the night—and pray that someday she would have many children, boys as well as girls, and that her children would all "become somebody." And in fact, Bu Dinar added pointedly, eventually her mother *did* have many children—twelve altogether—who all "became somebody."

Stories like these point repeatedly to the obligation to be *prihatin*, which is to say, to conserve something for one's descendants. Even as an unmarried teenager, Bu Dinar's mother was urged to make personal sacrifices for the good of her as-yet unconceived progeny. Not yet a mother, nor even a wife, she nevertheless was encouraged to work toward accumulating value for the children that she would, she and her parents hoped, someday bear.

It appears, then, that the same logic of gender that places women in charge of economic conservation for their families also operates in the spiritual domain. If few men can be expected to restrain their ordinary desires enough to accumulate material wealth for the family, then they can hardly be expected to exercise the more intensive self-discipline needed for ascetic practices on behalf of their offspring. This is not to say that men do not think about their children's welfare, or that they never make any sacrifice for the benefit of their descendants. Several people did actually tell me in retrospect that their fathers or grandfathers had been *prihatin* for the sake of their children and grandchildren. As a general rule, however, women feel that they have a naturally stronger bond with their offspring than their husbands do. This leads them to take the burden of securing their descendants' futures more heavily on their own shoulders. Most men seem quite happy to entrust this responsibility to their wives.

When we bear all of this in mind, the conjunction of the *arisan* and the *slametan* does not seem so strange after all. The *arisan*, as a savings association, provides its members a means of accumulating money. The social pressure to keep paying their weekly dues compels women to set aside some of their cash, which will eventually come back to them in a lump sum when they win the jackpot. They then use the money for some needed household item, for their children's school tuition, or as capital to invest in their businesses.[7] That most *arisan* are run by and for women stems from the woman's role as keeper of the family's money, the person who is supposed to be able to control her desires in order to ensure the family's continued financial well-being. We see as well that on the "spiritual" side of the economy of desire, women are also expected to be able to restrain their passions for the sake of their family and their future descendants. The ability to manage one's desires in this way is basic to the accumulation of what has been called "spiritual potency," although "spiritual capital" might be a more accurate term, since it is thought to be exchangeable for other kinds of benefits, including material ones.

The ritual efficacy of the *slametan* depends on the collective production of a kind of spiritual capital similar to that generated by individuals through ascetic practices and the control of desire. Both men and women can (and do) engage in the production of spiritual value through their participation in the *slametan*. But women take this as a serious duty that they must carry out with or without the help of their husbands. Women see the obligation to participate in ritual as a kind of "helping out" (*réwang*), something that they already do when they assist each other in cooking or preparing in other ways for a ritual celebration, a frequent and time-consuming social requirement for women of all classes. It is usually only mature adults who are expected to "help out" by preparing for or attending *slametan* and other such collective rites—one rarely sees children or young, unmarried adults at these events. Ritual responsibilities are tied to a person's adult status (of which marriage is an important marker) and position in the household and community. As the individuals who are most frequently assigned the work of generating and conserving value for their families, women in particular are also called upon to help generate spiritual value for others in the community. The "domestic economy," then, as an economy of value in both material and spiritual dimensions, extends well beyond the domain of the household, into the sphere of social and ritual life.

HISTORY, DESCENT, AND CULTURAL VALUE

In thinking about the creation and perpetuation of value, we need to consider how value is understood to be passed down from generation to generation. In comparison with some other Indonesian ethnic groups, kinship organization, marriage rules, and principles of descent and inheritance among Javanese are rather vague. With the exception of the royal houses and other select groups, most people do not keep formal genealogical records, nor do they ordinarily keep track of genealogical ties for more than three or four generations.[8] Corporate groups based on descent are notably rare. This does not mean, however, that descent is unimportant here; on the contrary, the importance of having descendants cannot be overemphasized. If a woman does not become pregnant within a few months after marrying, she, her husband, and both of their extended families worry endlessly that the union will be barren. Despite the government's generally successful campaign to promote the use of birth control in Indonesia, few couples would consider using it before the birth of at least one child. The idea of marriage is essentially inseparable from that of having children, and most people frown on the thought of deliberately postponing the first pregnancy, as if that would somehow be tempting fate and might result in the couple never having any children. That anyone would want a life without children at all is almost unthinkable.

The tremendous emphasis that is placed on having children goes beyond whatever emotional satisfaction people may derive from parenting (though children are much loved and pampered in Java), or their concerns for the household's economic welfare or for security in their old age. Pak Tridjono attempted to elucidate for me how vital having descendants is for Javanese. "Maybe for people in the West it's not so important to have children," he mused. "And when you think about it, children really are a kind of burden. But for a Javanese, not to have children is a terrible thing." I asked him why that is so. "We must have descendants, so that there's someone to continue where we leave off," he answered simply. "So that things don't just come to a stop" (*Supaya nggak mandheg*), his son added. *Mandheg* (to stop) implies not a gradual running down but a sudden halt, suggesting that without descendants, there is no continuity, no future: just a complete and irreversible end to a person's existence.

The desire to have descendants is not rooted only in the wish of individuals for self-perpetuation. An equally weighty consideration is the fulfillment of obligations to past as well as future generations. The individual person, as we have seen, is conceived of as a link in the chain that extends from ancestors to descendants. The present generation is responsible for paying back debts incurred to ancestors, and part of this payment is ensuring that continuity is maintained through the future. To have children is a sign of deference to one's forebears, an acknowledgment of the debt that they are owed for one's very existence. The second, equally important responsibility is to do everything possible to provide for the security and welfare of one's progeny; this starts, of course, with giving them life. As it turns out, these responsibilities are merely two moments of the same process. Attending to the well-being of descendants is an essential part of repaying one's ancestors, because it makes it possible for the spiritual and material blessings bestowed by past generations to flow uninterruptedly to their descendants.

It is thus understandable that Solonese often speak in hushed, pitying voices of childless people. In Laweyan there were several very wealthy couples who had been unable to have children. Although each of them had eventually adopted children, people in the neighborhood still shook their heads and remarked on how sad it was that they had no children of their own to whom they could bequeath their riches. The implication was that in the long run, all of their wealth and hard work would be for naught if they had no proper heirs to inherit it. For this reason, a tiny, white-haired lady who sold textiles in Pasar Klewer told me wistfully that because she was childless, her fifty-odd years of earning money as a market trader had been "useless" (*mboten wonten ginanipun*). Her wealth would not be passed down to her descendants and was therefore without inherent value. It was, in short, "empty" money.

As I mentioned earlier, one finds a strong connection in Java between the notion of historical legitimacy and that of cultural authenticity and value. The greatest value is attributed to knowledge and things that, it is claimed, have been passed down from previous generations to the present. From such a perspective, only those things said to have been received as a bequest from the ancestors—particularly ancestors of high status—may be considered to be of full cultural value. Value, according to this formulation, and even culture itself, is understood to be generated through the historical process. History becomes the very source of cultural legitimacy: to say that something is without history is to imply that it has no intrinsic worth.

Wealth, like everything else, is incorporated into the hierarchies that infuse so many dimensions of Javanese social and cultural life. Not all wealth, though, is valuable in a cultural sense. Money that is earned through commerce or labor, for instance, contains no trace of its origins— it has no legible history and provides no links to the past.[9] As the universal equivalent, money is "the absolutely alienable commodity, because it is all other commodities divested of their shape, the product of their universal alienation" (Marx [1867] 1977, 205). It is this quality of absolute alienability that ordinarily prevents money in its basic form from acquiring cultural value. As a rule money has value only in its exchangeability for other commodities, but as we have seen, cultural value in the Javanese context is acquired mainly through the process of *conservation*, the process of taking something *out of* the sphere of exchange and keeping it in reserve.

We saw in the last chapter, however, that money, ordinarily associated with the *kasar* realm of the marketplace—a realm that most Javanese would consider to be outside the domain of "culture" altogether—can be transformed into something *alus*, of cultural value, through the process of domestication and conservation. If value may be said to originate in conservation, then the continued act of conservation over time not only creates, but also increases and regenerates, value. It is by removing an object from circulation, and in particular, by refraining from exchanging it for something that would satisfy one's immediate desires, that it becomes culturally valuable. At the same time, taking money out of circulation by turning it into a *warisan* is the opposite movement from that of capital, where money must keep circulating. This basic means of generating cultural value from wealth, then, is fundamentally at odds with capitalist enterprise and its insistence on the perpetual reinvestment of money toward the pursuit of more money.

Simmel's intriguing comments on the subjectivity of value, which appear in *The Philosophy of Money* ([1907] 1990), have a distinct resonance here. Value, he notes, is not an intrinsic quality of objects "but a judgment upon them which remains inherent in the subject" (63). Value is created subjectively, in the process of imagining the satisfaction that the enjoyment of an object would provide; it arises through the desire that the not-yet-attained object incites in the subject. The value of an object, then, is engendered in the separation between subject and object—in that space in which the object is desired, but not yet consumed. "We desire objects," he proposes, "only if they are not immediately given to us for our use and enjoyment; that is, to the extent that they resist our desire" (66). It therefore follows that "we call those objects valuable that resist our desire to possess them" (67). Value is created only when the object remains at a distance from the subject, out of reach but still close enough to be desired. Viewing the economy as a particular case of the general form of exchange, "a surrender of something in order to gain something," he suggests that value accrues to an object partly or wholly from the extent of the sacrifice that is needed to obtain it (87).

Simmel's ideas—while obviously not intended as an explanation of anything specifically Javanese—strike me as curiously well suited to grasping how the economy of value is construed in Java. His explanation is especially useful in pointing to the inherent connections between the subjective experience of desire, sacrifice, and the assignation of value. It should be clear by now that the concept of desire, *nafsu*, bears a particular weight in Javanese notions of subjectivity. The ability to control one's desire is always viewed positively; this is seen as the key to producing value for oneself as well as for one's descendants. Value, as we have seen, has both a material aspect and a spiritual aspect to it. By restraining desire and deferring gratification, an individual accumulates both economic value and spiritual value for herself and her family, which can be called upon, if needed (cashed in, one might say), at a later time. Economic and spiritual resources are often considered exchangeable—involving a sacrifice in return for a gain—as, for example, when a Muslim gives alms or builds a mosque in the hope of accumulating religious merit (which Bu Hamzuri once described as "a savings account for heaven"), or when a person meditates all night at the tomb of a powerful figure in the hope of winning the lottery.

It follows, then, that the more a person restrains her desires, the more value she creates. The greatest value is accumulated by conserving resources over a long period of time and passing them down to one's descendants as a bequest. By doing so, an individual shows that she has made the ultimate sacrifice: she has renounced the possibility of satisfying her *own* desires for the sake of her children and future generations. The enjoyment of the object of desire is deferred indefinitely. Such a sacrifice generates the greatest concentration of value and brings the highest honor to the family. This is why, I would propose, a *warisan* (especially one that has been passed down over more than one generation) is often believed to have an almost sacred value, even a magical potency in the case of some objects. It stands as a material testimony to the spiritual strength of those who passed it down, people who repeatedly denied themselves the gratification of their own desires in order to keep something in reserve for their descendants.

Money itself, as we have seen, does not make a very appropriate *warisan*. It is too easily dispersed and, as the universal equivalent, it does not carry with it any traces of historical value or ancestral blessings. However, money that has been transformed into an object of value can been conserved and passed down from generation to generation as a *warisan*. Such an object of value, be it in the form of jewelry, land, a house, or a prized ceremonial dagger (*keris*), becomes a sign of continuity with the ancestral past. As such, it is also a sign of the sacrifice of ancestors on behalf of their descendants.

The comments of one Solonese woman may clarify how wealth seems to acquire cultural value as it is passed down over the generations. Bu Warsito was a loyal retainer of the Kraton who worked as the caretaker (*juru kunci*) of the royal cemetery in Laweyan, with the official title "Madame Caretaker of Souls" (Nyai Lurah Hamongsukma). She had lived in Laweyan all of her life, having inherited her position from her mother. As a servant of the palace, however, she chose to identify with the values of the Solonese nobility and their courtiers rather than with those of the local merchants. Bu Warsito shared her knowledge of Laweyan and its history with me on several occasions. In the eyes of the Kraton, she stated, no matter how much money Laweyan people had, they would never be more than common folk, because they were not of royal descent (*mboten kagungan turun ningrat*). However, she did feel that there was a difference between those entrepreneurs and traders who were "truly" wealthy (*sing sugih saèstu*), that is, those whose wealth was legitimate, and those who had come into their wealth illegitimately, through the use of magical means (*sing golèk pasugihan*).

The sign of "real" wealth, Bu Warsito explained, is that it never dries up. As she put it,

> The truly rich families stay rich generation after generation (*turun-tumurun sugih*). The wealth gets passed down from the ancestors to their children, grandchildren, great-grandchildren, great-great-grandchildren, and great-great-great-grandchildren. There's no end to it—it just keeps on going (*diturunaké nyang anak, putu, buyut, canggah, warèng, tetep isih waé*). But it's a different story with people who use magical means (*pasugihan*) to get their money. After one generation, their money usually runs out. When the person dies, that's it. It can't be handed down.

In Bu Warsito's opinion, most of the merchants of Laweyan fell into the category of those whose wealth had come down to them from their ancestors (*saking kakèk moyangipun dipunlangsungaken*). Few, she believed, had been reduced to using *pasugihan* to acquire their wealth. It was mostly just petty traders who resorted to the use of magic, she suggested, so that their goods would sell.

The distinction that Bu Warsito made between "real" wealth and illegitimate wealth reflects the importance of both hierarchy and history in establishing cultural legitimacy and value. Those people whose wealth was traceable to their ancestors automatically had a rightful claim to the *warisan* bequeathed to them by senior generations. The legitimacy of the *warisan* itself was firmly established by the fact that it had been passed down successfully over the generations. In other words, it was wealth with a history, which had been removed from circulation and conserved through a sustained sacrifice—wealth that had genuine value. In contrast, according to common belief, those whose money is obtained through diabolical means, rich though they might be in the short run, will not be able to pass their wealth down to their descendants, because illegitimate wealth can never be a source of perpetual value.

The corollary to this belief is that people who become rich all of a sudden (say, through a new and unexpectedly successful business venture) are immediately suspected of having come by their wealth through illicit means involving a *pasugihan*. Such illegitimate money is also believed to involve a sacrifice, because, consistent with the "law of conservation" that I discussed earlier, there can be no gain without a sacrifice of some kind, just as there can be no sacrifice without an eventual gain. However, in place of the sacrifice of ancestors for their descendants through the control of desire, which produces a positive, fertile, and long-lasting value, people who are said to have used magic to become rich are frequently accused of having done so by sacrificing the health, the mental faculties, or even the lives of their children or employees to various kinds of demonic beings.

People from other neighborhoods sometimes confronted me with rumors, for instance, that many children of Laweyan entrepreneurs were "not right in the head" (either mentally impaired or psychologically disturbed), having been sacrificed by their parents to the demands of a *pasugihan* (as the rumors had it) so that the parents could be wealthy. This implies a disruption of the rules of hierarchy, along with an obvious breach of morality, because in this case the source of wealth is believed to be the unwilling sacrifice on the part of juniors for people who are their seniors, rather than the voluntary sacrifice of seniors on behalf of their juniors, as it should be. A parent may not ask a child for blessings, since blessings must always flow from those of higher status to those of lower status, never in the opposite direction. Wealth acquired through the use of a *pasugihan* is believed to be barren wealth, wealth that cannot be regenerated, because it is not accumulated through the legitimate production and conservation of value.[10]

Despite the frequency with which Laweyan's residents dedicated themselves to fasting and other acts of abstinence, there was an overwhelming feeling in the merchant community that the days in which people truly knew how to make sacrifices were long gone. People spoke of their parents' and grandparents' ability to be *prihatin* with a quiet admiration, always adding ruefully that they themselves were not capable of such self-discipline. They contrasted the toughness, self-control, and frugality of their parents' and grandparents' generations with the present generation's softness, extravagant tastes, and unwillingness to work hard or to endure even the slightest deprivation. The ability to make deep sacrifices was always located at least a generation or two behind the speaker, no matter how old he or she was. This displacement of the *prihatin* ethic from the present to the past removed the burden of self-sacrifice away from members of the present generation, freeing them to engage in the conspicuous consumption that was the hallmark of the *sudagar* community in particular and of the New Order era in general.

"In the old days, Javanese entrepreneurs didn't like to spend a lot of money on consumption," declared Bu Hamzuri, as we sat on mats on the marble floor of her mansion, surrounded by expensive antiques, plates of Javanese sweets and fruit, and attended by a couple of frail female servants. "They liked to eat simply—rice with a piece of tofu—at most they'd eat a bit of fish and *sambal* (chili paste) with their rice. These days, people aren't satisfied unless they have meat at every meal. Back then, if you owned a house at all, it was a crummy one. And the rule of thumb was that unless you had enough money to buy *ten* cars, you wouldn't even buy one. Today, the minute people make a little money, they go out and buy a new car."

An illustration of the simultaneously material and spiritual aspect of the ethic of sacrifice—located again in the past—came from Pak Djohari and his wife, both retired batik workers. One day when they were talking about the ways in which ritual celebrations had changed since their youth, the two of them reminisced about the days when guests at a wedding would never finish the food served to them. To clean one's plate was strictly taboo. The reason for this, Bu Djohari informed me, was that "You had to leave some food behind, to make sure that your descendants would always have enough to eat, too" (*Kudu nurahi, ngèngèhi sisa, supaya anak-putu mèlu mangan, supaya anak-putu aja nganti ora mangan*). The logic behind this was, once again, that the act of restraining one's own desires would leave something in reserve for one's heirs. It was a sacrifice that generated an excess. Now, they added, the custom of leaving a little food behind on the plate was being abandoned by the younger generation; the newer idea that one should finish all of one's food was "an Islamic teaching" (*ajaran Islam*).[11]

A man who had married into a Laweyan family mentioned that his father, a rich diamond broker, ate poor-quality rice and drank tea without sugar—neither of which is a small sacrifice for someone from Solo, where rice is eaten at almost every meal and tea, sipped constantly throughout the day, is ordinarily served very sweet. "He did it for the future of his children and grandchildren, so they would be prosperous. But nowadays, people don't know how to be careful the way my father was. If they have a little extra cash, they'll spend it all on buying *saté* or snacks."

Some people drew an explicit connection between success in business, or lack thereof, and the ability or inability to be *prihatin*. One day I was escorted to the home of Pak Suwarno, an eighty-five-year-old retired *juragan* of substantial means whose parents had established one of the neighborhood's batik dynasties. During the course of our conversation, I inquired whether, in his opinion, there was one key to success in business. Expecting to be told about the merits of hard work or careful capital investment, I was unprepared for his answer:

> When I was still a boy, my parents told me that when I grew up I had to make sure to be diligent about doing *laku*. My father used to walk a long way at night to soak himself (*laku kungkum*) in the Solo River.[12] So, when I got older, I did this kind of *laku*, too—not in the Solo River, like my father, but in a big vat of water in my batik factory, every night. The reason for doing *laku* is to train yourself, so you're not easily led astray. If your heart isn't good, you can't be successful. I can always tell if someone doesn't have a good heart—if they've been doing things like fooling around with women or gambling. That's what causes their downfall.

Pak Suwarno acknowledged that in the end, the decline of his own business had resulted from his weakness for gambling; his *nafsu* had gotten the best of him. He was convinced that the owners of the one Javanese batik firm in Solo that was still very successful must surely be doing *laku* on a regular basis; otherwise they would never have fared so well.

The goal of these Solonese merchants was to be able to create lasting value through the conservation of material and spiritual resources, which would enable them and their descendants to reproduce status and prosperity for themselves continually. It is only through the perpetuation of the inheritance, in both its material and incorporeal aspects, that this can be accomplished. In an ideal scenario, the merchants of Solo would have continued to pass down their legacies—their jewels, their fine homes, and, equally important, their blessings—for many generations to come.

Unfortunately, the New Order ushered in a period of steady decline for the members of the old Javanese *sudagar* class, a downturn of fortunes from which most would be unable to recover. In Laweyan, the bankruptcy of such a large number of firms was attributed by many people, merchants and nonmerchants alike, to the overall moral and spiritual decline of the times, which was manifested in people's increasing greed—their *nafsu*—and lack of self-discipline. Of course, everyone recognized the disastrous effects on the batik industry of factors external to the community, such as the competition posed by printed imitation batik and, more generally, the expanding influence of big capital in the Indonesian economy. The prevailing mood in the neighborhood, though, once the thriving center of the city's most lucrative industry, was one of nostalgia for the days when people knew how to master their desires, for their own sake as well as for the sake of their descendants. The notion of a growing moral and spiritual decadence was underscored by the physical decay and abandonment of homes that had once been stately, and by the rapid decline of a business that, only a generation or two earlier, had seemed an inexhaustible source of wealth.

ANCESTRAL COMMODITIES AND THE REGENERATION OF VALUE

Even the most bountiful inheritance will soon dry up if it is not regenerated. This is especially true when there are many descendants, since by Javanese custom, all of the children produced by a married couple have a claim to an equal share of the *warisan* from both parents, regardless of sex or birth order. Theory does not always accord with practice, however. Because few people leave written wills, there are often acrimonious disputes between siblings, as well as any others who might claim rights to the inheritance, as each competes for a larger portion. One source of the conflict is that all of them share the same ancestors, but none share the same descendants, so it is up to each individual to make sure that his or her own descendants receive as much of the inheritance as possible. As a result, the *warisan* is divided with each subsequent generation. Efforts of siblings to keep the inheritance intact by maintaining joint property or businesses are, to my knowledge, quite rare among Javanese, and they seem to be doomed to failure in a relatively short time.

For wealth to be passed down in perpetuity, then, it must be reproducible with each generation. In Laweyan and other neighborhoods of Solo, the batik firms themselves appeared, at least until the 1970s, to provide the ideal means for regenerating wealth over time. It was a matter of course for the children of batik entrepreneurs to start their own firms when they reached adulthood and married; they saw this as the easiest and most natural path to follow. That the decline of the firms in the 1970s and 1980s was met with something akin to disbelief in the batik communities may be accounted for by the lingering, still-vivid memory of previous decades, when the batik business had produced seemingly limitless wealth.

Some people in Laweyan were convinced that batik still offered the surest source of livelihood, if not necessarily prosperity. Bu Hartati, whose once-vigorous firm had languished for several years, had halfheartedly tried to move into a few other businesses, such as raising quails and investing in a small fried chicken restaurant. After her failures in the poultry field, she had returned to producing and trading batik for small profits. She explained her reluctance to abandon batik for another line of business in the following way:

> Being in the batik business is tough (*cokot-cokot alod*; literally, "if you bite it, it's tough"). Lots of batik producers here have tried going into other businesses— opening fried chicken restaurants, raising quails, and that sort of thing. But all of those businesses are just fashion (*musiman*).[13] People get tired of fried chicken and the restaurant goes out of business. Or the quails catch some disease and die. Batik is different, though. Even at times when the market is slow, the business won't die out altogether. There are good times and not-so-good times, but you can always keep going, at least on a small scale. That's because batik isn't fashion, it's from our ancestors.

Bu Hartati was not the only person in Laweyan to tell me of batik's ancestral origins. When I would ask local entrepreneurs how long their families had been in the batik business, I often received the reply, "Oh, for a long time, since the time of my ancestors." Such an answer was of little use in my efforts to determine for how many generations certain families had been producing batik. At the same time, I soon came to realize that this answer was meaningful in itself. When a *juragan* told me that her family had been making batik since the time of her ancestors, she was marking her business as something of more than just economic value. She was transforming it from an ordinary business into a *warisan*, an almost sacred heirloom that had been passed down from time immemorial. It mattered little that for most batik families, "since the time of my ancestors" had been at most three or four generations, for few Javanese have any knowledge of or interest in the identities or occupations of their forebears beyond their grandparents or great-grandparents.[14] Nor did it matter to people like Bu Hartati that as early as 1918, when Laweyan entrepreneurs had only been manufacturing batik for a few decades, *Scribner's Magazine* was already noting that Javanese batik had "recently become a fad in New York," its patterns suitable for imitation in dresses, neckties, bathrobes, and even wallpaper and rugs (Sams 1918, 509). New York's fashion, it seems, was to become Solo's "tradition." One could argue that attributing the origin of the inheritance to ancestral time, a time before memory, increased its value. Unfettered by a bounded temporality, it could better stand as a sign of continuity with a lofty past, and consequently, as a sign of high status and cultural value.

By treating the batik business as a *warisan*, these producers and merchants were identifying their commodity, and the batik industry itself, as a powerful source of ancestral blessings. Its value lay in its ability to produce and regenerate value generation after generation. This was in marked contrast to the evanescence of businesses that depended on the whims of fashion, which might be very profitable in the short run but which could never be a source of everlasting value, as they saw it. Batik might well have been a fad in New York in 1918, but in Solo seventy years later it was an almost sacred inheritance, a bond that linked together ancestors and their descendants.

In her discussion of "inalienable possessions," Weiner (1992) points out that certain items—frequently in the form of cloth (especially relevant here), but also other objects or special types of knowledge—become particularly valuable when they are taken out of circulation and turned into signifiers of historical continuity with a transcendent past. Such objects acquire value not only through their conservation over time, but also through their "cosmological authentication" by true or fictive genealogies and historical events or through their association with the realm of sacred ancestors, origin myths, or gods. "What gives these possessions their fame and power," she writes, "is their authentication through an authority perceived to be outside the present" (42). Their histories and identities give them a subjective value superior to that of objects with ordinary exchange value. Weiner observes, however, that behind the value of these items also lies the ever-present danger of their loss (6), which means the loss of memory and the loss of continuity between the past, present, and future. Such objects become, then, a sign of cultural and social reproduction and continuity in the face of a fundamental instability. As she puts it, "the most that such possessions accomplish is to bring a vision of permanence into a social world that is always in the process of change" (8). They do not prevent change but instead acquire their value through its inevitability.

The concept of inalienable possessions provides one way to think about the valorization of batik. This entire industry became a *warisan* at the point when the danger of its loss—and the loss of an entire way of life and the community that had developed around it—seemed most acute. At a time of rapid social change and uncertainty about the future, the maintenance of the industry, weak though it was, could be made to serve as a sign of stability and continuity with the past. To insist that batik was not fashion, but something of eternal value, was to give it a permanence that put it outside the domains of both change and exchange. It could not simply be substituted for by something else. The associations of batik cloth itself, through its linkages with court culture and as an object of ritual significance in Java, lend it an aura of sanctity and cultural authenticity that makes it—as well as the industry that surrounds it—fitting as such an inalienable possession.

Weiner observes that in many societies, cloth has the status of a highly valued object that embodies cosmological, regenerative, and political as well as economic significance.[15] This has certainly been true in Indonesia and in many other parts of Southeast Asia and the Pacific. The ritual and economic importance of batik cloth in Java, and its historical association with the nobility, imparts an air of cultural value even to the commercial sides of batik production and trade. One can hardly imagine someone calling fried chicken a *warisan* from the ancestors, no matter how lucrative its sale happens to be, but the special status of batik in Java allows its producers and traders to claim it, even in its fully commodified form, as an emblem of ancestral value.

In most batik families, the firms themselves were not passed down from generation to generation; by convention, each generation began anew to build its own firms. What *were* passed down were the skills needed to make batik. These included the jealously guarded "batik secrets" that centered especially on the tricky matter of dye making, for even subtle nuances in the shade of the natural dyes could make or break a firm. The technical knowledge needed to make batik, then, was also treated as a most important *warisan*, one that would ideally enable the inheritor to reproduce time and time again the wealth that had been produced by his or her ancestors. Even after information about dye making and batik production techniques became readily available to the public, many children and grandchildren of batik entrepreneurs continued to guard and carefully follow the recipes and methods that they had acquired from their own parents. To reenact their predecessors' techniques of batik production was an act of faith and a gesture of deference. In return, they hoped to receive ancestral blessings in the form of abundant wealth and high status.

Where the knowledge of these techniques came from in the first place seemed of little concern to anyone, though. An interesting case is that of Bu Kartika, the Dutch-educated aristocrat who ran a workshop for dyeing high-quality *batik tulis* with *soga Jawa*, a golden-brown natural dye for which Solonese batik is well known. She boasted that her prized *soga* recipe had been passed down as a *warisan* through the maternal line from her aristocratic great-grandmother. It was a secret known only to the other women in her family, one that she planned to pass on to her own daughter when the proper time came. She also claimed, however, that her great-grandmother had originally acquired the recipe from a Dutch batik entrepreneur. "Back in those days," she said, "Javanese people didn't know how to make *soga* turn out the same color every time. Sometimes it would be a deep brown, other times it would end up yellowish. They didn't use precise measures—they just did it like cooking, throwing in some of this and a little of that. But my great-grandmother wanted to learn how to make it turn out the same each time. So she studied from a Dutch person. And her recipe is basically the same recipe that I use today."

Bu Kartika's *soga* recipe was no less valuable a *warisan* for having originated with a Dutchman.[16] Furthermore, she was careful to follow precisely not only the dye recipe itself but also the ritual steps that her mother had taken to ensure the success of the dyeing process. Once a month, at the finishing stages of this laborious process, she would call in neighbors to assist her and her permanent workers in hanging the freshly dyed and washed batik cloths out on long bamboo poles, scraping the excess wax from them with a fine metal tool, laying them out in the sun to dry, and stamping them in ink with her trademark. Like her mother, and perhaps her grandmother and great-grandmother as well, she burned incense in the work area, which was right outside her house, so that the process would be protected (*slamet*). Her mother had set out plates of Javanese sweets (*jajan pasar*, "market snacks"), a rainbow-colored assortment of snacks made of sticky rice, cassava, and agar, as ritual offerings (*sajèn*) to the spirits during this final stage of the process. Bu Kartika's modern adaptation of this practice was simply to offer the sweets directly to the people who came to work; the effect was "just the same," she declared. She would start the finishing touches of the dyeing process on Fridays, the Muslim holy day, so that the *soga* would come out with a nice golden hue. (In the old days, she told me, women would chew a wad of bright-red betel during the dyeing if they wanted their *soga* to have a reddish hue.) In addition, once a year she held a *slametan* (at her workers' urging, she insisted) to promote security and prosperity for herself and those who worked for her.

The emphasis on remaining in the same business as one's forebears and repeating their methods of production may well be seen as a kind of conservatism, but it is conservatism in the most literal sense of the word, based on the desire to *conserve* something of value from the past, something that has already been conserved and passed down by one's ancestors. The comment of Bu Usman from the Kauman, a fourth- or fifth-generation batik producer, was representative of many others: "Our ancestors (*mbah-mbah*; literally, 'grandparents') started making batik a long time ago. After that, all that was left for us to do was to continue it, to keep it going." Like the numerous other entrepreneurs who told me that their families had made batik "generation after generation" (*turun-tumurun*), she said this not with resignation but with a note of pride in her voice. The meaning behind this remark was that her ancestors had created something lasting, and therefore of great cultural (not to mention economic) value, for their descendants. Following the path that had been laid out for her, she had been able to reap their blessings and to prosper.

This is not entrepreneurship as it is typically understood in the context of the United States, which centers on the image of the "self-made man" forging his own path to riches through innovation and the sweat of his brow. Not that there was no effort involved—without question, Bu Usman *had* put a lot of work into her business. "I worked hard, day and night, but I never felt tired," she told me. In the 1950s and early 1960s, she had traveled frequently to other Javanese cities to trade her batik, often making the long, hot, round-trip journey by train or bus in a single day. Still, her story conveyed no sense of an upward struggle against the odds. Rather, as she saw it, she and her husband were simply fulfilling their destinies as the children, grandchildren, and great-grandchildren of batik producers. Tracing their ancestors' footsteps—using the same dye recipes and wax mixtures that their parents and grandparents had used, producing batik decorated with many of the same timeworn motifs—led to a feeling of security that stemmed from having taken their correct place in the line of descent. It was in this place that they were properly positioned to receive the blessings bestowed and the value created by their ancestors.[17]

Bu Usman mentioned to me that her devout Muslim parents had never slept much at night. "Mostly they stayed up and prayed for their children," she said, a sign of their willingness to make sacrifices for the benefit of their offspring. Their success in conserving something of value for their descendants was proven to Bu Usman's satisfaction by her own success in business, and by that of her children, who had become professionals in various fields at a time when the batik industry was no longer a reliable source of livelihood. Bu Usman had the contented air of one who knew that she had been well provided for by her ancestors, and that she in turn had dutifully upheld their honor by passing on to her own children the blessings, material and otherwise, that she had received from previous generations.

"Preserving Tradition"

The success of Bu Usman and her husband did not compare, however, with the success of a younger Javanese couple in Solo, Ibu Danar and Bapak Santosa, blood relatives whose families had been prominent producers of batik and *tenun* (woven cloth) in Solo for several generations.[18] Truly "enterprising" entrepreneurs, this husband-and-wife team had managed to turn their family firm, Batik Danar Hadi, into a multimillion-dollar company in the 1970s and 1980s. They had the only Javanese firm large and highly capitalized enough to compete with the two major companies run by Chinese Indonesians, both Solo-based, which dominated the Indonesian market for batik and imitation batik. The key to its flourishing at a time when most other batik firms were failing was the owners' quickness to diversify outside the field of traditional batik. Besides opening up a successful chain of upscale batik shops all over Indonesia, they also went into mass production and sales of ready-to-wear garments, printed imitations of batik fabric, undyed cloth, and other items. In addition, they opened a swank (by Solo's standards) restaurant and nightclub called Dynasty (at about the same time, they built a mosque behind their factory). By the mid-1980s only a small fraction of their profits came from the sale of traditional batik, most of which they did not even produce themselves.[19] In 1988 their company had more than two thousand employees.

Widely admired by the entire Solonese merchant community, they were believed to have brought untold honor to the names of their parents and grandparents. Although they were not from Laweyan, they were the object of high regard there and had relatives in the neighborhood. Yet no one from Laweyan—nor anyone else from the old Javanese batik communities—seemed capable of imitating them; many people wondered aloud how Pak Santosa and Bu Danar could be so progressive (*maju*) in their thinking. Some said that they had been advised by a parent or grandparent to emulate the Chinese rather than the Javanese in their methods of business management; that Pak Santosa's father had been a well-educated physician rather than a *juragan* may have contributed to a more progressive attitude as well. The extraordinary success of this couple was taken in the *sudagar* community to reflect not only their own formidable accomplishments as entrepreneurs, but also the power of their ancestors to provide for them through their blessings and a generous inheritance. Their success, then, proved that the mutual obligations between the couple and their forebears had been fulfilled to the utmost: their ancestors obviously had provided amply for their welfare, while they themselves had reciprocated the gift of the *warisan* by using it to uphold their ancestors' good names. The process of regenerating the *warisan* was to be continued by their children, who were being groomed to take over the business at some point in the future.

The deliberate effort of the couple themselves to draw attention to the "ancestral" origins of their business was highlighted by an impressive advertisement that they took out in Indonesia's largest daily newspaper, *Kompas*, published in Jakarta. The ad featured a half-page photograph of Pak Santosa's grandparents (who were also Bu Danar's relatives), Bapak and Ibu Raden Haji Saleh Wongsodinomo, who had been among the most successful textile entrepreneurs in Solo in their day. The accompanying text read as follows:

> Preserving Tradition (*Me'nembok' Tradisi*)
> *Me'nembok'*, to cover certain designs on the face of a cloth [with wax] so that they stay white, unpenetrated by dye. One episode (*satu episode*) in the process of creating batik. With the touch of a hand. With the fullest of care. Just as batik artists have done, since hundreds of years ago . . . preserved by Batik Danar Hadi. Starting with the Danar Hadi family's tradition of fine dressing. Whereby the attractiveness of the pattern, the loveliness of the color and the quality of the cloth . . . must radiate the enchantment of the wearer. Danar Hadi preserves the beauty of the tradition of fine dressing (*me'nembok' eloknya tradisi berbusana*). The tradition of genuine batik (*Tradisi batik asli*). The true tradition of Indonesia (*Tradisi Indonesia sejati*).[20]

The message of this advertisement, as communicated through the photograph of the ancestral couple (which was printed in sepia tint to appear "genuinely" old) and the text itself, is that Batik Danar Hadi is continuing the high "Indonesian" (read: Javanese) traditions of batik making and refined appareling (the text makes ample use of the loanword *tradisi*, from the Dutch *traditie*).[21] They appear not to be selling a commodity so much as preserving the integrity of an *alus* art form, a *warisan* from the past that was handed down to the owners by their ancestors.

In fact, there was nothing traditional about the Danar Hadi firm or most of their products, which was exactly the reason for their success. Their methods of production, management, marketing, and advertising were all distinctly modern. The language used in their advertisement, for example, has a style and rhythm to it that is strongly reminiscent of American advertising, snappy and upbeat. It provides a notable contrast to the "old-fashioned" photograph that the text accompanies, exemplifying a typical New Order Indonesian style of invoking the authority of tradition while welcoming modern progress. Unlike the majority of Solonese batik merchants, the owners of this firm sold their goods not in the hot, fiercely competitive, overcrowded marketplace but in quiet, air-conditioned retail shops with smartly dressed mannequins in the windows, crystal chandeliers dangling from the ceilings, and a bevy of uniformed salesgirls at the customer's beck and call—credit cards accepted, no bargaining allowed. Although they did sell some high-quality *batik tulis* in traditional colors and designs, much more of the firm's income depended on the sale of factory-manufactured textiles and Western-style garments—dresses, bathrobes, men's tailored shirts, and so on—made out of brightly colored rayon or cotton fabric printed with batik-style motifs.

The notion that a business or a commodity could be of ancestral, and therefore *alus*, origins fundamentally contradicts dominant *priyayi* ideologies of culture (not to mention popular Western notions about what constitutes "traditional" culture). According to *priyayi* formulations, as we have seen, business is dedicated to the quest for profit, a sign of self-interest; it is thus *kasar* and of low status. Nothing, it would seem, could be more antithetical to the *priyayi* ethos than the world of commodities, commerce, and wage labor. In the world of *priyayi* ideology, there can be neither honor nor cultural value in an occupation that takes as its highest goal the pursuit of money, because money in its pure form neither respects hierarchy nor acknowledges history, the two axes around which "culture" turns in Java.

However, the emphasis on maintaining—or perhaps fabricating—"tradition" in the batik industry suggests that Javanese batik producers have borrowed from, and in some cases selectively reinterpreted, *priyayi* cultural ideologies. Not just *any* commodity could be called a gift from the ancestors. Batik entrepreneurs are able to claim ancestral origins and a modicum of cultural legitimacy for their business precisely because of the *priyayi* associations of their commodity, its links to the *alus* culture of the palaces. Batik, like Javanese court dance or shadow puppet plays, is thought by many Javanese to embody the loftier moral, philosophical, and aesthetic values of a time past. Solonese from all walks of life were constantly telling me that as a student of Javanese cultural life with an interest in batik, I really ought to be studying the deep philosophical meanings of batik designs—meanings which almost no one could explain, but which they were absolutely certain existed. That they themselves were not privy to this esoteric knowledge was unimportant; if anything, it added to the mystique surrounding the designs.[22]

Such notions of high culture and tradition have also been thoroughly co-opted by the Indonesian state in its own quest for legitimation, political stability, and social control. A brochure titled "What Batik Means to Us" (*Arti Batik Bagi Kita*) was put out by the New Order government in 1967, shortly after the regime's ascent to power. It begins with the declaration, "How happy we all are that we have inherited Batik from our ancestors, which has put the Indonesian nation in the center of the international world. How could we not be! Because talking about Batik for Indonesia is just the same as talking about the Kimono for Japan, the Sari for India, or the Chongsam for China. Batik constitutes our national identity (*Batik merupakan indentity nasional kita*)" (Harjono 1967, 5). The success of this effort to make batik into a symbol of the Indonesian nation, which began in the Sukarno era,[23] was revealed in a comment made by a Solonese woman at a wedding I attended. When I remarked on the fact that this woman, who usually wore Western dress, was wearing a batik sarong and a *kebaya*, she replied matter-of-factly, "Well, what else can I do, for a wedding you have to wear national dress" (*Ya, bagaimana lagi, untuk perkawinan harus pakai pakaian nasional*, I.).

The Danar Hadi advertisement shows that the commodity batik is well adapted to the monumentalization of tradition and "national culture." If the company manufactured blue jeans instead of batik it could not proudly display a picture of the owners' ancestors and refer to "the true tradition of Indonesia" in a newspaper with national circulation. An appeal through advertising to the value of tradition is quite modern, but the attempt of Solo's merchant class to seek cultural legitimacy from a moral order that has explicitly denied them this privilege is not. By locating the origins of their commodity in the imagined ancestral past—which is to say, in the sphere of high culture—Javanese batik merchants have drawn on commonly recognized sources of cultural legitimacy in their endeavor to establish a claim to high status in the wider society. This appropriation of the *alus* has also allowed them to look to the business itself as a source of ancestral blessings. The value of batik lies in its signification of an unbroken continuity between past, present, and future, generated as a residue, one might say, of the historical process.

It is the belief in the batik industry both as a channel of ancestral value and as a way of asserting their own (tenuous) claims to cultural legitimacy, I would argue, that has led Javanese batik entrepreneurs to cling so tenaciously to this field of business even as they see their own once-substantial profits dwindle to a fraction of what they were in the heyday of the industry. We have already seen that many Javanese continued to produce batik long after the majority of ethnic Chinese entrepreneurs had switched to more profitable businesses. The Javanese merchant community had a certain relationship to the past, as well as to the actual commodity that they produced and exchanged, which led them to regard the batik industry as a source of value that could not be easily replaced. The designation of the batik industry as a *warisan*, in short, led to its fossilization. Though the industry was full of vitality in its earlier years, its heirs gradually became paralyzed by their unwillingness to alter it in any basic way, or to abandon it when it ceased to be viable. Ironically, the very desire to conserve the *warisan* was what led it to dry up. In Laweyan the virtual demise of the batik industry represented more than just the inability of an old-fashioned, labor-intensive technology to compete with modern techniques of mass production. For the members of the community, it signified their own failure to uphold the honor of their ancestors and to maintain continuity with future generations by perpetuating that which was passed down to them.

In this chapter, I have offered a glimpse of an economy that, although bound up with the production and exchange of commodities for the market, looks quite different from the rationalized capitalist economy that social theorists have conventionally identified with the modern age. Yet this economy exists within an urban milieu that has been quite modern for some time, by many, if not all, definitions of that term. My aim is neither to romanticize this Javanese economy nor to claim that it is untouched by capitalism, the mechanisms of the global market, or other modern economic institutions and practices. Rather, my intent is to rethink the meanings of "economy" and to redraw its boundaries for a society whose subjects have been drawn into capitalist relations without being entirely consumed by them. As Marilyn Strathern points out, a simple dichotomy between capitalist and noncapitalist systems fails to account for the many other symbolic strategies that may be at play in society (1985, 195). Indeed, the sharp edges between "capitalist" and "noncapitalist" systems become blurred when one considers the ways in which the logics of capitalism can intermingle with other kinds of logics, such as those of hierarchy, sacrifice, and cultural value that I have discussed for Java.

For example, the division between gift exchange and commodity exchange is not absolute, for the two spheres are not mutually exclusive (see Appadurai 1986). In Java the commodity batik, which is exchanged in the marketplace for money, is also treated symbolically as an ancestral gift, which creates, in the Maussian sense, a link between giver (progenitor) and receiver (progeny) and, also in keeping with Mauss's understanding of the gift, demands a return gift (of deference, propitiation, and the perpetuation of the *warisan* into future generations).[24] This sense of the gift is evoked even in the contemporary advertising strategies of a modern, highly capitalized firm like Danar Hadi: the "gift" of batik that the owners of the firm have received from their ancestors is also presented in the ad as their own valuable "gift" to the consuming public. While one could argue in this case that these strategies involve the co-optation of older meanings toward patently capitalist ends—a point with which I would certainly agree—such a strategy can succeed only because it calls on cultural discourses that are still in wide circulation about the relationship between past and present and the ways in which value is produced.

To be sure, the market operates here as part of a larger economic system that is heavily affected by such factors as economic growth or recession, the tightening or expansion of government credit, and devaluations of the Indonesian currency relative to the American dollar. But the market is also linked to the cycle of spiritual regeneration and conservation, and to the production of status within local social hierarchies. Money, commodities, and other forms of wealth circulate within and between these distinct but interrelated realms of value, undergoing transformations from financial to cultural capital and vice versa. Such ideas as the "ancestral" commodity, the firm as *warisan*, and asceticism or magic as a means of achieving success in business all cast doubt on the modern market's ability to mold everything in its path to the same shape.

Javanese batik entrepreneurs have formed buyers' cooperatives in order to obtain raw materials at lower prices, participated in complex and long-term credit relationships, and used clever ploys to avoid paying high taxes, at the same time that they have prayed to their ancestors and to other powerful souls for success in business, soaked themselves in pools of water in the middle of the night, and placed offerings of flower petals beside their dye vats and toilets to placate any spirits that might inhabit them. My point is not that Javanese entrepreneurs are sometimes "rational" and sometimes not (according to Western standards of rationality, that is); I wish, rather, to demonstrate the interconnectedness of these practices within an economy that is neither "traditional" nor strictly "modern," an economy that simultaneously partakes of and reconfigures the logics of the modern market.

In dislodging the usual boundaries of "economy," I also want to highlight the importance of the domestic sphere as a site where these various economies (in the broader sense of "regimes of value"; Appadurai 1986, 4) converge. The domestic economy does not merely involve the production and provisioning of the family with material goods; it also involves the production of such things as social status and power, and spiritual and cultural capital. As Weiner notes, the traditional boundaries between domestic and public spheres break down when we recognize that "domestic values such as biological reproduction and nurturance as well as the 'magical' values of cosmologies and gods" inform political and economic action (1992, 4).

The domestic sphere in Laweyan, as I have already suggested, revolves around the woman who stands at its core. As the main agents of domestication in the household, women often take on the burden of producing and accumulating not only material wealth but also social status and cultural capital for their families—the latter of which have been inadequately recognized in most studies of Javanese society. One might also say that women have primary responsibility for the transvaluation of money, turning money into the gift—in other words, into something of cultural value—and turning the gift back into money.[25] They occupy a position in which they are expected to maintain intergenerational continuity, making sure that the gift of the *warisan* (as a material or spiritual endowment, or as a form of knowledge) is handed down in perpetuity. If they are associated, perhaps more than men, with "tradition," it is not because they are more traditional or conservative by nature, but because they tend to assume somewhat greater responsibility for keeping the links between past and future generations strong and uninterrupted. I agree wholeheartedly with Weiner's (1992) point that anthropologists have often failed to recognize the centrality of women in processes of social and cultural reproduction, and as the possessors in their own right of the valued objects and forms of knowledge that come to embody those processes.[26]

The views of domestic economy that I have presented here are intimately linked to notions of subjectivity that are both historically and culturally situated. The idea of the domestic sphere as a realm where individuals can manage their own desires, as well as the desires of others, for the good of the family and its descendants presumes a certain autonomy and agency for the subjects who inhabit that sphere. Javanese concepts of personhood, as seen in particular through the emphasis on asceticism, self-denial, and the capacity for instinctual self-control, also affirm the ability of individuals to behave as self-determining subjects. This applies to women as well as to men. Even when women's autonomy is constrained by ideologies of male dominance and superior self-control, they assert their agency through their roles as domesticators of the forces of desire in the marketplace and in the domestic economy.

While these understandings of subjectivity are deep-seated, they are also subject to change, for subjectivity and its construction through public and private discourse is not a fixed state but an ongoing process. I will return to this issue in the final chapter of this book, when I discuss New Order constructions of gender, domesticity, and "modern" subjectivity. It will become apparent that the models of household and family promoted by the state and the mass media diverge sharply from the image that I have presented here, based on very different assumptions about individual agency, the proper roles of men and women, and the management of human desires toward desirable ends.

Chapter Six

THE MASK OF APPEARANCES

DISORDER IN THE NEW ORDER

ONLY A DAY after I had moved to Laweyan, I spent part of the afternoon talking to a young man, Mas Hendro, who lived across the street from my new home. Knowing that I had just recently arrived from America and that I had an interest in local culture, he invited me to accompany him to his friend's wedding, which was to take place later that evening. I accepted the invitation, pleased to have the opportunity to witness my first "ritual" in my new field site—my own rite of passage as an anthropologist.

What I had read and heard about Javanese weddings prior to that night, however, did not quite prepare me for this particular event. Suffice it to say that it was not quite the solemn, grand affair that I had expected. Arriving at a nearby hall—part of an old batik manufacturers' cooperative that, having fallen on hard times, was often rented out for receptions—Mas Hendro and I took our seats on the uncomfortable metal chairs and waited, endlessly it seemed, for all of the guests to arrive. As they slowly filed in, a tape of Arabic chanting played over the loudspeakers, a sign that this was to be a more "Islamic" atmosphere than was typical for most weddings (ordinarily the music on the stereo system would be Javanese gamelan music, not Arabic chants). I learned from Mas Hendro that the groom's father, who wore a white robe and turban, was a local *kiai*, a respected religious teacher in the community, while the groom himself ran a gas station in town.

The six hundred or so guests were listless in the stuffy wedding hall, apparently uninterested in the proceedings as they fanned themselves, looked around, and chatted loudly with each other, drowning out the flowery speech of the master of ceremonies (the *protokol*, as he is called). The only time that they showed a flicker of interest was when the groom's father's voice began to tremble as he intoned Arabic prayers before a microphone, seeming momentarily close to tears. Over the course of the evening, Mas Hendro, who sat next to me in the women's section of the seats (to his mild embarrassment), uttered a litany of complaints: it was too hot in the hall; the food was being served too slowly; there were only three courses of food instead of the usual four; the dancer (a young girl who performed in Balinese style to music from a cassette—a curious form of entertainment, I thought, to have at a wedding made by devout Javanese Muslims) wasn't moving forward enough for the men seated in the outer section to see her. It was also clear that he expected to be bored from the start, as, I believe, most of the other guests did, given the general feeling of restlessness that prevailed in the hall.[1] This was the height of the Javanese wedding season (as well as the height of the rainy season, which made everything feel a little soggy), it was well into the evening, and some people had been attending two—occasionally even three!—weddings a day in recent weeks, sitting elbow to elbow on hard metal folding chairs for hours on end. For most of the guests, attending weddings was a tiresome obligation, not a pleasure.

This was an arranged marriage (with the couple's consent), which may help to explain why the bride and groom were so palpably ill at ease. The groom, who should have looked serious, impassive, and stately, instead shifted nervously in his chair, twiddled his thumbs, glanced around the room and periodically appeared to be suppressing a laugh when he happened to catch the eye of a friend. The bride, who should also have kept her gaze more or less fixed ahead like the "queen" that she was dressed to imitate, kept peering out of the corner of her eye at the guests, while trying not to be obvious about it. The only time that the couple assumed the "properly" dignified bodily postures and composed facial expressions was when a photographer came to take their pictures. One could almost see them imagining what the photographs would look like, hanging on their wall or being shown to guests in an album.[2]

Indeed, *this* was the moment that was to be remembered and preserved as an image, not the hours of boredom or awkwardness that generally characterized the event, nor the nervous marriage negotiations and harried last-minute preparations that had undoubtedly preceded it. The memory of this event would be savored by the participants, and by the time I had attended a few weddings, I realized that the photographs, which preserved the memory as a series of images that would remain fixed over time, were almost as important as the events themselves. The photographic depiction of the wedding was more than just a recording of the event. It was, one might say, the key to establishing the authenticity of the event, while the actual wedding served almost as a backdrop for the photographs. Authenticity is always created in retrospect: the process of looking backward is what allows the authentic to be defined as such. The ritual life of the photographs would be nearly as significant as the ritual event that they documented: they would be framed or preserved in albums, passed around, and shown to visitors for years to come as proof of a culturally authentic (and personally and socially significant) moment, the wedding. They would

11. A Laweyan bridal procession. The bride and groom are at center.

serve as indisputable evidence of their subjects' ability to uphold "tradition" in an honorable fashion—even if it was a hodgepodge of Javanese, Middle Eastern, and Balinese elements, with food that combined Chinese, Javanese, and Dutch influences. Unchanging over time, the pictures would quickly replace fading memories of inattentive guests, a fidgety bridal couple, and a wedding that was not quite the majestic, dignified affair that a Javanese wedding should, in theory, be.[3]

At many Javanese homes that I visited, sooner or later (often during my first visit) my host would proudly produce an album of photographs of a wedding or other ritual event that her family had sponsored. The ubiquitous albums would also appear at informal gatherings of neighborhood women, especially when one of the women had just married off or circumcised her child and had new pictures to display. What struck me after being shown so many of these albums was how very similar all of the pictures were; after seeing a few one knew exactly what to expect from the others. The sequence of poses of the bridal party and the solemn expressions, stiff body postures, and styles of clothing were utterly predictable. Rarely did one find any candid shots—all had been carefully styled to fit a standard that was usually followed to the letter. The surprise or amusing shots, the embarrassing, cute, or touching shots that might have made their way into an American photograph album—and that I personally would have welcomed for a change of pace—were noticeably absent.

The aim of these pictures was not to surprise the viewer, to capture the range of emotions that might accompany an important rite of passage, or to establish the uniqueness of any particular ritual event. It was, rather, to reaffirm a vision of cultural order as people felt it *should* be. The pictures represented the family in its proudest moments, moments that it had labored for weeks, months, or even years to bring to fruition. (The Javanese term for putting on a ritual event such as a wedding, *nduwé gawé*, literally means "to have work.") All traces of work, though, had disappeared in the photographs, as had any signs of anxiety, strife, or urgency that might have led up to the event itself (if, for example, the bride happened to be several months pregnant and the marriage was an "emergency" wedding, put on in added haste because the month of Ramadan, when weddings are taboo, was quickly approaching). The pictures represented the family as its members wanted to be remembered: dressed in regal Javanese style, with an aura of calm and stately refinement that seemed to have been attained effortlessly. The pictures portrayed the family at the height of its glory, its members taking their place in the long line of forebears who had themselves participated in such rituals. This moment was what most *other* moments were not: a carefully orchestrated, meticulously arranged display of cultural refinement and dignity, representing a Javanese ideal that was difficult, if not impossible, to live up to in everyday life.

Relying on the photograph to establish a putative cultural authenticity epitomizes in my mind the ongoing process of re-imagining and re-presenting the past that saturated the life of the Javanese community in which I lived. This was a disintegrating community whose identity was maintained through hindsight. The image of its past, fixed in the memories of its inhabitants and in the architecture and furnishings of their homes, was what gave Laweyan a conviction of its own indelible authenticity as a community, and its residents the sense of being the heirs to a past to which they owed (like it or not) so much. There was a preoccupation with origins rather than destinations, a constant feeling of looking over one's shoulder at generations gone by. Laweyan itself was very much like the wedding photographs that people there were so fond of: the residents were obsessed with its image, an image that had become rather static over the years and that had effaced most signs of the labor, ingenuity, hardship, and dynamism which had been so integral to the making of the community in the first place. The imagined authenticity of the past, created through collective memory, was a product of the present, but it also pressed on that same present with an almost unbearable weight.

Individually and collectively, the merchant families of Laweyan put forth their best efforts to maintain their dignity and high status, and to uphold the "authentic" standards of tradition that they believed had been passed down to them from their parents and grandparents. The local elites in particular were concerned with concealing, as best as possible, any indication that things might not be quite right: that their businesses were failing, or their inheritances rapidly dwindling, or that some of their children showed little potential for success in any field. As with the wedding photograph, the reality of their situation rarely matched the ideal image that they wanted to present to the public eye. The image was almost as important as the reality, sometimes even more important; that is why so many entrepreneurs with businesses on the verge of bankruptcy were nonetheless willing to invest large sums of money, often borrowed, in elaborate engagement ceremonies, weddings, circumcisions, postmortem rites for the souls of the deceased, and a host of other ritual events—money that might otherwise have been used as capital for their businesses or to repay their mounting debts. It was through these rituals that a family could continue to count itself among the pillars of the community and to command respect from others. Although it was difficult to keep secrets here—everyone knew, more or less, who was prospering and who was not—there was a quiet complicity in the community, a willingness to accept outward appearances as evidence of "truth" (like the photograph) even when it was well known that they were just as likely to mask it.

Life in Laweyan, then, had a kind of duality to it, a life of appearances and a life behind the scenes. But life behind the scenes always threatened to erupt onto the stage, tearing away the flimsy mask of appearances and revealing the humbler realities that lay just beneath it. The complicity of Laweyan's families in holding onto the mask, I believe, was also their acknowledgment of the fragility of the community as a whole and of the extent to which it relied on the maintenance of appearances for its very existence. The gradual process of disintegration that was taking place could only be slowed by the collective efforts of the community to maintain its integrity, and that of its individual families, through images.

Signs of Failure in the Merchant Community

The failure that I witnessed during the period of my research was on a scale unprecedented in Laweyan's history: it was the failure of an entire community to reproduce itself. This was the end of the line for the *warisan*, at least in the form in which it had been passed down for almost a century; the social fabric of the community was disintegrating. Instead of teaching their children to be batik manufacturers, as their own parents had done, Laweyan's merchants were encouraging their children to go to college so that they could pursue other careers as white-collar workers or professionals. Many of the younger people who had grown up in Laweyan were marrying outside the community and moving away to other neighborhoods or even to other cities. Some of the large houses went uninhabited after their owners died, too expensive to be purchased or maintained by other people in the neighborhood, and too old and "eerie" to appeal to Solo's nouveaux riches, who preferred more modern homes. Former batik workers who had lost their jobs had become servants, *bécak* drivers, construction workers, or just unemployed people. Only a small number of those in the community were able to prosper, mostly the few entrepreneurs who had found success in other businesses outside batik production.

But, on a lesser scale, failure had always been an integral part of life in the community; the perpetual fear of loss was what had made the *warisan* so valuable in the first place. Merchants in Laweyan suffered the same turns in fortune that they are subject to everywhere. Individual families rose and fell—even in the heyday of the batik industry, one family's shining success could easily mean another family's dismal decline. Stories of failure were unavoidable. There were many kampong residents whose fortunes had taken a sharp downturn: a domestic servant who had briefly earned a living as a batik entrepreneur in the 1950s, for instance, or a chauffeur whose parents had been comfortable merchants. A number of people from former merchant families did not work at all—they simply lived off their inheritances in the large homes that many could not afford to maintain properly.

Some of the entrepreneurs-turned-laborers were from kampong backgrounds, initially batik workers or small-scale entrepreneurs who had managed to meet the minimum requirements to become members of the batik cooperatives in the 1950s and early 1960s. They had prospered as long as the cooperatives had supplied them with cheap raw materials, but had been unable to continue in business when the subsidies were taken away from them after 1965. Other people came from wealthy families but had failed in business themselves, or had so many siblings that they had been left with only a small portion of the inheritance from their parents. Those who could no longer pretend to any status above that of "kampong people" were basically resigned to their lot: everyone has their own luck (or lack thereof), they said; whether or not you like your fate you have to accept it. They focused instead on their children's futures, hoping that the latter might do well enough in school to secure a minor position in the civil service, which, if not well paying, would ensure at least a modicum of status and security.

Most of the elites of the *sudagar* community, however, especially those whose families had been successful for several generations, seemed to find their decline harder to accept. For the older people, it was difficult to come to terms with the realization that all the knowledge and wealth that they had inherited from their forebears could not be passed down to future generations. For some, the fall from great wealth to the brink of having nothing left at all—which is to say, of fading into the forgotten masses of the kampongs—was spectacular, occurring within a single generation. When a women's magazine with national distribution ran a series on "Stories of Rich People from the Past," which featured anecdotes on such well-known Indonesian entrepreneurs as "Cigarette King" Nitisemito of Kudus, a writer was sent to interview the aging brother of one of the "batik kings" of Laweyan, Atmosusilo, who had died some thirty years earlier, for details of this entrepreneur's life story.[4] When younger members of the family learned of the interview, however, they immediately called the editor of the magazine to request that the story not be printed. When I asked why they objected to the publication of the story, which presumably would have highlighted the great success of their ancestor, one of the family members responded rather bitterly, "What for? There's no point. There are other people whose stories are more interesting, aren't there? The batik industry is dead." She felt that it would be far more appropriate to interview those few entrepreneurs who were still prospering, such as the owners of Batik Danar Hadi, about *their* ancestors. Clearly, as she saw it, to focus attention on Atmosusilo's wealth and success would simultaneously draw attention to the fact that his offspring had been unable to maintain the status that he had achieved. His *warisan* had been exhausted, an indication of his inability to leave a legacy of lasting value for his descendants, as well as a sign of his descendants' failure to uphold his good name.

The fate of this family was known throughout Solo's merchant community. It was said that the Atmosusilos' home, formerly one of the finest in Solo, was almost empty, its furnishings sold off to cover the debts of the present owner, while the bank had put a lien on the house itself. The many other houses and parcels of land that the Atmosusilos had once owned in Solo had also been sold. As one man put it, "Riches that no one thought could be used up in two hundred years were gone in one generation, it turned out." There was broad speculation as to what had caused the downfall of this family. A former *juragan* of the Kauman suggested that this was God's retribution for Atmosusilo's greediness and his failure to give the alms (*zakat*) required of all Muslims who can afford it. (In fact, it was not uncommon to hear devout Muslims from outside the community, Arabs as well as Javanese, remark that the downfall of Laweyan as a whole had been brought about by its residents' unwillingness to give the obligatory alms despite their abundant wealth.) Other people observed that the children of rich entrepreneurs like the Atmosusilos were spoiled and had never learned how to work hard, spending their inheritance liberally but not regenerating it. Rumor also had it that one of the Atmosusilos' children had been swindled out of a large sum of money, hastening the dissipation of the *warisan.*

It was not easy to keep a secret in Laweyan. Although the neighborhood had a well-deserved reputation for hiding its secrets from the outside world behind high walls, the same inward-lookingness that spawned that reputation merely intensified the circulation of gossip within the community. The long-standing preference for endogamous marriages, which had ended only in the late 1960s and early 1970s, meant that many people were related to each other by blood or marriage, or at very least knew the intimate details of one another's family histories and fortunes. Production secrets for making batik may have been guarded successfully over the years, but news of personal triumphs and failures, scandals and good fortune spread quickly and inevitably through the neighborhood and its commercial extension a few miles down the road, Pasar Klewer.

Pasar Klewer was the hub for the exchange of news and gossip in the *sudagar* community at large, linking Laweyan to other pockets of merchants throughout the city and beyond. Reputations were made and broken here: everyone seemed to know whose business was doing well and whose was declining; whose checks were good and who was a bad credit risk; who had gone on the *haj* and whose house was in hock to the bank. It was general knowledge when a merchant's son had succeeded in becoming a doctor, an engineer, or a Jakarta bureaucrat—the sorts of prestigious, neo-*priyayi* positions that merchants now desired for their children. Likewise, if an entrepreneur's daughter had married beneath her family's status, there was endless speculation that it had been an "emergency" wedding—otherwise, people said, the parents would never have agreed to the union (this was sometimes confirmed when the *mitoni*, the ceremony marking the seventh month of pregnancy, was held only four or five months after the wedding).

Everyone knew. In the streets and back alleys of the kampongs, the servants, peddlers, *bécak* drivers, and day laborers took a lively interest in the affairs of local elites (although the reverse was rarely true), exchanging information among themselves. A *bécak* driver, commenting on the bankruptcy of a neighborhood entrepreneur, would remark with a touch of irony, "He always used to have four wheels under him when he went out, but now he only pedals two." Or the owner of a small food stall would shake her head over a merchant's penchant for womanizing, which was depleting his family's money.

Yet the effort to maintain appearances—*njaga praja*, to guard one's reputation and the good name of one's family—persisted, despite the speed with which gossip spread and the futility of trying to keep anything secret for long. The outward forms of status were almost indistinguishable from status itself; as long as a family could maintain the *appearance* of wealth and high status, it could continue to claim its place among the elites of the community. Whether or not there was any "real" wealth behind it was of secondary importance, at least in the short run. None of the elites was exempt from being gossiped about, but this was still preferable to being put out of the public mind altogether, to fading into the obscurity and anonymity of the kampong as many families had. Failure implied more than just financial ruin; it reflected unfavorably on past generations and boded darkly for future generations. To fail was the ultimate form of filial disrespect and irresponsibility to one's descendants: it meant leaving no *warisan*. Without a *warisan*, continuity with the past was lost, and history was in effect erased, for history was not an abstract set of past names and events in Laweyan, but a thread by which the names and events of the present could be traced to their sources. The price of failure was being lost from the community's memory and depriving one's descendants of a remembered history.

One instance of this came out in separate conversations that I had with two Laweyan women, from whom I had been trying to learn the name of the earliest known batik entrepreneurs in Laweyan. The first of the women, Bu Sukanto, recalled hearing of someone who had made batik "before Haji Samanhoedi" (the founder of Sarekat Islam), but who had been all but forgotten in the community. "His name was Haji Abdul Somebody-or-Other," she told me, adding that he was not remembered because he "had no descendants." Later in the same conversation, though, she mentioned that "Haji Abdul Somebody-or-Other" was said to have had eight wives. I pointed out that with eight wives, it was surprising that he had left no descendants. "But he lost everything, and probably left no *warisan*," she answered. Unlike the batik pioneers who had left large inheritances to their children and whose descendants were still prominent in the community, this man, his wives, and his offspring were lost to history because he had left no *warisan* with which to be remembered. There was little room in the community's collective memory for those who had failed.

Not long after this conversation took place I asked an elderly woman, Bu Wahid, whether she knew anything about this man. "Oh, she must be talking about Haji Abdul Ridha," Bu Wahid said.[5] It turned out that he had not been the first person to manufacture batik in Laweyan, nor did he have eight wives (he had only had two wives, she was fairly sure, and had married the second one after the first died), but he *did* have children. He had owned a fair amount of property in Laweyan, but had sold most of it off after he went bankrupt, and left little or no inheritance to his descendants. Some of them still lived in the Laweyan area. But his descendants did not "stand out" (*menjila*), she added. In other words, they were no longer numbered among the elites of the community—they blended in with the anonymous masses of kampong people. Having failed to conserve anything of value for his descendants, it was almost as if Haji Abdul Ridha had never existed.

Catching Fortune: Prestige and Conspicuous Consumption

The closer a family came to the brink of failure—of obscurity, like Haji Abdul Ridha—the more its members felt the need to project the image that they were prospering, even though the rest of the community usually knew that this was not true. The desire to maintain their prestige was what led many families to persist in making elaborate and very expensive ritual celebrations, with large numbers of guests—often six hundred or more—to commemorate weddings, engagements, death anniversaries, successful completion of the *haj*, and other rites of passage. They continued to make large ceremonies because that was the established tradition in the community, and to break with tradition would have invited gossip and signaled failure. Many families also poured large amounts of money into their ritual events to try to hide the degree to which their financial situation was deteriorating.

The social pressure to present these periodic ceremonial displays to the community overrode all economic considerations: for most people, investments in status were more important than investments in business, even though failure in business would eventually lead to the absolute decline of the family's status. Because Laweyan firms had never been rationalized to the point where business finances and household finances were kept entirely separate, money that might otherwise have been set aside as capital was frequently used instead for consumption and display. The obligation to display wealth, which had an almost moral imperative in Laweyan, did not cease when the wealth itself was nearly expended. In fact, just the opposite was true, for it was precisely at the moment when the *warisan* had almost dried up that the need to display its durability became most acute.

A number of Arab and Chinese merchants were critical of the tendency toward conspicuous consumption and display in the Javanese *sudagar* community. By spending too much on fancy cars, expensive rituals, and lavish homes, they said, the Javanese were letting their capital be "eaten" (*modalnya dimakan*, I.) instead of investing it in business. Arab entrepreneurs repeatedly observed that prestige was not as much of an issue in the Arab community as it was in the Javanese community. As one man commented, "Instead of going out and buying a new car, people here [in the Arab community] will walk, or at most buy a motorcycle. The important thing is to keep the money turning over as capital."

Many Javanese were themselves disapproving of the prodigality of their own ethnic group. In the words of a woman who sold textiles in Pasar Klewer, "Javanese borrow money from the bank for their businesses, but as soon as they have the money in their hands they think it's their own. They use it to fix up their house, or to buy a new car. Months turn into years and the interest keeps accumulating, reaching millions of *rupiah*, but the money is gone, so they can't pay it back. It's different with the Chinese— *they* use the money for capital." This was a recurring theme. One man, a former *juragan* and official of a local batik cooperative, estimated that a third of the bankrupt entrepreneurs he knew had fallen because of borrowing money (either from the bank or from a private moneylender), ostensibly for business purposes, and then spending it instead on consumption. "It's a particular way of thinking," he explained. "They say to themselves, 'I might as well use the money while I have it,' and then they go out and buy a new car or something."

People who borrowed money from banks or private moneylenders certainly realized at the time that it had to be paid back with interest. Yet money that appears suddenly, no matter what the source, tends to be assimilated to the notion of *rezeki*, unexpected good fortune or a windfall.[6] The point of *rezeki* is that it comes to one without apparent effort, although it is often believed to be a reward for an unselfish or charitable deed performed at some point in the past, or a return on some prior act of personal sacrifice or asceticism. Many Javanese Muslims believe that giving alms of one's own free will always has its eventual return in the form of *rezeki*, which usually arrives in excess of the original amount given. Bu Hartati, who was barely able to make ends meet, showed me a passage in the Qur'an which stated explicitly that a person who gives alms openly, without any hidden motive, will receive *rezeki* of at least seven times the value of what he or she originally gave away. She gave me a personal example of how this works:

> One day not long ago I took my son to school. I had only fifteen hundred *rupiah* [about ninety cents] with me—that was the last of my money. I spent a thousand *rupiah*, then I was only left with 500. At the school, we were asked for donations for the teacher's father, who was sick. I wondered if I should give her my last 500 *rupiah*, but then I went ahead and did it. And do you know what? When I got home, my husband told me that he had just been sent fifty thousand *rupiah* in the mail by his cousin, who owed him the money. How I thanked God for His generosity! It showed that He doesn't like to be in debt.[7]

Many people are convinced that to seek *rezeki* actively is a sure way to repel it; Solonese are fond of quoting the expression "People don't chase after *rezeki*, *rezeki* chases after *them*" (*Wong ora ngoyak rezeki, rezeki sing ngoyak wong*). But when *rezeki* appears, the lucky person knows that it is his due: it was just a matter of waiting patiently for it to arrive. Still, there are ways that people allow it to "find" them if it happens to be coming their way. Buying tickets for the national lottery (*Porkas*) was extremely popular in Solo and elsewhere in Java in the late 1980s; people appeared to see this as one way of making sure they could catch hold of *rezeki* if it happened to be "chasing" them.

Rezeki differs from a *warisan* or other gift in that it does not set into motion a cycle of exchange. The difference between *rezeki* and a *warisan*, for instance, is that the *warisan* clearly originates with one's ancestors and the sacrifices they have made, and the recipient of the *warisan* incurs a debt that must somehow be repaid. *Rezeki*, however, carries no similar obligation, which is precisely what makes it so attractive: because it has been earned with no obvious source, there is no one to repay. Even when a more Islamic interpretation of *rezeki* is applied, in which *rezeki* is seen as a direct gift from God, it is usually taken to be God's reward for a good deed already done, a sacrifice already made.

The sudden appearance of a large sum of money in the form of bank credit or a private loan resembles *rezeki* in that it seems to appear out of nowhere, even if it is received through a bank or moneylender. The attitude "I might as well use the money while I have it" reflects the uncertainty of *rezeki*, because the recipient never knows if or when such a windfall will appear again. Instead of investing their loans in their declining businesses, which might or might not have yielded eventual profits somewhere down the road, some people chose to convert the borrowed money into immediate sources of status by investing it in their homes or new cars. The ultimate goal of business was also to gain status, but the status returns to capital invested in business would have been much longer in coming—if they ever came at all.

I was told that the recurrent pattern of entrepreneurs borrowing substantial sums of money and then finding themselves unable to repay the loans had only become prevalent since the early 1970s. It coincided with two trends: generally, with the rise of consumer culture in New Order Indonesia; and specifically, with the decline of the local merchant community. The former was linked to the rapid expansion of the Indonesian economy in the 1970s and 1980s and to the capitalist orientation of the New Order. Some people I knew contrasted the current consumer mentality with an older ethic of not showing off one's wealth too openly (although, having seen the homes that Laweyan's entrepreneurs had built long before the New Order, I felt that this contrast with the past was probably somewhat exaggerated). That the decline of the merchant class coincided with the rise of the New Order's bureaucratic-capitalist elite, with its passion for consumerism, meant that the demand for Solonese merchants to display wealth in order to maintain their status was stronger than it had been before even as most members of the merchant class had less actual wealth to display.

In Laweyan and Pasar Klewer, those women who had been forced to sell off all of their valuable jewelry (in order to pay off their debts or to support

12. A prosperous batik trader displaying her wares in Pasar Klewer, attended by her assistants.

their families) borrowed, rented, or wore imitation diamonds because, as Bu Hartati put it, "People here always guard their prestige, they guard their status." Women also wore jewelry to the market, she said, "so that it looks like they can be trusted with credit, so that they can get their checks cashed easily" (especially by the Chinese moneylenders). Prestige and the appearance of financial solvency were closely intertwined. This was a long-standing convention among merchants, as demonstrated by Soerachman's observation in 1927 that the suppliers of raw materials looked at the clothing, and especially at the jewelry, of a female batik entrepreneur in order to assess her creditworthiness (*credietwaardigheid*, D.).[8] Sixty-odd years later, it was still true that almost no self-respecting Solonese batik entrepreneur would go to Pasar Klewer without wearing her jewels prominently displayed. Even older Muslim women who wore a long, gauzy scarf (*kerudung*) draped over their hair and shoulders usually wore it in such a way that it did not hide their diamond earrings; in fact, covering their hair in this way often seemed to accentuate their jewelry. However, as Bu Hartati also pointed out, "Of course, you never know—sometimes they might be wearing imitation jewels, which are hard to tell from the real thing, or they may be borrowed. There was a trader I knew in Pasar Klewer whose credit turned out to be bad—it turned out that all the stock in her stall and the diamond earrings that she wore had been borrowed."[9]

Like the wedding photograph, carefully styled not to represent "reality" but rather to project the image by which its subjects wished to be remembered, the diamond-encrusted bracelets, new cars, and extravagant rituals were intended to give the outward appearance that everything was just as it should be. Behind these outward appearances were often bankruptcies, scandals, numerous cases of fraud, and, not infrequently, a quiet desperation. But appearances were everything. The appearance of wealth was the next best thing to true prosperity. "As I've told you," Bu Hartati reminded me, "for people in Solo, prestige is everything. Lots of people will go to Pasar Klewer just to cash a check, when it would be a lot closer to go to the bank. They do it so that people there will *know* they're cashing a check, that they've got money. If they have to go somewhere, they'll only go in a car, since they'd be embarrassed to be seen riding in a *bécak* or anything else. Lots of them will only let their kids go to school by car. It's all for prestige. That's how people in Solo are." I asked her if most people who did business in Pasar Klewer knew which of the traders owned their own stalls and stock and which did not. "Oh, they know," she answered confidently. "Someone will comment on the nice things that one of the women has in her house, and then another person will tell her, 'You know, those things don't even *belong* to her.'" From Bu Hartati and many others, I learned that people also knew what financial shape the traders were in by knowing who paid cash for their goods (this earned a trader the most respect) rather than paying, as most traders did, with postdated checks; whose checks bounced; and who could not get their checks cashed at the market at all because their credit was known to be bad. This information circulated widely in the marketplace, and it was a constant subject of gossip among merchants and traders.

On the Inside: Swindling and Scandal

Cases of bad credit and of deliberate swindling (*penipuan*, I.) were common in Pasar Klewer and in the merchant community more generally—so common that, according to Bu Sukanto, almost everyone in Laweyan had been badly cheated at one time or another, although they did not like to talk about it. Some had lost large sums of money as a result, to the point of having to sell off one or more of the houses that they had inherited to cover their losses. Swindling had been around for a long time, certainly since before Indonesian independence, but the scale on which it was taking place in the New Order was unparalleled. Unlike simple defaults on loans, swindling was a calculated move, but Bu Sukanto speculated that if the local economy were in better shape, deliberate acts of swindling as well as unintentional defaults would happen less often. Frequently it was a case of "digging a hole to cover up a[nother] hole" (*gali lubang untuk tutup lubang*, I.), she remarked—people cheat others because they themselves have been cheated. She referred to Pasar Klewer as the "nest" of swindlers in Solo.

As she explained the intricate details of fraud in Pasar Klewer to me, Bu Sukanto would laugh occasionally at the surprised or blank expression on my face, commenting with a knowing air, "You don't understand, do you, Suzanne. You haven't lived here long enough. All you know is what you see on the outside. You don't know what really goes on *inside*, what you can't see." She was right, of course. No matter how long I lived in Laweyan (at the time of this conversation with Bu Sukanto I had lived there for a year), I would not be privy to all of the "secrets" that were, for insiders, common knowledge.

These scandals were not confined to the Javanese community; they also involved local Chinese and Arabs. A very frank Arab Indonesian man, Pak Jaffar, related his own experience of being swindled. Upon returning to Solo after several years of working in Saudi Arabia, he had opened a stall to sell textiles in Pasar Klewer. At first he was cautious, and most of his transactions were on a cash basis. But after a while he came to trust some of his regular customers, allowing them to buy from him on credit or partial credit. One such customer was a local Javanese woman. For a half year or so, she regularly bought quantities of batik wholesale from him with cash. By that point he trusted her enough to let her buy on a half-cash, half-credit basis. This went on long enough for her to build up a debt of four million *rupiah*. Finally she told him that she was broke and could not pay him back, at least not all at once. Since then she had been paying him back bit by bit, but the original loss had been substantial enough to force him out of business. I asked him if such stories were common. "It happens all the time," he smiled. "Every year at least one person at Pasar Klewer goes bankrupt because of swindling. Just last month a trader had to close down her stall for that reason."

Women, Pak Jaffar and his friend assured me, were just as likely to cheat people as men. "Oh, women here are plenty shrewd (*O, di sini wanita lihai-lihai*, I.). They wear big diamond earrings and talk sweetly, but they can be shrewd." I inquired whether the person who is cheated could not take the debtor to court. "The law isn't on the side of the person who's swindled," he explained. "If someone builds up a debt of ten million *rupiah*, and is taken to court, the court will be satisfied as long as they say they intend to pay back the debt, even if it's only at the rate of fifteen thousand *rupiah* per month. That doesn't do the person who has been cheated much good. The other thing is that in a lot of cases the person who has lost the money knows the debtor well. Maybe they're even friends. So the person is reluctant to take the debtor to court. In the end, it has to be settled in a family-like way (*dengan cara kekeluargaan*, I.)."

One afternoon, while I was sitting with another trader, Bu Minul, a village woman came to her stall. After a polite exchange in high Javanese, the woman handed Bu Minul the small sum of two thousand *rupiah* and took her leave. Bu Minul, who looked mildly amused after the woman departed, told me that fifteen years earlier, a woman from the village of Boyolali had incurred a debt to her of nine thousand *rupiah*, "which was a lot of money in those days." Afterward, the woman had never appeared again, and she never paid off her debt. Quite recently she had become ill, and was now close to death. Only now had the woman decided to pay off the debt—but without interest or adjustment for inflation, even though nine thousand *rupiah* now was only equal to a fraction of what it had been worth at the time. Recently she had returned seven thousand *rupiah*, but Bu Minul had checked her books from the early 1970s and discovered that the debt was actually nine thousand. So the woman who had just come to her stall was paying the remaining two thousand *rupiah* on behalf of the debtor. It struck Bu Minul as funny that the debtor was only now making good on her fifteen-year-old debt, but she said that it was quite common for people to default on loans until they are very sick, and then suddenly "remember" them (apparently out of fear for the consequences that they might face in the afterlife, as Muslims, if they die while they are still in debt). Sometimes debts are paid off by the family of the debtor after he or she has died—those are the *good* people, she emphasized, indicating that many people never pay off their debts at all.

The increasing frequency of people cheating others and defaulting on their debts was a sign, not the cause, of the merchant community's decline. However, because so many businesses were linked together through extended networks of credit relations, a single instance of swindling or bankruptcy could cause a chain reaction, one business after another falling like dominoes. Although many cases in which people cheated others were surely motivated by greed—by *nafsu*—other instances were desperate attempts to preserve the last of the family's wealth. People who were about to go bankrupt would often act rashly, amassing a very large debt in a short period of time in a frantic attempt at speculation. The victims of such actions frequently suffered great losses. Because there was no clear separation of the domestic sphere and the sphere of business, the desire to save the family's reputation at all costs sometimes led people to act in ways that might benefit the family in the short run, but that in the long term would probably have the opposite effect. Conspicuous consumption and defrauding others were both means—one socially sanctioned, the other not—of attempting to maintain the family's status. Even if the business went under, the family could continue the public displays of wealth that would enable it to maintain its status until the next generation—or at least until its money was truly gone.

The longer I lived in Solo, the more apparent it became to me that personal scandals, cases of swindling, and bankruptcies were the dark underside of the smooth, repetitive, and seemingly unruffled pattern of life that everyone worked so hard to maintain on the surface. Vast amounts of financial, social, and emotional resources were invested in maintaining the image of high status, of a state of equilibrium, of carrying on revered traditions that had come down from the past. No matter what indignity one had suffered, what scandals one had become embroiled in, or how anxious one was about the future, the important thing was always to present publicly the photograph-like image of pure refinement, high status, and unwavering dignity that would ensure one's place in the community. On many fronts people tried to pretend that little had changed, that things could go on just as they had in the past. Nevertheless, the contradiction between the desire for perfect order, on the one hand, and the realities of life in a declining community, on the other, created social and psychological tensions that took their toll on everyone. As we sat at the dinner table one evening, Bu Wiyono told me about a friend of hers who had been suffering from stress (she used the English word "stress"), adding that nowadays was the "season for stress," what with the economy declining and so forth. "Besides," she observed wistfully (and a bit more philosophically than usual), "these days, you can't tell whether civilization is advancing or going backward."

Indeed, the numerous cases of swindling and other forms of scandal seemed to be signs that a new era of unbridled desire—an uncontrolled *nafsu*—had taken over in spite of all efforts to maintain a semblance of order and control. "Corruption" (*korupsi*) was everywhere. Several women reported that in a neighborhood *arisan* that had been meeting since the 1950s, the practice of setting aside a portion of the group's money for loans to its members had recently been stopped because too many of the women had not paid back what they owed. The current situation had given rise to a commotion among the members, many of whom were now old women, as they accused each other of cheating the rest of the group.

Even relatives sometimes charged each other with cheating and deception. Bu Hartati and her husband, who had been enthusiastic some months earlier about a cooperative business venture that they were embarking on with relatives, now complained bitterly about not having seen a penny of the money that their far-richer relations owed them. Bu Hartati's husband announced that he was thinking of going to the police over the matter, but she asked him not to, because the people who had cheated them were relatives and it would cause an unpleasant situation. Bu Hartati mentioned with some small satisfaction that the particular people who owed them money frequently lost things to theft. You'd think they'd figure out, she huffed, that the reason they were always losing things was because God was punishing them for their stinginess. It is written in the Qur'an, she insisted, that people who spend their money generously on others will receive *rezeki*, while those who are miserly will end up losing more than they saved.

Not even the mosques were free of scandal. A local *bécak* driver commented that at Idul Adha (Eid al-Adha), an important Islamic holiday when goats are slaughtered and distributed to the needy, the distribution of the meat was often "corrupted" (*dikorupsi*) by members of the mosque committees who, "driven by *nafsu*," he said, kept most of the meat for themselves.

By many people's accounts, swindling and corruption were not really recent developments in Laweyan or elsewhere. But the growing frequency of swindling (at least according to the tales that I heard), and the scale on which it was occurring, belied the community's efforts to keep up appearances of order. A fundamental disorder was undermining the heroic public displays that seemed to announce, "All is as it should be." Swindling, like other forms of scandal, was taken by local people as just one more indication that the moral order of the past—an imagined era of sacrifice and self-denial that had always generated an excess for future generations—had been replaced by an age of self-indulgence and moral laxity. The forces of desire, and the disorder with which desire was associated, appeared to be gaining the upper hand in spite of all efforts to bring them under control. In short, the ideal of domesticating desire so as to create value for the family and a surplus for its heirs was becoming increasingly difficult to realize.

The spreading disorder in Solo's merchant enclaves also ran counter to the New Order regime's staunch insistence that order and discipline are the keys to the creation of a prosperous, stable, and "developed" nation. Through the apparatuses of the state, the educational system, the mass media, and various religious institutions (such as the state-sponsored neighborhood *pengajian*, Muslim prayer meetings that usually include a sermon), these messages of order, discipline, and development were repeatedly inserted into daily life. While the corruption of the government itself was well known, far outweighing the relatively petty forms of *korupsi* that were affecting Solo's merchants, the regime's ceaseless campaigns to promote order and discipline in all aspects of Indonesian life cast an uncomfortable light on the increasing disorder that accompanied Laweyan's decline. Physically, the somewhat dilapidated, walled-in neighborhood was surely a thorn in the side of the city's development-minded government, which was conducting a vigorous public campaign to make Solo *berseri* (I.), shining—also an acronym for *bersih* (clean), *séhat* (healthy), *rapi* (neat), and *indah* (beautiful). In an effort to make Solo appear modern, particular streets and neighborhoods were targeted for "development." In the 1980s and 1990s, this included replacing old markets with shopping malls; removing sidewalk food stalls, *bécaks*, and other signs of "disorder" from certain major thoroughfares; and forcing *bécak* drivers to paint over their colorful, individually decorated pedicabs in a uniform red and white (the colors of the Indonesian flag).

Laweyan, in this sense as well, was disorderly; it did not have the tidy, exposed, and carefully regulated look of the neighborhoods on which the city government had managed to impose its particular sense of order. Rarely were banners with slogans touting development or national pride hung in Laweyan's kampongs, and no one paid much attention when local officials requested that neighborhood residents remove the massive walls surrounding their homes, at their own expense, so that the kampong roads could be widened. Most of the roads in the kampongs remained narrow and unpaved, and the neighborhood kept its unmodern, and relatively unregulated, feel. Its physical unruliness and apparent indifference toward city hall's plans for urban development could hardly have come as a surprise, since even in better times Laweyan had always represented a certain disorderliness in its avowed independence from the centers of power and unwillingness to be regulated by the state.

But there were limits to how long this corner of Java could put off the penetration of "Indonesia" as it was envisioned by the New Order state and those who identified with its agendas. Under a regime as dedicated to the ordering of disorder—and the reordering of prior orders—as the New Order has been, Laweyan was the sign of a backwardness, an undesirable marginality outside the mainstream of development and modernity. Sites like Laweyan were ripe for domestication, less by the direct intervention of the state, perhaps, than by the ideologies and practices that it promoted, which were becoming, along with the regime itself, ever more firmly entrenched.

In the next and final chapter, I want to consider a final form of domestication—the domestication of the domestic sphere itself in the New Order. I have maintained throughout this book that the domestic sphere, as a site of economic, social, and cultural production, was central in defining both the merchant family and the larger community of which it was a part. One would expect the process of its domestication, then, to have fairly dramatic consequences for the life of the community and its members. The disciplining of the domestic sphere in Laweyan, however, is just one example of a process that is taking place on a much larger scale in New Order Indonesia under the rubrics of "modernization" and "development." I will look as well, then, at the shift in the meanings and the practices of the domestic, in Laweyan specifically and in New Order Indonesia more generally. It is to these processes of refiguring the domestic, both locally and nationally, that I now turn.

Chapter Seven

DISCIPLINING THE DOMESTIC SPHERE, DEVELOPING THE MODERN FAMILY

ONE STICKY March afternoon, I was invited to attend a neighborhood event: a government-sponsored campaign to persuade Laweyan women to have IUDs inserted—right there on the spot, in a curtained-off room. The New Order regime is well known for its aggressive efforts to promote "family planning" (*keluarga berencana*, I., usually abbreviated to KB), and such a public event is by no means unusual. By the time I arrived at the "clinic" (which was actually a kampong home) there was already quite a gathering, mostly of the less-affluent women from the kampongs. To what extent they had been pressured to attend, I do not know; I do know, however, that the more elite women of the neighborhood, who rarely participated in government-sponsored activities of any sort, were nowhere in sight.

Tea and snacks were served, and the atmosphere was closer to that of a party than a medical clinic. A cheerful, loquacious, middle-aged woman acted as the emcee of the lively event. Standing up with her microphone, she rambled on in rapid-fire Javanese, much like a hawker of patent medicines, about the benefits of using an IUD over other methods of birth control: "Come on, ladies. It only takes five minutes. Just five minutes! *You* know what happens if you forget to take the pill—'it' happens! (*Dadi!*). Or if your husband doesn't feel like using a condom? 'It' happens!" A nervous volunteer for the procedure was led into the adjacent room by a nurse. When she emerged a few minutes later looking slightly pale, the nurse (still in surgical gloves) right behind her, the emcee pushed the microphone in her face and asked brightly, "Well, how was it, Ibu?" "It was okay" (*Ora apa-apa*), the woman answered weakly, as another replaced her in the curtained-off room.

While I sat watching this spectacle with a mixture of amusement and dismay, a man who had been sent from city hall to observe the proceedings chatted with me. In the past, he informed me, of all the wards of Solo, Laweyan (the smallest ward) had been the most resistant to the government's birth control campaign, although lately they had been having more success there. He explained that because people in Laweyan lived behind high walls, the area was "difficult to penetrate" (*sulit ditembus*, I.). In retrospect the metaphor of penetration seems especially apt, given what was taking place in the next room, just a few feet from where we sat. The image of the phallic state endeavoring to penetrate a once-impregnable sphere was also oddly appropriate for understanding the significance of Laweyan's walls.

As I have already asserted, the domestic sphere enclosed by those high walls was the site of the family's power in the community and in the wider society. It was the place where merchant families could symbolically claim their independence from the political and cultural authority of the state and its representatives, and could escape the prying eyes of the regime—no matter which regime happened to be in power at the time. The comment of the man from city hall was reminiscent of de Kat Angelino's complaint more than half a century earlier that "much discretion and patience was required . . . in order to break a path into this ground, which was almost closed through distrust" (1930–31, 2:130; see chapter 2). The idea that the state needed to put forth considerable effort to "penetrate" Laweyan was not a new one.

This was not the first time that I had heard a government official complain about those high walls. A few months earlier, a bureaucrat at the provincial capital who had once been stationed in Laweyan had also grumbled to me about the inconvenience they caused: "If one of those houses caught fire, you know, those walls would make it hard for firemen to put it out." I also heard a rumor that the city government was no longer allowing citizens to build tall, opaque walls of the kind found in Laweyan; the reason given was that they "didn't look nice." Obviously, local officials were unhappy that they could not scrutinize whatever activities might be taking place behind the walls; the notion of a truly private sphere beyond their gaze did not fit with their understanding of how the Indonesian polity should work. It seems that the walls were, both to those who dwelled within them and those who did not, a potent symbol of a sphere shielded from the state's watchful eye and penetrating grasp—though, to be sure, the power of the walls to keep out the state was something of a fantasy on both sides.

It was not only Laweyan, of course, that the regime was interested in penetrating. There is no question that the remarkable staying power of the present regime, and its success in carrying out so many of its political, social, and economic agendas, has depended in large measure on its ability to insert itself deep within the domestic sphere throughout Indonesian society. While the state has regularly flexed its political and military muscle, harnessing the power of the army and the regime's enormous network of bureaucrats to maintain internal "security" and to implement its programs with a dogged determination from the top down, it has also managed to impose its will through subtler means directed at securing the willing cooperation of its citizens. One of the major ways in which this has been carried out is through attempts to co-opt the family into the state's ideologies of development and order. Through the educational system, the mass media, state-sponsored religious activities, and various organizations and activities aimed primarily at women, the family has become a focal point of the New Order's efforts to "develop" Indonesian society.

Among the more obvious examples of the state's efforts in this regard is its birth control program, which operates through a combination of positive and negative incentives and by essentially redefining what is considered public or private. That reproduction is *not* considered a private matter is made plain, for instance, by the fact that village and neighborhood headmen keep careful, often publicly displayed records of how many children each household has and what forms of birth control particular married couples use (see, e.g., Blackwood 1995, 137); those who have had their quota of two children are likely to be visited by a concerned headman who strongly suggests that they refrain from having any more. The public, celebratory atmosphere of the IUD campaign that I witnessed in the kampong also demonstrates the state's determination to make reproduction (and its prevention) a matter of public record. John Pemberton argues that prior to the New Order such campaigns would have been unlikely "because the machinery of state operation simply could not reach *so* intimately into Javanese lives" (1994, 230).

The regime's long-term goals of capitalist development, modernization, and the creation of its own stark versions of social order and stability cannot be met through forceful intervention alone; these goals can only be achieved by refashioning society from the inside out, so to speak. The New Order's endeavors to domesticate the domestic sphere hinge on bringing it under ideological as well as practical bureaucratic control. Apparently operating from the assumption that control over society begins with control over the family, the state and its sympathizers have invested tremendous energy toward this end. Significantly, while the state almost always takes for granted that the head of the Indonesian household is male, it is women, in their roles as wives and mothers, who have been treated as the linchpins of the family's domestication.

In this chapter I will explore both the means and the effects of this disciplining of the domestic sphere and of women, in Laweyan as well as in Indonesia more broadly. Throughout this book I have tried to paint a portrait of a distinctive way of life in Java, now fading, which centered around a certain understanding of family and household and their place in society. The domestic economy, through which were transacted not only money and material goods, but also human passions, spiritual substance, and cultural value, was closely bound up with Solo's market economy as well as with its social economy of hierarchy and prestige. I have maintained that women, in whose person the family and the family firm were typically conjoined, played a crucial role in each of these distinct but interwoven economies. Women's centrality to each of these spheres, however, was contingent upon their *not* being confined to the domestic sphere; the female *juragan*'s freedom to move between the household, the workshop, the marketplace, and the wider society was what enabled her to assert her influence within each of these domains.

New Order images of the modern woman and the modern family present a striking contrast to the thinking and practices of merchant women and families that I have presented in this book. As I have made plain, I do not claim that Laweyan was entirely typical of Javanese communities—nor would I suggest that it was completely unique in its woman-centeredness, since social life in Java seems to revolve around women more than has generally been acknowledged. However, the state-sponsored and popular portrayals of the family that have emerged during the New Order resemble neither the families that I saw in Laweyan nor the vast majority of other Javanese (or other Indonesian) families. When the concept of "family" is deployed in the ideological work of modernization, it is aimed not at accurately representing the diverse social entities that we call families but at presenting a model that *all* families are supposed to emulate, directed toward the furthering of goals that always exceed the boundaries of the family itself. In the development policies and rhetorics of New Order Indonesia, the family often takes the foreground as the site on which the seeds of a "modern," "orderly," and "developed" nation can be planted. It also becomes the focus of ideological contestations over the course of the nation's future, a stage on which competing models of modernity can be played out. The family, then, bears a heavy burden in the transformation of Indonesia's population into "modern" citizens of the nation-state.

However, the New Order state's images of modern society are also deeply conservative in their reliance on older Javanese notions of social order. Although the Indonesian nation includes hundreds of ethnic groups, the political domination of the government by ethnic Javanese is well known. That the Suharto regime should place itself at the apex of a vast political and social hierarchy comes as no surprise to those who have observed the state's Javacentric and patrimonial tendencies: the modern Indonesian state is itself positioned within a much older discourse of hierarchy. The regime's promotion of modernist ideas about progress and development must be considered with this in mind. Instead of trying to break down traditional ideas about hierarchy, the state depends on them in attempting to garner allegiance to itself and its objectives. The state's success—notable, although not complete—at disseminating its ideologies and securing the loyalty of its citizens is tied to its ability to replace other, often locally based hierarchies with its own centralized authority. Its efforts to reorient the family toward national rather than local hierarchies, goals, and centers of authority can be better understood against this background; by co-opting the allegiance of the family, the state's power becomes more firmly entrenched at both the national and local levels. The regime's relative success, at least in Java, can be partly explained by the willingness of many Javanese to accept the state's hierarchy above all others, with government bureaucrats seen as a privileged neo-*priyayi* class.

The domestication of the family in the New Order has been an ongoing process that operates on many levels. The state has not been alone in targeting the domestic sphere: religious institutions, the mass media, and the capitalist interests that the state supports (and in which many of its officials have a large personal stake) have also aimed at reshaping the family's goals and desires. A basic similarity underlies their efforts, in that each is working to reorient Indonesians away from local hierarchies and sources of power, toward nonlocal institutions and sources of authority. Although these sources of authority are frequently at odds with one another—as can be seen by the state's anxiousness to co-opt popular Islamic leaders and to suppress any Islamic factions that might challenge its political power, as well as in the attempts of the regime to maintain firm control over the most powerful capitalist interests—their attempts to redefine the family are often mutually reinforcing. In the pages that follow, after identifying some of the forms and effects of this process in contemporary Indonesian society, I will draw out their implications for both Laweyan and New Order Indonesia as a whole.

MODERNIST ISLAM, NEW ORDER IDEALS

Religion is one sphere in which we can see the effects of Indonesia's modernizing forces on the domain that I would broadly define as domestic. Changes in religious practices and doctrines are related to the state's policies in complex ways, but they are also tied to religious politics on a global scale. One of the most obvious changes in New Order Indonesia has been the deepening influence of Islam, especially modernist or reformist Islam. Reformist Islam has a long history in Indonesia; since 1912 it has been disseminated most widely under the banner of the large modernist organization Muhammadiyah, which has many adherents throughout the country. The efforts of Muhammadiyah to modernize and purify Islamic practices of their local syncretic and heterodox tendencies, however, had for decades generally met with a cold or indifferent reception in Laweyan, which was "Javanese Islamic" (*Islam Jawa*) through and through. Although most of Laweyan's residents were Muslims who affirmed their faith in a single God whenever they prayed, many of those same people also believed there were other supernatural beings in their environment that required their own Javanese—*kejawèn* (from the root word *Jawa*, "Java" or "Javanese")—forms of propitiation. People did not see their *kejawèn* practices as conflicting with their faith in Islam or in God; they were simply different sets of practices and beliefs with somewhat different, but complementary, aims.

The Wiyonos, for instance, were practicing Muslims who prayed regularly and fasted during Ramadan. Every Thursday night, though, they had a servant place small offerings of fragrant flower petals on banana leaves around their home: near the toilet, at the foot of the stairs, next to the dye vats in the workshop, and in other spots that seemed likely to harbor spirits. Bu Wiyono was also dutiful in making offerings every Friday morning at the graves of her parents and grandparents, and during Ruwah she visited the graves of others whose spirits needed to be propitiated only once a year. Reformist Islam sharply condemns such practices of spirit propitiation, but many Javanese, including many from Laweyan, were loath to abandon them. As one man summed it up, "In the past, people in Laweyan considered Muhammadiyah too modern for the Javanese, too progressive (*kemajon*). They liked the old ways, they didn't want to change things."

In the 1980s, however, these attitudes had started to change. The active practice of Islam had been on the rise throughout Indonesia since the beginning of the New Order, in part because of the government's campaign to foster organized religion among the populace as a means of achieving social stability and discouraging the return of communism, which is closely linked to atheism in state ideology. All Indonesians were required to embrace an "officially" recognized, monotheistic religion—monotheism being identified with progress, literacy, sophistication, and power, as opposed to "pagan" beliefs and customs (Guinness 1994, 295)—and many people who had never been observant in the past began to engage in the practice of Islam, Christianity, or another world religion.[1] Eventually the religious upsurge acquired its own momentum, especially in the wake of the Iranian Revolution in 1979 and the global Islamic movement that followed. Java's mainly Muslim population became noticeably more orthodox in the 1980s than it had been earlier.

In Laweyan, signs of this religious change were unmistakable. A number of people who had never before prayed regularly took to carrying out the obligatory five daily prayers. Some middle-aged people who had not learned how to read Arabic as children began studying it in small groups. Through the mass media and the influence of a growing number of Islamic study and prayer groups, many of which were linked to national Islamic organizations like Muhammadiyah or were sponsored by the government's Department of Religion, reformist doctrine also started to seep into the community, though it continued to meet with some resistance. These gatherings were attended mostly by women (although the majority were led by men), who carried the reformist message back to their homes. Even Bu Wiyono, who was a staunch Javanese traditionalist in many ways, was influenced by reformist ideas. After I had lived with her and her family for quite some time, I noticed that the usual Thursday night spirit offerings were no longer appearing around the house. When I asked her about this, she answered (with a hint of regret, I thought) that she had learned that making such offerings was not an appropriate practice for Muslims, so she had decided to put a stop to it in her home.

The most controversial impact of reformism was found in the attitudes of the members of the community toward various rites for the dead. The advocates of modernist Islam insisted that attempts to communicate with the dead in any form were polytheistic (*syirik*) and therefore fundamentally misguided, even sinful.[2] Some people I knew echoed the standard reformist line on rites for the dead by saying, "When someone's dead, they're dead—there's nothing that they can do for you or you can do for them." This simple formulation shook the foundations of the Laweyan merchant community's beliefs, because it denied the ability of ancestors to look after the well-being of their descendants, and at the same time denied the ability of descendants to see to the comforts of their deceased parents and grandparents in the afterlife, thereby nullifying a basic relationship of exchange between the living and the dead. To visit graves was still considered acceptable, but "feeding" the dead was definitely not. Most fundamentally, one was not permitted to ask the spirits of the dead for blessings, for only God could grant favors and answer prayers.

According to reformists, it is acceptable to pray to God to accept the good deeds (*amal baik*, I.) of the dead, to forgive their sins, and to grant them a place in heaven, but even these sorts of prayers are of limited use, for in the end God will judge people primarily on the basis of what they did during their lives rather than on the basis of others' efforts at intervention. In a similar vein, another Javanese Islamic tradition, the series of *slametan* following an individual's death, was also criticized by reformists. The main purpose of these rites, as they were explained to me, is to ask God to forgive the sins of the dead, but it is also widely believed that those who attend the *slametan* and recite the prayers will accumulate religious merit (*pahala*) for themselves as well as for the deceased. These were among the most frequent and important rituals observed in Laweyan. Reformists denounced these postmortem rites for being based in heterodox Javanese traditions rather than Islamic law; they condemned them for being wasteful and essentially useless. The taking of a ritual meal at such gatherings was considered particularly offensive and clearly "Javanese" as opposed to "Islamic." There was strong resistance in Laweyan, however, to doing away with the cycle of rites for the dead, especially among the older members of the community. Most people simply continued to hold the series of *slametan*, accusing those who wanted to abandon them of being *fanatik* (fanatical) or *ékstrim* (extreme) in their religious beliefs.

Responses to the reformist conviction that it is wrong to ask blessings from the dead were more mixed. Older traditionalists like the Sapardis tended to ignore the reformist message altogether; they continued their regular offerings at the graves of their ancestors and other powerful figures, acknowledging quite openly that they were asking the spirits of the dead for blessings. They did not try to hide their belief in the close connection between the souls of the deceased and the prosperity of the living. For example, at a Laweyan clan's visit during Ruwah to their family cemetery, one of the older women revealed that if the graves in that site were ever covered by tombs or roofs, the descendants of those buried there would not lead happy or prosperous lives. Some of the graves had once been covered, but the coverings had been removed for this reason.

Most of the oldest people did not even distinguish between certain "Islamic" and "Javanese" practices. The elderly Pak Suwarno, who diligently visited dozens of graves during Ruwah, informed me without hesitation that making offerings of flowers, incense, and prayer at graves during Ruwah is something that "only Muslims do; it's an Islamic custom." This even included making requests to the spirits of the dead—"of course, you always ask them for something, whatever you need." Younger, modernist Muslims, however, not only denied adamantly that this was an "Islamic" practice but also insisted that it was contrary to the basic tenets of Islam.

Many middle-aged people continued to visit the graves, but they sometimes rationalized doing so by insisting (slightly defensively) that their only purpose was to "remember" the dead and to pray that their souls would be accepted into heaven. Their intent, they stressed, was *not* to ask the dead for things—for how can someone who is dead give you anything? they added perfunctorily, following the reformist line. They claimed that their prayers were directed to God, not to the deceased. As Pak Djohari remarked with his usual air of mild sarcasm, "In the old days, people around here used to go to their parents' graves to ask that their work run smoothly. Nowadays, with the influence of [reformist] Islam, they go to ask God for forgiveness instead."

Reformism seemed to have taken hold most strongly among the younger members of the community. A few young female entrepreneurs even took to wearing modern styles of "Islamic clothing" (*jilbab* or *pakaian Islam*, I.), large headcloths and loose garments that covered them from head to foot, leaving only their faces and hands exposed—a notable departure from the tightly wrapped sarongs and rather revealing blouses that had been the traditional, very feminine dress of Solonese merchants.[3] Women who adopted these new styles of Islamic clothing were branded *fanatik* by many residents of the neighborhood, who felt that they were falsely pious and had exceeded the bounds of what was proper for a Javanese. Wearing this style of clothing was a Middle Eastern custom, most of the older people argued, which had no place in Indonesia; one could be a good Muslim without "dressing like an Arab."

The decision of Laweyan's merchants, however reluctant, to turn to a remote God for help rather than to their ancestors, as they had done in the past, seemed to indicate a basic shift in their attitude toward the future as well as the past of the community. It was an implicit acknowledgment that their ancestors could no longer provide for their welfare, because the *warisan* of batik, of wealth, of spiritual substance had been all but exhausted. The failure of the *warisan* was the failure of the domestic—a sign that the family could no longer consider itself self-contained and self-reliant. To an ever-greater extent the family depended on others outside itself, especially the state, for its economic and social well-being: hope for the future lay in educating children to become professionals and civil servants, so that they, too, could partake of the wealth and status that was concentrated in the hands of those with power. This marked a radical departure from the ideologies that had declared the independence of the *sudagar* community from the centers of political power. With the rise of bureaucratic capitalism in the New Order, maintaining the autonomy of the family firm and the authority of ancestral tradition had grown ever more difficult. The family could not continue to conceive of itself as independent of the state, as it found itself increasingly dependent on the government for its economic welfare, and at the same time more deeply subjected to the state's regulating practices.

The regime's insistence that all Indonesians adhere to a world religion and profess their faith in one God (which is incorporated into Pancasila, the official state ideology), and that religious organizations acknowledge the supremacy of Pancasila over all other credos, led to a heightened association of religion with the state.[4] An abstract God was, in a sense, the religious equivalent of the state: remote, demanding unequivocal deference, potentially benevolent, but also frightening in a way that ancestors were not. The concept of sin (*dosa*), which is a cornerstone of Islamic doctrine and a key to determining the nature of an individual's relationship with God, is conspicuously lacking in the relationship between ancestors and descendants, and is downplayed in Javanese (as opposed to Islamic) thought more generally. (A woman I knew commented that one "benefit" to come out of the political upheaval of 1965–66 was that it prompted many people to embrace religion, and as a result they "became aware of the notion of sin.") Ancestors required deference, but their role was to look after their descendants, even to indulge them as a parent indulges a child, not to mete out punishment as God might do. One could bring shame

upon ancestors but one could not sin against them. The relationship between ancestors and descendants was based on continuity and a feeling of
personal connection; it was conceived of as a mutually beneficial relationship of reciprocal exchange.

Like the state, God was a distant but formidable power that had to be
reckoned with, whether or not one really wished to do so. The gradual
replacement of ancestor propitiation and the practices of Javanese Islam in
Laweyan with those of reformist Islam meant the substitution of a modern,
rationalized form of deference—not unlike that required of a civil servant
toward his superiors—for the personal, more intimate forms of deference
that characterize familial relations. The idealized household of the New
Order did not look to itself for material support or to its ancestors for
spiritual support and blessings. It looked, rather, to the state and to the
capitalist structures with which the state collaborated for its material welfare, and to God (and to formal religious institutions—often linked to the
state as well) for its spiritual guidance.

This rationalization of domestic religious practice can be seen in other
arenas besides those of reformist Islam. In my mind it was epitomized by
Laweyan's new ways of carrying out *halal bihalal*, the custom at Lebaran
(the holiday at the end of Ramadan) of people asking and offering forgiveness of each other for any wrongdoings over the past year. In Laweyan, as
is common elsewhere in Java, people had formerly made visits at this time
to the homes of their relatives for the purpose of ritually asking forgiveness; junior relatives would show their respect by paying visits to those who
were senior to them. The visits had been fairly informal, with members of
one household visiting another for a short time, then moving on to visit
others. Sometime around the early 1980s, however, this practice of informal visits had become formalized among Laweyan's elites as a group gathering of all the available members of a single clan (*trah*, several generations
who are descended from a single pair of ancestors) along with their
spouses. The gatherings usually included about four generations of men,
women, and children; the ones that I attended had as few as 50 or as many
as 150 people, depending on the size of the clan.

The atmosphere at the group *halal bihalal* was quite stiff; everyone sat in
neat rows of chairs, half-listening to stilted, somewhat mind-numbing
speeches amplified through a public address system and eating the kinds of
rich, bland foods (often Western-type fare such as macaroni drowned in a
heavy butter sauce, or *korkèt*, "croquettes") that were common at such
events. The ritual climax of the gatherings was a dramatic enactment of the
clan's internal hierarchy, as each member of the clan asked forgiveness of
every other person who was senior to him or her. It began with the most
senior members of the group, usually an elderly couple, standing up at the
front of the room. One by one, in order of seniority, each member of the

family would approach the senior couple and the others who had followed them, ask them for forgiveness with a standard set of phrases and the touching of hands known as *salaman* (forgiveness was inevitably granted, with another stock set of phrases), and then join them at the end of the line. The final result was a very long line of people that wrapped around the room, which included the whole clan in perfect hierarchical order, from the elders at the beginning of the line down to the most junior members at the end.

Such a formal, collective demonstration of hierarchy would in the past have been quite unnecessary in Laweyan. People already knew how they were related to others in the community, and used a range of kinship terms to indicate their relationships; they had not needed to display their relationships in a semipublic setting. The quiet visits to individual homes had been enough for the *halal bihalal*. But times had changed. A number of the younger people had moved away and produced children of their own; Lebaran was the time of year that they would return to their natal homes with their children to visit their families. The group *halal bihalal* was obviously intended to reaffirm the solidarity of the clan, recreating the hierarchical relations within it in ways that froze them—rather like the conventional wedding photograph—and made them tangible for the whole group. It appears to have been a kind of social glue that was meant to hold together a disintegrating community.

However, this ritual display also bore the distinct signs of the New Order's emphasis on hierarchy and order. It was the perfect bureaucratization and reification of relationships that had once been conceived of as personal and dyadic. The process of asking one's seniors for forgiveness had in the past been a simultaneous expression of deference and a request for blessings, the sort of mutual exchange in life that would later be continued by making offerings to the spirits of the dead in the hope of receiving their blessings. Although this exchange between juniors and seniors was ostensibly maintained in the group *halal bihalal*, the public, perfunctory nature of moving through what looked like a long reception line, mechanically asking for and granting forgiveness in rank order, replaced the personal relationship between two people with a collective, exemplary enactment of hierarchy. Perhaps it was intended as an antidote to the increasing disorder of life in Laweyan and to the centrifugal forces that were dispersing its residents, but it also had the effect of voluntarily subjecting the community's families to the kind of institutional ordering of society that is the trademark of the New Order.[5]

The formal, bureaucratic style of the *halal bihalal* as it was conducted by elite Laweyan clans was entirely different from another event that I witnessed, the group visit of the members of a local clan to the graves of their elders during Ruwah. As the members of the clan gradually drifted into the small, neighborhood graveyard early in the morning, they were each handed a bottle of tea and a small box of snacks by two women. The first people to arrive sat down casually right among the marble tombstones, then a few mats were spread out on the ground, still amid the graves, for the later arrivals. Each family brought a basket or tray of flower petals, mostly pink roses, to sprinkle on the graves, while a few of the older people, most of them women, also burned chunks of incense, fanning the sweet, heavy smoke in the direction of the graves. Seven *santri* men were brought in to lead the whole group in chanting prayers for the dead. After the chanting was over, people talked and laughed, ate their snacks and drank their bottled tea while still sitting among the graves. No one looked sad. It was a quiet remembrance, something that they did every year during Ruwah. A simple affair by Laweyan standards, it was over within an hour or so.

This graveyard outing bore no signs of bureaucratization. The relaxed, picniclike atmosphere, in which living members of the clan mingled comfortably and intimately with each other as well as with those members who were deceased, reaffirmed the close bonds that brought together the living and the dead. It is probably no coincidence that these ties were being collectively renewed by a clan that was still the wealthiest and most powerful in Laweyan. The vast *warisan* that had been passed down by their ancestors was still partially intact, and some members of the clan had become quite successful in businesses outside the batik industry. No doubt the members of this clan felt especially well provided for by their ancestors; this feeling inspired a sense of gratitude and debt.

The contrast between this small, loosely structured rite and the highly formalized *halal bihalal* also points to the fact that Laweyan had not yet been fully "ordered," either by the ideologies of the New Order state or by the influence of reformist Islamic doctrine, the latter of which seemed to reinforce the state's emphases. People were still attempting to harness the power of the domestic and the local, disregarding for the moment the demands for stringent uniformity that issued from the state and religious institutions alike. In the confines of that small graveyard—which was also enclosed by high walls—ancestral power and the bonds between the living and the dead had not yet been eroded by the abstract but ineluctable forces of development.

The Domestic Sphere Revisited

While Laweyan continued to stave off some of the New Order's attempts to develop Indonesian society, it is clear that new economies were beginning to take hold here: economies that centered not on the household and the family, nor on the community, but on sources of power that stood far outside them. The locus of the circulation of value was shifting from the domestic sphere and all that it signified—including the intergenerational links that were forged through it—to other, more remote and diffuse sites. True, the family and the family firm had always been tied into broader circuits of value and power, and had been influenced by the politics and economics of the Netherlands East Indies and the early Indonesian state as well as by distant sources of Islamic authority. But there had still been a space, if only a small one, within which the family and its members could preserve a sense of independence and moral authority. Material, spiritual, and cultural value had been generated and reproduced within the family and the domestic economy over the generations, a process that had continued through colonial and postcolonial regimes as well as through great fluctuations in the national and global economies.

Merchant families had been linked to others like them in the wider community through relationships of reciprocal exchange, credit, and debt; networks of trade and gossip; ties of kinship, marriage, and friendship; mutual competition in business; and involvement in local status hierarchies. Even through their interdependence, however, people had always held a fundamental respect for the autonomy and privacy (to whatever extent it could be maintained) of the domestic sphere, and of the individuals and families that inhabited it. The family occupied a crucial role, ideologically and in practice, in the constitution of local domains of value. Women, who in their pivotal positions defined both the family and the family firm, were also accorded a basic respect as generators and guardians of value in both family and community. Yet, as the New Order regime embarked confidently on its third decade in power, its own economies were having a pronounced effect on all sectors of society. Through the state's heavy stress on capitalist development as the key to modernizing Indonesian society, and its simultaneous insistence on maintaining strict forms of social, political, and moral order at any cost, new configurations of gender, family, and community were coming into being.

The New Order regime has concentrated much of its ideological effort to develop Indonesian society on the family, but it has reconceptualized the family in a way that is intended to drain it of its local significance and to gear it toward the fulfillment of national goals. In an article on sexuality and the New Order state, Julia Suryakusuma cites the following passage from an official government publication, which demonstrates the deliberateness of the state's attempts to co-opt the family into its agendas: "The family household is the smallest unit of a nation. . . . The (nation) state can only be strong if it is made up of strong families. A just nation can only be achieved through a just arrangement of families. For that reason, building a family implies participation in the building of the foundation of a nation" (quoted in 1996, 97). As Suryakusuma shows, such statements are more than just rhetoric; they underlie a systematic effort on the part of the state to manage the family through concrete and mutually reinforcing laws, policies, and programs.

The simple idea that "the family household is the smallest unit of a nation" signals a basic reconfiguration of the household from how, I believe, it had been conceived by members of Solo's merchant community as well as by many other Javanese. In the ideologies of the New Order, the family/household is not considered to be autonomous in any way; it is merely a fraction of a national whole, a unit that has no independent meaning or existence apart from the nation-state. In contrast, the identity and integrity of the family and the family firm in Laweyan had rested on two foundations. The first was the basic autonomy of the family, the firm, and the entrepreneur, at least in theory, with regard to the state. In practice, the family and its firm had never been completely autonomous, for both had always been tied to the economic policies and political agendas of the state, colonial or postcolonial. Through the state, the family and the family firm had been registered, taxed, inspected, given (or refused) credit, or subsidized. But the family firm, limited in size and integrated with the household economy, had to some extent always been able to evade the control of the government and carry on in the interstices of the national economy.

The second foundation on which the Laweyan family and firm had rested was the unity of the firm and the household, brought together in the person of the female *juragan*. Her jewels were simultaneously the firm's liquid assets, a generator of status for her family, and a potential *warisan* for her children: when she wore her diamond earrings and bracelets to the marketplace, they served both as a sign of her firm's reputability and as an indication of her ability to conserve something of value for her descendants. The domains of firm and household were inseparable, even though their unity was at times a liability, especially when capital accumulation and investment were sacrificed for investments in the family's status.

In New Order visions of modern society, the home is rarely seen as an appropriate place for material production. Through the combined efforts of the state, the mass media, and the forces of an emergent capitalism, home is being transformed into the site of a reified domesticity where loyal and docile citizen-consumers are produced. The household is being pried apart from the economy of production and resignified as a place whose only proper economic function, as the domain of the imagined bourgeois family that inhabits it, should be that of consumption. The image of the modern, capitalist economy that has been adopted by the Indonesian state and mass media, an image that is clearly modeled on the West, assumes a basic separation between household and workplace.

According to these conceptions of a well-ordered, modern society, the production of commodities should take place in large factories, not in small workshops attached to the back of the house, and work more generally should be separated from the domain of the household, which functions mainly as a realm of citizenship, socialization, nurturance, and emotion. This separation of household and workplace has been seen in the West as a critical moment in the development of modern capitalist society (see Weber 1958, 21–22). Indonesian rhetorics of development envision a similar process of transition, following the path of the industrial nations of the West. The small family batik firm does not fit the New Order model of a highly capitalized, industrialized, and rationalized business; nor can it compete with the many multimillion-dollar textile factories that have sprung up around Solo and elsewhere in Indonesia.

The increasing control of bureaucrats and their business associates over the economy has paralleled the progressive insinuation of the state into the domestic sphere. The few Javanese merchant families that have actually been successful by New Order standards—which is to say, the families that have diversified their businesses and expanded into the fully capitalist sector, beyond the sphere of petty commodity production—no longer manage their businesses like the old family firms. They have rationalized their firms and separated them from the household. These entrepreneurs have typically cultivated close contacts with bureaucrats at various levels of the government and have taken ample advantage of state credit programs; it is also significant that men are gaining a much more important role in these businesses than they usually played in the old-style batik firms.[6] A not-so-subtle sign of this new breed of entrepreneur is a photograph, prominently displayed on an office or home wall, of the entrepreneur shaking hands with President Suharto.[7] A comparable picture would have been unimaginable in a past era. These icons of the state replace the inevitable portraits of ancestors that gaze unflinchingly at their descendants from the walls of old Laweyan homes, suggesting that whereas the prosperity of the family was once attributed to ancestral blessings, now it is tied to the "blessings" bestowed by the state.

The insistence on the separation of workplace and home is accompanied by gender ideologies that associate women primarily with the domestic work of caring for the family, and men with the task of going out of the home to the workplace to earn a living for their families. Although it is recognized that women may also work outside the home to "supplement" their husbands' incomes, their foremost duty is to tend to their husbands' needs, nurture the family, and socialize their children to become loyal and obedient citizens of the nation-state—as well as good consumers, one of the keys to promoting capitalist economic development. The "ideal" New Order woman is portrayed as a dedicated wife and mother who devotes her energies to serving her husband and bolstering his career by joining an organization like Dharma Wanita (Women's Duty, a huge national organization for the wives of male civil servants),[8] and to raising the next generation of good Indonesian citizens. In short, the domestic sphere is being recast ideologically to fit an image that more closely resembles the stereotypes of American middle-class family life in the 1950s than any social reality in Java's (or Indonesia's) history.

A number of authors have written about the gender ideologies and programs of the New Order state and their effects on various sectors of Indonesian society.[9] There is a great deal of consensus among these writers on the content and broad implications of state policies. Suryakusuma uses the term "State Ibuism" to describe the regime's gender ideologies, which define women "as appendages and companions to their husbands, as procreators of the nation, as mothers and educators of children, as housekeepers, and as members of Indonesian society—in that order" (1996, 101).[10] These ideologies derive from a combination of *priyayi* gender ideologies and Western-style bourgeois ideologies of domesticity, or "housewifization." Suryakusuma argues that the Indonesian state places women first and foremost in the category of wife, as a means of containing both women and the family itself (1996, 100).[11] Diane Wolf, who discusses the state's gender ideologies in her study of Javanese factory women, points out that the regime's portrayal of women's roles offers "a middle-class image completely divorced from the difficult realities and limited possibilities that most women in Indonesia must confront throughout their lives" (1992, 68).

In Laweyan I saw the impact of New Order models of gender less on the older women, who were quite addicted to their own economic independence, than on the younger generation—women in their late teens, twenties, and thirties who had grown up in the New Order and seen their parents' and grandparents' ways of life languishing. The new emphasis in the community was on educating children—especially, although not exclusively, sons—in the hope that they would enter the professional or administrative sectors of the economy, and on marrying daughters off to men who worked in high-status, high-paying professions, such as doctors, engineers, or bankers. Those young women who married well but did not pursue lucrative professions themselves became increasingly dependent on their husbands for financial support. This pattern fit well with the New Order's promotion of middle-class wifeliness for women.

Both Ibu Wiyono and her mother had been very active entrepreneurs, but none of her four daughters had followed in their footsteps. Several of them married, became housewives, and moved out of Laweyan (two moved to other cities) to follow their husbands. The category of "housewife" had simply not existed for previous generations of Laweyan women, so closely was the family's prosperity tied to a work ethic for women—indeed, almost all Solonese women had worked outside the home—but it was now becoming an accepted lifestyle for their children. To the extent that the category of housewife (translated into Indonesian as *ibu rumah tangga*, roughly, "mother of the household") had any basis in Solonese history at all, it was for the elite wives of colonial and postcolonial *priyayi*: the aristocrats, court retainers, and civil servants of the Dutch and postindependence regimes.

New Order gender ideologies, like all gender ideologies, are concerned with defining appropriate and inappropriate social roles and identities for males and females. What makes ideologies of domesticity so powerful is that they often present, as if conveying timeless truths, gender arrangements that are socially, historically, and politically produced. Local histories are erased or revised to fit particular visions of what the present and future should look like. To control the domestic sphere is to gain the upper hand on the future: the closer one gets to home, so to speak, the deeper the impact one may have on present as well as future generations. The domestic sphere, often represented as if it were wholly outside the sphere of political discourse, is, on the contrary, an inherently political domain. In contemporary Indonesia, an autonomous and economically productive domestic sphere, with an autonomous and economically productive woman at its core, is one that is inadequately domesticated or disciplined. Both such a sphere and such a woman are disruptive to a vision of social order that imagines the household as a place where the goals of national and capitalist development are internalized and reproduced in microcosm.

Modernity and the *Karier* Woman

One of the most effective means for the dissemination of the New Order regime's gender ideologies and policies is through the mass media. This includes media that are directly controlled by the state, such as the national television and radio networks and various state-affiliated publications, as well as those that are independent but still closely tied, whether by ownership or by common interests, to the government's bureaucrats and their goals. New Order ideologies of domesticity resonate with particular force when they recur repeatedly in all forms of mass media at the same time that they are being promoted through the apparatuses of the state. Scholars who have studied the Indonesian mass media have found the domestication of women to be a prominent theme. Krishna Sen (1993), for instance, finds that in modern Indonesian cinema, social and familial disorder is represented by a reversal of the usual gender paradigm associating women with the home and men with the workplace (see also Heider 1991, 118). Similarly, Saraswati Sunindyo remarks that Indonesian television offers negative portrayals of women who devote themselves too passionately to their careers, thereby reinforcing an ideology of female domesticity (1993, 138).

In spite of the state's ideologies of domesticity, many Indonesian women of all classes, including those in Laweyan, have continued to work outside the home in the New Order. The "career woman," *wanita karier* (I.), is a particular focus of anxiety and debate in the popular media. The concept of the career woman is, like the category of housewife, rather peculiar in the Indonesian context. Throughout the Indonesian archipelago since early recorded history, women of almost all classes have worked outside the home, yet the imported concept of career woman is applied as if women's extradomestic work were an entirely modern phenomenon, a mark of Indonesia's progress in becoming developed. From another angle, however, the notion of "career woman" *is* a fairly recent development, since this category usually only includes women who work in white-collar jobs in the modern sectors of the economy. A market trader, farmer, or Laweyan-style *juragan* would not be considered a "career woman" regardless of how much money she earns from her trade, whereas a professional secretary, bank employee, or corporate executive would each qualify for inclusion. Discussions of the career woman always ignore the historical precedents for women's productive—and sometimes powerful—roles in Indonesian society, treating (middle-class) working women as if they were an entirely new breed, a by-product of modernization.

A typical comment on modern women's "advancement," found in a newspaper article titled "Taking a Look at the Pattern of Career Women," begins, "Lately the role and position of women has become increasingly established. They have been able to prove their abilities with a number of contributions that have helped to further the nation's development."[12] The sense that one gets from this remark is that women themselves have had to be "developed"—by men and by the state—in order to be able to make such contributions to national development. That "they have been able to prove their abilities"—only lately—implies that their abilities were, and perhaps still are, in question.

The career woman has been made into a larger-than-life symbol of the positive and negative aspects of modernization. *Wanita karier* ambiguously signifies a woman who is admired for her ability to participate in the modern economy, but who is at the same time fundamentally suspect for her presumed selfishness and lack of attention to her family. According to popular portrayals, her role as career woman may interfere with her duties as wife and mother; she may become overly engrossed with her work, causing her to neglect her family's needs. An even greater fear is that her independence might lead her into adulterous affairs that could destroy her marriage and family. Depictions of career women often stress the dangers and fears that they and their families face. Such concerns are never aimed at men (the category of "career man" is conspicuously absent from Indonesian discourse) because men are primarily held to be the providers for the family rather than its nurturers, as well as the motors of Indonesia's economic development. There is nothing controversial about a man who follows a career; he is simply fulfilling his duties as a good citizen, husband, and father.

That so much attention has focused on the figure of the career woman in Indonesia should give us pause. In a society in which working outside the home has been quite customary for women over the centuries, and where women as well as men have conventionally helped to support their families with their productive activities, one would not expect women's employment to generate so much controversy. As Anthony Reid makes clear in his study of Southeast Asia from 1450 to 1680, women in Java and in Southeast Asia more broadly already enjoyed a high degree of economic autonomy during this period, working not only as farmers, craftswomen, traders, and entertainers, but also as political envoys, courtiers, and soldiers (1988, esp. 162–72). One could say with some confidence, then, that working for a living outside the home has been traditional for many women in this part of the world.

In light of this, it is somewhat astounding to find statements like the following, taken from another Indonesian newspaper: "[We need to] understand that the duty of wives nowadays in this modern era *is no longer just to be 'at home and in the kitchen'*; rather, they engage in many activities outside the home. For instance, [they participate in] functional organizations, social or professional; *there are even many who work, too*, to add to their husbands' income, in order to meet the needs of the household."[13] Such statements have become part of everyday discourse about women in Indonesia. It is as if the forces of modernization and national development have only recently released women from their long-standing role as housewives, authorizing them to step into the public sphere for the first time.

How can we explain this revisionist view of Indonesian women's historical position in household and society, which amounts to the traditionalization of a way of life that is not at all traditional? And what are we to make of the public anxiety that centers on the career woman? I would submit that the idea of the "career woman" becomes a problem at precisely the moment when such a category is *recognized* and opposed to another imported category, that of "housewife." Ideologies of domesticity in the New Order present the concept of housewife as if this were the traditional status of all Indonesian women. The career woman then becomes a modern, and potentially risky, alternative to women's default position as housewife— thereby reproducing in Indonesian society the same debates that have historically occurred in Western, middle-class society over women's work outside the home. The sharp delineation of public and private domains that accompanied the rise of capitalism in the West led to an equally sharp gender division that placed bourgeois women squarely within the private sphere and men within the public sphere. These divisions have been adopted and underscored in the New Order's systematic attempts to make Indonesia "modern." Ironically, the clear ideological separation of domestic and public spheres has occurred at the same time that the state has insisted upon the full incorporation of the household/family into the nation-state, thus erasing the public/private distinction even as it is persistently regenerated by the ideologies of the New Order.

In May 1991 a seminar was sponsored by the women's magazine *Kartini* on "The Successes and Problems of the Career Woman (Dilemmas of the Modern Era)" (*Sukses dan Problematika Wanita Karier [Dilema dalam Era Modern]*, I.). An advertisement for this seminar that ran in a moderate, middle-class Muslim women's magazine read:

> In a society that is rapidly moving forward, various issues emerge at life's threshold and become problems that require our collective attention. One of them is the appearance of the career woman, who until now remains the subject of debate. . . . This is a big advancement, a rapid evolution.
>
> On the other hand, the challenges aren't minor: their dual roles as housewives and workers, challenges from their husbands or other relatives, and, just as important, the temptation to become involved in extramarital affairs. This has become the subject of gossip in certain circles. But is this really how things are? If so, is the situation truly all that bad?[14]

The "big advancement" that is imagined to have allowed women to cross the boundary between domestic and public spheres has also led them into dangerous territory, apparently. The concern with the career woman's sexuality is especially telling in this respect. By leaving the domestic sphere and entering the public sphere of the modern workplace, which is also the sphere of true power, her motherly and wifely qualities are diminished and her independence and undomesticated sexuality are enhanced. Her frequent contact with men to whom she is not related threatens the domestic ideal for middle-class women, and she becomes associated with the easy, unconstrained sexuality of men in public space.

Ideologies of domesticity displace onto the figures of woman and the family a complex set of social anxieties and problems that are intertwined with the process of modernization as well as with political authoritarianism and repression. The domesticated woman serves as a sign of social stability—and as a real means for achieving it—by becoming the incarnation of morality and virtue in her newly exalted roles as mother and wife. Women actually become part of the state apparatus of social control by embodying the ideologies of the nation-state and incorporating them into the daily life of the household. They are told that they must control their desires and make sacrifices on behalf of the family and the nation: the locus of the control of desire, formerly in the family, now shifts to the state, with the family serving as a constituent element of the larger nation-state. This "function" of women is elemental to the success of the regime in fulfilling its goals of development and stability.

Given the extremely volatile decades that preceded the New Order, the present regime has never taken social order or political stability for granted. The severe social and economic inequities of contemporary Indonesia—where corruption is rife, a very small percentage of the population controls the vast bulk of the nation's economic resources, and most political power is held by members of one ethnic group in a multiethnic nation—have created an atmosphere that, while almost eerily quiescent for more than three decades, could be potentially explosive. Rapid modernization has also caused strains in the social fabric and in individuals' lives. In such an environment, the domestication of women and the family becomes not incidental but crucial to the establishment of order and stability.[15] It is therefore no surprise to see the great effort that the regime has invested toward this end. In addition to workplace-based women's organizations like Dharma Wanita, the government also sponsors a number of organizations and activities for women at the neighborhood and village level that aim at implanting them with the skills and values of virtuous domesticity. These include the ubiquitous PKK (*Pembinaan Kesejahteraan Keluarga*), or Family Welfare Guidance, which teaches poorer women especially how to be good (that is, middle-class) mothers and wives (see Wolf 1992, 68–71), and the Project for Mental/Religious Guidance (*Proyek Pembinaan Mental/Agama*, or P2A), which sponsors local Islamic prayer meetings whose sermons have a distinctly New Order tone. There are no comparable local-level organizations for men.

Concern over the morality and propriety of women's behavior deflects attention from larger and potentially more divisive social issues, such as those of class, ethnicity, and widespread political corruption. The propriety of women's behavior is presented as an issue that transcends all social, economic, or cultural divisions; the domesticated woman and harmonious New Order family become the representations of a pan-Indonesian, class-blind, social and moral order. The underlying proposition seems to be that if all Indonesian families could be "developed" to the point at which they could follow the middle-class domestic model, then development of every other sort would simply fall into place. By serving as guarantors of the family's orderliness and morality, women would also, in effect, guarantee the orderliness and morality of the entire society.

While the career woman contributes to economic growth and modernization, she is not the model of domestic virtue that is represented by the New Order housewife. She cannot dedicate herself fully to the needs of her husband and children at the same time that she is devoting herself to her career. Just at the moment when a firm divide has been established between public and private spheres, the career woman has transgressed that divide. The persistent concern over the figure of the career woman highlights that transgression by focusing attention on the risks that such women face as well as pose to others, including the nation at large.

NATURE IS DESTINY: REORIENTING THE MODERN SUBJECT

The career woman is depicted so ambivalently in public discourse not only because she crosses the boundary between domestic and public spheres, but also because she is seen as violating her own *nature* as a woman. The effective inculcation of domestic ideologies depends on making the social roles and identities that they endorse appear as if they are deeply rooted in human nature. Such ideologies do not simply exist as ideas; rather, they acquire tangible form in the institutions and practices of social life, and thereby "constitute both the experience of social relations and the nature of subjectivity" (Poovey 1988, 3). To the extent that the New Order's programs aim at reconfiguring the domestic sphere, they do so in large part by attempting to reshape the subjectivity of those who inhabit that sphere. New, "modern" visions of subjectivity relocate individuals within unfamiliar regimes to control human energies and passions and to harness them for political and social purposes. Female subjectivity in particular is reoriented toward the state's goals through the discourses of gender that are simultaneously disseminated through such diverse channels as the educational system, the mass media, women's organizations, and religious institutions.

Through the "guidance" of political and religious figures, educators and clinicians in fields like psychology and medicine, popular writers and advice columnists, and the leaders of organizations like Dharma Wanita and PKK, women and men learn how they are supposed to behave toward one another and toward their children; what their "natural" attributes, strengths, and weaknesses are (or should be); and how they can best serve family, community, and nation by making use of their inborn character in the manner that God and nature intended. The term *kodrat*, "God-given nature or destiny," is commonly invoked in discussions of gender differences, especially in reference to *women's* nature/destiny, *kodrat wanita*. The notion of *kodrat* embodies the sense of something decreed from above and therefore timeless and unchangeable. "Women's nature/destiny" is defined primarily by their status as mothers (a woman who has no children is one who has not fulfilled her *kodrat*). No matter what else they do besides raise children, women are maternal beings, according to the notion of *kodrat*, and this shapes every facet of their lives.

The headline of an article from a Central Java newspaper, for instance, strongly warns women, "Don't Forget Your Destiny (*Kodrat*) as Mother Even If You Have a Career."[16] The article reports on the contents of the opening speech prepared by the head of the Central Java section of Dharma Wanita, at a seminar titled "The Role of Mothers in Raising the Younger Generation to Become Quality Cadres of the Nation" (*Peranan Ibu dalam Pembinaan Generasi Muda Menjadi Kader Bangsa yang Berkualitas*, I.). Women's role in raising the future generation is central to the success of national development (*pembangunan nasional*, I.), the article states. "Because of this, a mother, who is also the companion of her husband, must always be prepared to guide and educate her children at home." The article explains that the target of Phase II of the state's Five-Year Plan for development is to improve the level of human resources, a process in which mothers are to play a special part:

> In this effort . . . one of the elements that plays an important role, even a very great role, lies in the hands of the women of the household. It can even be said that mothers are the determining factor in the success of shaping quality human resources.
>
> Toward that end, it is hoped that mothers will understand their meaning and function, and add to their knowledge and skill, so that they can give or do as much as possible for their children.

Women's nature, it would seem, is conveniently adaptable for use in the state's official plans for development, a happy meeting of the state's needs and women's natural "meaning and function."

The reorientation of individual subjectivities as a basic element in the "development" of Indonesian society and its citizens works through many different channels. The popular print media are quite influential in this process, especially among the middle classes. This can be seen, for instance, in the advice of "experts" that appears so frequently in Indonesian newspapers and magazines. These experts, whose qualifications are proven to the reader by their professional degrees and titles (always prominently attached to their names), bring an aura of scientific validity to their pronouncements on such matters as marriage, sexual relations, and psychological problems. The political implications of this personal advice are shrouded beneath the veneer of the "caring" but at the same time "objective" (in the name of science) tone of the writer.

A notable example of this is found in an advice column called "Consultation with a Psychiatrist" (*Konsultasi pada Psikiater*, I.), which was published in the Jakarta weekly *Buana Minggu*.[17] Writing on the topic of "Character and Marriage" (*Karakter dan Perkawinan*, I.), the columnist, Dr. Dadang Hawari, a psychiatrist and member of the medical school faculty at the University of Indonesia, offers his advice on how a couple (read: wife) can prevent marital problems by understanding the fundamental psychology and proper roles of husband and wife. The article begins:

> Rapid social change as a result of modernization, industrialization, and progress includes within it marital problems. In modern society the problematics of marriage are more and more complex and tend to increase, requiring preventive measures and professional intervention.
>
> Among the various problems that arise, typically the factor of character or personality plays an important role. Disturbances in marital/family life (family dysfunction [*disfungsi keluarga*]) are ordinarily caused by psychopathological disorders (*kelainan psikopatologis*) in one or another member of the family. However, before approaching the aforesaid psychopathological problems, one needs to understand normal matters, that is, male and female psychology. This is necessary whenever one approaches cases concerning marriage.

The author proceeds to outline the basic personality traits of males and females. With an air of clinical detachment, he presents these traits as undisputed facts: "Physically, males are indeed different from females; this is also true from the perspective of psychology." Men are more rational than emotional, he writes; their thinking or reason is shaped by their experiences and their creativity. "In his life a man does more and works more [than a woman]; it is often the case that 'his home is outside,' that is, in the place where he works." "Men are 'active aggressive' ('*aktif-agresif*') whereas women are 'passive-aggressive' ('*pasif-agresif*'). Men are driven more by the fulfillment of biological needs, while women place greater value on the fulfillment of love and attention, and feeling secure and protected."

Women, he asserts, are more intuitive than men, but their ability to use reason (*rasio*) is weaker. They are more adaptable than men. In matters of love, women emphasize the psychological side, while men emphasize the biological (i.e., sexual) side. Women are more detail-oriented, preferring to deal with small matters, whereas men prefer matters that are more abstract and global in nature. Dr. Dadang further comments, "The husband, as the head of the household and as an executive at the office, frequently faces problems that lead him to experience stress." Women, he adds (in a passage that I quoted earlier), may also experience stress, because "their role is no longer just to be 'at home and in the kitchen.'"

Dr. Dadang claims that he is going to discuss the ways that both husband and wife may help each other if they experience stress (he repeatedly uses the English term "stress" rather than an Indonesian equivalent). However, the remainder of the article focuses exclusively on "what a wife can do when her husband, as an executive, is experiencing stress . . . with the hope that the stress won't be so extensive as to cause a disturbance in the relationship of husband and wife, which can end up in a household crisis (*krisis rumah tangga*)." His professional recommendations are as follows (note that terms in italics appear in English rather than Indonesian in the original text): a wife should be skilled at "*empathic listening*," so that her husband can "vent" to her about the problems that he faces at the office. She should be "*helping*," "*caring*," "*sharing*," and full of understanding in order to lighten his burden when he is experiencing stress. She should not act selfishly or be indifferent toward her husband's troubles, which will only add to his problems. Although her primary role is as a wife, there are many other roles that she can play in order to better look after her husband: for example, "as a 'woman' in fulfilling a husband's biological as well as psychological needs (*how to be a good lover*)"; as a "girlfriend" when he is feeling nostalgic for the days of his youth; as a "*motivator*" who encourages him to be creative and constructive; and as a "*stabilizer*" when he is experiencing anxiety or depression. She should be happy to serve as a "nurse" when he is ill, as a "*mother figur*" [*sic*] when he wants to feel secure, or as a "*lady*" who can be invited to attend various social affairs and guard her husband's "*standing*" in society.

Dr. Dadang's high status as a psychiatrist and educator at Indonesia's most prestigious university, combined with his frequent use of English phrases and scientific jargon ("empathic listening," "psychopathological disorders"), marks his advice as modern, scientific, and beyond question, at least by people who lack his expert qualifications. His prescriptions have a Western ring to them, appropriating concepts that obviously have their origins outside Indonesia, yet they also reflect a conception of domestic relations that is tailored to New Order sensibilities. The "natural" role of a woman is to make sacrifices on behalf of her family—in this case, specifically on behalf of her husband. In the ideologies of national development, such sacrifices are always seen, implicitly or explicitly, as sacrifices on behalf of the nation as well. It is a given that a husband should always be in control, dominant even when he needs his wife to mother him, nurse him, stabilize him, or treat him like an adolescent. A woman's selfhood is defined by her husband's needs rather than her own; she must be adaptable and chameleon-like, sensitive to her husband's every mood and ready to play any role that he requires, even if it means effacing her own needs and desires.

The presumed status of a husband is that of "head of the household" as well as "executive at the office"; a woman's "primary role," however, is merely that of wife. In the credits following the article, it is mentioned that the author had previously presented its contents at a seminar sponsored by the Jakarta chapter of Dharma Wanita. That the author initially addressed himself to an organization to which all civil servants' wives (but never husbands) are expected to belong helps explain his one-sided emphasis on the role of "wife," but the article is offered as general advice to any Indonesian reader who wants to learn about the relationship between "character and marriage."

This depiction of the relationship between husband and wife, and of the innate character of men and women, differs starkly from the understandings of marriage and gendered subjectivity that I encountered in Laweyan. In accordance with the strict delineation of domestic and public spheres so clearly in evidence here, women appear as the self-sacrificing but essentially powerless sentinels of a domain that is obviously subordinate to the public realm of the modern workplace, to which their husbands naturally belong. In Laweyan, as we have seen, women derived power from their status as *juragan* and from their dealings in the marketplace. Women's task, according to Dr. Dadang, is not to domesticate men and the antisocial forces of desire, or to generate wealth and status for their families, as I argued were basic to women's identities in Laweyan. They are expected, rather, to graciously accept their own domestication as a consequence of their female nature/destiny, and to provide mainly emotional support to their families, while their husbands serve as the primary producers of wealth and status.

Nor does women's guardianship of the domestic sphere, on this account, stem from their ability to conserve economic and cultural value for their children and future descendants. Instead of being defined by their role in maintaining intergenerational continuity, they are defined foremost by their position as wife. While both roles can be broadly identified as "domestic," there is a fundamental distinction between the former, which assigns women a productive position in family and society, enabling them to actively create value for their descendants, and the latter, which places a woman in the role of "companion" to her husband and defines her primarily in relation to *his* needs, interests, and desires.

Furthermore, although both roles place a premium on women's willingness to make sacrifices for their families, a woman's deliberate sacrifice on behalf of her descendants through the control of her own instincts and passions, which is accorded much cultural value in Java, has a very different significance from the kind of self-effacing sacrifices for the sake of pleasing a husband that Dr. Dadang promotes for women. I found that many Laweyan women were quite devoted to their husbands, and often took pleasure in serving them, but they did not define themselves as their husbands' dependents, nor did they cater to their husbands at the expense of everything else in their lives. In truth, the idea of being dependent on a man for a living was something that the majority of women there found distasteful. Instead, their aim was to earn money and to generate status for their families, a far different way of placing oneself in the domestic sphere.

The Dharma Wanita model of womanhood was very unappealing to the women of Solo's merchant class, who preferred to make their sacrifices on their own terms.

The potential impact of New Order images of womanhood like Dr. Dadang's, however, should not be underestimated, even in places like Laweyan. In a nation where modernization is touted as the ultimate goal, to be reached in as short a time as possible, the "modern" advice of experts with advanced degrees like Dr. Dadang carries considerable weight. Such advice is also strongly supported by the pronouncements of religious and political leaders, as well as by the gender portrayals found in other forms of mass media. Inscribed in print and on screen, these depictions of the appropriate gender roles for women and men also play a critical part in efforts to inscribe new subjectivities onto Indonesian women and men.

Certain themes, like the ones I have just discussed, emerge time and again in New Order discourses of gender. Dr. Dadang's emphasis on wifely complaisance and unwavering support for her husband, for instance, was echoed in the words of a woman who delivered a sermon at an Islamic prayer meeting that I attended. This all-female gathering, which met twice a month in different sites in the city, was regularly attended by some of Solo's most elite women—the wives of high-ranked bureaucrats, doctors, and businessmen, as well as a few wealthy female traders, entrepreneurs, and professionals. On this occasion, after the recitation of prayers, a junior high school teacher delivered the sermon to the hundred or so women who had assembled inside a small mosque that had been built by the owners of the Danar Hadi company. As she spoke, a number of the women took notes.

Her sermon had a noticeably Dharma Wanita–ish flavor to it. Besides urging the women to behave as faithful Muslims, to serve as good role models for their children and to raise them to be devoted Muslims, and to avoid the temptations of the devil, she repeatedly reminded them that "You have responsibilities in the household, in society, in the nation, and in the state." She warned them to restrain their bad desires (*menahan nafsu yang batil*, I.) and to exercise self-control (she added that the terminology from the government's training program in Pancasila, or state ideology, was "self-restraint," *pengendalian diri*, I.). Then she gave an example to the women of how they should exercise such restraint. "You notice that your husband has started coming home late from the office. First he comes home at six o'clock, then at eight, then at nine, then at eleven, and finally, at one in the morning. It turns out that your husband is keeping a woman on the side. The way to deal with this is not to get angry at him. Instead, as a wife, you should serve him heart and soul, even if he comes home very late. Make your husband feel like a king! With this kind of treatment— making coffee and food for him no matter what time he comes home, and treating him well—he'll start coming home at eleven, and then at nine, then at eight, then at six—and eventually he won't go out at night at all."

Whose desire *is* it, then, that needs to be restrained? The issue of male passions, the need for men to control their desires, is never raised here. The problem of men's *nafsu* is turned into a matter of women's self-restraint: by controlling her own impulse to become angry, the domesticated woman is thereby able to (partially) domesticate her husband. But this is domestication of a very different order from what we saw in Laweyan, where a woman's presumed power to control the forces of desire—her own as well as that of others—was simultaneously the source of her power in the family, the marketplace, and the community. Implied in the scenario of the unfaithful husband is that by failing to treat her husband "like a king" in the first place, a wife drives her husband to seek his pleasures elsewhere; the only way that she can convince him to return is by "serving him heart and soul." As in Dr. Dadang's prescriptions for a happy marriage, women's sacrifices, as well as their domesticating moves, are located within an economy in which they play only a tangential part. Power is ultimately centered elsewhere—outside the home, where men, not women, are in control. In New Order representations, the domestic sphere is never seen as a source of its own power; all of its power (and that of the woman who dwells within it) derives from its connections to the public sphere of the state and the modern economy, filtered through the figure of the man who, in the end, rules both domains.

It would be naively deterministic—and simply wrong—to argue that the gender ideologies of the New Order have been able to completely supplant local, alternative constructions of gender, or that they will do so in the near future. I proposed earlier, in my discussion of Javanese gender ideologies (chapter 4), that even dominant gender ideologies are not monolithic, that they fully determine neither the everyday practices of gender nor how people understand their own gendered subjectivity. At the same time, though, it would also be naive to deny the power of New Order ideologies, which are constantly circulating in the public (and private) domain, to bring about changes in people's thoughts and actions as gendered subjects. While alternative understandings of gender will always exist, challenging, contradicting, or just circumventing dominant representations, they may be increasingly constrained by the weight of an ideological system that so thoroughly embeds itself in both official and popular discourse as to be inescapable in daily life.

In her analysis of the ideologies and "technologies" of gender, Teresa de Lauretis observes that "the movement in and out of gender as ideological representation . . . is a movement back and forth between the representation of gender . . . and what that representation leaves out, or, more pointedly, makes unrepresentable" (1987, 26). This book has been dedicated in part to describing the alternatives to dominant representations of gender, whether "Javanese" or "New Order" (there is, in fact, some overlap between them), by looking in some depth at the life of a particular community and the practices of gender that have prevailed within it. Although Laweyan is a community in decline, the traces of its past, and of particular forms of subjectivity that seem not to have their origins in the New Order, can still be read in the actions and words of those who belong to that community. The decline of Laweyan, I would propose, should be seen not just as the decline of one community, but as a figure for the decline of a particular way of life and of distinctive forms of gendered subjectivity that, I believe, are becoming increasingly "unrepresentable" (to use de Lauretis's term) under the social and political conditions of "modern" Indonesia. Although Laweyan is unusual in some ways, the changes that have been taking place here can nevertheless be taken as an indication of changes that are occurring in Java, and Indonesia, more broadly.

In Laweyan, change has occurred neither rapidly nor uniformly. In the mid-1990s, the community was still considered a bastion of tradition by the rest of Solo's population. Some people continued to look to their ancestors for blessings, and some still declared their disdain for those who made a living by serving the state. A few women still went to Pasar Klewer to trade batik while their husbands stayed at home; those who no longer had any goods to sell occasionally went there out of habit and for companionship, saying that they felt "lonely" if they stayed at home. But even those who rejected change knew that it was inevitable. Built on the foundations of a new modernity at the turn of the twentieth century, Laweyan could not keep pace with modernity's demands at the century's end.

NOTES

INTRODUCTION

1. The common pronunciation of "Laweyan" is something like "LA-way-an," although there are several variations on this.

2. The day-to-day language used in the home and in informal conversations among ethnic Javanese in Laweyan, as in most of Central Java, is Javanese. Indonesian is the language of schools, the government bureaucracy, and the mass media throughout the Indonesian archipelago. The inability to speak "proper" Indonesian is often associated with lack of education or a traditional outlook (among older people or villagers, for instance).

3. This account is found in vol. 2 of P. de Kat Angelino's *Batikrapport* (1930–31).

4. The topic of marginality has come to the fore recently in Indonesian studies. Anna Tsing, for example, writes about Meratus Dayaks of South Kalimantan as "exotic subjects" living at the margins of the Indonesian nation-state. In the eyes of those located at Indonesia's center, people like the Meratus are hopelessly backward, a thorn in the side of a nation that wants to be a respected player on the modern stage of the global economy. As Tsing puts it, the Meratus are "a *displacement* within powerful discourses on civilization and progress" (1993, 8). The notion of displacement is also evoked in Mary Steedly's study of Karo, in North Sumatra. The phrase "hanging without a rope" (also the title of her book) describes the feeling of Karo spirit mediums and others "of being out of place . . . in a time officially designated as Indonesia's Age of Development" (1993, 38). Earlier studies examining groups that are marginalized within the larger power structures of Indonesian society also include works by Robert Hefner (1985) and Jane Atkinson (1989).

Marginality, it would seem, is a by-product of the very forces that seek to contain it, and it comes in many forms. If we define the margins as sites of displacement or exclusion, they can be found not only in what Tsing calls "out-of-the-way places" but also as gaps in the centers of power, of development, of so-called civilization—such as the urban Javanese community about which I write in this book.

5. For two insightful studies that examine, in two very different contexts, how the notion of tradition is deployed in particular "national-cultural" projects, see Pemberton 1994 and Ivy 1995 (the phrase is Ivy's).

6. As Gayatri Spivak writes, "the deconstruction of the opposition between the private and the public is implicit in all, and explicit in some, feminist activity" (1988, 103).

7. According to *The New Shorter Oxford English Dictionary* (1993), "economy" stems from the Greek *oikonomia*, itself derived from *oikonomos*, "manager of a household, steward" (s.v. "economy"). The Greek *oikos* is equivalent to the Latin *domus*, "house," from which derives the term "domestic."

8. Dorinne Kondo makes a similar comment about the women she came to know in her study of urban Japan, whose identities "were constituted through a

variety of specific subject-positions—wife, mother, part-time worker, resident of the Shitamachi, or downtown, district of Tokyo, and worker in a small enterprise, to name only a few. And these subject-positions are shaped in history and in specific interactions on the shop floor" (1990, 44).

CHAPTER ONE
A NEIGHBORHOOD COMES OF AGE

1. The Kraton Surakarta is also commonly called the Kraton Solo (Solo Palace).

2. For accounts of the events leading up to and following the move of the Kraton from Kartasura to Solo, see Ricklefs 1981, chaps. 8, 9; see also Ricklefs 1978, esp. 10–11; Darsiti 1989; Shiraishi 1990. An alternative and thoroughly enlightening account of these events, based primarily on Javanese sources, is also found in Pemberton 1994, chap. 1.

3. Eventually a fourth principality, the Pakualaman, was established in Yogyakarta in 1812. It was subordinate to the Sultanate of Yogyakarta.

4. Indonesia's independence was proclaimed by Sukarno (who became Indonesia's first president) and Hatta (the first vice president) on August 17, 1945. However, the Netherlands did not officially cede full sovereignty to the new nation until 1949.

5. For two valuable discussions of the development of the Dutch colonial field of "Javanology," which located the golden age of Javanese culture and literature in the pre-Islamic past and designated the Javanese aristocracy, particularly those associated with the palace of Surakarta, as its heirs, see Tsuchiya 1990; Florida 1995. Pemberton also notes that the practices of Solo's elites became Javanology's model for the standardization of generic "Javanese" practices, just as the dialect of Javanese spoken in Solo became the model for a standard "Javanese" language to be taught in schools (1994, 140).

6. In her powerful ethnography of Karo of North Sumatra, Mary Steedly (1993) offers compelling arguments against the ethnographic privileging of generic representation at the expense of partial, shifting, and sometimes discordant "mappings of the social terrain" (238). The delicate complexity of her own study of what she terms "narrative experience" underscores the value of such an approach.

7. As someone from Solo pointed out to me, this woman had confused Laweyan people with the so-called Galgendu or Kalang people of the Kotagede area, near Yogyakarta, who constituted another very wealthy and marginal Javanese group. According to local legend, these people had tails because they were descended from the union of a Balinese princess with an ape. For more on the Kalang people, see M. Nakamura 1983, esp. 38–40.

8. The words *bapak* (father) and *ibu* (mother), which also mean "Mr." and "Mrs." (and which are broadly used to designate adult males and females, regardless of their marital or parental status) are often shortened to *Pak* and *Bu* when they are used as terms of address.

9. K. R. T. Harjonagoro, interview, October 23, 1986. Three short studies on the early history of Laweyan, based on both oral and written sources, are Samsudjin 1981, Mlayadipura 1984, and Sarsono 1985.

10. According to de Graaf, who bases his conclusions on the *Serat Kandha*, the *Babad Tanah Jawi*, and other court chronicles, the appanage was given to Kyai

Ageng Anis (which may alternatively be spelled Henis or Ngenis) by Jaka Tingkir, the son-in-law and vassal of the sultan of Demak. Jaka Tingkir later became Sultan Hadiwijaya of Pajang, a short-lived kingdom that was based just a few kilometers west of Laweyan, in what is now an unremarkable village. See de Graaf 1985, esp. 5–7, 19–20.

11. Kyai Ageng Anis is credited with bringing Islam to Laweyan, whose residents are assumed to have been Hindu Javanese until that time. The mosque dates to the sixteenth century, although it has since been rebuilt.

12. According to Samsudjin Probohardjono (1981, 35–36), the mosque and cemetery have been treated as royal property since the early days of Mataram, when Senapati was still the ruler. A court retainer (*abdi dalem*) was sent to care for the cemetery, and an Islamic official of the court (*penghulu*) was installed to look after the mosque and the religious affairs of the local people.

13. See chapter 2 for an account of Pakubuwana II's brief visit to Laweyan. Although his tombstone is still prominently displayed in the cemetery at Laweyan, he was reinterred in the royal cemetery at Imogiri, near Yogyakarta, during the reign of Pakubuwana III. See Mlayadipura 1984, 12.

14. Most trace their ancestry to villages outside Solo, such as Nusupan, once a prosperous entrepôt on the banks of the Solo River, and home to many well-to-do merchants, until the construction of the railroad through Solo made river transport obsolete in the early 1870s (see Soerachman 1927, 23). Others trace their roots to Tembayat in the area of Klaten, southwest of Solo.

15. I have no information as to when the market at Laweyan disappeared; however, it is quite possible that it lost its importance as a result of the shrinking of the local waterways to the small streams that they are today, unsuitable for passage by boat.

16. It is beyond the scope of the present study to discuss the much-debated issue of the origins of batik in Indonesia. On the history of batik making in the Netherlands East Indies, see Rouffaer and Juynboll 1914; Jasper and Pirngadie 1916; Adam 1934; Tirtaamidjaja 1966; Gittinger 1980; Elliott 1984; Fraser-Lu 1986; Kitley 1987, 1992; Boow 1988.

17. W. F. Wertheim writes, "In his [1656] account of a mission to Mataram Rijcklof van Goens describes how some thousands of female workers were employed at the *kraton* [palace] in the *batik* industry and other crafts. To a certain extent . . . these *kraton* trades have the character of large-scale industries carried on with slave labour" (1956, 231–32). Whether the workers were actually slaves is questionable; they may well have been paid artisans in service to the court.

18. According to one account, batik cloth was originally worn principally by men (Poensen 1887, 1–21; cited in Kitley 1987, 9).

19. Sumptuary laws designating certain batik motifs for the exclusive use of the royalty were first put into effect in the mid– to late eighteenth century in the palaces of Solo and Yogyakarta. Kitley (1987) points out that once batik began to be made and worn widely outside the courts, status no longer attached to the product itself, making it necessary for the royalty to create these sumptuary laws to maintain a clear distinction between themselves and other wearers of batik.

20. "Batikken" 1917. Kitley (1987) suggests that English textile firms used the information on batik making in Raffles's *History of Java* to learn how to make imitations, but if the date that appears in the *Encyclopaedie van Nederlandsche-Indië* is

correct, English manufacturing of imitation batik predated the publication of *The History of Java* by three years.

21. Although no one seems to know precisely when the *cap* was invented, Rouffaer and Juynboll (1914) date its first use to 1845 (cited in Soerachman 1927, 8). Soerachman names the neighborhood of the Kauman, near the city's central mosque, as the "birthplace of the *cap* firm" (*de bakermat der tjapperij*, D.), although it appears to have been invented in the nearby city of Semarang. He attributes the first use of the *cap* in Solo to an entrepreneur named Ngabei Resodipo Djiwangono. Apparently the latter tried to keep the process secret—the story goes that he kept his workers shut in on the upper floor of his workshop—but word quickly got out and soon the process was being imitated widely by other entrepreneurs (Soerachman 1927, 30–31). See also Kat Angelino 1930–31, 2:96.

22. For descriptions of the techniques of Javanese batik making, see Adam 1934; Tirtaamidjaja 1966; Hamzuri 1985; Elliott 1984; Fraser-Lu 1986. Although the actual process is fairly complicated, a good, short layman's description is found in Banner: "Baticking is, first and last, a dyeing process. For the present, without going into detail, it may be described as a method whereby cotton fabric is adorned with patterns of variegated colour by successive dippings in different dyes, a layer of wax being laid, prior to each dipping, upon those portions of the surface not intended to come into contact with that particular colour" (1927, 98).

23. According to the system of Javanese orthography that I follow in this book, the term should properly be spelled *bathik tulis*. However, I have opted to use instead the common spelling, *batik*, which is often used in Javanese and always used in Indonesian.

24. The process is made even more laborious because it must be done twice: after the designs are applied to one side of the cloth, it is then turned over, and the entire design is retraced in detail on the opposite side (*diterusi*). Even cheap batik has the design applied to both sides of the cloth; this is considered an aesthetic imperative in Java, even though only one side of the cloth is revealed when it is actually worn. One of the reasons that imitation batik was never as popular as genuine batik was that the designs were only printed on one side of the cloth, making it a less pleasing substitute by local standards.

25. A comment made by Raffles in 1817 is telling in this regard: "A very extensive and valuable assortment of [English printed] cottons, imitated after the Javan and Malayan patterns, was recently imported into Java by the East-India Company, and on the first sale produced very good prices; but before a second trial could be made, the natives had discovered that the colours would not stand, and the remainder were no longer in any demand" ([1817] 1965, I:216–17).

Synthetic (aniline) dyes began to be used in the batik industry around 1900 (see "Batikken" 1917, 196); by that time the quality of artificial dyestuffs had improved to the point that they could satisfy the local population. Although artificial dyes soon replaced natural dyes almost completely in Pekalongan and many other cities, and were substituted for indigo fairly early in Solo, many batik makers of Solo and Yogyakarta continued to use to the deep yellow-brown vegetable dye called *soga Jawa*, which they still preferred to its imitations even though its use was more costly and required much more labor than synthetic dyes. *Soga Jawa* is still used today in some firms in Solo and Yogyakarta, although it may be mixed with synthetic dyes.

26. Originally all aspects of batik production in the palaces, including dyeing, were carried out by women, but this changed after batik began to be produced outside the courts. The shift in the sexual division of labor in batik production is discussed in Dunham 1982.

27. I say "more or less full-time" because batik production fluctuated seasonally. During times of peak demand—for example, right before the harvest or before Lebaran (Idul Fitri, the holiday at the end of Ramadan), when it is customary to purchase new clothing and to give gifts—the workshops operated at maximal capacity and work was easy for a batik laborer to find. During slower periods, many of the workshops dismissed a portion of their workers, or even closed down temporarily until the demand for batik increased again. Men from the villages also went home to help out during the harvest or at other times when their labor was needed.

28. For those who could not afford the higher-quality *batik tulis*, there was also the option of buying a coarse, inexpensive style of *batik tulis* that was mostly produced in the villages.

29. The Vorstenlanden, or Principalities, was the region of south Central Java that was nominally under the rule of the four royal houses of Solo and Yogyakarta, the Kasunanan (Sunanate) and Mangkunagaran in Solo and the Kasultanan (Sultanate) and Pakualaman in Yogyakarta. The region was, in fact, controlled by the Dutch through a system of indirect rule.

30. Apparently imported cambrics have been used for making batik in Indonesia since the seventeenth century. Furnivall writes, "The older batiks were worked on a rough indigenous homespun, but the importation of fine cambric from China or British India began about three hundred years ago, coinciding more or less with the coming of the Dutch" (1936, 373). During the later colonial period, most cambric and other undyed cloth of lesser quality for making batik was imported from the Netherlands, England, and Japan.

31. In a government study conducted in 1915 of batik firms with a total of five employees or more, Solo had the largest number of firms (225), followed by Pekalongan (114) and Yogyakarta (69) ("Batikken" 1917, 198–99). Since there were undoubtedly many batik firms with fewer than five workers that went uncounted, however (as well as other, larger firms that managed to avoid being surveyed by the government), these figures do not indicate the full extent of the industry in any of the batik centers. In 1922 Koperberg wrote, "it is a fact that the center of the batik (*cap*) industry is Central Java and in particular Solo and Djokja [Yogyakarta], where an estimated two-thirds of the batik firms are established" (150). The batik industry of Yogyakarta was smaller than Solo's both in the number and size of the firms (see Soerachman 1927, 13).

Yet the industry was expanding rapidly in this period, and some other towns and cities seem to have quickly surpassed Solo in the number of firms that they had, at least according to official estimates. In 1930, for example, it was noted that Pekalongan was by far the largest center of batik production in Central Java, with a total of 1,195 firms, followed by Solo with 387, Tegal with 226, and Yogyakarta with 209. According to the same study there were also cities in other parts of Java with more batik firms than Solo, including Cirebon, Batavia, and Tasikmalaya in West Java (Kat Angelino 1930–31, 1:203, 2:321). Each of these cities had their own regional styles of batik, which were favored in different markets. The batik produced in Pekalongan and in West Java used bright colors and bold designs that became very popular throughout much of the Indies and abroad; these were often preferred to Solo's more subdued brown and indigo dyes and designs.

32. Most ethnic Chinese and Arab batik entrepreneurs were so-called *peranakan*, the descendants of mixed unions between local women and immigrant men from China or Hadramaut (South Yemen, the place of origin of most of Indonesia's Arab population), whose families had lived in the Indies for at least two generations. Although I have no information about the identity of the Europeans in the industry—according to surveys of the period and the memory of older residents of Solo there were three European firms there around the 1920s and 1930s—it is possible that they were Indies-born Eurasians, since the off-spring of local women and European men were also classified under the general category of "Europeans." Interestingly, several distinctive styles of batik dyeing (*soga*) were named after European entrepreneurs in Solo who made them popular—*jonasan*, *gènesan*, and *maèran*, reputedly based on the names Johannes, van Geuns, and Mayer. These terms are still in general use in Solo. See Soerachman 1927, 38.

33. Koperberg 1922 cites a local survey of the batik industry in Solo and Yogyakarta held in 1920, which found in Solo, out of 283 firms in total, 158 Javanese firms, 85 Chinese firms, and 37 Arab firms. (The article also mentions that there were 37 European firms, but this is clearly a misprint; the correct number was 3.) The same study counted 208 indigenous firms in Yogyakarta (this included Javanese and quite a few Sumatran-owned firms, apparently) and 17 Chinese firms; no Arab firms were mentioned.

Notably, some of the highest-quality *batik tulis* was produced by Chinese- rather than Javanese-owned firms. Chinese firms tended to produce batik in colors and motifs preferred by non-Javanese, like the extraordinary *tiga negeri* (three countries) style, which combined design and color elements from three cities with distinctive batik styles. Taste in batik was determined not only by region but also by ethnic group, since Chinese, Arabs, Eurasians, and Javanese often wore different styles of batik. Batik sarongs were commonly worn by mestizo (*peranakan*) women of each of these groups until fairly recently.

34. Although Solonese batik was marketed all over the Indies and to other countries, many producers had little or no idea of where their product ended up after they sold it to the local Chinese or Arab wholesaler, who would in turn market it to Surabaya or Batavia, whence it might be marketed to regions farther afield. One older batik entrepreneur remembered how surprised he was when he visited North Sumatra for the first time and discovered that wherever he went, people were wearing the batik manufactured by his firm. He described his reaction: "I thought to myself, so *this* is where my batik is going!"

35. On the ethnic division of the colonial economy, see, e.g., Furnivall 1944; Rush 1990; Alexander and Alexander 1991.

36. Soerachman (1927, 30) lists the neighborhoods of Solo where batik production was concentrated: Sorogenen, Warung Pelem, Samaan, Kauman, Keprabon, Pasar Kliwon, Soniten, Telukan, Singosaren, Kabangan, Tegalsari, Laweyan, Pasar Kembang, and Priobadan. These neighborhoods are scattered all over the

city. Most Chinese-owned firms were found in the northeastern section of the city, although there were some in the central part as well; the Arab firms were concentrated in the neighborhood of Pasar Kliwon, in the southeastern section, where much of the city's Arab population lived.

37. Tegalsari, Kabangan, and Laweyan are all located very close to each other; Kabangan, in fact, is often considered to be part of the neighborhood of Laweyan.

38. According to one colonial government publication, the population of Solo in 1934 was 165,500, making it the fifth-largest city in the Indies (*Statistisch Zakboekje voor Nederlandsch Indië 1934* 1934, 8).

39. These communities included West Kudus, on Java's north coast, and Kotagede, in the region of Yogyakarta (south Central Java). On Kudus, see Castles 1967, Weix 1990; on Kotagede, see M. Nakamura 1983.

40. Remarkably, de Kat Angelino mentions Solonese batik firms that had 500–600 employees before the early 1920s; after that time, however, the firms shrank as a result of the ensuing recession (1930–31, 2:98).

41. For an excellent study of the opium revenue farms and the Chinese business communities in nineteenth-century Java, see Rush 1990.

42. Hawkins (1961, 45), citing Purcell (1951, 539), writes that the depression of the 1930s tended to push the Chinese out of the batik industry and other trades, as the indigenous Indonesians returned to older methods of barter. Whether or not this was indeed the reason, many Chinese did leave the production side of the batik industry in the 1930s and especially after World War II and the Indonesian Revolution, although they retained their prominent roles as suppliers of raw materials and batik wholesalers. A retired Chinese batik entrepreneur in Solo told me that most Chinese had left the batik industry for more lucrative businesses as soon as the once-spectacular profits from batik production began to diminish.

43. Koperberg mentions that in 1892, several Residents (the highest Dutch official in a given region) of Java and Madura had discussed "the desirability of extending help to the batik industry out of economic and aesthetic considerations" (1922, 151).

44. Sams 1918, 510. Encouraging the production of batik can be seen as an extension of the more general "Ethical Policy" of the Dutch that began around the turn of the century, and which aimed at improving the welfare of the native population of the Indies. The move to protect the artistic aspects of batik making was in keeping with other Dutch efforts to preserve or restore what they perceived as "traditional" in the Javanese arts and literature—a task that they felt could not be left to Javanese people alone (see Florida 1995).

45. On the economic importance of the Indies' market for Dutch cottons at the end of the nineteenth century, see Hoëvell 1896.

46. The 1930 census figures place the population of Java and its small island neighbor Madura at a combined total of 40.9 million, up from about 34.4 million in 1920 (Ricklefs 1981, 147).

47. For a detailed account of the political events of these two decades in Solo, see Shiraishi 1990. The following information on political activity in Laweyan and

Solo is drawn primarily from this source, except where otherwise indicated. Another useful source on Sarekat Islam and the events of this era is Noer 1973.

48. Haji Samanhoedi was so successful in the batik trade that he was able to establish branches of his business in cities all over Java. Eventually, however, his business failed, and he also removed himself from the active leadership of Sarekat Islam. For a profile of Haji Samanhoedi, see Noer 1973, esp. 106–7, 111. A few of his descendants still live in Laweyan.

Deliar Noer cites November, 11, 1911, as the founding date of the Sarekat Islam (1973, 102). Shiraishi, however, believes that this date is too early, and that the actual date of Sarekat Islam's establishment was around February 1912 (1990, 42).

49. The Javanese radical journalist Marco Kartodikromo describes a large Sarekat Islam rally held in Kabangan (adjacent to Laweyan, and part of the same extended neighborhood), and attended by people from all over Java, in his Malay-language novel *Student Hidjo* (Marco 1919, 95–96). An English translation of the passage is found in Shiraishi 1990, 65.

50. Extensive analyses of the communist movement in the Indies during this period are found in McVey 1965 and Shiraishi 1990.

51. Rinkes was adviser for native affairs; cited in Shiraishi 1990, 71–72.

52. Most children of Laweyan merchants attended HIS (Hollandsch-Inlandsche School, or "Dutch-Native School") for primary school; those who continued on to middle school attended MULO (Meer Uitgebreid Lager Onderwijs, or "More Extended Lower Instruction [School]"). Only a few went to high school.

53. Marriage between first cousins (and more distant relatives) was in the past generally deemed acceptable in Javanese society, with the exception of patrilateral parallel cousin marriage, which most people consider taboo—interestingly, a pattern of marriage that is often considered preferable among Arabs, but that was not imported with Islam. Marriage between first cousins in Laweyan was not prescribed, but it did take place from time to time.

54. I know of two other communities of formerly rich Javanese merchants that were also largely endogamous in the past, possibly even more so than Laweyan. One was the devout Muslim merchant community of West Kudus (Weix 1990); the other was the community of very rich pawnbrokers and moneylenders who lived in Kotagede and other Javanese cities (including Solo), the so-called Kalang or Galgendu people. Among the latter group, the preferred pattern was for cousins, including first cousins, to marry each other (see M. Nakamura 1983). Price also observed a tendency toward endogamy among a community of textile entrepreneurs in an unspecified village on Central Java's north coast (Price 1983, 104). Endogamy is found as well among certain occupational groups in Java, including the families of shadow puppeteers (*dhalang*)—a highly skilled and often respected occupation—as well as traditional Islamic teachers (*kiai*).

55. A common exception to the general rule of neolocal residence and the establishment of new firms with each generation was that a youngest or only child tended to remain in his or her parents' house, together with spouse and children, after marriage, in order to look after the parents and to help them out in business until they were ready to retire. At that point, the child and the child's spouse sometimes assumed control of the business. By custom, after the eventual death of the parents, the business and house would often fall to that child.

CHAPTER TWO
HIERARCHY AND CONTRADICTION

1. Ruwah is also called Sadran or Syaban (its Arabic name). The ritual of visiting graves during this month is known in Java as *sadranan* or *ruwahan*.

2. Kotagede was established by Kyai Ageng Mataram, also known as Pamanahan (died 1575), the son of Kyai Ageng Anis (see chapter 1). The kingdom of Mataram was founded at Kotagede in 1587 by Panembahan Senapati Ingalaga, Kyai Ageng Mataram's son, after he destroyed the kingdom of Pajang (the capital of which had been located just west of Laweyan). Senapati died in 1601 and was buried in the graveyard of the town mosque, next to the grave of his father. Other members of the royal family and high officials of the kingdom were buried there as well. This graveyard was subsequently made into a special compound and designated a royal cemetery. Even after the seat of Mataram was moved from Kotagede to Kerta by Sultan Agung, who built a new royal cemetery at Imogiri, the cemetery at Kotagede continued to be treated as a venerated site housing the graves of the ancestors of Later Mataram. Following the division of Later Mataram into the Sunanate of Surakarta (Solo) and the Sultanate of Yogyakarta in 1755, it was agreed that the royal cemeteries at Kotagede and Imogiri would be maintained jointly by the two courts as "ancestral lands" (*tanah pusaka*). For more on Kotagede and its royal cemetery, see Mook 1958; M. Nakamura 1983.

3. For discussions of the workings of language levels in Javanese, see C. Geertz 1960; H. Geertz 1961; Soepomo 1968; Wolff and Soepomo 1982; Keeler 1984, 1987; J. Errington 1985, 1988; Siegel 1986; Smith-Hefner 1988.

4. In linguistic situations where people wish to avoid acknowledging status distinctions openly, they may decide to use Indonesian, in which status differences are not marked as they are in Javanese. However, the majority of Javanese people in Solo seem to prefer using Javanese rather than Indonesian for most interactions, with a few exceptions (such as dealing with government bureaucrats).

5. For two very different but complementary studies that examine language and hierarchy in Solo (Surakarta), see Siegel 1986 and J. Errington 1988.

6. Anderson's article was originally published in 1972.

7. This conception of the relationship between wealth and power corresponds to a broader understanding of that same relationship in the precolonial Malay world, including, but not limited to, Java. Writes the historian Pierre-Yves Manguin, "political power and wealth cannot be dissociated in a Malay World context. The symbolic value of the ruler's 'treasure' is essential in this regard. Wealth is an attribute of the ruler, one of the requisite sources of his power (wealth, however, is not an accumulative process: it should flow towards the ruler as well as from him)" (1991, 47). Anthony Reid confirms this, commenting that "in Southeast Asian languages wealth and power were not sharply distinguished. Wealth could be obtained only through power, in the sense of inner strength and an intimate relationship with the spiritual world" (1993, 115).

8. The Java War is also known as the Diponegoro War. As Nancy Florida notes, the end of this war marked "the final defeat of indigenous Javanese royal power." The war, which was led by Prince Diponegoro and supported by a network of rural *kiai*, or Islamic teachers, was "the last concerted Javanese rebellion against colonial

authority (prior to the Indonesian national revolution)"; the lives of over 200,000 Javanese are said to have been lost (1995, 23–24).

9. For an analysis of the events that determined the political fates of the Solo and Yogyakarta royal houses after independence, see Anderson 1972, esp. 350–69.

10. According to one man, a Kraton courtier of high rank, the sunan said to the people of Laweyan, "In the future, you will never become one with me" (*Sésuk, kowé ora isa manunggal karo aku*).

11. Writing in the 1920s about Kotagede, a town that, like Solo, had both a strong indigenous Javanese bourgeoisie and many *priyayi* in service to the courts (both the Yogyakarta Sultanate and the Sunanate of Solo), the colonial administrator H. J. van Mook remarked of the richer merchants and entrepreneurs that "In them nothing is to be detected of the obsequiousness usual in the Principalities, for many of them are, on a lesser scale, what Rothschild was on a grand scale: the creditors of princes" (1958, 288). He also commented, "The administrative officials [in Kotagede] have much less influence there than elsewhere, especially when they are not well-to-do. It is often difficult, and financially disastrous, for them to keep up with the wealthier inhabitants of Kuta Gede" (287). See also M. Nakamura 1983, 53.

12. Just such a wedding is described in an extremely amusing Javanese poem from the early nineteenth century, *Suluk Mas Ngantèn*, written in 1818 by Raden Mas Riya Jayadiningrat I, a member of Solo's *priyayi* literati. This poem describes, among other things, the disastrous (and very comical) efforts of a petty Javanese merchant to make a grand, *priyayi*-style wedding for his child. The poem is a sarcastic comment about people who try to be something that they are not—in this case, a merchant trying to pretend that he is a *priyayi*—but it is also a biting denunciation of the self-indulgent, arrogant tendencies of members of the *priyayi* class to which the author himself belonged. The poem is reprinted in *Serat Wulang* (Jakarta: Departemen Pendidikan dan Kebudayaan, 1981), 131–201. For a partial translation and commentary, see Brenner 1991.

13. One cannot make generalizations in this regard for the whole of Java, because the situation in the agrarian interior of the island, where Solo is located, differed from that of the commercially oriented coastal polities. In the trading ports of Java's north coast in the centuries prior to colonization, where Javanese and foreigners—Malays, Chinese, Arabs, Persians, Indians, and Portuguese—had engaged in a thriving international trade in spices, cloth, and other products, political power and access to revenue among Javanese coastal rulers had depended on their ability to attract traders to their ports and to exercise control over commerce. There was little basis for a deep ideological conflict between merchants and aristocrats because both depended in one way or another on trade for their livelihood and social status (see Manguin 1991; Reid 1993). Only when colonization permanently altered the face of socioeconomic relations in the region by shifting trade into the hands of Europeans and Chinese did commerce cease to be a major source of political and economic strength for local elites. Beginning in the seventeenth century, Dutch competitors used military force to wrest control of the highly profitable international trade that had been conducted by Javanese and others from the north coast (Alexander and Alexander 1991; Reid 1993); this was the start of

Dutch colonial penetration of Java, as well as the decline of Javanese participation in large-scale trade.

In the fertile inland of Java, where economic and political power were based less on commerce and more on control over land and labor, it is quite possible that even before colonization, the occupation of trader may have been disparaged by political elites. When Sultan Agung (r. 1613–45) of the inland kingdom of Mataram conquered the coastal polities of North Java, he is reported to have expressed his disinterest in trade, stating, "I am a prince and a soldier, not a merchant like the other princes of Java" (Reid 1993, 284). Evidence from the poem *Suluk Mas Ngantèn* (1818) strongly suggests that the social categories of merchant and *priyayi* were already considered to be fundamentally at odds with each other by that time (see Brenner 1991), but whether this was a legacy of a long-standing rivalry dating back to the precolonial period or a product of colonialism is difficult to determine.

14. For more on the effects of the agrarian reorganization in the Principalities, see Anderson 1972, 348–51; Shiraishi 1990, chap. 1; Larson 1987, 20–22; M. Nakamura 1983, 40–44; Mook 1958, 320–31.

15. Both Sutherland (1979) and Kumar (1980b) point out that over the course of the nineteenth century, the period during which the Dutch consolidated their control over the whole of Java and over the Javanese ruling class, the ideal of being a warrior (*satria*) in service to a powerful Javanese ruler gave way to an ideal of being an aristocrat-cum-bureaucrat in service to the colonial state (through the palaces), i.e., a *priyayi*.

16. The pattern of women dominating local trade during this period was not limited to Java. Reid notes that the domestic markets of rural Southeast Asia in the fifteenth through seventeenth centuries were "almost entirely an affair of women. Local men would appear in the market to browse, to flirt, to gossip and socialize, but they were not usually concerned with buying and selling except at the highest level. . . . In the cities, however, there was always an abundance of foreign men selling in the market." He reports that in the port city of Banten (in West Java, on the north coast of the island), there were separate cloth markets in which the sellers were either local women selling local cloth or foreign men selling imported cloth (1993, 93).

17. De Kat Angelino, for instance, describes Solonese *batik cap* workers as being of weak physical constitution, addicted to opium, and perpetually in debt. If they earned a little money, he writes, they would fritter it away on opium, gambling, or other frivolous spending—buying *saté*, going to movies or to the amusement park—rather than bringing it home to their families or investing it wisely (1930–31, 2:106–9).

18. In her research on divorce practices in Java, Hisako Nakamura (1983) found that "sharing husband with another wife" (this included the prospect of being made a co-wife as well as the fact of already having been made a co-wife) was recorded as the second most common cause of divorce in Kotagede from the years 1964–71. The one reason cited more commonly as the cause of divorce was "neglecting marital obligations" (on the part of either husband or wife).

19. The best-known instance of female seclusion in Java is that of Radèn Ajeng Kartini (1879–1904), the daughter of a Jepara regent whose letters in Dutch were

published under the title *Door Duisternis tot Licht* (Through darkness into light) seven years after her death at the age of twenty-five. Much has been made of the figure of Kartini, who attained the stature of a national hero after Indonesian independence. An English translation of her letters, with a useful introduction, is found in Coté 1992. In general, though, the practice of seclusion for women was uncommon among Javanese, except among the highest echelons of the *priyayi* and in some devout Muslim enclaves on the north coast.

20. As Shiraishi comments, "in central parts of the city such as Kauman there emerged no independent class of native bourgeoisie, even though there were numerous batik workshops and many batik entrepreneurs amassed wealth. In Marco Kartodikromo's words, batik entrepreneurs in this area were 'still in the family' with sunan's officials" (1990, 25; quoting Marco 1919, 6). A similar pattern existed in Yogyakarta, where batik families of the Kauman were often in service to the Sultanate as well.

21. Another commodity that was "respectable" for high-status women to trade was jewelry (especially gold and precious stones), which, like batik, had associations with court culture.

22. The rest of this passage from Furnivall is also worth citing: "'Formerly,' remarked the head of the Batik Station at Jokya [Yogyakarta], 'the education of a well-bred girl was not regarded as complete unless she could do batik. Now, the Foxtrot and Charleston have taken its place.' Presumably the common people, as at Solo at the present day, went about in rags dyed with indigo and looking as if they had stolen their garments from a dead Chinese cooly" (1936, 373).

23. Batik workers and servants in such households addressed their employers deferentially as "Dèn" (from Radèn) or "Ndara" (from *bendara*, master or mistress) instead of "Mbok Mas," the term of address commonly used in Laweyan for female employers without aristocratic rank.

24. Peter Carey and Vincent Houben, for example, remark that in the early nineteenth century, members of the sultan of Yogyakarta's elite corps of women soldiers (*prajurit èstri*; see Kumar 1980a,b on the late-eighteenth-century diary of a woman soldier in Solo) were involved in "frenetic trade in gold and precious stones between Yogya[karta], Kutagede, Surakarta and the north coast" (1987, 23).

25. I found a deep and almost primordial fear of tax collectors in the *sudagar* community, "passed down from generation to generation," as one outsider put it. One elderly, retired entrepreneur, after describing to me how extensive her business had been in the 1930s, made me promise that I "wouldn't tell anyone," apparently out of fear that someone might seek back taxes that she had avoided paying to the colonial government at the time. De Kat Angelino remarks on a strategy used by Laweyan batik entrepreneurs in 1930 to limit the amount of taxes they had to pay: when an inspection to assess taxes on the business was to be held, the *juragan* would send a portion of the workers home under the assumption that the tax inspectors would estimate the income of the business on the basis of how many workers were found in the workplace that day (1930–31, 2:131).

26. The story about Tjokrosoemarto wanting to cover his floor with coins is also mentioned in a magazine article titled "Laweyan, the Story of Your Past," (*Laweyan, Riwayatmu Dulu*), which appeared in the trendy men's magazine *Matra*, July 1992, p. 66.

27. Nancy Florida observes that the walls surrounding the Kraton compound produced "the image of an inviolable difference beween court and countryside" (1995, 307). She argues, however, that the impenetrability of Kraton walls was something of a myth. Again, the issue of gender is a central one: it was women, she notes, who were able to pass most freely through the supposedly closed palace walls. Her argument parallels my own, which is that the sharp "differences" that appeared to exist between social categories in Javanese society tended to break down on close scrutiny, particularly where women were concerned.

28. Ruth McVey suggests that members of such groups, already "losers under the colonial order, were if anything more marginalized by independence, when their interests were neglected for those of the political-bureaucratic elite" and others better served by the new regime (1992, 22).

CHAPTER THREE
THE SPECTER OF PAST MODERNITIES

1. *Dandanggula* is a classical Javanese verse form said to have been sung frequently by batik workers in the past.

2. "Laweyan, Riwayatmu Dulu," *Matra*, July 1992, p. 66. Another "nostalgia" piece on Laweyan that was published at about the same time is Nanang Junaedi, "Sisa-sisa Kejayaan Laweyan" (The remains of Laweyan's glory), *Editor*, August 22, 1992, p. 89.

3. One finds it, for example, in the well-known letters of Kartini (1879–1904), the young, Dutch-educated Javanese noblewoman who was designated posthumously as one of the first Indonesian nationalists and feminists (see Tsuchiya 1990; Coté 1992). Kartini writes (in Dutch) of her desire for her and her people to become part of the modern era. In a collection of her letters that was published after her death, the first begins: "I have so longed to make the acquaintance of a 'modern girl'" (*Ik heb zóó verlangd kennis te maken met een "modern meisje"*; cited in Tsuchiya 1990, 76). As Tsuchiya remarks, "The Dutch word *modern* demarcates the new age of the twentieth century from the colonial society of the nineteenth" (76).

4. According to Robison, most estimates put ethnic Chinese ownership of private corporate capital in Indonesia at about 70 percent of the total; the large corporate sector in particular is dominated by Chinese capital (1986, chap. 9; 1992, 68). For discussions of the roles of ethnic Chinese in the New Order Indonesian economy, including their relationship with political elites, see Mackie 1991, 1992; Robison 1986, 1992. For broader, comparative discussions of the position of ethnic Chinese in the economies of contemporary Southeast Asia, see Mackie 1992; McVey 1992.

5. Economic Research Bureau 1958, 377; Elliott 1984, 178. The few firms that continued to operate during the occupation produced only very low quality batik for government orders; on the north coast, especially in the Pekalongan area, an expensive style of *batik tulis*, known as batik Hokokai, was also produced for the few people who could afford it.

6. Of the 1,191 firms in Solo, all but 192 were owned by indigenous (almost all Javanese) entrepreneurs. Of the remainder, most were apparently Arab owned, al-

though there were still some Chinese involved in the industry. See Economic Research Bureau 1958, 352, 372, 388.

7. In a survey of batik manufacturers conducted in Yogyakarta in 1956, it was found that about 90 percent of the respondents in the sample were the direct descendants of batik entrepreneurs, and that at least 75 percent of the respondents' parents also came from batik-producing families (Economic Research Bureau 1958, 387).

8. On the Indonesian batik cooperatives and GKBI, see Economic Research Bureau 1958; *Dua-puluh Tahun G.K.B.I.* 1969; Robison 1986.

9. There was a vigorous black-market trade in white cloth. One reason for the demand was that the allocations made available to individual firms that were still genuinely engaged in batik production were often insufficient to meet their needs. There was also a demand for cloth from Chinese batik entrepreneurs, who were not provided with the subsidies that indigenous producers were given. Many Chinese traders were also involved in speculative wholesale buying and selling of black-market cloth. It appears that Arabs, unlike Chinese, were also eligible for allocations of cloth even though they were not included in the category of "indigenous Indonesians" (*pribumi, bumiputera*, I.), because they were considered to be part of the "weak economic group."

10. For further discussion of this period, see Economic Research Bureau 1958, 371. That article refers to the years 1954–55 as the "golden age" for batik producers, when they were making substantial profits simply from reselling their cloth allocations, and characterizes the years 1956–57 as a recession in the batik industry. One man in Laweyan, however, recalled the period between 1958 and 1964 as having been the strongest for the batik industry, because of the cooperatives.

11. In order to qualify for significant allotments of raw materials from the cooperative, the *juragan* had to produce (or pretend to produce) *batik cap*, because the allocations of cloth to producers of *batik tulis* were quite small, based on the assumption that the volume of production was much lower. A large number of people who were not engaged in batik production at all managed to get themselves certified as batik entrepreneurs during this period in order to obtain allocations of cloth and other materials. This was only one form of the deception that went on in connection with the cloth allocations. The cooperatives themselves were rife with corruption; apparently many individuals paid bribes to the cooperatives' managers in order to secure larger allocations of cloth than was their due. Athough allocation of materials was supposed to be strictly on the basis of how large one's firm was, those who received the biggest quotas were usually those who paid the biggest bribes. The extent to which GKBI itself and some of its member cooperatives were mismanaged came to light when they eventually declared bankruptcy some years later; GKBI's debt was staggering.

12. GKBI nearly crumbled from within as a result of political tensions at this time, especially during the so-called Nasakom period in Indonesian politics, when nationalists, Muslims, and communists were engaged in furious power struggles. In Laweyan, political factionalism caused an uproar in the local batik cooperative, PPBS, in 1965 (see *Dua-Puluh Tahun G.K.B.I.* 1969, 89).

13. It was not easy to get people in Laweyan to talk about this period in local history. I attributed their reticence to the psychological and social scars left by the trauma of this dark period, as well as to the continued fear of government reprisals for any "political" activity or even its open discussion in the New Order. I was unwilling to force people to talk about issues that made them so obviously uncomfortable. However, a few people were willing to discuss briefly the events that had taken place in Laweyan at that time. The PKI was quite strong among the poorer people in Laweyan and in the bordering villages, Banaran and Pajang, which were the source of many laborers for Laweyan batik firms. Some middle-class people also joined the movement, though the majority of well-to-do Laweyan entrepreneurs belonged to the Nationalist Party (PNI) or to Masyumi, a prominent Muslim party. Relatives, friends, and neighbors were at sharp odds with each other over their political differences.

Both men and women were involved in these political activities; at the time, the only women's organization in the community was Gerwani (Indonesian Women's Movement), which was affiliated with the PKI. One woman I knew recalled an unmarried woman in her thirties, the daughter of a Laweyan batik entrepreneur and communist sympathizer, who had been a local leader of Gerwani. She had been sent to the Soviet Union and to East Germany for training, which impressed people in a community where few unmarried women had even been outside of Solo, let alone outside the country, on their own. In the upheaval of 1965–66, however, she disappeared, no doubt a victim of the mass slaughters. A number of other Laweyan people were also killed or imprisoned at that time.

14. Even for good *batik tulis*, the market was limited; furthermore, because the highest-quality batik was largely distributed through Jakarta elites and fancy boutiques (most of which were in Jakarta as well), marketing expensive batik required personal contacts and knowledge that many merchants lacked. The decline in the market for *batik cap* was gradual but steady. During the period in which I lived in Laweyan (February 1986–August 1988), I observed a noticeable decrease in the demand for *batik cap* and the cheaper *batik tulis*, as more and more people turned to printed imitations as well as to Western-style clothing.

15. One turning point in the 1980s may have been when Ibu Tien Suharto, the president's wife, began to appear in public wearing Western dresses after many years of wearing only Javanese dress; this made Western clothing into a more "respectable" option than it had seemed in the past for middle-aged and older Javanese women. The rise of Islamic reformism and of Islamic activity in general also brought about a change in women's dressing habits: various forms of modern Islamic clothing had by the mid-1980s become decidedly fashionable (although still worn by a minority of the population), clearly influenced by similar trends in Malaysia and other Muslim countries.

16. A good deal of the production of imitation batik also shifted from the old centers of the batik industry—Solo, Yogyakarta, Pekalongan, and elsewhere—to Jakarta.

17. However, amicable long-term, or *langganan*, business relationships—between suppliers of raw materials and manufacturers, or between manufacturers and wholesalers, for instance—were very common. For a description of *langganan* (reg-

ular customer) relationships in a Javanese marketplace, see Alexander 1987, chap. 5.

18. The survey, conducted in December 1987, recorded a total of 2,177 inhabitants, which included 530 heads of household (*kepala keluarga*). The vast majority of Laweyan's residents are ethnic Javanese; however, according to the 1987 survey there were also 62 ethnic Chinese living in the neighborhood. Of the residents, 2,008 were registered as Muslims, while the remainder were registered as Catholics (68), Protestants (83), Buddhists (5), and Hindus (5) (the other 8 were unaccounted for in the survey). These statistics are on record at the Laweyan Ward (*kelurahan*) Office.

19. When I use the word "entrepreneur" here and elsewhere, I mean simply "one who owns and manages a business enterprise," particularly an enterprise that involves the production of goods rather than just trade. The term *juragan*, which I translate in various places as "employer," "boss," "entrepreneur," "producer," or "manufacturer," does not have the added connotation of "an enterprising and innovative person" that the word entrepreneur often carries in English—it simply designates the owner of a business (one that employs other people).

Batik manufacturers are called both *juragan* and *sudagar*, since manufacture and trade are seen as integrally related. The word *sudagar*, or *saudagar* in Indonesian, usually means a medium- to large-scale merchant. When I refer to the merchant or *sudagar* class, this includes people who participate in manufacturing as well as trade. Throughout this book I use the terms "merchant," "producer," and "entrepreneur" more or less interchangeably.

20. The less-wealthy people in the community often referred to the elites as *wong gedhongan*, which translates loosely as "people who live in big houses."

21. For a good, general discussion of *pasugihan*, see Keeler 1987, 113–14. In fact, a *pasugihan* can be any sort of magical means for gaining wealth; entering into a deal with a demonic being is just one example. Poerwadarminta defines *pasugihan* as "a means (talisman, etc.) for making one rich" (*sarana [djimat lsp] sing ndjalari bisa soegih*) (Poerwadarminta 1939, 570). The practice of seeking such a magical means for gaining wealth is called *golèk pasugihan*, "to seek a *pasugihan*."

22. For more on *thuyul* and other supernatural beings, see C. Geertz 1960, esp. 16–29. Geertz also notes that most people he encountered believed that one must enter into "a kind of devil's pact" in order to secure the *thuyul's* assistance (21).

23. In her study of young female factory workers in Java, Diane Wolf (1992) also makes the case that recent capitalist relations of production in Java are not necessarily experienced by workers as significantly more exploitative than other forms of production. She writes, "For centuries the Javanese peasantry has been exploited by the Javanese aristocracy, the Dutch, and the Japanese; contemporary industrial capitalism is just one more link in a long chain of extractive relations. Indeed, the low expectations of female workers accustomed to inadequate returns to their labor in the village have made for a relatively quiet recent history of industrial disputes." Changes in labor regimes from agricultural production to factory production, she observes, "were somewhat less dramatic than such images of precapitalist work [in the literature on Third World industrialization] suggest" (134).

24. On the organization and conditions of labor in the batik industry in the late 1920s, see Kat Angelino (1930–31). For more recent studies on labor organization in the batik industries of Central Java, especially among women, see Wieringa 1979 and Joseph n.d.

25. These steps include outlining the basic design in wax (*ngèngrèng*, which takes considerable skill and is usually done by women with the most experience), filling it in with fine patterns (*ngisèni*), retracing the design on the back side of the cloth (*nerusi*), and covering over parts of the cloth that have already been dyed (*mbironi*) with wax in order to protect them from dye baths of different colors—not to mention the laborious process of dyeing the cloth itself and removing the wax, the latter steps of which are often carried out by men.

26. *Mas*, which means "older brother," is a term of address commonly used for young men or males who are not significantly senior to the speaker.

27. I found this generalization about wages to be true. For instance, batik workers' wages in the neighborhood of Pajang, which bordered on Laweyan, were said to be lower than those in Laweyan because Laweyan was considered "city" and Pajang "village," despite their close proximity.

28. Joel Kahn, for instance, criticizes the way that "the grand narrative of capitalist development argues teleologically for capitalist development from the presence of the commodity in seed form. Once present, the realm of the commodity expands inexorably until full capitalist development has been 'achieved'" (1993, 26).

29. Although this definition of capitalism may appear somewhat black-and-white from the vantage point of the late twentieth century, the emphasis on the profit motive does not significantly differ in contemporary perspectives. For example, in her recent edited volume *Southeast Asian Capitalists*, Ruth McVey defines capitalism as "a system in which the means of production, in private hands, are employed to create a profit, some of which is reinvested to increase profit-generating capacity" (1992, 8).

30. Cf. Castles 1967 on the Javanese entrepreneurial community of West Kudus, which was involved in the clove cigarette (*krètèk*) industry: "Capital accumulated in the *[krètèk]* industry appears to be spent on land, houses, automobiles, and other such . . . items or dissipated in periods of unprofitable production" (30).

31. See Osborne 1995, xii. Kahn 1993 discusses this notion with specific regard to Indonesia; in his study of Minangkabau (in West Sumatra), Kahn argues against the assumption that "tradition" and "modernity" lie at two ends of an evolutionary continuum, and that apparently traditional social forms that exist alongside modern ones are merely the residues of a premodern past. In the case of Minangkabau, he suggests, certain socioeconomic patterns that are usually thought of as premodern should instead be seen as the products of modern colonial state formation and ideology in the late nineteenth and early twentieth centuries. He makes the case that "traditional" Minangkabau culture is largely a modern creation.

32. For a detailed discussion of the *slametan*, see C. Geertz 1960.

33. Anderson observes that "there is no good reason to believe that there was any dramatic change in the class structure between, say, 1955 and 1975. It is generally agreed that in Java the dominant class has all along been the so-called *priyayi*,

deriving genealogically from the court, provincial, and village elites of precolonial times and overwhelmingly identified in this century with white-collar occupations" (1990e, 116).

CHAPTER FOUR
GENDER AND THE DOMESTICATION OF DESIRE

1. The gendered divisions of trade that hold for ethnic Javanese in Solo do not apply to ethnic Chinese and Arabs. There are also regional differences in this respect among the Javanese. On the north coast of Java, for instance, where Islam has had a more pervasive influence on people's lifestyles and where long-distance trade has been carried on for many centuries, more Javanese men participate in trade than they do in the regions of Solo and Yogyakarta.

2. Collecting and caring for birds of various types is a favorite hobby of members of the traditional *priyayi* aristocracy, especially *priyayi* men. Many non-*priyayi* males also devote their leisure time, and often considerable sums of money, to caring for birds.

3. This novel, which is written in Indonesian, originally appeared as a serial in the Jakarta daily newspaper *Kompas*.

4. See, e.g., H. Geertz 1961, 123; Jay 1969, 61, 92; Stoler 1977; Koentjaraningrat 1985, 139–40; Siegel 1986, 198–201; Keeler 1987, 1990; Papanek and Schwede 1988; Hatley 1990.

5. For more on the inheritance and ownership of property, as well as the division of a married couple's property upon death or divorce, see H. Geertz 1961, chap. 2.

6. See, e.g., Jay 1969; Hatley 1990; Keeler 1987, 1990.

7. See Anderson 1990c; Keeler 1987, 1990; Djajadiningrat-Nieuwenhuis 1987; Hatley 1990; S. Errington 1990.

8. For a specific analysis of gender differences with regard to speech styles in Java, see Smith-Hefner 1988, 535–54.

9. The household in Java often coincides with the nuclear family, although frequently there is an added member or two—a grandparent, perhaps, or a niece or nephew. The nuclear family is the basic unit of Javanese kinship.

10. It should be mentioned that the term "capitalist" means more than just "moneymaker" here. Given the period in which the novel is set, a time when the Indonesian Communist Party (PKI) was competing for power with other political factions, the term "capitalist" carries its full political (and derogatory) implications. I should add that Arswendo Atmowiloto is a social satirist who describes the interchange between the two men in a rather tongue-in-cheek tone.

11. The Javanese ideological declaration that men are better able than women to control themselves dovetails well with certain Islamic gender ideologies. These conceptions of male and female nature, which are found in Indonesia and Malaysia as well as in the Middle East and elsewhere in the Islamic world, portray men as innately more capable than women of controlling their base passions and instincts, *nafs* (Arabic) or *nafsu* (Indonesian/Malay). Although men as well as women have natural desires that may threaten to overcome them, it is believed that men have

greater rationality and reason, *akal* (Indonesian/Malay), which enables them to suppress those desires and to hold fast to the guidance of the Qur'an (see, e.g., Siegel 1969; Rosen 1984; Abu-Lughod 1986; Mernissi 1987; Ong 1987, 1990; Peletz 1995, 1996). Women are said to be more emotional, sexual, and irrational than men by nature; hence they must be carefully controlled by men so that they do not lead the latter astray from the proper path, thereby wreaking havoc on the social and religious order.

12. *Nafsu* also has finer religious and philosophical associations that are beyond the scope of this study. For a detailed discussion of the significance of *nafs/nepsu* in Javanese philosophy, see Woodward 1989, 190–92.

13. Javanese tend to view men's irrepressible sexual desire with a degree of ambivalence. Anderson (1990c) has suggested that there is a conceptual link between male sexual potency, spiritual potency, and political power in Javanese thought, whereby a political leader's virility—and, more important, fertility—may be taken as an indicator of his true power. At the same time, he also notes that sexual indulgence, like greed or excessive political ambition, is considered a type of *pamrih*, or personal indulgence, that leads to the dispersion of one's power and consequent diminishment of status. Acknowledging the apparent contradiction in these two views of men's sexual prowess, Anderson proposes that one possibility for its resolution may lie in the direct linkage of sexuality and fertility, such that sexuality that does not lead to pregnancy becomes politically valueless, with the number of children that a ruler sires serving as an indication of his true potency.

14. Rarely did I hear any Solonese women defending the practice of polygamy. One woman who did was a young, devoted Muslim who had been much influenced by the Islamic reformist movement. In her opinion, polygamy was a somewhat unfortunate but necessary institution. "It's not recommended by Islam," she explained, "but it's accepted. Islam recognizes that men have strong desires (*nafsu*), so one wife might not be enough to satisfy them. If they weren't permitted more than one wife, they might run to prostitutes. So they're allowed up to four wives. But each wife must be treated fairly."

15. The literal translation of this is, roughly, "It's okay to eat out, but don't bring your banana-leaf container (*pincuk*) home."

16. *Asmara*, which I have translated here as "love," may have been this man's euphemistic term for something more along the lines of "lust."

17. To my knowledge, the seclusion of women has never been widespread in Southeast Asia, where there is a very long history of women's active involvement in trade, agriculture, and other productive activities outside the home (see Reid 1988). Seclusion of women among the Javanese in the past was fairly rare, and was generally confined to the ranks of high nobility (see, e.g., Coté 1992). Seclusion was also occasionally practiced among nonaristocrats in parts of Java that were devoutly Islamic, such as the orthodox merchant community of West Kudus. Vestiges of the practice of female seclusion were still found in Kudus in recent years (G. G. Weix, conversation, 1988).

18. For a description of the *arisan* in Java, see C. Geertz 1962.

19. For similar observations on women traders in Haiti, see Mintz 1971. One still sees an occasional Javanese girl or young woman accompanying her *juragan*

mother on her rounds in the marketplace or helping to mind her mother's market stall.

20. "Memburu Kepuasan: Seks di Kalangan Wanita Jawa," *Wawasan*, April 3, 1988, p. 1.

21. Hildred Geertz found during her fieldwork in the 1950s that among Javanese adultery was widespread but carried little moral weight. She observes that "each partner is constantly on the watch to catch the other in a misstep, and both are also looking out for a chance for an illicit affair—although women are less likely either to have such a chance or to take advantage of it after they have children" (1961, 128).

22. For a more extensive discussion of the domestication of money in Java, see Siegel 1986, esp. chap. 7. My own thinking on this subject owes much to Siegel's work.

CHAPTER FIVE
THE VALUE OF THE BEQUEST

1. A few *arisan* were attended by mixed couples, but as far as I know there were no *arisan* that were attended strictly by men.

2. The practice of putting money into a savings account in the bank seems to be growing among middle- and upper-class Javanese, but my impression in the 1980s was that in Solo, many people preferred to deal with banks as infrequently as possible. A further consideration is that because the price (and therefore resale value) of gold is calculated according to its dollar value on the international market, the instability of the *rupiah* does not affect it.

3. In a more general discussion of exchange, Georg Simmel points to a comparable idea when he writes that "the isolated individual who sacrifices something in order to produce certain products, acts in exactly the same way as the subject who exchanges, the only difference being that his partner is not another subject but the natural order and regularity of things which, just like another human being, does not satisfy our desires without a sacrifice" ([1907] 1990, 83).

4. The preference for fasting on Mondays and Thursdays derives from Islam, though it is common among both devout and nondevout Javanese Muslims. In Solo it was also practiced by people in the Arab community. A young woman of Arab descent explained to me that "Rasulullah (the Prophet Muhammad) used to fast every Monday and Thursday, so we do it too, to try to model ourselves after Rasulullah. It is *puasa sunnah* (a meritorious but optional fast). We do it to learn how to restrain our desires (*menahan nafsu*, I.)."

5. The word *laku* has several meanings. Besides meaning "ascetic practice," it can also mean "walk" or "step" as well as "behavior," "conduct," "to act," "to take steps," or "to conduct oneself." (In trade, *laku* also means that an object is selling well.) In referring to ascetic practice, people often make the noun *laku* into the verb form *nglakoni*, "to engage in ascetic practice."

6. It is notable that Bu Sapardi, one of the traditionalists of Laweyan who had been little influenced by the wave of Islamic reformism sweeping Indonesia, did not distinguish between *sholat hajat*, a practice associated with Islamic devotion, and other types of *laku* that are more strictly "Javanese"—for instance, staying up all

night, eating only rice and other white foods, or immersing oneself in a pool of water at night.

7. This was especially true for market traders, who used the *arisan* as an important means of accumulating capital. Some traders I knew in Pasar Klewer belonged to as many as eight *arisan*, several of which were organized in the marketplace among a large group of traders. (The *arisan* inside the marketplace did not have a social dimension to them; they were strictly financial, and did not require that the traders gather together in one place.) One trader I knew estimated that she put about 700,000 *rupiah* a month, a substantial sum by local standards, into various *arisan*.

8. For a discussion of Javanese *trah*, groups based on shared genealogical descent, see Sjafri 1982.

9. As Marx observes, "Since every commodity disappears when it becomes money it is impossible to tell from the money itself how it got into the hands of its possessor, or what article has been changed into it. . . . If it represents, on the one hand, a commodity which has been sold, it also represents, on the other hand, a commodity which can be bought" ([1867] 1977, 205).

10. Cf. Taussig (1980), who writes that for Colombian sugarcane workers, money obtained through contracts with the devil is thought to be inherently barren, to the effect that if it is invested in land or livestock the land will become sterile and the animals will die.

11. Based on my own observations at weddings and other ceremonies, many people still consider it bad form to finish everything that is served them in a ritual context. Some people actually eat a full meal at home before attending a ritual celebration, so that they will not be hungry (and, as a result, eat with too much desire) when the food is served.

12. *Laku kungkum* is a form of *laku* that involves immersing oneself at least chest-deep in water at night for a sustained period of time. It is thought to be very demanding, both physically and spiritually, especially when it is done at a powerful spot in a river or stream. It seems to be practiced more commonly by men than by women, though at least one woman I knew had tried it.

13. As a result of the sharp decline of the batik industry in the early to mid-1980s, a number of Laweyan batik entrepreneurs were forced to enter other businesses in an attempt to supplement their incomes from batik production and trade, or to replace their batik businesses altogether. Some turned to raising poultry on a limited scale, selling feed for poultry, or opening small restaurants. These businesses may have been appealing because they were perceived as requiring relatively little capital or technical expertise, as opposed to other types of manufacturing, for instance. Few of these businesses had a long life span, however.

14. Clifford Geertz comments that "Javanese claim they reckon kinship ascent eight generations back and have terms for each level (father, grandfather, great-grandfather . . .); but I never knew anyone who knew his ancestors by name back farther than his grandfather" (1960, 76).

15. For detailed discussions of the role of cloth in social life, see Schneider and Weiner 1989; Weiner 1989, 1992.

16. Indeed, many objects of cultural value in Java have non-Javanese origins. Take, for example, the ornate royal carriages that are kept on display at the Kraton

museum in Solo. Manufactured in Europe during the colonial period, they are nonetheless given honorary Javanese titles and designated as *pusaka*, heirlooms imbued with an almost sacred power. Like other Kraton *pusaka*, they are propitiated with offerings every Thursday night.

17. See also Siegel 1986, 185–86.

18. Because their company is well known in Indonesia as the only very large, indigenously owned batik firm, Ibu Danar, Bapak Santosa, and their firm, Batik Danar Hadi, would be immediately recognizable from the description here whether or not a pseudonym is used; I therefore have used their real names.

19. Like their two large Chinese competitors, Batik Keris and Batik Semar, the owners of Batik Danar Hadi made the shrewd decision to leave most of the labor-intensive, time-consuming production of batik to smaller firms in Solo and other cities. Many smaller batik producers sold their products wholesale to Danar Hadi, often through a system of subcontracting. Danar Hadi then resold the goods at much higher prices through their large chain of retail stores.

20. *Kompas*, October 30, 1986, p. 5.

21. Significantly, there is no single indigenous term, either in Indonesian or Javanese, that conveys the same sense as the word *tradisi*, "tradition." W. J. S. Poerwadarminta's (1985) Indonesian dictionary defines *tradisi* (s.v.) as "everything (such as customs, beliefs, habits, teachings, and so on) that has been [passed down] generation after generation from the ancestors" (*segala sesuatu [seperti adat, kepercayaan, kebiasaan, ajaran dsb.] yang turun-temurun dari nenek moyang*). As I have shown, however, the notion of "ancestral origins" is very much subject to interpretation as well as to manipulation. For a study of the creation of the concept of *tradisi* in colonial and postcolonial Java, see Pemberton 1994.

22. Cf. Florida 1995, introduction, on common Javanese attitudes toward what has been monumentalized as "Traditional Javanese Literature," which is widely assumed to be culturally valuable but basically impenetrable for the general population.

23. President Sukarno personally promoted a new style of batik in the 1950s, called "Batik Indonesia" (see Kitley 1987), which blended batik motifs from different parts of Java with untraditional colors (including shocking pink, lime green, and bright orange) in a deliberate attempt to divorce it from its regional specificity. The unorthodox style of this batik suggests that the creation of a bold, modern, yet still recognizably "indigenous" form of clothing was more important here than the invocation of tradition, in keeping with the broad tenor of this early postindependence period. Notably, I was told by batik entrepreneurs that there was a marked tendency after the fall of the Sukarno regime and its violent aftermath for batik manufacturers and consumers to return to traditional styles of batik. This was just one aspect of the recuperation of high Javanese "tradition," as a movement toward political control and stabilization, that occurred during the New Order period (see Anderson 1990a; Pemberton 1994).

24. Cf. Bayly 1986, who notes that in India, the full commoditization of cloth did not preclude its being considered an object that could retain and transmit the qualities of people who produced or transacted it—an anthropomorphic trait that is also a primary attribute of the gift as Mauss describes it.

25. See also Carsten 1989, who similarly explores Malay women's roles in converting money into objects of cultural value.

26. See also Weiner 1976 for her earlier treatment of this issue.

CHAPTER SIX
THE MASK OF APPEARANCES

1. One might even go so far as to argue that boredom is an integral part of many Javanese rituals. A Javanese man in Solo once told an American friend of mine that if he did not reach the point of boredom at a wedding, he didn't feel satisfied (Marc Perlman, conversation, March 1986)! Pemberton also remarks upon the rather numbing predictability of most Javanese weddings, which seem to elicit the genuine interest of guests only when something goes amiss (1987, 18–20; for a more detailed discussion of weddings in New Order Indonesia and their antecedents, see Pemberton 1994).

2. See Roland Barthes's comment about the power of photography to transform the subject: "Now, once I feel myself observed by the lens, everything changes: I constitute myself in the process of 'posing,' I instantaneously make another body for myself, I transform myself in advance into an image" (1981, 10).

3. On the power of photography to authenticate more than to represent, and to replace memory rather than to enhance it, see Barthes 1981, esp. 89, 91.

4. The name "Atmosusilo" is a pseudonym. We should note that both Atmosusilo and his wife were active in their family business, but accounts that focused on well-known entrepreneurs of the past always seemed to ignore the important roles of women.

5. The name "Haji Abdul Ridha" is a pseudonym.

6. The term *rezeki* (sometimes written *rejeki*) can also mean livelihood or daily food/basic necessities of life.

7. An Arab man I knew was critical of Javanese understandings of *rezeki*. Many Javanese make the *haj*, he told me, in the belief that it will bring them *rezeki*, which is inappropriate according to the tenets of Islam. "We Arabs believe that the amount of *rezeki* we can receive has been preordained by God—it's in the hands of Allah. But *rezeki* doesn't just come to you; you have to work hard for it. If you don't work for it, you won't get it."

8. The "most important point," he wrote, "lay in the possession of brilliant [diamond] earrings. These sparkling jewels formed, so to speak, a part of the firm's capital, by which the creditworthiness of the entrepreneur was judged" (Soerachman 1927, 39).

9. Arswendo Atmowiloto (1986) writes in his novel of the lengths to which traders in Pasar Klewer will go to uphold their honor in the eyes of others—a passage that I found rather uncanny in its similarity to what I had learned firsthand from Bu Hartati and others in Solo. He observes, for example,

> It was usual for these traders to wear only large ornaments made of gold with all sorts of diamonds and gems. This was a kind of status symbol and showed that their business was prospering. These were stories of success. A diamond-stud-

ded bracelet was a measure of success. It didn't matter if it belonged to someone else. It didn't matter if they had to sell off all their wares, or even sell their stall, in order to wear it. It didn't matter if the next month they sold off the bracelet at a cheaper price, and then added their business capital just to buy another style, which would make it appear as if they owned several sets of jewelry. (1986, 307)

CHAPTER SEVEN
DISCIPLINING THE DOMESTIC SPHERE, DEVELOPING THE
MODERN FAMILY

1. Initially these religions included Islam, Christianity, Buddhism, and Hinduism—the last of which had to be standardized according to state guidelines in order to meet the requirement that it be monotheistic. Later, certain indigenous religions of various Indonesian ethnic groups were also certified as officially recognized religions (see Guinness 1994, esp. 295–98).

2. On the concept of *syirik* (or *shirk*) in Javanese Islam, see Woodward 1989, chap. 7.

3. For an analysis of the significance of women's Islamic clothing in contemporary Java, see Brenner 1996.

4. In 1985 the government passed legislation requiring that all sociopolitical and religious organizations formally recognize Pancasila as their sole ideological basis (*azas tunggal*, I.) or risk losing their legal permission to exist. This law guaranteed that no political or religious organization could legally challenge the primacy of the state (Zifirdaus 1990). Most groups ultimately accepted the new law, even though it led to violent disagreement and protests.

5. For a detailed discussion about the inscribing of New Order structures of authority on contemporary Javanese weddings, see Pemberton 1994.

6. In some firms the position of the wife is subordinate to her husband's, or she does not participate at all in the business—an unusual state of affairs by past standards. Although there are modern, highly capitalized firms in which women do play an active part (the Danar Hadi firm is one example), it appears that the capitalist sector, unlike the marketplace, is the domain of men more than the domain of women.

7. These are not as uncommon as one might imagine—I saw several of them in people's homes. Whenever a group or individual visited the Suhartos on "official" business, there was always a photographer on hand to capture the moment of shaking hands with the president or his wife.

8. See Saraswati 1996; Suryakusuma 1996. All female government employees and the wives of all male government employees are expected to join Dharma Wanita; failing to do so can hinder a civil servant's career.

9. See, e.g., Wolf 1992; Blackwood 1995; Saraswati 1996; Suryakusuma 1996.

10. This definition of State Ibuism follows the official "Five Responsibilities of Women" (*Panca Dharma Wanita*) endorsed by the state and adopted by all state-affiliated women's organizations. See also Djajadiningrat-Nieuwenhuis 1987 on the notion of "Ibuism."

11. The category of mother is also important, she notes, but it is considered subordinate to that of wife.

12. Dwi Arjanto, "Melongok Pola Wanita Karier," *Jawa Pos* (Java Post), August 9, 1992, p. 5. *Jawa Pos* is published in Surabaya (East Java).

13. Dadang Hawari, "Karakter dan Perkawinan" (Character and marriage), *Buana Minggu*, April 28, 1985, p. 11; my emphasis.

14. *Amanah*, May 3–16, 1991, p. 3.

15. As Joan Scott remarks, "The connection between authoritarian regimes and the control of women has been noted but not thoroughly studied" (1988, 47).

16. "Jangan Melupakan Kodrat sebagai Ibu meski Berkarier," *Suara Merdeka*, August 13, 1992, p. 2.

17. Dadang, "Karakter dan Perkawinan," p. 11.

GLOSSARY

abdi dalem — servant of the palace

akal — reason, rationality, intellect

alus — refined, smooth, cultured

arisan — rotating savings (or credit) association; the social gathering of such a group

bapak — father, adult male; term of address for adult male (usu. capitalized)

batik — method of dyeing cloth using wax-resist process; cloth that has been decorated with this method

batik cap — batik decorated with a copper stamp

batik tulis — batik decorated with a small handheld tool

bécak — bicycle-powered pedicab

Bu — Mrs.; term of address for an adult female (from *ibu*)

buruh — worker, employee

canting — small handheld, spouted tool used for applying molten wax to cloth

cap — copper stamp used for applying molten wax to cloth

dagang — trade, commerce

désa — village, rural area

Dharma Wanita — government-sponsored organization for the wives of civil servants

haji — a man who has made the pilgrimage (*haj*) to Mecca

hajjah — a woman who has made the pilgrimage to Mecca

halal bihalal — to ask and grant forgiveness at the end of Ramadan (the Muslim fasting month); social gathering for this purpose

ibu — mother, adult female; term of address for adult female (usu. capitalized)

ibu rumah tangga — housewife

jajan — a snack; to eat out; slang for visiting prostitutes or having illicit sex

juragan — owner of an enterprise

kasar — coarse, crude, unrefined

kebaya — tailored, long-sleeved blouse usually worn with a sarong

keris — ritual dagger with wavy blade

kiai — respected Islamic teacher; title used for a venerated man or object

kodrat — God-given nature or destiny

korupsi — corruption

kota — (see *kutha*)

krama — high level of Javanese language

kraton — royal palace

kutha — city

laku — ascetic practice (also: behavior; walk; step; to sell well)

langganan — regular customer

madya — middle level of Javanese language

Mas — term of address for young man or a man who is not significantly older than the speaker; older brother (not capitalized)

Mbok Mas — respectful term of address for a female *juragan* (owner of a firm)

mori — unbleached cloth used for making batik

nafsu — desire, passion, natural instincts

nékad — strongly determined, willful

ngoko — low level of Javanese language

Pak — Mr.; term of address for an adult male

pasar — market

pasugihan — magical means of gaining wealth, sometimes in the form of a demonic creature

pembangunan — development (economic, social, etc.)

pendhapa — main sitting area of a Javanese-style house (often an open veranda in front of the house)

pendopo — (see *pendhapa*)

penghulu — Muslim leader or official

pribumi — person of native Indonesian ancestry

prihatin — concerned, anxious, prayerful; to make a sacrifice or strong effort in order to bring about a desired outcome

priyayi — member of elite aristocratic/bureaucratic class

rezeki — good fortune, windfall; daily food, necessities of life

rupiah — unit of Indonesian currency

Ruwah — eighth month of the year according to the Javanese Islamic calendar

santri — student at a traditional Islamic school; devout Muslim

saté — small pieces of meat grilled on skewers

saudagar — (see *sudagar*)

sembah — an obeisant gesture made by holding the hands before the face, palms together, with the head slightly bowed

slamet — safe, protected

slametan — a communal ritual meal

soga — a reddish-brown or yellow-brown dye used for batik (*soga Jawa* is made of all natural ingredients)

sudagar — merchant (usually large-scale)

sunan — king of Solo (Surakarta) (short for *susuhunan*)

tradisi — tradition

wanita karier — career woman

warisan — legacy, inheritance

wong — person, people

BIBLIOGRAPHY

Abu-Lughod, Lila. 1986. *Veiled Sentiments: Honor and Poetry in a Bedouin Society.* Berkeley: University of California Press.

Adam, Tassilo. 1934. "The Art of Batik in Java." *The Bulletin of the Needle and Bobbin Club* 18(1–2): 3–74.

Alexander, Jennifer. 1987. *Trade, Traders, and Trading in Rural Java.* Asian Studies Association of Australia Southeast Asia Publication Series no. 15. Singapore: Oxford University Press.

Alexander, Jennifer, and Paul Alexander. 1991. "Protecting Peasants from Capitalism: The Subordination of Javanese Traders by the Colonial State." *Comparative Studies in Society and History* 33: 370–94.

Anderson, Benedict R. 1972. *Java in a Time of Revolution: Occupation and Resistance, 1944–1946.* Ithaca, N.Y.: Cornell University Press.

———. 1990a. "Cartoons and Monuments: The Evolution of Political Communication under the New Order." In Anderson 1990d: 152–93.

———. 1990b. "Further Adventures of Charisma." In Anderson 1990d: 78–93.

———. 1990c. "The Idea of Power in Javanese Culture." In Anderson 1990d: 17–77.

———. 1990d. *Language and Power: Exploring Political Cultures in Indonesia.* Ithaca, N.Y.: Cornell University Press.

———. 1990e. "Old State, New Society: Indonesia's New Order in Comparative Historical Perspective." In Anderson 1990d: 94–120.

———. 1991. *Imagined Communities: Reflections on the Origin and Spread of Nationalism.* Rev. ed. London: Verso.

Appadurai, Arjun. 1986. "Introduction: Commodities and the Politics of Value." In *The Social Life of Things: Commodities in Cultural Perspective,* edited by Arjun Appadurai, 3–63. Cambridge: Cambridge University Press.

Armstrong, Nancy. 1987. *Desire and Domestic Fiction: A Political History of the Novel.* New York: Oxford University Press.

Arswendo Atmowiloto. 1986. *Canting.* Jakarta: PT Gramedia Press.

Atkinson, Jane M. 1989. *The Art and Politics of Wana Shamanship.* Berkeley: University of California Press.

Atkinson, Jane M., and Shelly Errington, eds. 1990. *Power and Difference: Gender in Island Southeast Asia.* Stanford: Stanford University Press.

Banner, Hubert S. 1927. *Romantic Java as It Was and Is.* London: Seeley, Service.

Barlow, Tani. 1996. "Theorizing Woman: *Funü, Guojia, Jiating* (Chinese Women, Chinese State, Chinese Family)." In *Feminism and History,* edited by Joan W. Scott, 48–75. Oxford: Oxford University Press.

Barthes, Roland, 1981. *Camera Lucida: Reflections on Photography,* translated by Richard Howard. New York: Hill and Wang.

"Batikken." 1917. In *Encyclopaedie van Nederlandsche-Indië,* 1:199–200. 3rd ed. The Hague: Martinus Nijhoff.

Bayly, C. A. 1986. "The Origins of Swadeshi (Home Industry): Cloth and Indian Society, 1700–1930." In *The Social Life of Things*, edited by Arjun Appadurai, 285–321. Cambridge: Cambridge University Press.

Berman, Marshall. 1988. *All That Is Solid Melts into Air: The Experience of Modernity*. New York: Penguin Books.

Blackwood, Evelyn. 1995. "Senior Women, Model Mothers, and Dutiful Wives: Managing Gender Contradictions in a Minangkabau Village." In *Bewitching Women, Pious Men: Gender and Body Politics in Southeast Asia*, edited by Aihwa Ong and Michael G. Peletz, 124–58. Berkeley: University of California Press.

Boow, Justine. 1988. *Symbol and Status in Javanese Batik*. Asian Studies Centre Monograph Series no. 7. Nedlands: University of Western Australia.

Bourdieu, Pierre. 1977. *Outline of a Theory of Practice*, translated by Richard Nice. Cambridge: Cambridge University Press.

Brenner, Suzanne. 1991. "Competing Hierarchies: Javanese Merchants and the *Priyayi* Elite in Solo, Central Java." *Indonesia* 52: 55–83.

———. 1996. "Reconstructing Self and Society: Javanese Muslim Women and 'the Veil.'" *American Ethnologist* 23: 673–97.

Butler, Judith. 1992. "Contingent Foundations: Feminism and the Question of 'Postmodernism.'" In *Feminists Theorize the Political*, edited by Judith Butler and Joan W. Scott, 3–21. New York: Routledge.

Carey, Peter, and Vincent Houben. 1987. "Spirited Srikandhis and Sly Sumbadras: The Social, Political, and Economic Role of Women at the Central Javanese Courts in the 18th and Early 19th Centuries." In Locher-Scholten and Niehof 1987: 12–42.

Carsten, Janet. 1989. "Cooking Money: Gender and the Symbolic Transformation of Means of Exchange in a Malay Fishing Community." In *Money and the Morality of Exchange*, edited by Jonathan Parry and Maurice Bloch, 117–42. Cambridge: Cambridge University Press.

Castles, Lance. 1967. *Religion, Politics, and Economic Behavior in Java: The Kudus Cigarette Industry*. Cultural Report Series no. 15. New Haven: Southeast Asia Studies, Yale University.

Comaroff, John, and Jean Comaroff. 1992. "Homemade Hegemony." In *Ethnography and the Historical Imagination*, 265–95. Boulder, Colo.: Westview Press.

Coté, Joost, ed. and trans. 1992. *Letters from Kartini: An Indonesian Feminist, 1900–1904*. Clayton, Australia: Monash Asia Institute, Monash University.

Darsiti Soeratman. 1989. *Kehidupan Dunia Kraton Surakarta 1830–1939*. Yogyakarta: Penerbit Tamansiswa Yogyakarta.

de Lauretis, Teresa. 1987. "The Technology of Gender." In *Technologies of Gender: Essays on Theory, Film, and Fiction*, 1–30. Bloomington: Indiana University Press.

Deventer, C. Th. van. 1904. *Overzicht van den Economischen toestand der Inlandsche Bevolking van Java en Madoera*. The Hague: Martinus Nijhoff.

Djajadiningrat-Nieuwenhuis, Madelon. 1987. "Ibuism and Priyayization: Path to Power?" In Locher-Scholten and Niehof 1987: 43–51.

Dua-Puluh Tahun G.K.B.I. 1969. Jakarta: Koperasi Pusat Gabungan Koperasi Batik Indonesia.

Dunham, S. Ann. 1982. "Women's Work in Village Industries on Java." Photocopy.

Echols, John M., and Hassan Shadily. 1989. *An Indonesian-English Dictionary*, revised and edited by John U. Wolff and James T. Collins. 3rd ed. Ithaca, N.Y.: Cornell University Press.

Economic Research Bureau of Gadjah Mada University. 1958. "The Batik Industry in Central Java." *Ekonomi dan Keuangan Indonesia* (Economics and finance in Indonesia) 11: 345–401.

Elliott, Inger McCabe. 1984. *Batik: Fabled Cloth of Java*. New York: Clarkson N. Potter.

Errington, J. Joseph. 1984. "Self and Self-Conduct among the Javanese *Priyayi* Elite." *American Ethnologist* 11: 275–90.

———. 1985. *Language and Social Change in Java: Linguistic Reflexes of Modernization in a Traditional Royal Polity*. Monographs in International Studies, Southeast Asia Series no. 65. Athens: Ohio University Center for International Studies.

———. 1988. *Structure and Style in Javanese: A Semiotic View of Linguistic Etiquette*. Philadelphia: University of Pennsylvania Press.

Errington, Shelly. 1989. *Meaning and Power in a Southeast Asian Realm*. Princeton: Princeton University Press.

———. 1990. "Recasting Sex, Gender, and Power: A Theoretical and Regional Overview." In Atkinson and Errington 1990: 1–58..

The Far East and Australasia 1991. 1990. 22nd ed. London: Europa Publications.

Felski, Rita. 1995. *The Gender of Modernity*. Cambridge, Mass.: Harvard University Press.

Flax, Jane. 1990. "Postmodernism and Gender Relations in Feminist Theory." In *Feminism/Postmodernism*, edited by Linda Nicholson, 39–62. New York: Routledge.

———. 1993. *Disputed Subjects: Essays on Psychoanalysis, Politics, and Philosophy*. New York: Routledge.

Florida, Nancy K. 1995. *Writing the Past, Inscribing the Future: History as Prophecy in Colonial Java*. Durham, N.C.: Duke University Press.

Fock, D. 1904. *Beschouwingen en Voorstellen ter Verbetering van den Economischen toestand der Inlandsche Bevolking van Java en Madoera*. The Hague: Martinus Nijhoff.

Foucault, Michel. 1978. *The History of Sexuality*. Vol. 1, *An Introduction*, translated by Robert Hurley. New York: Random House.

Fraser-Lu, Sylvia, 1986. *Indonesian Batik: Processes, Patterns, and Places*. Singapore: Oxford University Press.

Furnivall, J. S. 1936. "The Weaving and Batik Industries in Java, with Notes on Hat Making and Soap Boiling." *Asiatic Review* 32: 365–76.

———. 1944. *Netherlands India: A Study of Plural Economy*. New York: Macmillan.

Geertz, Clifford. 1960. *The Religion of Java*. Chicago: University of Chicago Press.

———. 1962. "The Rotating Credit Association: A 'Middle Rung' in Development." *Economic Development and Cultural Change* 10: 241–63.

———. 1963. *Peddlers and Princes: Social Development and Economic Change in Two Indonesian Towns*. Chicago: University of Chicago Press.

———. 1973. "Ritual and Social Change: A Javanese Example." In *The Interpretation of Cultures*, 142–69. New York: Basic Books.

Geertz, Hildred. 1961. *The Javanese Family: A Study of Kinship and Socialization.* Glencoe, Ill.: Free Press.

George, Edwin B. 1925. *Cotton-Goods Market in the Netherlands East Indies.* [Washington, D.C.?]: United States Department of Commerce.

Gittinger, Mattiebelle, ed. 1980. *Indonesian Textiles.* Irene Emery Roundtable on Museum Textiles 1979 Proceedings. Washington, D.C.: Textile Museum.

Graaf, H. J. de. 1985. *Awal Kebangkitan Mataram: Masa Pemerintahan Senapati.* Jakarta: Grafiti Pers.

Guinness, Patrick. 1994. "Local Society and Culture." In *Indonesia's New Order: The Dynamics of Socio-Economic Transformation,* edited by Hal Hill, 267–304. St. Leonards, Australia: Allen and Unwin.

Habermas, Jürgen. 1987. *The Philosophical Discourse of Modernity: Twelve Lectures,* translated by Frederick G. Lawrence. Cambridge, Mass.: MIT Press.

Hamzuri. 1985. *Batik Klasik* (Classical batik). 2nd ed. Jakarta: Djambatan.

Harjono. 1967. *Arti Batik Bagi Kita.* Jakarta: Direktorat Pengembangan Ditdjenkra.

Hatley, Barbara. 1990. "Theatrical Imagery and Gender Ideology in Java." In Atkinson and Errington 1990: 177–208.

Hawkins, Everett D. 1961. "The Batik Industry: The Role of the Javanese Entrepreneur." In *Entrepreneurship and Labor Skills in Indonesian Economic Development: A Symposium,* 39–74. Southeast Asia Studies Monograph Series no. 1. New Haven: Southeast Asia Studies, Yale University.

Hefner, Robert W. 1985. *Hindu Javanese: Tengger Tradition and Islam.* Princeton: Princeton University Press.

Heider, Karl G. 1991. *Indonesian Cinema: National Culture on Screen.* Honolulu: University of Hawaii Press.

Hoëvell, W. R. Baron van. 1896. "De Nederlandsche katoenen in Indie." *Tijdschrift voor Nederlandsch Indië,* 4th ser., 25: 478–81.

Horne, Elinor Clark. 1974. *Javanese-English Dictionary.* New Haven: Yale University Press.

Ingleson, John. 1986. *In Search of Justice: Workers and Unions in Colonial Java, 1908–1926.* Singapore: Oxford University Press.

Ivy, Marilyn. 1995. *Discourses of the Vanishing: Modernity, Phantasm, Japan.* Chicago: University of Chicago Press.

Jasper, J. E., and M. Pirngadie. 1916. *De Inlandsche Kunstnijverheid in Nederlandsche Indië.* Vol. 3, *De Batik Kunst.* The Hague: Mouton.

Jay, Robert. 1969. *Javanese Villagers: Social Relations in Rural Modjokuto.* Cambridge, Mass.: MIT Press.

Jayadiningrat I, Raden Mas Riya. [1818] 1981. "Suluk Mas Ngantèn." In *Serat Wulang,* 131–201. Jakarta: Departemen Pendidikan den Kebudayaan.

Joseph, Rebecca. n.d. [1986?]. *Worker, Middlewomen* [sic], *Entrepreneur: Women in the Indonesian Batik Industry.* Bangkok: Population Council.

Kahn, Joel S. 1993. *Constituting the Minangkabau: Peasants, Culture, and Modernity in Colonial Indonesia.* Providence: Berg.

Kartini, Raden Adjeng. 1911. *Door Duisternis tot Licht: Gedachten over en voor het Javaansche volk van Raden Adjeng Kartini* (Through darkness to light: Considerations about and in the interests of the Javanese by Raden Adjeng Kartini), edited by J. H. Abendanon. Semarang: Van Dorp.

Kat Angelino, P. de. 1930–31. *Batikrapport: Rapport betreffende een gehouden enquête naar de arbeidstoestanden in de batikkerijen op Java en Madoera* (Batik report: concerning an inquiry held into the labor conditions in the batik firms of Java and Madura). 3 vols. Publicatie no. 6 van het kantoor van arbeid. Weltevreden: Landsdrukkerij.

Katrak, Ketu H. 1992. "Indian Nationalism, Gandhian 'Satyagraha,' and Representations of Female Sexuality." In *Nationalisms and Sexualities*, edited by Andrew Parker, Mary Russo, Doris Sommer, and Patricia Yaeger, 395–406. New York: Routledge.

Keeler, Ward. 1984. *Javanese: A Cultural Approach*. Athens: Ohio University Center for International Studies.

———. 1987. *Javanese Shadow Plays, Javanese Selves*. Princeton: Princeton University Press.

———. 1990. "Speaking of Gender in Java." In Atkinson and Errington 1990: 127–52.

Kitley, Philip. 1987. "Batik and Popular Culture." *Prisma* (English ed.) 43: 8–24.

———. 1992. "Ornamentation and Originality: Involution in Javanese Batik." *Indonesia* 53: 1–19.

Koentjaraningrat. 1985. *Javanese Culture*. Singapore: Oxford University Press.

Kondo, Dorinne K. 1990. *Crafting Selves: Power, Gender, and Discourses of Identity in a Japanese Workplace*. Chicago: University of Chicago Press.

Koperberg, S. 1922. "De Javaansche Batikindustrie" (The Javanese batik industry). *Djawa* 2(3): 147–56.

Kumar, Ann. 1980a. "Javanese Court Society and Politics in the Late Eighteenth Century: The Record of a Lady Soldier." Part 1, "The Religious, Social, and Economic Life of the Court." *Indonesia* 29: 1–46.

———. 1980b. "Javanese Court Society and Politics in the Late Eighteenth Century: The Record of a Lady Soldier." Part 2, "Political Developments: The Courts and the Company, 1784–1791." *Indonesia* 30: 67–112.

Larson, George D. 1987. *Prelude to Revolution: Palaces and Politics in Surakarta, 1912–1942*. Dordrecht: Foris Publications.

Leur, J. C. van. 1955. *Indonesian Trade and Society: Essays in Asian Social and Economic History*. The Hague: W. van Hoeve.

Lévi-Strauss, Claude. 1969. *The Elementary Structures of Kinship*, translated by James Harle Bell, John Richard von Sturmer, and Rodney Needham. Rev. ed. Boston: Beacon Press.

Locher-Scholten, Elsbeth. 1987. "Female Labour in Twentieth Century Java; European Notions—Indonesian Practice." In Locher-Scholten and Niehof 1987: 77–103.

Locher-Scholten, Elsbeth, and Anke Niehof, eds. 1987. *Indonesian Women in Focus: Past and Present Notions*. Dordrecht: Foris Publications.

MacIntyre, Andrew. 1991. *Business and Politics in Indonesia*. Asian Studies Association of Australia Southeast Asia Publication Series no. 21. North Sydney, Australia: Allen and Unwin.

Mackie, Jamie. 1991. "Towkays and Tycoons: The Chinese in Indonesian Economic Life in the 1920s and 1980s." *Indonesia* (special issue on the Role of the Indonesian Chinese in Shaping Modern Indonesian Life): 83–96.

———. 1992. "Changing Patterns of Chinese Big Business in Southeast Asia." In *Southeast Asian Capitalists*, edited by Ruth McVey, 161–90. Ithaca, N.Y.: Cornell University Southeast Asia Program.

Manderson, Lenore. 1983. Introduction to *Women's Work and Women's Roles: Economics and Everyday Life in Indonesia, Malaysia and Singapore*, edited by Lenore Manderson, 1–14. Development Studies Centre Monograph no. 32. Canberra: Australian National University.

Manguin, Pierre-Yves. 1991. "The Merchant and the King: Political Myths of Southeast Asian Coastal Polities." *Indonesia* 52: 41–54.

Marco Kartodikromo. 1919. *Student Hidjo*. Semarang: N. V. Boekhandel en Drukkerij, Masman & Stroink.

Marx, Karl. [1867] 1977. *Capital: A Critique of Political Economy*, translated by Ben Fowkes. Vol. 1. New York: Vintage Books.

Mauss, Marcel. 1990. *The Gift: The Forms and Reason for Exchange in Archaic Societies*, translated by W. D. Halls. New York: Norton.

McVey, Ruth. 1965. *The Rise of Indonesian Communism*. Ithaca, N.Y.: Cornell University Press.

———. 1992. "The Materialization of the Southeast Asian Entrepreneur." In *Southeast Asian Capitalists*, edited by Ruth McVey, 7–33. Ithaca, N.Y.: Cornell University Southeast Asia Program.

Mernissi, Fatima. 1987. *Beyond the Veil: Male-Female Dynamics in Modern Muslim Society*. Rev. ed. Bloomington: Indiana University Press.

Mintz, Sidney W. 1971. "Men, Women, and Trade." *Comparative Studies in Society and History* 13: 247–69.

Mlayadipura, Raden Tumenggung (Samsudjin Probohardjono). 1984. "Sejarah Kyai Ageng Anis—Kyai Ageng Laweyan." Mimeographed pamphlet.

Mook, H. J. van. 1958. "Kuta Gede." In *The Indonesian Town: Studies in Urban Sociology*. The Hague: W. van Hoeve.

Nakamura, Hisako. 1983. *Divorce in Java: A Study of the Dissolution of Marriage among Javanese Muslims*. Yogyakarta: Gadjah Mada University Press.

Nakamura, Mitsuo. 1983. *The Crescent Arises over the Banyan Tree: A Study of the Muhammadiyah Movement in a Central Javanese Town*. Yogyakarta: Gadjah Mada University Press.

Naniek Widayati. 1992. "Rumah Tinggal Pengusaha Batik di Laweyan Surakarta" (The homes of batik entrepreneurs in Laweyan, Surakarta). Typescript, Gadjah Mada University.

The New Shorter Oxford English Dictionary on Historical Principles. 1993. 2 vols. New York: Oxford University Press.

Nicholson, Linda. 1986. *Gender and History: The Limits of Social Theory in the Age of the Family*. New York: Columbia University Press.

Nietzsche, Friedrich. [1874] 1980. *On the Advantage and Disadvantage of History for Life*, translated by Peter Preuss. Indianapolis: Hackett Publishing.

Noer, Deliar. 1973. *The Modernist Muslim Movement in Indonesia, 1900–1942*. Singapore: Oxford University Press.

Ong, Aihwa. 1987. *Spirits of Resistance and Capitalist Discipline: Factory Women in Malaysia.* Albany: State University of New York Press.

———. 1990. "Japanese Factories, Malay Workers: Class and Sexual Metaphors in West Malaysia." In Atkinson and Errington 1990: 385–422.

Osborne, Peter. 1995. *The Politics of Time: Modernity and Avant-Garde.* London: Verso.

Papanek, Hanna, and Laurel Schwede. 1988. "Women Are Good with Money: Earning and Managing in an Indonesian City." In *A Home Divided: Women and Income in the Third World*, edited by Daisy Dwyer and Judith Bruce, 71–98. Stanford: Stanford University Press.

Parry, Jonathan, and Maurice Bloch. 1989a. "Introduction: Money and the Morality of Exchange." In *Money and the Morality of Exchange*, edited by Jonathan Parry and Maurice Bloch, 1–32. Cambridge: Cambridge University Press.

———, eds. 1989b. *Money and the Morality of Exchange.* Cambridge: Cambridge University Press.

Peletz, Michael G. 1995. "Neither Reasonable nor Responsible: Contrasting Representations of Masculinity in a Malay Society." In *Bewitching Women, Pious Men: Gender and Body Politics in Southeast Asia*, edited by Aihwa Ong and Michael G. Peletz, 76–123. Berkeley: University of California Press.

———. 1996. *Reason and Passion: Representations of Gender in a Malay Society.* Berkeley: University of California Press.

Pemberton, John. 1987. "Musical Politics in Central Java (or How Not to Listen to a Javanese Gamelan)." *Indonesia* 44: 17–29.

———. 1994. *On the Subject of "Java."* Ithaca, N.Y.: Cornell University Press.

Poensen, C. 1887. "Iets over de kleeding der Javanen." *Tijdschrift voor Zendingswetenschap 'Mededeelingen'* 21: 1–21.

Poerwadarminta, W. J. S. 1939. *Baoesastra Djawa.* Batavia: J. B. Wolters'.

———. 1985. *Kamus Umum Bahasa Indonesia.* Jakarta: Balai Pustaka.

Ponder, H. W. [1934] 1989. *Java Pageant: Impressions of the 1930s.* Singapore: Oxford University Press.

Poovey, Mary. 1988. *Uneven Developments: The Ideological Work of Gender in Mid-Victorian England.* Chicago: University of Chicago Press.

Price, Susanna. 1983. "Rich Woman, Poor Woman: Occupation Differences in a Textile Producing Village in Central Java." In *Women's Work and Women's Roles: Economics and Everyday Life in Indonesia, Malaysia, and Singapore*, edited by Lenore Manderson, 97–110. Development Studies Centre Monograph no. 32. Canberra: Australian National University.

Probyn, Elspeth. 1990. "Travels in the Postmodern: Making Sense of the Local." In *Feminism/Postmodernism*, edited by Linda J. Nicholson, 176–89. New York: Routledge.

Purcell, Victor. 1951. *The Chinese in Southeast Asia.* London: Oxford University Press.

Raffles, Thomas Stamford. [1817] 1965. *The History of Java.* 2 vols. Kuala Lumpur: Oxford University Press.

Reid, Anthony. 1988. *Southeast Asia in the Age of Commerce, 1450–1680.* Vol. 1, *The Land below the Winds.* New Haven: Yale University Press.

Reid, Anthony. 1993. *Southeast Asia in the Age of Commerce, 1450–1680.* Vol. 2, *Expansion and Crisis.* New Haven: Yale University Press.

Ricklefs, M. C. 1974. *Jogjakarta under Sultan Mangkubumi, 1749–1792: A History of the Division of Java.* London: Oxford University Press.

———. 1978. *Modern Javanese Historical Tradition: A Study of an Original Kartasura Chronicle and Related Materials.* London: School of Oriental and African Studies, University of London.

———. 1981. *A History of Modern Indonesia c. 1300 to the Present.* London: Macmillan Press.

Robinson, S. 1969. *A History of Dyed Textiles.* Cambridge, Mass.: MIT Press.

Robison, Richard. 1986. *Indonesia: The Rise of Capital.* Sydney: Allen and Unwin.

———. 1992. "Industrialization and the Economic and Political Development of Capital: The Case of Indonesia." In *Southeast Asian Capitalists*, edited by Ruth McVey, 65–88. Ithaca, N.Y.: Cornell University Southeast Asia Program.

Rosaldo, Michelle Z. 1980. "The Use and Abuse of Anthropology: Reflections on Feminism and Cross-Cultural Understanding." *Signs* 5: 389–417.

Rosen, Lawrence. 1984. *Bargaining for Reality: The Construction of Social Relations in a Muslim Community.* Chicago: University of Chicago Press.

Rouffaer, G., and H. Juynboll. 1914. *De Batikkunst in Nederlandsch Indië.* Utrecht: Oosthoek.

Rubin, Gayle. 1975. "The Traffic in Women: Notes on the 'Political Economy' of Sex." In *Toward an Anthropology of Women*, edited by Rayna R. Reiter, 157–210. New York: Monthly Review Press.

Rush, James. 1990. *Opium to Java: Revenue Farming and Chinese Enterprise in Colonial Indonesia, 1860–1910.* Ithaca, N.Y.: Cornell University Press.

———. 1991. "Placing the Chinese in Java on the Eve of the Twentieth Century." *Indonesia* (Special issue on the Role of the Indonesian Chinese in Shaping Modern Indonesian Life): 13–24.

Sams, Camilla C. 1918. "Javanese Batik Designs." *Scribner's Magazine* 63: 509–12.

Samsudjin Probohardjono. 1981. "Sejarah Laweyan." Photocopy.

Saraswati Sunindyo. 1993. "Gender Discourse on Television." In *Culture and Society in New Order Indonesia*, edited by Virginia Matheson Hooker, 134–48. Kuala Lumpur: Oxford University Press.

———. 1996. "Murder, Gender, and the Media: Sexualizing Politics and Violence." In *Fantasizing the Feminine in Indonesia*, edited by Laurie J. Sears, 120–39. Durham, N.C.: Duke University Press.

Sarsono Suyatno. 1985. *Suatu Pengamatan Tradisi Lisan dalam Kebudayaan Jawa: Studi Kasus Masyarakat Laweyan di Surakarta.* Yogyakarta: Departemen Pendidikan dan Kebudayaan.

Schneider, Jane, and Annette B. Weiner. 1989. Introduction to *Cloth and Human Experience*, edited by Annette B. Weiner and Jane Schneider, 1–29. Washington, D.C.: Smithsonian Institution Press.

Scott, Joan W. 1988. *Gender and the Politics of History.* New York: Columbia University Press.

———. 1992. "Experience." In *Feminists Theorize the Political*, edited by Judith Butler and Joan W. Scott, 22–40. New York: Routledge.

Sen, Krishna. 1993. "Repression and Resistance: Interpretations of the Feminine in New Order Cinema." In *Culture and Society in New Order Indonesia*, edited by Virginia Matheson Hooker, 116–33. Kuala Lumpur: Oxford University Press.

Shiraishi, Takashi. 1990. *An Age in Motion: Popular Radicalism in Java, 1912–1926*. Ithaca, N.Y.: Cornell University Press.

Siegel, James T. 1969. *The Rope of God*. Berkeley: University of California Press.

————. 1986. *Solo in the New Order: Language and Hierarchy in an Indonesian City*. Princeton: Princeton University Press.

Simmel, Georg. [1907] 1990. *The Philosophy of Money*, edited by David Frisby, translated by Tom Bottomore and David Frisby. 2nd enlarged ed. London: Routledge.

Sjafri Sairin. 1982. *Javanese Trah: Kin-Based Social Organization*. Yogyakarta: Gadjah Mada University Press.

Smith-Hefner, Nancy J. 1988. "Women and Politeness: The Javanese Example." *Language in Society* 17: 535–54.

Soedarmono. 1987. "Munculnya Kelompok Pengusaha Batik di Laweyan pada Awal Abad XX." *Pasca Sarjana* thesis, Gadjah Mada University.

Soepomo Poedjosoedarmo. 1968. "Javanese Speech Levels." *Indonesia* 6: 54–81.

Soerachman, R. M. P. 1927. *Het Batikbedrijf in de Vorstenlanden*. Weltevreden: Landsdrukkerij.

Spivak, Gayatri. 1988. "Explanation and Culture: Marginalia." In *In Other Worlds: Essays in Cultural Politics*, 103–17. New York: Routledge.

Statistik Indonesia 1988 (Statistical yearbook of Indonesia 1988). 1988. Jakarta: Biro Pusat Statistik.

Statistisch Zakboekje voor Nederlandsch Indië 1934. 1934. Departement van Economische Zaken, Centraal Kantoor voor de Statistiek. Batavia: De Koninklijke Boekhandel en Drukkerijen, G. Kolff.

Steedly, Mary M. 1993. *Hanging without a Rope: Narrative Experience in Colonial and Postcolonial Karoland*. Princeton: Princeton University Press.

Stoler, Ann. 1977. "Class Structure and Female Autonomy in Rural Java." In *Women and National Development: The Complexities of Change*, edited by the Wellesley Editorial Committee, 74–89. Chicago: University of Chicago Press.

Strathern, Marilyn. 1985. "Kinship and Economy: Constitutive Orders of a Provisional Kind." *American Ethnologist* 12: 191–209.

Suryakusuma, Julia I. 1996. "The State and Sexuality in New Order Indonesia." In *Fantasizing the Feminine in Indonesia*, edited by Laurie J. Sears, 92–119. Durham, N.C.: Duke University Press.

Sutherland, Heather. 1975. "The Priyayi." *Indonesia* 19: 57–80.

————. 1979. *The Making of a Bureaucratic Elite: The Colonial Transformation of the Javanese Priyayi*. Singapore: Heinemann.

Tanner, Nancy. 1974. "Matrifocality in Indonesia and Africa and among Black Americans." In *Women, Culture, and Society*, edited by Michelle Zimbalist Rosaldo and Louise Lamphere, 129–56. Stanford: Stanford University Press.

Taussig, Michael T. 1980. *The Devil and Commodity Fetishism in South America*. Chapel Hill: University of North Carolina Press.

Tilly, Louise A., and Joan W. Scott. 1978. *Women, Work, and Family*. New York: Holt, Rinehart and Winston.

Tirtaamidjaja, N. 1966. *Batik: Pola dan Tjorak* (English text by Benedict R. O'G. Anderson). Jakarta: Djambatan.

Tönnies, Ferdinand. 1964. *Community and Society* (Gemeinschaft und Gesellschaft), translated and edited by Charles P. Loomis. East Lansing: Michigan State University Press.

Tsing, Anna L. 1993. *In the Realm of the Diamond Queen: Marginality in an Out-of-the-Way Place*. Princeton: Princeton University Press.

Tsuchiya, Kenji. 1990. "Javanology and the Age of Ranggawarsita: An Introduction to Nineteenth-Century Javanese Culture." In *Reading Southeast Asia*, edited by Ruth McVey, 75–108. Ithaca, N.Y.: Cornell University Southeast Asia Program.

Van Kol, H. H. 1904. "Soerakarta." *De Indische Gids*, tevens nieuwe serie *Tijdschrift van Nederlands Indie* 26: 1149–74.

Veblen, Thorstein. [1899] 1979. *The Theory of the Leisure Class*. New York: Penguin.

Vries, E. de, and H. Cohen. 1938. "On Village Shopkeeping in Java and Madura." *Bulletin of the Colonial Institute of Amsterdam* 1: 263–73.

Weber, Max. 1958. *The Protestant Ethic and the Spirit of Capitalism*, translated by Talcott Parsons. New York: Scribner's.

Weiner, Annette B. 1976. *Women of Value, Men of Renown: New Perspectives in Trobriand Exchange*. Austin: University of Texas Press.

———. 1989. "Why Cloth? Wealth, Gender, and Power in Oceania." In *Cloth and Human Experience*, edited by Annette B. Weiner and Jane Schneider, 33–72. Washington, D.C.: Smithsonian Institution Press.

———. 1992. *Inalienable Possessions: The Paradox of Keeping-While-Giving*. Berkeley: University of California Press.

Weix, Gretchen G. 1990. "Following the Family/Firm: Patronage and Piecework in a Kudus Cigarette Factory." Ph.D. diss., Cornell University.

Wertheim, W. F. 1956. *Indonesian Society in Transition: A Study of Social Change*. The Hague: W. van Hoeve.

———. 1964. *Indonesian Society in Transition: A Study of Social Change*. 2nd rev. ed. The Hague: H. van Hoeve.

Wieringa, Saskia. 1979. "Batik: Money Maker or Time Filler? The Ideology of Women's Labour in the Batik Industry of Central Java." Mimeograph.

Wit, Augusta de. [1912] 1984. *Java: Facts and Fancies*. Singapore: Oxford University Press.

Wolf, Diane. 1992. *Factory Daughters: Gender, Household Dynamics, and Rural Industrialization in Java*. Berkeley: University of California Press.

Wolff, John U., and Soepomo Poedjosoedarmo. 1982. *Communicative Codes in Central Java*. Data Paper no. 116. Ithaca, N.Y.: Cornell University Southeast Asia Program.

Woodward, Mark R. 1989. *Islam in Java: Normative Piety and Mysticism in the Sultanate of Yogyakarta*. Tucson: University of Arizona Press.

Yanagisako, Sylvia Junko, and Jane Fishburne Collier. 1987. "Toward a Unified Analysis of Gender and Kinship." In *Gender and Kinship: Essays toward a Unified*

Analysis, edited by Jane Fishburne Collier and Sylvia Junko Yanagisako, 14–50. Stanford: Stanford University Press.

Zifirdaus Adnan. 1990. "Islamic Religion: Yes, Islamic Ideology: No! Islam and the State in Indonesia." In *State and Civil Society in Indonesia*, edited by Arief Budiman, 441–78. Monash Papers on Southeast Asia no. 22. Clayton, Australia: Monash Asia Institute, Monash University.

INDEX

abdi dalem, 53
advertising, 200, 202–3
Alexander, Jennifer, 73
Alexander, Paul, 73
alus, 58, 61, 77, 113–14, 142, 144–45, 148,
  168–69, 176, 187, 201–2
Anderson, Benedict, 45, 61, 147–48, 271n.
  33, 273n. 13
anthropology, urban. *See* urban anthropology
Arab Indonesians, 28, 45, 111, 157–58, 215,
  220, 260n. 32; batik firms of, 37–38, 157
Arabic. *See* language, Arabic
architecture. *See* Laweyan, architectural
  styles of
arisan, 32, 100, 141, 160, 173–76, 184–85,
  222, 274n. 1, 275n. 7
Armstrong, Nancy, 17
Arswendo Atmowiloto, 136, 143, 272n. 10,
  277n. 9
art deco, 6, 46
asceticism, 180–82, 185, 191–93, 274nn. 4
  and 5, 275n. 12; women's practices of,
  182–84
authenticity, cultural. *See* cultural authenticity
autonomy, 80–83, 85–86, 93, 205, 225, 233,
  237–38. *See also* women, autonomy of

bargaining, 144–47, 159
Barthes, Roland, 277n. 2
batik cap, 36, 39, 89–90, 92, 109–10, 113,
  258n. 21, 268n. 11, 269n. 14
batik cloth: aesthetics of, 35, 39, 41–42, 49,
  68, 92, 113–14, 116–18, 259n. 31,260n.
  33; as an American fashion, 195; association with court culture, 77–78, 113–14,
  201; as a commodity, 34–36, 39, 77, 113,
  203; imitations of, 35, 89, 91–93, 193, 199,
  258nn. 24 and 25; made by noblewomen,
  34, 77, 113, 259n. 26; marketing of, 36–
  37, 199–200, 260n. 34, 269n. 14; as national culture, 35, 91, 201–2, 276n. 23; as
  a prestige good, 34, 36, 92, 257n. 19; production techniques of, 35–36, 258nn. 22,
  24, and 25, 271n. 25

batik cooperatives, 90–91, 93, 95, 211,
  268nn. 9 and 11
Batik Danar Hadi, 199–200, 202–3, 212,
  251, 276nn. 18 and 19
batik industry: access to raw materials, 37–
  38, 41–42, 90, 259n. 30; as an ancestral inheritance, 171, 194–202; conditions of labor in, 109–12, 114, 259n. 27; decline of,
  28, 87–89, 91–92, 120, 202, 275n. 13; description of firms, 40, 157–58; ethnic division of, 37, 199, 260nn. 32 and 33, 267n.
  6; government protection of, 89–91; history of, 34–37, 39, 91, 93, 257n. 17,
  258nn. 21 and 25, 259nn. 30 and 31, 268n.
  10; indigenous entrepreneurship in, 39;
  integration with colonial economy, 41–42;
  labor in, 31, 36–37, 39–42, 90, 261n. 40; in
  postcolonial period, 90–91; unions in, 44;
  women's roles in, 27, 49–50
batik printing. *See* batik cloth, imitations of
Batik Research Station, 42
batik tulis, 35–36, 39, 109, 112–13, 197, 201,
  258nn. 23 and 24, 260n. 33, 268n. 11,
  269n. 14
Batikrapport, 42
bequest. *See* inheritance
Berman, Marshall, 124
birth control, 186, 225, 227
black magic, 130, 156
blessings, 52, 54–55, 98, 177–78, 180, 187,
  191, 195, 198, 202, 232
bourgeoisie. *See* merchant class, Javanese
bureaucratic capitalism, 94, 217, 233. *See also*
  capitalism
business partnerships, avoidance of, 80–81,
  93

Canting, 143
capitalism, 6, 11, 21, 89, 95, 105, 107, 119–
  21, 132, 143, 188, 193, 203, 217, 239, 244,
  271nn. 28 and 29, 272n. 10. *See also* bureaucratic capitalism
Carey, Peter, 79, 266n. 24
cemeteries, royal, 33–34, 52–55, 68, 175,
  189, 257n. 13, 263n. 2
children, value of, 186–87

ABOUT THE AUTHOR

Suzanne April Brenner is Associate Professor of Anthropology at the University of California, San Diego.